TEACHER EXPECTANCIES

TEACHER EXPECTANCIES

Edited by

JEROME B. DUSEK

in conjunction with

Vernon C. Hall
William J. Meyer

SYRACUSE UNIVERSITY

LEA LAWRENCE ERLBAUM ASSOCIATES, PUBLISHERS
1985 Hillsdale, New Jersey   London

Lawrence Erlbaum Associates, Inc., Publishers
365 Broadway
Hillsdale, New Jersey 07642

Library of Congress Cataloging in Publication Data
Main entry under title:

Teacher expectancies.

  Includes index.
  1. Teachers—Psychology.   2. Expectation (Psychology)
3. Motivation in education.   I. Dusek, Jerome B.
LB2840.T44 1985   371.1'22   84-25866
ISBN 0-89859-443-X

10   9   8   7   6   5   4   3   2   1
Printed in the United States of America

Contents

SECTION 5: TEACHER EXPECTANCIES: BACKWARD AND FORWARD

List of Contributors

Sharon A. Barger, *University of Wisconsin-Madison*
Reuben M. Baron, *University of Connecticut*
Jere E. Brophy, *Michigan State University*
Harris M. Cooper, *University of Missouri-Columbia*
Jerome B. Dusek, *Syracuse University*
Jacquelynne Eccles, *University of Michigan*
Maureen J. Findley, *University of Missouri-Columbia*
Thomas L. Good, *University of Missouri-Columbia*
Vernon C. Hall, *Syracuse University*
Gail Joseph, *Syracuse University*
Stephen P. Merkel, *Syracuse University*
William J. Meyer, *Syracuse University*
Alexis L. Mitman, *Far West Laboratory for Educational Research and Development*

Penelope L. Peterson, *University of Wisconsin-Madison*
Robert Rosenthal, *Harvard University*
Julian B. Rotter, *University of Connecticut*
Richard E. Snow, *Stanford University*
David Y. H. Tom, *University of Missouri-Columbia*
Rhona S. Weinstein, *University of California, Berkeley*
Allan Wigfield, *University of Michigan*
David C. Zuroff, *McGill University*

Preface

The study of teacher expectancy effects on childrens' learning and school performance is a volatile pursuit. This was true 15 years ago when the initial study was published and reported in the popular press, and it is true now, when there are renewed concerns over the quality of education received by our youngsters. Regardless of the events of the times, parents want the best for their children, including the best possible education. Of course, for most parents educational quality is seen as a function of the role of the teacher. Hence, the teacher becomes an easy scapegoat for the poor performance of children in our educational system. Indeed, several articles in the popular press have indicated that if parents could get teachers to have higher expectancies for their children, the children would achieve at higher levels. One purpose of this volume is to examine the relevant literature, theoretical, methodological, and practical, in an attempt to present clearly the evidence on this issue.

A second purpose of this compilation is to provide a summary of knowledge available on the topic of teacher expectancy effects. This is a new area of study, as time goes in the sciences, but it has been researched with great vigor and energy. As a result, the literature has grown by leaps and bounds. The time is ripe for an authoritative summary of the state of the field.

We have aimed our summary at several audiences. First, the researcher interested in teacher expectancy will find up-to-date descriptions of knowledge and theory, including critical reviews of literature areas. Second, teachers will find insights into the impact of their daily interactions with students. Finally, parents will find valuable information describing the world about which they know so little—the school classroom.

Contributing to a book of this type is a novel experience because the subject area touches virtually everyone. We all go to school and have varieties of interactions with teachers. Many of us have children and we are concerned with their school encounters. In all likelihood, those who read this book will have had at least one conference with a teacher about a child of concern to them. In part, we hope that what we have written will enlighten all of us, teachers and non-teachers, to the nature of in-classroom teacher and student behavior.

The complexity of the classroom situation has, in part, determined the nature of study of teacher expectancy effects and the organization of this book. Hence, we try to spell out the etiology of the study of expectancy effects, in general, and teacher expectancy effects in particular. We provide chapters detailing theoretical perspectives about the nature of teacher–student interactions from both the standpoint of the teacher and the students. Finally, some chapters are devoted to substantive research issues, including the formation of expectancies, the impact of expectancies on teacher–student interactions, and the role of expectancies on student learning. In providing this set of perspectives we have tried to make the material meaningful to an audience with widely ranging interests.

The work of many people makes a volume of this type possible. Our most sincere thanks go to the authors who contributed the chapters. Each is an expert in one or another aspect of teacher expectancy effects. It is their contributions that make this volume the most authoritative source available. We thank them deeply for their efforts.

Jerome B. Dusek
Vernon C. Hall
William J. Meyer

1 Introduction to Teacher Expectancy Research

Jerome B. Dusek
Syracuse University

Most areas of educational research are multifaceted. An initial study or two reveals an interesting and important phenomenon that is further investigated in an attempt to explain it and its implications. Knowledge about the topic of interest builds and is extended in order to link it to other important concerns. Theoretical perspectives grow in an attempt to fit the phenomena into current explanatory systems. Methods of investigation become increasingly sophisticated and complex as new ramifications of the phenomena become evident. After several years of such activity it usually can be determined if the phenomenon under investigation is worthy of further research efforts or if investigation is best abandoned in favor of other pursuits. If continued research effort is the choice, knowledge and theory continue to grow.

With the growth of knowledge, the time ultimately becomes ripe for an attempt at integration and consolidation of what is known and what is yet to be found out. That time has come with respect to research on teacher expectancy effects. The past decade and a half has seen considerable research and theory revolving around this topic as investigators have followed the typical trend in educational research. This book is our attempt to consolidate knowledge, integrate current theoretical and empirical information, and point to avenues for future consideration.

THE START OF A RESEARCH AREA

The study of teacher expectancies was born with the publication of Rosenthal and Jacobson's (1968) initial study. As Rosenthal points out in Chapter 3 of this volume, the study grew from a more traditional set of experiments focused on expectancy effects in general. The publication of the findings of the "Oak School" study stirred considerable controversy. Foremost among the challenges

1

to the study was a series of criticisms (e.g., Elashoff & Snow, 1971; Jensen, 1969; Thorndike, 1968) concerning the methodological and analytical procedures used. While the disputes continued among the principles, new research efforts were initiated by many others. As is customary, investigators from a variety of disciplines—educational psychology, developmental psychology, and social psychology—and perspectives undertook efforts to clarify the major concerns.

The findings of the past 15 years of research allow the firm conclusion that teachers do, indeed, form expectancies for student performance. In retrospect, this should not be a surprising conclusion; we all form expectancies about people. What makes teacher expectancies special is that they correlate, albeit only moderately, with student achievement. This finding has led some researchers (e.g., Dusek, 1975; Rist, 1970, 1973) to conclude that teachers may bias, positively or negatively, the education of some children. Given this possibility, research efforts were increased as the issue of teacher expectancies took on a more applied tone.

The directions taken by those investigating teacher expectancy effects have been diverse; the major issues and questions many. Some have researched the issue of how teachers form expectancies for student achievement (see Chapter 9). Among the many individual difference variables of concern to these researchers was social class. Do teachers use this information to decide if some students are likely to do less well than others in the educational system? Other information, such as a previous teacher's estimates of likely success, test scores, family background information, and race have been examined for their contribution to the expectancies teachers hold for students.

Other researchers have attempted to elaborate how expectancy effects are communicated to students. Many studies have shown that teachers treat high- and low-expectancy students differently during classroom interactions. In a sense, high expectancy students receive a higher quality interaction with the teacher, which likely leads to greater achievement. Hence, the students' behavior begins to fulfill the teacher's prophecy.

Still other researchers have focused their efforts on theoretical concerns. Theory development has progressed very rapidly in the area of teacher expectancies. Cooper (see Chapter 6) reviews these attempts to provide conceptual models linking child characteristics to expectancies and expectancies to teacher behavior.

These areas of emphasis have shaped, to a degree, the structure of this book. Several chapters representing work in each area are presented.

MAJOR THEMES

There are, of course, a variety of ways in which extant information about teacher expectancies may be organized. Any system used to structure the information has its advantages and disadvantages. We have chosen to include chapters that revolve around several major areas of importance.

Historical Trends

Although the study of teacher expectancies is a relatively new field of inquiry, the expectancy construct has a long and rich history in psychology. Zuroff and Rotter (Chapter 2) provide a summary of the history of expectancy research and place research on teacher expectancies into this historical perspective. As they point out, nearly every area of psychology has made use of the expectancy concept. With regard to its use in educational psychology research, Zuroff and Rotter illustrate a number of potential pitfalls that may be faced by the researcher. In particular, they argue strongly for well articulated definitions of expectancy constructs.

The historical development of the concept of teacher expectancies is chronicled by Rosenthal (Chapter 3). The initial study with Jacobson was an outgrowth of earlier research on experimenter expectancy effects. The findings of research on experimenter expectancy (bias) effects rocked the psychological research community. Were the findings on which our theories were based influenced by the predelections of the researcher? As researchers began to unravel this question a more broadly pertinent one came from the Rosenthal and Jacobson study. Was the achievement of our children determined by the predelections of the teacher? Although the study of experimenter expectancy effects, and hence teacher expectancy effects, occurred almost by accident, it has been at the center of research in educational psychology since its emergence.

The relationship between research on teacher expectancies and the mainstream of educational psychology is the subject of Chapter 4 by Hall and Merkel. In their chapter, they place research on teacher expectancies into the more general area of research in educational psychology. Acknowledging that there is no question teachers treat students differently, they suggest that differential teacher behaviors toward students may reflect appropriate responses to the needs of individual students. Research to examine this question is, they argue, at the heart of the field of educational psychology because it represents an attempt to elaborate and understand the nature of learning and the impact of the school environment on the student.

In sum, the authors of the previously noted chapters point out that research on teacher expectancy effects is simply an extension of other types of research. The expectancy construct has a long history in psychological research, and the study of teacher expectancy effects is simply a logical extension of earlier reseach. The study of teacher expectancy effects should enlighten us considerably about the nature and impact of schooling on the student.

Theoretical and Methodological Issues

The prevailing view in educational and psychological research, as in other fields of scientific inquiry, is that empirical knowledge should advance theory in order to enhance understanding. The initial studies of teacher-expectancy effects were guided by general expectancy theory. As further research was conducted, theoretical conceptualizations specifically dealing with teacher expectancy effects developed. Several theoretical perspectives are presented in this book.

The most broad model of teacher expectancy effects is Cooper's (Chapter 6). Borrowing from achievement attribution theory and the learned helplessness literature, Cooper has built a model of how expectancies are communicated to students and how they are sustained. The central focus of the theory is the teacher and how he or she dispenses praise and criticism, controls the climate of the classroom, and interacts with students.

Peterson and Barger (Chapter 7) have elected to concentrate on elaborating the utility of attribution theory for understanding teacher expectancy effects. The major thrust of their perspective is that the teacher forms attributions for students' successes and failures. These attributions are part of the basis for forming expectancies regarding students' academic, as well as other, behavior. The expectancies then cause the teacher to behave in specific ways, which are interpreted by the student, who forms certain attributions for the teacher's behavior. These attributions relate to how the student views his or her own performance and guide future behavior. The cycle then continues.

Eccles and Wigfield (Chapter 8) have focused on a specific aspect of theory, namely, the role played by student motivation. Noting that student motivation affects achievement, they suggest that students behave in ways to preserve self-esteem, specifically with respect to failure experiences in the classroom. In general, they argue that beliefs held about the stability of ability and the failure to consider other factors influencing achievement lead to negative teacher expectancy effects and a feeling of immanent failure on the part of the student.

As with any research area, concerns of methodological and scientific rigor have surfaced with respect to investigations of teacher expectancy effects. Mitman and Snow (Chapter 5) point out many of the potential pitfalls of research on teacher-expectancy effects, including those involving student perceptions, the value of analog research designs, basing causal inferences on correlational data, and the generalizability of existing in-classroom and nonclassroom research. In addition, they address issues concerned with observing teacher–student classroom interactions and relating such observations to teacher expectancies.

As is clear from reading these chapters, methodological advances and theoretical sophistication have taken diverse courses. Some of the avenues followed have been more profitable than others and much still needs to be accomplished. However, it is difficult to find another field of inquiry that has progressed so rapidly.

Individual Difference Factors

The remaining chapters address more specific questions. Dusek and Joseph (Chapter 9) present a meta-analysis of the bases of teacher expectancies. Drawing on research conducted primarily in the context of teacher expectancies, as opposed to more general social psychology research on expectancy formation, they conclude that we have identified several bases of teacher expectancies. However, it is clear that research with in-classroom teachers judging their own students is needed before we shall know with confidence how teachers form expectancies.

Just as gender is related to learning, socioeconomic background and race also are related to school performance. Indeed, many have suggested that social class and race are primary student characteristics related to teacher expectancies. Baron, Tom, and Cooper (Chapter 10) address this issue in a meta-analysis of the literature.

Sex differences in student achievement are well documented. Good and Find-ley (Chapter 11) address these differences within the context of teacher expecta-tions and expectations of students. More specifically, they examine teacher and student expectancies for performance in mathematics and reading, two areas in which differential performance for the sexes occurs.

It is well documented that teacher expectancies are communicated to students during times of teacher–student interactions. Brophy (Chapter 12) reviews re-search on teacher student interactions with an eye toward identifying teacher behaviors that mediate self-fulfilling prophecy effects.

Of course, the student is an important character in the study of teacher expec-tancy effects. Weinstein's contribution (Chapter 13) is on the topic of the percep-tions of students. As is pointed out, little research has been directed at examining student perceptions in the teacher expectancy literature. Research on student perceptions, however, is likely to point the way to further understanding of the import of teacher-expectancy effects on student behavior, learning, and achieve-ment.

WHERE DO WE GO FROM HERE?

In the last chapter Meyer presents an integration of the theoretical and substan-tive aspects of the field. In his critique he points out deficiencies in knowledge and directions for future research. As with any highly researched area, much knowledge has accrued. However, the ecological validity of some aspects of what we know is questionable. As research progresses, we shall come closer to providing the answers to such questions.

OUR INTENTS

In organizing a book such as this it is the hope of the editors to provide a balanced and knowledgable view of a research domain. The authors of the contributed chapters are all experts in the field of teacher expectancies. The summary of knowledge they provide is state of the art and up-to-date. As a result, this volume represents a current summary of the major developments in the research area.

In summarizing the research in their various areas of expertise, each of the authors has pointed ways for investigation for the future. We hope that current and future researchers find this volume a valuable source book, not only for summaries of research done to date, but also for valuable insights for future research endeavors.

Finally, it is our hope that practitioners who read this book will gain understanding of the teacher expectancy phenomenon. School psychologists, teachers, and administrators should find valuable information for furthering their understanding of the role of the teacher. Hopefully, we have done our tasks well and will enlighten all concerned individuals to the complexity of the issues involved.

REFERENCES

Dusek, J. Do teachers bias children's learning? *Review of Educational Research,* 1975, *45,* 661–684.

Elashoff, J., & Snow, R. *Pygmalion reconsidered.* Worthington, OH: Jones. 1971.

Jensen, A. How much can we boost IQ and achievement? *Harvard Educational Review,* 1969, *39,* 1–123.

Rist, R. Student social class and teacher expectations: The self-fulfilling prophecy in ghetto education. *Harvard Educational Review,* 1970, *40,* 411–451.

Rist, R. *The urban school: A factory for failure.* Cambridge, MA: MIT Press. 1973.

Rosenthal, R., & Jacobson, L. *Pygmalion in the classroom: Teacher expectation and pupils' intellectual development.* New York: Holt, Rinehart, & Winston.

Thorndike, R. Review of Pygmalion in the classroom. *American Educational Research Journal,* 1968, *5,* 708–711.

Section 1
Historical Trends and
Methodological Concerns

The expectancy construct has a long and rich history in the psychological literature. Zuroff and Rotter (Chapter 2) trace this history in three areas of inquiry, each relevant to a complete understanding of teacher expectancies. It is instructive to note that in each of the three areas the definition of expectancy is quite consistent with common usage of the term in the teacher-expectancy literature. More than 50 years ago Tolman discussed the term in the context of theories of learning in both humans and animals. More recently, expectancy-value theorists have discussed expectancies as being based on past experiences in situations perceived to be the same. Finally, researchers interested in interpersonal perceptions—an area of inquiry obviously relevant to teacher expectancies—have argued that person perception is in part a function of beliefs about properties of individuals or groups of individuals, a concept consistent with notions concerning teacher expectancies.

It is, of course, the study of person perception, at least in a broad sense, that started Rosenthal (Chapter 3) on the pursuit of teacher expectancies. His "attack of studently compulsivity" led to his intensive study of experimenter-expectancy effects. The initial research was done with human subjects (the experimenters) interacting with humans, looking at pictures and stating various expectancies for the individual shown, and running rats in mazes. As Rosenthal details in his chapter, these initial studies lead him to consider the possibility that teachers' expectancies for student learning might become self-fulfilling prophecies. This possibility led to the study conducted by Rosenthal and Jacobson, which was the initial study in the field. Following Rosenthal and Jacobson's publication of their study, numerous attempts at replication, extension, and clarification were conducted. The resultant research has raised many questions and answered some.

7

Regardless of the ultimate outcome of these research endeavors, one fact remains unquestionningly true: The field of educational psychology, and specifically teacher training, was changed for all time.

It is the influence of teacher expectancy research on the field of educational psychology and teacher training that is the subject of Hall and Merkel's contribution (Chapter 4). Drawing on studies aimed at assessing teacher expectancy, and on studies of classroom teacher–student interaction, Hall and Merkel discuss a variety of issues related to teacher training. In their chapter they argue, in effect, that research evidence bearing out the suggestion of teacher expectancies being responsible for individual student variation in learning is weak. More specifically, they contend that evidence demonstrating that differential teacher behaviors toward students reflect teacher expectancies is particularly weak. In other words, they feel the link between teacher expectancies and differential teacher behavior has not been sufficiently demonstrated. They go on to argue that differential teacher behaviors may well reflect attempts by the teacher to provide optimal learning environments for students with differing needs.

This issue, of course, strikes at the heart of a number of measurement issues that have been raised about the area of teacher expectancies because it bears directly on the validity of the concept. Mitman and Snow (Chapter 5) attack this issue in their discussion of logical and methodological problems in the study of teacher expectancy effects. Their critique of the research points out the complexity involved in conducting research on teacher expectancies and addresses the issue of the validity of the measurement techniques and experimental manipulations that have been employed. Following a review of the validity of both classroom and nonclassroom experiments, they go on to suggest that the inclusion of individual difference measures of both teachers and students may help attenuate some of the logical problems that plague researchers in the area.

The four chapters in this section trace the roots of the study of teacher expectancy to the classical literature in experimental psychology and demonstrate the tie between research in applied educational psychology to the more theoretically oriented research in experimental psychology. Because of the peculiarities of the research domain there are a variety of methodological and measurement problems that have been encountered, and, to a degree, solved. As advances in measurement of teacher expectancies are made, the direction of causality in the relationship of teacher expectancies to student achievement will become clarified.

2 A History of the Expectancy Construct in Psychology

David C. Zuroff
McGill University

Julian B. Rotter
University of Connecticut

Almost every area of psychology has made use of the concept of expectancy. Rather than attempting a comprehensive review, we discuss in some detail the histories of expectancy research in three areas that might be of particular interest to those concerned with teachers' expectancies. In particular, we propose to narrate the histories of expectancy constructs in learning theories, expectancy-value theories, and theories of person perception. Within each area, major theoretical statements that employed expectancy or closely related concepts are reviewed in chronological order. The reviews will focus on (a) the formal characteristics of the theories and (b) hypotheses that appear to be particularly relevant to teacher expectancy research. By formal characteristics of the theories, we mean the degrees to which a theory is explicit, operationalized, and falsifiable; a major theme is that expectancy theories have had the greatest heuristic value when they have been most systematically developed. We hope that this dual focus leads to a history that can provide some guidance, not only for students of teachers' expectancies, but also for cognitively oriented theorists in other domains.

Before beginning the historical survey, it may be useful to state what we mean by a systematically developed theory. The principle point to be made has to do with the definition of theoretical terms. The second author has suggested that psychological constructs require three types of definition, one being the familiar operational definition and the other two being the "ideal" and the "systematic" definitions.

The ideal definition of a construct is an ordinary language definition; it contains the surplus meaning of the construct and must be capable of operationalization. The ideal definition makes explicit the types of referents that the construct is intended to subsume. It also allows the theorist to state what Rotter has called the "working hypotheses" of a theory, which together comprise the systematic definition. The systematic definition of a construct X defines it by stating it is that which stands in this relation to construct Y, that relationship to construct Z, and so on. Well-developed theories provide a rich array of explicit linkages among their constructs; that is, each construct has a well-developed systematic definition. As for the operational definition, its importance hardly needs to be emphasized. However, theorists sometimes neglect to consider whether their operations systematically sample referents that are logically related to their ideal definitions. An objective, reliable set of operations is of little use if the referents they sample are not appropriate given their constructs' ideal definitions.

THE EXPECTANCY CONSTRUCT IN LEARNING THEORY

Tolman (1932) is considered to be the originator of expectancy theories of learning. Tolman himself did not cite any previous writers as sources of the notion of expectancy (Tolman, 1932) and later in his career he stated that his theorizing was largely based on his own phenomenology (Tolman, 1959). Thus, Tolman's principal source for the expectancy concept may have been the informal notion of expectancy as it appears in ordinary language. Gibson's (1941) scholarly review of the history of the concept of "set" suggests that there was some use of concepts related to expectancy prior to Tolman, but that it is doubtful that these were of more than indirect influence on him. Gibson (1941) treated Tolman's "expectation" as a member of a family of related concepts that could be subsumed by the term set. He traced set back to the early studies of the Wurzburg school. In the general sense that students of set believed that they had identified a cognitive determinant of behavior, which could not be reduced to principles of association, they can be said to be precursors of Tolman's ideas. For example, the preparatory set in reaction time experiments was believed to include the expectation that the stimulus was to be presented. Gibson (1941) also described an early study by Lewin (1926) that purported to demonstrate that learning was not automatic, but required a "mental act, intention, or set" (p. 787). Gibson also indicated that the early literature on human classical conditioning contained occasional references to cognitive nonassociative learning processes. Hamel (1919) discussed the role of insight into the conditions of the experiment and Schilder (1929) reported that his subjects described expectations of the occurrence of the US. Regardless of the degree to which these studies should be looked on as influences on Tolman or as independent borrowings from everyday language, it is fair to say that Tolman (1932) was the first to construct even a semiformalized theory in which expectancy appeared as a theoretical term.

Tolman provided two detailed theoretical statements, one in the classic book of 1932, *Purposive Behavior in Animals and Men,* and the other published in 1959, shortly before his death. In between these two works there appeared several shorter papers, which introduced changes in terminology and minor changes in the laws of learning. Expectancies were renamed hypotheses (Tolman, 1938) and the concept of a "cognitive map" (Tolman, 1948/1958) was put forward, but never elaborated. Since there was little substantive change in the theory between 1932 and 1959, we will discuss only early and late Tolman.

Early Tolman

Tolman's book of 1932 introduced numerous concepts, but we are concerned only with those of a means-end-expectation and a means-end-readiness. Tolman's avowed goal was to develop definitions of mentalistic terms that were purely behavioral and cleansed of any mentalistic or subjective denotations. His attempt to achieve such a definition for means-end-expectation read as follows: (they are) "expectations that such and such of the immediately presented means-objects (discriminanda and manipulanda) are going to be better or worse for reaching (or avoiding) the given goal object . . . The experimental definition and evidence of a means-end-expectation is to be found, in other words, in the fact of an animal's selectivity among some array of actually presented means-objects" (p. 95). A means-end-readiness was defined as a generalized version of an expectation that referred to "a 'judgment' that commerce with such and such a 'type' of means-object should lead on by such and such direction-distance relations to some instance of the given demanded type of goal-object" (p. 451). Tolman also provided a definition of cognition, which included both expectations and readinesses: "(a cognition) is present in a behavior in so far as the continued going-off of that behavior is contingent upon environmental entities . . . proving to be 'so and so.' And such a contingency will be testified to whenever, if these environmental entities do not prove to be so and so, the given behavior will exhibit disruption and be followed by learning" (p. 440).

Expectancies were linked to other constructs at two points in Tolman's exposition of the theory. First, there was a list of "laws of learning." That these laws were far from precise was pointed out repeatedly (Hilgard & Bower, 1966; MacCorquodale & Meehl, 1954) and was acknowledged by Tolman (1959). Second, the cognitive variables were linked to other theoretical constructs such as demand, past training, physiological state, and running back and forth by a sort of flow chart describing the process of an animal's "choice" of a final behavior. MacCorquodale and Meehl's (1954) evaluation of the total postulate system was that it was too sketchy to permit anything approaching formal derivations of hypotheses. This amounts to saying that there was little in the way of systematic definition to supplement the ideal and operational definitions.

How adequate were Tolman's ideal and operational definitions of his cognitive constructs? Expressions such as "reaching (or avoiding) the goal object" and "direction-distance relations" had reasonably clear interpretations in the maze context, but they required increasingly metaphorical interpretation when applied to other forms of rat behavior and most forms of human behavior. Consequently, Tolman and his followers were forced to employ increasingly loose linkages between ideal and operational definitions in the interpretation or design of experiments in those other behavioral realms.

The looseness of fit between Tolman's ideal and operational definitions had another source as well. One cannot escape the feeling that the ideal definitions carried, despite Tolman's protestation, a substantial load of mentalism; the use of expressions such as "expectations that such and such . . . are going to be better or worse . . ." and "He expects that this means-object will lead on to . . . (the) goal-object" certainly seem to have as their referents the goings-on in the rat's mind. Tolman's "experimental definitions" succeeded in reducing some of the referents of his cognitive constructs to empirical terms, but there remained a core of mentalistic referents that resisted reduction and contributed to the looseness of fit between the ideal and operational definitions.

An example of the looseness of definition might be useful. MacCorquodale and Meehl (1954, p. 188) discussed an example in which Tolman (1932, p. 72) interpreted a disruption in maze performance that followed shifting animals from water to food deprivation as a consequence of the "old cognitive expectation of water." They pointed out that the disruption definition of expectancy referred to changes in goal-objects, not to changes in drive state. Accordingly, "the explanation in terms of the expectation of a non-demanded goal object has a certain common-sense appeal; but it requires common-usage connotations, exceeding those of Tolman's formal definition, to do the explaining job it is given here" (MacCorquodale & Meehl, 1954; pp. 188–189).

To summarize, Tolman's theorizing suffered from three main problems: (1) His ideal definitions were only partially capable of reduction to empirical referents; (2) His constructs were connected by so few explicit hypotheses that they were not systematically defined; and (3) His operational definitions were frequently related not to the stated ideal definition, but rather to portions of the common-usage meanings of his terms.

Late Tolman

Following their analysis of Tolman's theorizing through 1949, MacCorquodale and Meehl (1954) attempted to outline a Tolman-like expectancy theory that they hoped would have greater definitional precision. MacCorquodale and Meehl felt that the best way to clarify the meaning of expectancy was to provide a detailed implicit (systematic) definition by way of an explicit postulate set. They acknowledged that a common-sense, surplus-meaning-laden concept of expectancy might be a necessary background for fruitful theorizing and experimenting, but they sought to separate these connotations from the formal structure of the theory. They provided an illuminating example in which they were able to deduce the occurrence of a simple spatial inference that rats are capable of making. One can be struck either by the fact they elevated Tolmanian theorizing to a level of rigor comparable to that of Hullian theory or by the extraordinary effort required to "deduce" what is obvious to common sense. In either case, the contrast with Tolman's style of theorizing is striking.

Tolman (1959) stated that the final version of his theory had been influenced by MacCorquodale and Meehl's attempt to formalize his views. One does find an increased use of formulas and symbols; for example, means-end readinesses and expectations were represented by symbols such as $(S_1 R_1 \rightarrow S_2)$. A distinction was also introduced between the latter types of expectancy and a simple expectancy that one stimulus will follow another $(S_1 \rightarrow S_2)$. On the other hand, the cognitive constructs were still given definitions laden with mentalistic surplus meaning, rather than being defined implicitly, as recommended by MacCorquodale and Meehl. The postulates connecting the constructs remained inexact. The defining experiments (operational definitions) remained sketches for experiments rather than true operational definitions. In summary, the fundamental lack of systematic development that we ascribed to the 1932 theory persisted through the theory's final statement.

Points at Issue Between Expectancy and S–R Theorists

So far, we have been concerned with the formal properties of Tolman's theorizing. We now briefly enumerate the major substantive points that divided expectancy and nonexpectancy theorists, and then consider the extent to which recent years have produced a consensus concerning "who was right."

Theoretical Issues. Tolman returned repeatedly to four points in differentiating his views from others'. First, he insisted that behavior should not be analyzed in terms of muscular movements or glandular outpourings, but rather in terms of "performances." Performances were to be defined in terms of outcomes or achievements, for example, depressing a lever, entering an alleyway, or writing a sentence. Second, he distinguished sharply between learning and performance. Third, he believed that learning did not consist of acquiring a set of habits, that is, a set of S–R connections. He believed, of course, that learning consisted of the acquisition of information (expectations) concerning the outcomes of various responses. The fourth point is closely related to the third. The role of outcomes (reinforcements) in learning was to be understood in terms of confirmation or disconfirmation of expectancies, not the automatic strengthening of connections between stimuli and responses.

Empirical Issues. Five major classes of empirical results were used by Tolman to support the positions outlined above (Hilgard & Bower, 1966). Research on what are today called contrast effects began with Tinklepaugh's (1928) demonstration that a monkey that had been trained to select the one of two cups that hid a piece of banana exhibited "searching" behavior when a piece of lettuce was substituted for the preferred banana. Disruption of maze-running in rats when the magnitude of reward was decreased was later demonstrated by Crespi (1942). Tolman viewed these findings as evidence that animals formed expectancies about goal-objects. Experiments on place learning were designed to show that animals did not learn sequences of movements, but rather the direction or place in which rewards could be found. Latent learning experiments (Blodgett, 1929; Tolman & Honzik, 1930) showed that animals could learn about a maze in the absence of any reward; the learning was demonstrated by abrupt improvements in performance when appropriate demand conditions were introduced. A fourth line of evidence was provided by Krechevsky's (1932, 1938) studies of "hypotheses" in rats engaged in discrimination training in a maze. Tolman interpreted these studies as evidence that the animals successively formed and discarded hypotheses (tentative expectancies) concerning the correct solution to the problem of reaching the goal box. Lastly, Tolman (1948/1958) argued that "vicarious trial and error" (the rat's looking back and forth at choice points in a maze) indicated that the "animal's activity is not just one of responding passively to discrete stimuli, but rather one of the active selecting and comparing of stimuli" (pp. 253–254). We now examine the histories of post-Tolmanian animal and human learning to see how Tolman's views fared against the alternative S–R positions.

Post-Tolmanian Animal Learning

Since Tolman's death there has been very little systematic theorizing in the field of animal learning using the expectancy construct. Bolles (1972) presented a general learning theory based on S–S* and R–S* expectancies and Seligman and Johnston (1973) presented a theory of avoidance learning that used Irwin's (1971) concept of stimulus-act-outcome expectancies. Seligman and Johnston's work is more formalized than Bolles', but neither represents a major advance over the positions of Tolman (1959) and MacCorquodale and Meehl (1954). Irwin's (1971) work is an impressive attempt to define expectancy, intention, and preference without recourse to mentalistic surplus meaning, but there is little development of systematic definitions of these terms. The contrast between this lack of theoretical progress and the numerous theoretical contributions of neo-Hullians such as Miller, Amsel, and Logan is striking.

Equally striking is the fact that on almost every major issue, the current consensus of students of animal learning is Tolmanian rather than Hullian. The learning-performance distinction was incorporated into Hull's (1952) later theorizing, and the definition of response in terms of achievement rather than movements was accepted in practice, if not in principle, by most S–R psychologists (MacCorquodale & Meehl, 1954). With regard to the question of "what is learned?", Estes (1978) concluded that, "like habituation, conditioning is coming to be interpreted by many investigators in terms of processes of memory and response selection rather than as an automatic strengthening of connections . . ." (p. 248). Estes also acknowledged that the field has adopted a fundamentally Tolmanian conception of reinforcement: ". . . reinforcement can only be effectively understood in terms of distinct processes of acquiring information regarding stimulus-outcome and response-outcome contingencies and employing this information in conjunction with overt or covert search or exploratory behavior in order to allow choices among actions to be guided by information concerning probable consequences" (p. 261).

Without denying that there are dissenters, it is also interesting to examine the conclusions reached by Mackintosh (1974) after his exhaustive review of the animal learning literature. His review of the classical conditioning literature led him to reject an S–R interpretation in favor of an S–S interpretation: "Exposure to a contingency between two stimuli results in the formation of an association between them" (p. 91). The widely cited classical conditioning theory of Rescorla and Wagner (1972) is also based on CS–US associations. Mackintosh also rejected an S–R view of instrumental learning: ". . . the role of reinforcement in instrumental learning is not to strengthen antecedent responses: reinforcers do not increase the strength of an association between stimulus and response; they are themselves associated with those responses" (p. 216). Contrast effects (Mackintosh, 1974) and discrimination learning (Medin, 1976) have also received increasingly cognitive interpretations.

Despite the convergence of the animal learning field on basically Tolmanian positions, little use has been made of the expectancy construct, per se. Rescorla and Wagner (1972), for example, referred to a CS–US association rather than to an expectancy of the US. Similarly, Mackintosh referred to the learning of an association between the response and reinforcement, rather than to an expectancy that the response will lead to the reinforcement.

To summarize, there has been little systematic theorizing in the animal learning field using the expectancy construct. However, S–R psychologists have arrived at fundamentally Tolmanian positions, which they have expressed in associationist language rather than expectancy language. Thus, although Tolman appears to have been basically correct, his work has had less direct influence than one would expect (Hilgard & Bower, 1966). We try to understand why this occurred after we review the history of post-Tolmanian human learning.

Post-Tolmanian Human Learning

Classical Conditioning. Excellent reviews of the history of cognitive approaches to classical conditioning have been presented by Gibson (1941), Bandura (1969), and Ross and Ross (1976). Ross and Ross (1976) identified four main periods of research. In the period of the 1920s and 1930s, the roles of the subject's set and awareness of CS–US contingencies were well known (Cook & Harris, 1937), but they were generally viewed as artifacts to be controlled so that pure processes of conditioning could be investigated. Two important exceptions were a series of studies (Hilgard, Campbell, & Sears, 1938; Humphreys, 1939a, 1939b) that investigated the relations between expectancies and the acquisition and extinction of eyeblink responses, and the interaction of subjects' expectancies and intentions in controlling the eyeblink response. During the 1940s and 1950s, experimenters were generally content to control awareness (expectancies) through techniques such as masking tasks, and little research was done on cognitive factors in classical conditioning. A renewed interest in awareness of CS–US relationships developed in the 1960s. This group of investigators (Grings, 1960; Nelson & Ross, 1974) believed that, far from being artifacts, expectancy effects were important, even necessary, for conditioning. In recent years, the interest in cognitive factors has persisted, but information processing models have become increasingly prominent.

Instrumental Conditioning.   Reviews of research on expectancy factors in human instrumental conditioning have been provided by Bandura (1969) and Nelson (1976); we simply highlight a few trends in this literature. Prior to the 1950s, research of human learning was dominated by S–R and, to a lesser extent, Gestalt theories. The expectancy construct did not begin to be widely discussed until Greenspoon's (1955) study of awareness of reinforcement contingencies in verbal operant conditioning. Greenspoon himself concluded that conditioning occurred without awareness, but a flood of subsequent investigations led to a consensus that awareness greatly facilitated learning, although it was perhaps not necessary (Bandura, 1969). Discrimination learning was studied by Levine (1975), who developed a hypothesis theory that was avowedly Tolmanian and which has attracted considerable attention. In recent years there has been an increased use of information processing concepts, with researchers beginning to ask questions such as how expectancies are stored and retrieved from memory. It is noteworthy that the expectancy construct seems to have been more widely used and more heuristic in this field than the others which we have reviewed.

Social Learning Theories.   Tolman's theorizing, along with Kurt Lewin's, was crucial for the development of the social learning theories of Bandura (1977b), Mischel (1973), and Rotter (1954). These theories will be reviewed in the next section of the chapter; at present, we merely wish to note that the concept of expectancy plays a central role in these theories. The success of the social learning theories attests to the heuristic value of the expectancy concept, at least when it is applied to human behavior.

CONCLUSIONS

Our review has led us to two conclusions. The last half century of research has shown that Tolman was basically correct in his views of animal and human learning and those views have been more influential and more heuristic in the human field than in the animal field.

What were the problems in applying Tolman's theory to animal learning? First, the paucity of systematic definition had the consequences that: (1) The theory did little "work," in the sense of generating nonobvious predictions through the interaction of several postulates; and (2) the theory did not entail any hypotheses strongly enough to be disconfirmed if they were not supported by data. Second, the intuitive appeal of the mentalistic surplus meaning of expectancy was seductive, leading experimenters to feel that they understood phenomena rather than leading them to ask more probing, analytic questions. Third, expectancy was difficult to operationalize with nonhuman subjects, whereas the surplus meaning of expectancy could be operationalized in humans by asking about their beliefs.

The surplus meaning of expectancy that seduced animal researchers was an asset for students of human learning, because it permitted them to elaborate more explicit sets of hypotheses about expectancies (i.e., systematic definitions) and to develop multiple operational definitions, each logically related to the ideal definition. We would predict that the history of research on teachers' expectancies will be consistent with the history we have reviewed; the field will flourish if systematically developed theory replaces loose theorizing and the mere accumulation of empirical results.

EXPECTANCY-VALUE THEORIES IN PERSONALITY AND SOCIAL PSYCHOLOGY

Over 20 years ago, Feather (1959) recognized that a surprising variety of theorists had converged on formulations that attempted to predict action from a joint consideration of expectations concerning the consequences of acts and the values placed upon those consequences. Theories of this type have come to be called expectancy-value positions and have occupied central places in the recent histories of personality and social psychology. Although the concept of expectancy has certainly been used outside the context of such theories, Feather's (1982a) recent book documents the pervasive and ongoing influence of expectancy-value theories. Most expectancy-value theorists acknowledge major intellectual debts to Tolman and Kurt Lewin. Having considered Tolman's work at length, we turn now to Lewin's.

Lewin's theoretical vocabulary differed considerably from Tolman's, as did the phenomena that he studied. Lewin described the "life-space" of the individual in terms of "valenced" regions, "paths" connecting those regions, and "forces" or vectors acting on the person. The strength of a psychological force towards a region or goal was determined by the valence of the goal and the psychological distance between the person and the goal. It was soon recognized, however, that there were important parallels between Tolman's and Lewin's theories. White (1943) identified two assumptions that they shared: (1) Learning involves the acquisition of information about the relationships between means and ends, not the acquisition of habits; and 2) behavior is determined by the organism's goals and its knowledge of paths towards those goals. In short, Lewin viewed humans, and Tolman viewed rats, as cognitive, goal-seeking organisms; the two theorists were viewed by their contemporaries as providing alternatives to S–R psychologies.

Lewin's contribution to the development of expectancy-value theories was twofold. First, numerous fruitful lines of empirical research were opened up by him and his students, including research on conflict resolution, decision-making, and level of aspiration. Second, his attempt to develop a formal, explicit theory (Lewin, 1935, 1936, 1938, 1951) produced a number of widely used concepts and principles. Lewin's theorizing had the important general consequence of conferring intellectual legitimacy upon cognitive, non S–R approaches to complex human behavior. However, expectancy was not part of Lewin's theoretical vocabulary in his early work (Lewin, 1935, 1936); he spoke, instead of "cognitive structures" and "paths" towards valenced regions of the life space. Later in his career, the concept of expectancy became more prominent (Lewin, Dembo, Festinger, & Sears, 1944). A major limitation of Lewin's theorizing was that his metatheoretical position led him to place much greater emphasis on conceptual and systematic definitions than on operational definitions (Atkinson, 1964). This may be the reason why Lewin's influence, like Tolman's, remains largely indirect; his theory has not stood the test of time. Nevertheless, many of his ideas live on in contemporary expectancy-value theories.

Of Lewin's empirical contributions, level of aspiration (LOA) research was the most important for the development of expectancy-value theories. Rotter developed many of the ideas that were later incorporated into his social learning theory while working with the LOA paradigm (Rotter, 1943, 1945). Phenomena that would later preoccupy need for achievement researchers, such as goal-setting, reactions to success and failure, and persistence, were first investigated in the context of LOA (Atkinson, 1982). LOA research was also crucial for the development of operations to measure expectancy; we will return to this point later. We turn now to a summary of the histories of several expectancy-value positions that were influenced by both Tolman and Lewin.

Rotter's Social Learning Theory

Rotter's (1954) social learning theory (SLT) was the first attempt to develop a systematic theory of human behavior that used the expectancy construct. Since then, the theory has been elaborated and applied to a variety of issues in personality, social, and clinical psychology (Rotter, Chance, & Phares, 1972; Rotter, 1982). It appears to us that the principal contributions of SLT to the development of expectancy as a systematic construct have been: (1) the careful conceptual definition of several types of expectancies; (2) the analysis of situational determinants of expectancies and, on the other hand, the generalization of expectancies; (3) the statement of numerous principles relating expectancies to other variables, thereby providing a systematic definition of expectancy; and (4) the development of operational definitions of expectancy.

Types of Expectancies. In the initial statement of SLT (Rotter, 1954), expectancy was defined as "the probability held by the individual that a particular reinforcement will occur as a function of a specific behavior on his part in a specific situation or situations" (p. 107). The focus on subjective rather than objective probability reflected Tolman and Lewin's emphases on the environment as perceived by the organism, together with Rotter's (1943, 1945) observation of large individual differences in LOA, despite identical objective probabilities. Although Tolman at one point defined expectancy probabilistically (Tolman & Brunswik, 1935), in practice he did not emphasize the continuous nature of expectancies. Rotter's definition of expectancy in terms of probabilities, rather than all-or-none beliefs, reflected Lewin's later theorizing (Lewin et al., 1944; Lewin, 1951) and Krechevsky's (1932) concept of a hypothesis.

Rotter (1954) went on to distinguish two determinants of expectancy: the specific expectancy, which is "based on past experience in situations perceived to be the same" and generalized expectancies "for the same or similar reinforcements to occur in other situations for the same or functionally related behaviors" (p. 166). In later work, Rotter (1966, 1971, 1978) distinguished between generalized expectancies based on perceived similarity of reinforcements and those based on perceived similarity of the situation. Perceived similarity among situations is frequently based on common decisions to be made or problems to be solved; consequently, the latter type of expectancy was called a problem-solving generalized expectancy. The concept of generalized expectancies for problem-solving gave rise to research on locus of control (Rotter, 1966, 1975) and interpersonal trust (Rotter, 1971, 1980). The final type of expectancy in SLT is the expectancy for reinforcement-reinforcement sequences, that is, the expectancy that some reinforcer will lead to the occurrence of other reinforcers. Although they are of considerable theoretical importance and laboratory investigations of the basic hypotheses have been made, there has been little application of this type of expectancy to practical problems.

In considering how to change teachers' expectancies, separate study may be needed of specific expectancies (I will not succeed in teaching Johnny arithmetic through rote learning), generalized expectancies for reinforcement (I will not succeed in teaching Johnny anything useful through rote methods), problem-solving generalized expectancies (I will not succeed in teaching Johnny anything by any of the usual methods) and expectancies for reinforcement-reinforcement sequences (Even if Johnny learned to read, he'd never be able to hold a job).

Specificity and Generality.   SLT embodied the principle that behavior is best predicted by considering both the effects of the immediate situation and the generalized characteristics that the individual brings to the situation. In other words, it rejected both extreme trait and extreme situationist positions, respecting Lewin's formula that B = f(P,E). With regard to expectancies, SLT acknowledged the roles of both specific and generalized expectancies; the contribution of the latter was hypothesized to vary inversely with the amount of prior experience in the situation. This formulation had its origin in LOA research, in which it was observed that: (1) Subjects' initial goals, and the changes in their goals, depended upon their prior experience with the task; (2) there were large individual differences in subjects' changes in LOA in response to success and failure; and (3) there was a moderate degree of generality from task to task in subjects' changes in LOA. The second and third observations suggested that personality characteristics, that is, relatively stable, generalized properties of the person, were involved in LOA (Rotter, 1943, 1945). Eventually, the study of generalized expectancies as personality variables emerged from this LOA research.

A study by Dean (1953, described in Rotter, 1954) was particularly important, because it illustrated both the importance of generalized expectancies and the limitations of predicting behavior without considering the situation. Dean attempted to predict discrepancies between a subject's stated expectancies in an LOA paradigm and the scores actually obtained. He found that discrepancies could be predicted by measures of generalized expectancy for reinforcement, but that prediction was greater the more closely related the measure of generalized expectancy was to the specific task to be performed. With regard to the effects of teachers' expectancies, this research suggests that expectancy change can best be predicted if the teacher's (and the student's) generalized expectancies are considered as well as the specific expectancies induced by particular events or outcomes. Large increments (or decrements) in expectancy will not take place quickly if environmental events are inconsistent with generalized expectancies.

Systematic Definition.   The initial statement of SLT included principles of expectancy acquisition, change, and generalization, as well as principles linking expectancies, reinforcement values, and situational parameters to the strength of response tendencies. A considerable number of investigations were undertaken on such issues as the effects on expectancy change of the patterning of outcomes and the size of the discrepancy between expectancy and outcome; need-relatedness as a determinant of generalization of expectancy change; and amount of previous experience as a determinant of expectancy change. Much of this research, together with a summary of the principles involving expectancy, can be found in Rotter, Chance, and Phares (1972). One principle, so central that it is easily overlooked, deserves mention: Optimal prediction of behavior requires a consideration of both expectancies and reinforcement values. Theories that focus exclusively on beliefs or needs cannot achieve a high level of prediction. This implies that a full understanding of the effects of teachers' expectancies depends upon understanding the values students and teachers place upon various goals. Those values, like the expectancies, may vary considerably as a function of the situation being investigated.

Operational Definitions. Recognizing the need for operations that were logically related to the theory's constructs, Rotter and his associates developed a variety of procedures for measuring subjective expectancies as continuous variables. Measures were constructed to assess both expectancies for individual trials on laboratory tasks (as in LOA paradigms) and subjects' generalized expectancies. The history of these efforts to operationalize expectancies began with early LOA work. In 1930, Hoppe, a student of Kurt Lewin, published a monograph seeking to study the effect of success and failure on the setting of future goals. American psychologists became interested in this research very early and goal setting behavior was widely studied in the 30s and early 40s, both by social psychologists and personality psychologists interested in individual differences. It became clear, however (Rotter, 1942a), that when a subject was asked what goal (score or level of difficulty) he would seek following a success or failure on some task, some subjects responded by stating a goal they hoped to achieve, some a goal they expected they were most likely to attain and some a goal which they were reasonably sure would avoid any public failure. Instructions for these investigations varied, some emphasizing hope and some expectancy, but recognition of the ambiguity of typical instructions was slow in developing.

One exception was the work of Hausman (1933), who was interested in individual differences in "abnormal responses to success and failure." To reduce the ambiguity of typical LOA instructions, Hausman penalized subjects for overbidding or underbidding, thereby pressuring them to state scores on a task that they were most likely to obtain. After doing this, he still found (clinical analysis) that some subjects deviated from normal patterns of response to success and failure in stable and consistent ways. Interestingly enough, Hausman did not use the term expectancy nor did he describe the differences among his subjects as having anything to do with generalized differences in expectancies for success or failure as a function of long term past experiences. Frank (1935a, 1935b) began the quantification of scores from a set of repeated trials, focusing on the average difference between stated goals and performance, and was able to show some generality of this difference score from one task to another. Using a prearranged sequence of scores (thereby controlling performance), Gardner (1939) was able to show significant generality of difference scores over a variety of tasks.

The use of the LOA method to study generalized differences in expectancies began with Rotter (1942b), who attempted first to compare four different methods of measuring expectancies in level of aspiration situations, in a task involving 20 trials. He concluded that the most reliable and consistent results were obtained using Hausman's instructions. He found in subsequent studies that patterns of responses to a task, including difference scores and frequency and kinds of changes in verbalized expectancies after success and failure (Rotter, 1943, 1945) were reliable and could predict subject characteristics in widely different life situations. It should be noted that Rotter's measure of expectancy was a measure of which of a series of possible scores was given the highest probability—not a measure of probability for a single event. But it was a measure of expectancy, nevertheless, and as Rotter, Fitzgerald, and Joyce (1954) were able to show later, it could be translated into a probability score.

Subsequent efforts to operationalize expectancy within an SLT framework proceeded in two directions. There was continued effort to develop both verbal and nonverbal (e.g., betting on outcomes) measures of expectancy for discrete events; Rotter et al. (1954) showed that there was good convergent validity among these methods. Second, numerous measures of generalized expectancy were developed. These included behavioral, interview, and projective test methods (see Rotter, 1954, pp. 169–174). Later on, questionnaires were devised to measure the generalized expectancies for locus of control (Rotter, 1966) and interpersonal trust (Rotter, 1967a).

We think that it would be fruitful to develop measures of teachers' subjective expectancies, both specific and generalized, to supplement experimental designs that attempt to manipulate expectancies. Individual differences in response to such manipulations are likely to be large, because of individual differences in prior experiences, expectancies, and generalization gradients.

Social Learning Theories of Mischel and Bandura

Mischel, who was a student of Rotter's, was initially interested in situational determinants of the generalization of expectancies (Mischel, 1958) and the effects of generalized expectancies on delay of gratification (Mischel & Staub, 1965). Among his later contributions were his focusing of attention on the psychological situation as a determinant of behavior (Mischel, 1968) and his elaboration of a cognitive-social learning theory (Mischel, 1973). Mischel's cognitive-social learning theory made use of five main concepts: cognitive and behavioral construction competencies, encoding strategies, behavior-outcome and stimulus-outcome expectancies, subjective stimulus values, and self-regulatory systems and plans. Behavior-outcome expectancies and stimulus values were conceptualized in ways similar to the analogous concepts in Rotter's SLT. Mischel's analysis of self-regulation drew on both the SLT concept of minimal goal level and Bandura's discussions of self-regulation. Competencies, encoding strategies, and plans were defined in accordance with contemporary cognitive psychology. This effort to synthesize the SLT tradition and the work of experimental cognitive psychologists appears to have considerable promise. Mischel's recent empirical research has principally been concerned with encoding strategies; we discuss the relationship between the concepts of schema (or prototype) and expectancy later.

Bandura and Walters (1963) described a social learning theory with a central emphasis on modeling, theoretically explained in S–R terms. Later, Bandura (1969) accepted a more cognitive view, emphasizing the role of expectancies in predicting behavior. Both Rotter and Bandura regard expectancy as a principal determinant of which of a person's available behaviors are performed, but Bandura's theory pays less explicit attention to reinforcement values and to stable, individual differences. Recently, Bandura (1977a) has suggested that there is an important distinction between outcome and efficacy expectations. An outcome expectation is "defined as a person's estimate that a given behavior will lead to certain outcomes"; an efficacy expectation is "the conviction that one can successfully execute the behavior required to produce the outcomes" (p. 193). Thus, one might describe a socially anxious male as holding the outcome expectation that a smooth, self-assured approach to a woman would lead to a date, but lacking the efficacy expectation that he is capable of executing that self-assured approach.

In comparing Rotter and Bandura's formulations, it should be remembered that Rotter's outcome expectancy is a subjective probability for a behavior-reinforcement sequence for oneself, *not for someone else*. Obviously, even if a person holds the outcome expectancies that investing in a particular stock will make one rich and that running a mile in 3 minutes will make one famous, the person will not invest the money if *he* doesn't have it nor will he enter a race if *he* cannot run the mile in less than 6 minutes. In both cases, the person's behavior-reinforcement expectancy would be zero. For Rotter, efficacy is included in the broad construct of expectancy.

The distinction between efficacy and outcome expectancies is not needed in Rotter's social learning theory because the concept of locus of control serves to distinguish between cases in which a low expectancy is perceived as due to one's own deficits and those in which it is perceived as due to external forces that would affect anyone. Nevertheless, Bandura's formulation appears to be at least logically tenable. Closer examination reveals that the concept of a belief that "one can successfully execute the behavior" is actually quite ambiguous. Consider first the case of an ordinary cook who believes that he "cannot execute" the behaviors needed to construct a sauce bearnaise. In this context it is clear that cannot execute refers to a perceived lack of skill. Now consider the cases of (1) a person who believes that he cannot execute the response of approaching a snake; (2) a person who believes that he cannot execute the response of abstaining from dessert for a day; and (3) a person who believes that he cannot execute the response of asking the waiter to have his steak cooked more. In each of these cases the person would surely acknowledge that he could execute the response if placed under sufficient threat or if offered sufficient incentives. In these contexts the meaning of cannot execute has shifted from lacks the skill to lacks the motivation. Subsuming beliefs related to skill, and beliefs related to motivation under the single construct of self-efficacy, produces a construct whose meaning, both conceptually defined and systematically defined, is likely to differ in different contexts. In other words, the determinants and consequences of self-efficacy beliefs may be considerably different when efficacy refers to perceived skill to perform an act than when it refers to motivation to perform an act. Furthermore, the determinants of self-efficacy in its motivational sense will be exactly the outcome expectancies (Will the snake bite? Will the waiter bite?) that were supposedly distinct from the efficacy expectancies.

Recent experimental work has confirmed the ambiguous nature of the efficacy/outcome distinction. Maddux, Sherer, and Rogers (1982) showed that measures of self-efficacy were not independent from those of expectancy for successful outcome. Kirsch (1982) showed that in the context of approaching feared stimuli, measures of self-efficacy for approach behavior actually assessed subjects' intentions to approach or avoid. Those intentions were themselves determined by subjects' expectancies concerning the consequences of their acts and the reinforcement values of the consequences. In our opinion, the measurement of self-efficacy cannot be significantly improved until the construct itself is better defined. Kirsch's study also illustrates that measures of efficacy can predict behavior, but they may do so for different reasons from those proposed by self-efficacy theory.

Achievement Motivation

Atkinson (1982) recently presented an informative survey of the history of the theory of achievement motivation. We have drawn heavily from that work and the interested reader is referred there for additional information.

Research on achievement motivation began with McClelland, Atkinson, Clark, and Lowell (1953), who developed a projective measure of the need for achievement and studied its correlates. Surprisingly, they did not relate their work to LOA research, nor did they attempt a systematic use of the expectancy construct to explain their results. While McClelland and his colleagues went on to study achievement motivation in relation to entreprenurial activity, Atkinson attempted to construct a theory of achievement-related behavior.

Atkinson (1982) reported that his early thinking was influenced by Tolman and Lewin's concepts of expectancy, but that until 1955–56 his theory remained relatively informal. In 1957, Atkinson published a seminal paper that related achievement motivation to the product of expectancy, incentive, and motive, the latter conceptualized as a relatively stable individual difference. Feather (1959) quickly realized that the theory was a member of the expectancy-value family, since the product of incentive and motive could be treated as equivalent to the value of an outcome.

Several of the key ideas in Atkinson's theory were suggested by Lewin et al.'s (1944) work on LOA, including the postulate of an inverse relationship between expectancy of success and incentive value of success, and the distinction between the motive to succeed and the motive to avoid failure. The definition of expectancy as a subjectively held probability reflected the influences of Lewin et al. (1944), Rotter (1954), and Tolman (1955). The postulated multiplicative relationship between expectancy, motive, and incentive reflected the influences of Edwards (1954), Lewin et al. (1944), MacCorquodale and Meehl (1954), and Tolman (1955). Edwards' (1954) mathematical statement of subjective expected utility theory eventually led Atkinson (1964) to restate his theory in more formal, precise terms.

The similarities between Atkinson's (1957, 1964) theory and other expectancy-value theories far outweigh their dissimilarities. However, the newly developed "dynamics of action" (Atkinson & Birch, 1970) was a genuine departure from prior theories. Although expectancy, motive, and incentive remained central concepts, the new theory suggested that motives, once aroused, persist until they are expressed in action. Atkinson (1982) contrasted the traditional view of the organism as "dead" until activated by a stimulus with the new view of the "behavioral life of an individual as a continual stream characterized by change from one activity to another even in a constant environment" (p. 34). The theoretician's task was defined as accounting for changes from activity to activity, in terms of both persisting motives and newly aroused action tendencies.

Throughout the development of the theory of achievement motivation, expectancy has, in one regard, been treated in a fashion more similar to Mischel and Bandura's use of the term than Rotter's. Specifically, Atkinson and his colleagues have generally viewed expectancies as situationally determined and have neglected stable individual differences in expectancy. Rotter's SLT, in contrast, recognizes both situational determinants of expectancies and personality differences in generalized expectancies. The theories are not contradictory, but there is a difference in emphasis.

Other Contexts

Feather (1982a) documented the wide range of contexts in which expectancy-value theories have been applied. We cannot survey each of these contexts, but we briefly note several of the most active areas of research.

Organizational Psychology.   According to Mitchell (1982), expectancy-value approaches to organizational psychology were initiated by Vroom's (1964) widely cited analyses of occupational choice, satisfaction, and performance. Vroom (1964) explicitly identified his work as a cognitive theory in the expectancy-value tradition of Tolman, Lewin, Rotter, and Atkinson. The first of Vroom's two postulates related the valence of an outcome to the individual's expectations concerning its instrumentality for producing other outcomes and the valences of those outcomes. The concept of instrumentality is analogous to Rotter's (1954) concept of expectancies for reinforcement-reinforcement sequences. The second postulate related the "force" on a person to perform an act (e.g., accepting a job or working hard at a job) to the person's expectations that various outcomes would be produced and the valences of those outcomes. This formulation spurred a great deal of research, as well as a number of reformulations; the interested reader is referred to Mitchell's (1982) review.

Decision Making.   Feather's book (1982a) contains several chapters reviewing the history of theory and research concerned with decision making. Students of decision making are interested in the situation in which an individual makes a conscious, deliberate choice among explicitly defined alternatives, the outcomes of which are uncertain. Edwards (1954) is credited with initiating research in this area and with bringing to psychologists' attention the work of economists and games theorists on subjective expected utility (SEU) theory. SEU theory predicts the attractiveness of alternatives from the sum of the products of subjective probabilities of the possible outcomes and the subjective utilities of the outcomes.

Although SEU theory is similar in form to other expectancy-value theories, decision theorists have been preoccupied with different research problems. Some of the major research topics have been: The relation between objective probability and subjective probability; the degree to which subjective probabilities conform to the principles of mathematical probability theory; the stability of utilities; the question of the independence or nonindependence of expectancies and utilities; and the form of the function relating expectancies and utilities to expected utility (Fischhoff, Goitein, & Shapira, 1982). These topics are generally investigated using highly controlled laboratory tasks rather than real-life decisions. A point of difference from social learning theories, especially Rotter's (1954), is that decision theorists have been little interested in individual differences as determinants of either expectancies or utilities.

Attitudes.   From the perspective of Rotter's (1967b, 1982) social learning theory, much of the confusion surrounding the relation of attitudes to behavior, and the relation of attitude change to behavior change, is a consequence of failing to distinguish among behavior potentials, expectancies, and reinforcement values. Social psychologists have applied the term attitude to measures of action tendencies, beliefs about groups, affective/evaluative responses to groups, and mixtures of the preceding elements. Only recently have systematic analyses of attitude from an expectancy-value perspective become prominent.

Rosenberg (1956) was the first to attempt such an analysis. He suggested that one's attitude toward an object depended upon the perceived instrumentalities of the object for obtaining various goals and the values placed upon those goals. Fishbein (1963) presented a similar theory that related attitude toward an object to beliefs about the object and implicit evaluative responses linked to each belief.

Rotter (1967b) attempted a social learning analysis of the relation between a subject's privately held expectancies about an object (his or her attitude) and both overt statements of attitude and behavior toward the object. He argued that the prediction of either statements of attitudes or actual behavior required the consideration of (1) reinforcement values as well as expectancies and (2) the multiple sources of reinforcement that may be at stake for the subject. A study by Feather (1982b) demonstrated that behavior was indeed better predicted by joint consideration of expectancies and values than from either alone.

Fishbein and Ajzen's (1975) theory is probably the most influential of the current theories of attitude. They postulated that the intention to perform a behavior is determined by the individual's attitude towards the behavior and his or her subjective norm concerning the behavior. Attitude towards the behavior was defined, as in Fishbein's (1963) theory, as a function of beliefs about the consequences of the act and evaluations of the consequences. According to Fishbein and Ajzen (1975) the subjective norm is "determined by the perceived expectations of specific referent individuals or groups (that the act should or should not be performed), and by the person's motivation to comply with those expectations" (p. 302). Thus, Fishbein and Ajzen's theory could be described as a twofold expectancy-value theory, since it considered expectancies about the consequences of an act, evaluations of the consequences of the act, expectations about others' reactions to the act, and evaluations of the importance of those reactions.

THE EXPECTANCY CONSTRUCT IN THEORIES OF INTERPERSONAL PERCEPTION

We chose to review the history of theories of interpersonal perception for two reasons. First, work on interpersonal perception can illuminate the processes by which teachers' expectancies affect their own behavior and their students' behavior. Second, this research area presents a clear example of an evolutionary process that can be detected in many areas of psychology, that is, successive transformations from unsystematic theorizing, to cognitive theorizing based on the expectancy construct, to cognitive theorizing based on information processing concepts.

Much of the research on interpersonal perception can be viewed as an elaboration, or occasionally a refutation, of the commonsense maxim that we perceive that which we are expecting to see. The earliest attempts to test this maxim took place in the first years of the century and led to the concept of set as a determinant of perception (Gibson, 1941). We briefly summarize this line of research and then discuss the "New Look" movement, which produced theories of the role of expectancy in perception, but did not apply those ideas to the perception of persons. We conclude with a discussion of the current wave of interest in "social cognition," which integrates certain New Look ideas with the field of person perception. We are particularly interested in examining the advantages and disadvantages of adopting the information processing approach. Before beginning our review, it may be useful to indicate what we perceive to be the differences between expectancy theories and information processing theories.

The central construct in information processing approaches to interpersonal perception (Hastie, Ostrom, Ebbesen, Wyer, Hamilton, & Carlston, 1980; Wyer & Carlston, 1979) is that of the schema. Schema and expectancy are, of course, used in different ways by different authors, but we compare Rotter's (1967b) expectancy analysis of social attitudes with some current definitions of schema. Rotter (1967b) began with the notion of a "simple expectancy," which he defined as a belief "regarding a property of an object or series of objects or events" (p. 114). For Rotter, therefore, person perception could be described in terms of expectancies concerning the properties of individuals or classes of individuals. Fiske and Linville (1981) stated that schema "refers to cognitive structures of organized prior knowledge, abstracted from prior experience with specific instances" (p. 544). Wyer and Carlston (1979) gave a more detailed definition, suggesting that schemas consist of attributes that "may be verbally or nonverbally coded physical characteristics . . . general traits and behaviors . . ., or specific behaviors manifested towards particular objects in particular situations . . ." (p. 74). At this level of definition, schema appears to be simply a name for a set of expectancies about an individual or class.

The differences between schemas and expectancies emerge in terms of their systematic and operational definitions. The crucial difference is that schema is embedded in a more or less explicit theory of information processing. Associated with the concepts of information processing are some operational definitions of schema that one would not ordinarily think to apply to expectancy. In Markus' (1977; Markus & Smith, 1981) work, for example, schemas are inferred from differences in the time required to process schema-related and nonschema-related information and from differences in recall of the two types of information. These operations seem quite removed from expectancy. On the other hand, another operation used by Markus (1977) to infer the presence of schemas, the subject's prediction of his or her behavior in a series of hypothetical situations, could easily be used to measure the subject's expectancies. In summary, then, the currently popular concept of schema is only partially distinguishable from certain types of expectancies. Schema becomes a distinct, and potentially valuable construct, only when it is provided with systematic and operational definitions that are both explicit and different from those associated with expectancy.

Set as a Determinant of Perception

According to Gibson's (1941) review, four major types of studies were performed to demonstrate the influence of set on perception. In general, these studies could be interpreted as having aroused certain expectations in the subject concerning the stimuli to be presented. Several studies examined the effects of set on what today would be called selective attention. The largest body of research was concerned with the effects of set on the perception of ambiguous or nonsense stimuli. A third line of research demonstrated that memory was affected by the set adopted by the subject when initially presented with the stimuli (Bartlett, 1932; Zangwill, 1937). A fourth group of investigators studied what Gibson (1941) called relatively permanent sets; these more permanent sets included occupational interests (Dearborn, 1898), emotional state (Murray, 1933) and the state of hunger (Sanford, 1936). This last group of studies represents a link between the older experimental literature's interest in task sets and the New Look's interest in the effects of organismic variables. It is interesting to note that many dependent variables used in contemporary studies of social cognition (e.g., measures of selective attention, encoding of ambiguous stimuli, and selective recall) were anticipated by the early students of set.

The theoretical issues that concerned these researchers are also strikingly similar to some contemporary concerns. For example, attempts to determine the stage of information processing at which schema-related distortions take place are reminiscent of an early debate over whether set affects either or both perception and primary memory (Chapman, 1932). Siipola (1935) performed a study that was conceptualized in terms of the persistence of sets, but which closely resembles contemporary studies of the effects of priming of semantic categories (Srull & Wyer, 1979). Another example is the theory of preperception, which Gibson (1941) summarized as follows: "A prearoused visual image, present at the time of perception, assimilated the incoming sensory data and thereby determined the nature of the total perception" (p. 794). The similarity between this theory and schema theories is apparent. Finally, it should be noted that the schema concept was introduced by Bartlett (1932) and was used to account for a variety of selective memory effects that are today being reexamined in the context of memory for social information.

Despite the similarities to, and anticipations of, contemporary research, the lines of research mentioned above failed to advance much beyond the common-sense maxim that gave birth to them. Numerous issues were debated hotly, remained unresolved, and then slowly receded from psychology's collective consciousness, until they were reactivated by the cognitive revolution. Once again, we would attribute the stagnation in the field to the failure (or inability) to create systematically developed theories.

The New Look in Perception

New Look researchers focused on inner (organismic) determinants of perception, especially the subject's motives and expectancies. Bruner (1951/1973) developed what he referred to as a hypothesis (or expectancy) theory of perception. He defined hypothesis as "a highly generalized state of readiness to respond selectively to classes of events in the environment" (p. 93). Hypotheses were anchored on the antecedent side to several variables and were described as "tuning" the organism's cognitive activity, including perceiving.

In Bruner's (1957/1973) restatement of the theory, perception was considered to be a "process of categorization in which organisms move inferentially from cues to categorical identity . . . perceptual categorization . . . permits one to go beyond the properties of the object or event perceived to a prediction of other properties of the object not yet tested" (p. 14). Categorization was believed to be strongly affected by perceptual readiness, also called category accessibility, which depended upon "the expectancies of the person with regard to the likelihood of events to be encountered in the environment, and the search requirements imposed on the organism by his needs and ongoing enterprises" (p. 19).

It is interesting to note that Bruner (1951/1973) clearly recognized that his theory could be applied to the perception of social stimuli. He wrote, for example, that "the fact that some parents see the obstreperous behavior of their children as fatigued, some as naughty, some as expressing sibling rivalry, . . . is perhaps of the same order (as differential perception of nonsocial stimuli)" (p. 103). Nevertheless, Bruner and the other New Look researchers did not develop the implications of their ideas for social perception.

The theory appears to predict that teachers who expect a particular type of behavior from a student will be more attentive to consistent cues, will require less information to perceive the expected behavior, will more quickly begin to discount inconsistent behavior, and will infer more characteristics that are consistent with the expected behavior. These sorts of predictions are quite similar to those that might be generated from a schema theory of social cognition.

Social Cognition and the Transformation of Expectancy into Schema

Prior to 1970, there was little explicit use of the expectancy concept in research on person perception (Tagiuri, 1969). The cognitive revolution of the 1970s transformed the field of person perception into the still emerging field of social cognition. Hamilton's (1979) analysis of the cognitive processes involved in stereotyping provides a particularly interesting example, because it is a transitional case between expectancy and schema theories of person perception. Hamilton (1979) moved back and forth between two modes of theorizing. In the first mode, he simply postulated relations between the perceiver's stereotype-based expectancies and his or her interpretations of, memory for, and attributions for the others' behavior; in the second mode, he attempted to introduce a process theory to explain the postulated effects of expectancies. For example, he wrote that "Deaux (1976) has proposed that the successful or unsuccessful performance of an actor is evaluated . . . in terms of the expectancies held by the perceiver . . . behavior which is consistent with expectations . . . will be attributed to a stable cause'' (p. 66). Following that, he wrote (p. 68) that ''A full understanding of this relationship requires empirical investigation of the cognitive mediating processes that might underlie this effect; that is, if the schema-based expectancies do bias the perceiver's use of the information available to him then it is important to determine at what point(s) in the cognitive processing system this bias is occurring.''

Either of the two styles of theorizing in Hamilton's (1979) article could be applied to understanding the effects of teachers' expectancies. Researchers could look for lawful relations between expectancies and dependent variables such as attention, encoding, memory, and attribution, or they could attempt to deduce those relations from process theories in which the schema concept plays a central role.

The final step in transforming Bruner's (1951/1973) expectancy theory of perception into a schema-based theory has been taken by a number of recent authors, including Wyer and Carlston (1979) and Wyer and Srull (1980). Their theories attempt to account for the basic findings that subjects' expectations affect their encoding of social information, their memory for that information, and the inferences or judgments that they base on the information. Theories of social cognition make use of concepts such as schemas, scripts, memory nodes, spread of excitation, encoding, and retrieval. The crucial question is whether these elaborate process models are more powerful than simpler expectancy theories such as Bruner's (1951/1973). In Fiske and Linville's (1980) words, ''what does the schema concept buy us?''

Schema theories promise to describe the processes that underlie relations that expectancy theories can only summarize, for example, the effects of a person's expectations on subsequent attributions. In the absence of truly explicit process theories, however, schema theories encounter two problems. First, they risk becoming no more than currently fashionable ways of summarizing the same kinds of results that can be summarized by an expectancy theory such as Bruner's (1951/1973). Second, they risk becoming more complex without becoming more explicit, and in so doing they risk becoming less falsifiable. In moving from expectancy theories to schema theories, researchers are trading off the promise of eventually obtaining a more detailed understanding of social cognition against the risk of becoming lost in untestably complex theories. If schema theorists can elaborate and refine the systematic and operational definitions of schema, they may win the gamble.

Progress has already been made in operationalizing some of the processes hypothesized in schema theories. Researchers who have adopted the tools of the cognitive psychologist such as reaction time measures, measures of false alarms in recognition memory, semantic priming manipulations, and ratings of prototypicality, have been able to demonstrate some effects that could not easily be deduced from an expectancy theory (Hastie et al., 1981). It is also true, however, that the ability of theoreticians to postulate mental apparatus has outrun the ability of experimentalists to operationalize the apparatus and their own ability to describe its workings fully and explicitly. Researchers in the field of social cognition might do well to recall the history of the expectancy construct in learning theories. Specifically, we found that oversimplified, yet systematically developed, theories were frequently more heuristic than their unsystematic rivals, despite the greater truth value of the later theories.

SUMMARY

Research described elsewhere in this book makes it clear that teachers' expectancies regarding pupils' intellectual capacities affect the teachers' behavior in predictable ways. What this chapter hoped to provide was the recognition that such effects are only one instance of a long history of theorizing and research on the relationship between expectancy and behavior. Relevant to the problem of teachers' behavior are many types of expectancies and systematic theories of how these expectancies are acquired and changed. It appears from our historical review that hypotheses regarding the effects of these expectancies on behavior will be most fruitful if investigators provide careful definitions, with at least suggestive logical operations for measurement and systematic statements of the relationship of expectancies to other variables.

REFERENCES

Atkinson, J. W. *Motivational determinants of risk-taking behavior. Psychological Review,* 1957, *64,* 359–372.

Atkinson, J. W. *An introduction to motivation.* New York: Van Nostrand, 1964.

Atkinson, J. W. Old and new conceptions of how expected consequences influence actions. In N. T. Feather (Ed.), *Expectations and actions.* Hillsdale, N.J.: Lawrence Erlbaum Associates, 1982.

Atkinson, J. W., & Birch, D. *The dynamics of action.* New York: Wiley, 1970.

Bandura, A. *Principles of behavior modification.* N.Y.: Holt, Rinehart & Winston, 1969.

Bandura, A. Self-efficacy: Toward a unifying theory of behavioral change. *Psychological Review,* 1977a, *84,* 191–215.

Bandura, A. *Social learning theory.* Englewood Cliffs, N.J.: Prentice-Hall, 1977b.

Bandura, A., & Walters, R. H. *Social learning and personality development.* New York: Holt, Rinehart & Winston, 1963.

Bartlett, F. C. *Remembering: A study in experimental and social psychology.* Cambridge, England: University Press, 1932.

Blodgett, H. C. The effect of the introduction of reward upon the maze performance of rats. *University of California Publications in Psychology,* 1929, *4,* 113–134.

Bolles, R. C. Reinforcement, expectancy, and learning. *Psychological Review,* 1972, *79,* 394–409.

Bruner, J. S. On perceptual readiness. In J. M. Anglin (Ed.), *Beyond the information given.* N.Y.: Norton, 1973. (Reprinted from *Psychological* Review, 1957, *64.*)

Bruner, J. S. Personality dynamics and the process of perceiving. In J. Anglin (Ed.), *Beyond the information given.* N.Y.: Norton, 1973. (Reprinted from R. R. Blake & G. V. Ramsey, (Eds.), *Perception—An approach to personality,* N.Y.: Ronald Press, 1951.)

Chapman, D. W. Relative effects of determinate and indeterminate *Aufgaben. American Journal of Psychology,* 1932, *44,* 163–174.

Cook, S. W., & Harris, R. E. The verbal conditioning of the galvanic skin reflex. *Journal of Experimental Psychology,* 1937, *21,* 202–210.

Crespi, L. P. Quantitative variation of incentive and performance in the white rat. *American Journal of Psychology,* 1942, *55,* 467–517.

Dearborn, G. A study of imaginations. *American Journal of Psychology,* 1898, *9,* 183–190.

Deaux, K. Sex: A perspective on the attribution process. In J. H. Harvey, W. J. Ickes, & R. F. Kidd (Eds.), *New directions in attribution research* (Vol. 1). Hillsdale, N.J.: Lawrence Erlbaum Associates, 1976.

Edwards, W. The theory of decision-making. *Psychological Bulletin,* 1954, *51,* 380–417.

Estes, W. K. On the organization and core concepts of learning theory and cognitive psychology. In W. K. Estes (Ed.), *Handbook of learning and cognitive processes* (Vol. 6). Hillsdale, N.J.: Lawrence Erlbaum Associates, 1978.

Feather, N. T. Subjective probability and decision under uncertainty. *Psychological Review,* 1959, *66,* 150–164.

Feather, N. T. (Ed.). *Expectations and actions.* Hillsdale, N.J.: Lawrence Erlbaum Associates, 1982a.

Feather, N. T. Human values and the prediction of action: An expectancy-influence analysis. In N. T. Feather (Ed.), *Expectations and actions.* Hillsdale, N.J.: Lawrence Erlbaum Associates, 1982b.

Fischhoff, B., Goitein, B., & Shapira, Z. The experienced utility of expected utility approaches. In N. T. Feather (Ed.), *Expectations and actions.* Hillsdale, N.J.: Lawrence Erlbaum Associates, 1982.

Fishbein, M. An investigation of the relationships between beliefs about an object and the attitude toward that object. *Human Relations,* 1963, *16,* 223–240.

Fishbein, M., & Ajzen, I. *Belief, attitude, intention and behavior: An introduction to theory and research.* Reading, Mass.: Addison-Wesley, 1975.

Fiske, S. T., & Linville, P. W. What does the schema concept buy us? *Personality and Social Psychology Bulletin,* 1981, *6,* 543–557.

Frank, J. D. Individual differences in certain aspects of the level of aspiration. *American Journal of Psychology,* 1935a, *47,* 119–126.

Frank, J. D. Some psychological determinants of the level of aspiration. *American Journal of Psychology,* 1935b, *47,* 285–293.

Gardner, J. W. Level of aspiration in response to a prearranged sequence of scores. *Journal of Experimental Psychology,* 1939, *25,* 601–621.

Gibson, J. J. A critical review of the concept of set in contemporary experimental psychology. *Psychological Bulletin,* 1941, *38,* 781–817.

Greenspoon, J. The reinforcing effect of two spoken sounds on the frequency of two responses. *American Journal of Psychology,* 1955, *68,* 409–416.

Grings, W. W. Preparatory set variables related to classical conditioning of autonomic responses. *Psychological Review,* 1960, *67,* 243–252.

Hamel, I. A. A study and analysis of the conditioned reflex. *Psychological Monographs,* 1919, *27,* Whole No. 118.

Hamilton, D. A cognitive-attributional analysis of stereotyping. In L. Berkowitz (Ed.), *Advances in experimental social psychology* (Vol. 12). N.Y.: Academic Press, 1979.

Hastie, R., Ostrom, T. M., Ebbesen, E. B., Wyer, R. S., Jr., Hamilton, D. L., & Carlston, D. E. *Person memory: The cognitive basis of social perception.* Hillsdale, N.J.: Lawrence Erlbaum Associates, 1980.

Hausmann, M. F. A test to evaluate some personality traits. *Journal of Genetic Psychology,* 1933, *9,* 179–189.

Hilgard, E. R., & Bower, G. H. *Theories of learning* (3rd ed.). N.Y.: Appleton-Century-Crofts, 1966.

Hilgard, E. R., Campbell, R. K., & Sears, W. N. Conditioned discrimination: The effect of knowledge of stimulus-relationships. *American Journal of Psychology,* 1938, *51,* 498–506.

Hull, C. L. *A behavior system: An introduction to behavior theory concerning the individual organism.* New Haven: Yale University, 1952.

Humphreys, L. G. The effect of random alternation of reinforcement on the acquisition and extinction of conditioned eyelid reactions. *Journal of Experimental Psychology,* 1939a, *25,* 141–158.

Humphreys, L. G. Acquisition and extinction of verbal expectations in a situation analogous to conditioning. *Journal of Experimental Psychology,* 1939b, *25,* 294–301.

Irwin, F. W. *Intentional behavior and motivation: A cognitive theory.* New York: Lippincott, 1971.

Kirsch, I. Efficacy expectations or response predictions: The meaning of efficacy ratings as a function of task characteristics. *Journal of Personality and Social Psychology,* 1982, *42,* 132–136.

Krechevsky, I. "Hypotheses" in rats. *Psychological Review,* 1932, 39, 516–532.

Krechevsky, I. A study of the continuity of the problem-solving process. *Psychological Review,* 1938, *45,* 107–133.

Levine, M. *A cognitive theory of learning: Research on hypothesis testing.* Hillsdale, N.J.: Lawrence Erlbaum Associates, 1975.

Lewin, K. *A dynamic theory of personality.* N.Y.: McGraw-Hill, 1935.

Lewin, K. *Principles of topological psychology.* N.Y.: McGraw-Hill, 1936.

Lewin, K. *The conceptual representation and the measurement of psychological forces.* Durham, N.C.: Duke University, 1938.

Lewin, K. *Field theory in social science.* New York: Harper, 1951.

Lewin, K., Dembo, T., Festinger, L., & Sears, P. S. Level of aspiration. In J. McV. Hunt (Ed.), *Personality and the behavior disorders.* N.Y.: Ronald, 1944.

McClelland, D. C., Atkinson, J. W., Clark, R. W., & Lowell, E. L. *The achievement motive.* N.Y.: Appleton-Century-Crofts, 1953.

MacCorquodale, K., & Meehl, P. E. Edward C. Tolman. In W. Estes, S. Koch, K. MacCorquodale, P. Meehl, C. Mueller, W. Schoenfeld, & W. Verplanck (Eds.), *Modern learning theory.* N.Y.: Appleton-Century-Crofts, 1954.

Mackintosh, N. J. *The psychology of animal learning.* New York: Academic Press, 1974.

Maddux, J. E., Sherer, M., & Rogers, R. W. Self-efficacy expectancy and outcome expectancy: Their relationship and their effects on behavioral intentions. *Cognitive Therapy and Research,* 1982, *6,* 207–212.

Markus, H. Self-schemata and processing information about the self. *Journal of Personality and Social Psychology,* 1977, *35,* 63–78.

Markus, H., & Smith, J. The influence of self-schemata on the perception of others. In N. Cantor & J. F. Kihlstrom (Eds.), *Personality, cognition, and social interaction.* Hillsdale, N.J.: Lawrence Erlbaum Associates, 1981.

Medin, D. L. Theories of discrimination learning and learning set. In W. K. Estes (Ed.), *Handbook of learning and cognitive processes* (Vol. 3). Hillsdale, N.J.: Lawrence Erlbaum Associates, 1976.

Mischel, W. The effect of the commitment situation on the generalization of expectancies. *Journal of Personality,* 1958, *26,* 508–516.

Mischel, W. *Personality and assessment.* N.Y.: Wiley, 1968.

Mischel, W. Toward a cognitive social learning reconceptualization of personality. *Psychological Review,* 1973, *80,* 252–283.

Mischel, W., & Staub, E. Effects of expectancy on working and waiting for larger rewards. *Journal of Personality and Social Psychology,* 1965, *2,* 625–633.

Mitchell, T. R. Expectancy-value models in organizational psychology. In N. T. Feather (Ed.), *Expectations and actions.* Hillsdale, N.J.: Lawrence Erlbaum Associates, 1982.

Murray, H. A. The effect of fear upon estimates of the maliciousness of other personalities. *Journal of Social Psychology,* 1933, *4,* 310–339.

Nelson, M. N., & Ross, L. E. Effects of masking tasks on differential eyelid conditioning; A distinction between knowledge of stimulus contingencies and attentional or cognitive activities involving them. *Journal of Experimental Psychology,* 1974, *102,* 1–9.

Nelson, T. O. Reinforcement and human memory. In W. K. Estes (Ed.), *Handbook of learning and cognitive processes* (Vol. 3). Hillsdale, N.J.: Lawrence Erlbaum Associates, 1976.

Rescorla, R. A., & Wagner, A. R. A theory of Pavlovian conditioning: Variations in the effectiveness of reinforcement and nonreinforcement. In A. H. Black & W. A. Prokasy (Eds.), *Classical conditioning II: Current theory and research.* N.Y.: Appleton-Century-Crofts, 1972.

Rosenberg, M. J. Cognitive structure and attitudinal affect. *Journal of Abnormal and Social Psychology,* 1956, *53,* 367–372.

Ross, L. E., & Ross, S. M. Cognitive factors in classical conditioning. In W. K. Estes (Ed.), *Handbook of learning and cognitive processes* (Vol. 3). Hillsdale, N.J.: Lawrence Erlbaum Associates, 1976.

Rotter, J. B. Level of aspiration as a method of studying personality. I. A critical review of methodology. *Psychological Review,* 1942a, *49,* 463–474.

Rotter, J. B. Level of aspiration as a method of studying personality. II. Development and evaluation of a controlled method. *Journal of Experimental Psychology,* 1942b, *31,* 410–422.

Rotter, J. B. Level of aspiration as a method of studying personality. III. Group validity studies. *Character and Personality,* 1943, *11,* 254–274.

Rotter, J. B. Level of aspiration as a method of studying personality. IV. The analysis of patterns of response. *Journal of Social Psychology,* 1945, *21,* 159–177.

Rotter, J. B. *Social learning and clinical psychology.* Englewood-Cliffs: Prentice-Hall, 1954.

Rotter, J. B. Generalized expectancies for internal versus external control of reinforcement. *Psychological Monographs,* 1966, *80,* (1, Whole No. 609).

Rotter, J. B. A new scale for the measurement of interpersonal trust. *Journal of Personality,* 1967a, *35,* 651–665.

Rotter, J. B. Beliefs, social attitudes, and behavior: A social learning analysis. In R. Jessor and S. Feshbach (Eds.), *Cognition, personality, and clinical psychology.* San Francisco: Jossey-Bass, 1967b.

Rotter, J. B. Generalized expectancies for interpersonal trust. *American Psychologist,* 1971, *26,* 443–452.

Rotter, J. B. Some problems and misconceptions related to the construct of internal versus external control of reinforcement. *Journal of Consulting and Clinical Psychology,* 1975, *43,* 56–67.

Rotter, J. B. Generalized expectancies for problem solving and psychotherapy. *Cognitive Therapy and Research,* 1978, *2,* 1–10.

Rotter, J. B. Interpersonal trust, trustworthiness, and gullibility. *American Psychologist,* 1980, *35,* 1–7.

Rotter, J. B. Social learning theory. In N. T. Feather (Ed.), *Expectations and actions.* Hillsdale, N.J.: Lawrence Erlbaum Associates, 1982.

Rotter, J. B. *The development and applications of social learning theory: Selected papers.* N.Y.: Praeger, 1982.

Rotter, J. B., Chance, J. E., & Phares, E. J. *Applications of a social learning theory of personality.* N.Y.: Holt, Rinehart, & Winston, 1972.

Rotter, J. B., Fitzgerald, B. J., & Joyce, J. A comparison of some objective measures of expectancy. *Journal of Abnormal and Social Psychology,* 1954, *49,* 111–114.

Sanford, R. N. The effects of abstinence from food upon imaginal processes: A preliminary experiment. *Journal of Psychology,* 1936, *2,* 129–136.

Schilder, P. Conditioned reflexes. *Archives of Neurological Psychiatry,* 1929, *22,* 425–443.

Seligman, M. E. P., & Johnston, J. C. A cognitive theory of avoidance learning. In F. J. McGuigan and D. B. Lumsden (Eds.), *Contemporary approaches to conditioning and learning.* Washington, D.C.: Winston, 1973.

Siipola, E. M. A group study of some effects of preparatory set. *Psychological Monographs,* 1935, *46,* Whole No. 210, 27–38.

Srull, T. K., & Wyer, R. S. The role of category accessibility in the interpretations of information about persons: Some determinants and implications. *Journal of Personality and Social Psychology,* 1979, *37,* 1660–1672.

Tagiuri, R. Person perception. In G. Lindzey & E. Aronson (Eds.), *The handbook of social psychology* (Vol. 3). Reading, Mass.: Addison-Wesley, 1969.

Tinklepaugh, O. L. An experimental study of representative factors in monkeys. *Journal of Comparative Psychology,* 1928, *8,* 197–236.

Tolman, E. C. Cognitive maps in rats and men. In E. C. Tolman, *Behavior and psychological man.* Berkeley: University of California Press, 1958. (Originally published, 1948).

Tolman, E. C. Principles of performance. *Psychological Review,* 1955, *62,* 315–326.

Tolman, E. C. Principles of purposive behavior. In S. Koch (Ed.), *Psychology: A study of a science* (Vol. 2). N.Y.: McGraw-Hill, 1959.

Tolman, E. C. *Purposive behavior in animals and men.* N.Y.: Appleton-Century-Crofts, 1932.

Tolman, E. C. The determiners of behavior at a choice point. *Psychological Review,* 1938, *45,* 1–41.

Tolman, E. C., & Brunswick, E. The organism and the causal texture of the environment. *Psychological Review,* 1935, *42,* 43–77.

Tolman, E. C., & Honzik, C. H. Introduction and removal of reward, and maze performance in rats. *University of California Publications in Psychology,* 1930, 257–275.

Vroom, V. H. *Work and motivation.* N.Y.: Wiley, 1964.

White, R. K. The case for the Tolman-Lewin interpretation of learning. *Psychological Review,* 1943, *50,* 157–186.

Wyer, R. S., Jr., & Carlston, D. E. *Social cognition, inference, and* attribution. Hillsdale, N.J.: Lawrence Erlbaum Associates, 1979.

Wyer, R. S., Jr., & Srull, T. K. The processing of social information: A conceptual integration. In R. Hastie, T. Ostrom, E. Ebbesen, R. Wyer, D. Hamilton, & D. Carlston (Eds.), *Person memory: The cognitive basis of social perception.* Hillsdale, N.J.: Lawrence Erlbaum Associates, 1980.

Zangwill, O. L. A study of the significance of attitude in recognition. *British Journal of Psychology,* 1937, *28,* 12–17.

3

From Unconscious Experimenter Bias to Teacher Expectancy Effects

Robert Rosenthal
Harvard University

The general purpose of this chapter is to describe the early history of experiments designed to test the hypothesis of interpersonal expectancy effects. Interpersonal expectancy effects refer to the effects of one person's expectations for the behavior of another person on that other person's behavior. Early experiments on interpersonal expectancy effects were designed to learn whether psychological experiments might unintentionally influence their research subjects to respond in accordance with the experimenters' hypotheses or expectations.

The specific purpose of this chapter, located as it is in a volume on teacher expectancy effects, is to trace the early history of experiments on experimenter expectancy effects from their inception to experiments on teacher expectancy (Pygmalion) effects. In addition, the historical tracing goes somewhat beyond these Pygmalion experiments to consider some of the methodological, the substantive, and the social consequences of this research. To be more precise it is not *the* history that will be traced but *a* history; A personal history of experiments and other studies. In this chapter I have been licensed to provide the recollections of an oldtimer.

PYGMALION EFFECTS: WHERE FROM?
EXPERIMENTER EXPECTANCY EFFECTS AND AN
UNNECESSARY STATISTICAL ANALYSIS

As a graduate student at UCLA in the mid 1950s I was much taken with the work of two giants of personality theory, Freud and Murray. I was taken with Freud, as were so many others, for the richness and depth of his theory. I was taken with Murray, as were not enough others, for similar reasons, but also because of

Murray's brilliant way of inventing whatever tool was needed to get him along in his inquiry. Thus, the Thematic Apperception Test was invented simply as a tool to further his research though it has become recognized as a major contribution in its own right. My dissertation was to depend on the work of both these great theorists.

Sigmund Freud's Projection.   As a graduate student in clinical psychology I was (and still am) very much interested in projective techniques. Murray's TAT, Shneidman's Make a Picture Story Test, and, of course, the Rorschach, were exciting methods for understanding people better. Shneidman, a brilliant researcher and clinician, was my first clinical supervisor during my VA clinical intership. Bruno Klopfer, one of the alltime Rorschach greats, was the chair of my doctoral committee. It was natural, therefore, for me to be concerned about the defense mechanism of projection for the part it might play in the production of responses to projective stimuli.

Harry Murray's Party Game.   Freud's defense mechanism of projection, the ascription to others of one's own states or traits (Freud, 1953; Rosenthal 1956) is only one of the mechanisms that has been isolated as contributing to the process of producing responses to projective stimuli. Another mechanism is complementary apperceptive projection, that is, finding in another the reasons for one's own states or traits. It was this mechanism that Harry Murray investigated in his classic paper on "The Effect of Fear Upon Estimates of the Maliciousness of Other Personalities" (Murray, 1933). At his 11 year old daughter's houseparty, Murray arranged a game called "Murder" that tended to frighten delightfully the five party-going subjects. After the game Murray found the children perceived photographs as more malicious than they did before the game of Murder. Murray's wonderfully direct and deceptively simple procedure of assessing projective processes by means of assessing changes in perceptions of photographs was the basic measuring device I adopted for my dissertation.

"An Attempt at the Experimental Induction of the Defense Mechanism of Projection."   With the foregoing as its almost unbearable title, my dissertation employed a total of 108 subjects: 36 college men, 36 college women, and 36 hospitalized patients with paranoid symptomatology. Each of these three groups was further divided into three subgroups receiving success, failure, or neutral experience on a task structured as and simulating a standardized test of intelligence. Before the subjects' experimental conditions were imposed, they were asked to rate the degree of success or failure of persons pictured in photographs. Immediately after the experimental manipulation, subjects were asked to rate an equivalent set of photos on their degree of success or failure. The dependent variable was the magnitude of the difference scores from pre to post ratings of the photographs. It was hypothesized that the success condition would lead to the

subsequent perception of other people as more successful while the failure condition would lead to the subsequent perception of other people as having failed more as measured by the pre/post difference scores.

In an attack of studently compulsivity, an attack that greatly influenced my scholarly future, I did a statistical analysis that was quite extraneous to the main purpose of the dissertation. In this analysis I compared the mean pre treatment ratings of the three experimental conditions. These means were:

Success: −1.52
Neutral: −0.86
Failure: −1.02

The pretreatment rating mean of the success condition was significantly lower than the mean of either of the other two conditions. It must be emphasized that these three treatment groups had not yet undergone their treatment; they were only destined to become the subjects of the three conditions. If the success group started out lower than the other conditions, then, even if there were no differences among the three conditions in their posttreatment photo ratings, the success group would show the greatest gain, a result favoring one of my hypotheses, namely that projection of the good could occur just as well as projection of the bad. Without my awareness, the cards had been stacked in favor of obtaining results supporting one of my hypotheses. It should be noted that the success and failure groups' instructions had been verbatim identical during the pretreatment rating phase of the experiment. (Instructions to the neutral group differed only in that no mention was made of the experimental task, since none was administered to this group.)

The problem, apparently, was that I knew for each subject which experimental treatment he or she would subsequently be administered. As I noted in 1956 with some dismay: "The implication is that in some subtle manner, perhaps by tone, or manner, or gestures, or general atmosphere, the experimenter, although formally testing the success and failure groups in an identical way, influenced the success subjects to make lower initial ratings and thus increase the experimenter's probability of verifying his hypothesis" (Rosenthal, 1956, p. 44). As a further check on the suspicion that Success subjects had been differentially treated, the conservatism-extremeness of pretreatment ratings of photos was analyzed. The mean extremeness-of-rating scores were as follow:

Success   3.92
Neutral   4.41
Failure   4.42

The success group rated photos significantly less extremely than did the other treatment groups. Whatever it was I did differently to those subjects that I knew were destined for the success condition, it seemed to affect not only their mean level of rating, but their style of rating as well.

The Search for Company.   When I discussed these strange goings-on with some faculty members they seemed not overly surprised. A not very reassuring response was "Oh yes, we lose a few Ph.D. dissertations now and then because of problems like that." There followed a frantic search of the literature for references to this phenomenon that I then called "unconscious experimenter bias." As far back as Ebbinghaus (1885) psychologists had been referring to something like this phenomenon and Table 1 lists some of these workers and their phenomena. Unfortunately, none of these investigators (or even later ones) had explicitly designed and conducted an experiment to test the hypothesis of unconscious experimenter bias; that remained to be done.

Table 3.1 is intended to be illustrative, not exhaustive, and it is in large degree self-explanatory. There is something I do want to add, however, about the last entry, the paper by Rosenzweig (1933), which appeared the same year that Harry Murray's paper (cited earlier) appeared, and, incidentally, the same year that I appeared. In my own several reviews of the literature (e.g., 1956, 1966) I had completely missed the Rosenzweig paper. I believe it was my good friend, long time collaborator and scholarly tutor, Ralph Rosnow, who called my attention to Rosenzweig's extraordinarily insightful and prophetic paper. Not only did Rosenzweig anticipate the problem of unconscious experimenter bias, but he also anticipated virtually the entire area now referred to as the "social psychology of the psychological experiment." The Rosenzweig paper makes good reading even

TABLE 3.1
Early Discussions of Phenomena Related to Unconscious
Experimenter Bias: 1885–1933

Dates	Authors	Phenomena
1885	Ebbinghaus	Early data returns became bases for self-fulfilling prophecies.
1898	Moll	Hypnotized subjects responded as expected to respond.
1911	Pfungst	Questioners of Clever Hans unwittingly communicated their expectations to Hans.
1927	Clark	More athletic survey interviewer obtained reports of higher levels of athletic participation by respondents than did less athletic interviewer.
1929	Pavlov	Experimenters' expectations affected learning by their mice (Gruenberg, 1929).
1929	Rice	Interviewers' expectations about causes of poverty affected responses obtained.
1929	Marine	Investigated degree of acquaintance with the experimenter as a factor in subject test performance.
1932	Barr	Studied individual differences among experimenters in data obtained from standard experiment.
1933	Rosenzweig	Anticipated not only unconscious experimenter bias but virtually the entire area of the social psychology of the psychological experiment.

today, some 50 years later. There is a superb appreciation of the Rosenzweig paper in Ralph Rosnow's recent and brilliant book about the methodology of social inquiry: *Paradigms in Transition* (Rosnow, 1981).

The Production of Company

If it was my "unconscious experimenter bias" that had led to the puzzling and disconcerting results of my dissertation then presumably we could produce the phenomenon in our own laboratory and with several experimenters rather than just one. Producing the phenomenon in this way would yield not only the scientific benefit of demonstrating an interesting and important concept, it would also yield the very considerable personal benefit of showing that I was not alone in having unintentionally affected the results of my research by virtue of my bias or expectancy.

Human Subjects.   In the first of our studies employing human subjects, 10 undergraduate and graduate students of psychology served as the experimenters (Rosenthal & Fode, 1963b). All were enrolled in an advanced course in experimental psychology and were already involved in conducting research. Each student-experimenter was assigned as his or her subjects about 20 students of introductory psychology. The procedure was for the experimenters to show a series of 10 photographs of people's faces to each of their subjects individually. Subjects were to rate the degree of success or failure shown in the face of each person pictured in the photos. Each face could be rated at any value from −10 to +10, with −10 meaning extreme failure and +10 meaning extreme success. The 10 photos had been selected so that, on the average, they would be seen as neither successful nor unsuccessful, but quite neutral, with an average numerical score of zero.

All 10 experimenters were given identical instructions on how to administer the task to their subjects and were given identical instructions to read to their subjects. They were cautioned not to deviate from these instructions. The purpose of their participation, it was explained to all experimenters, was to see how well they could duplicate experimental results which were already well-established. Half the experimenters were told that the "well-established" finding was such that their subjects should rate the photos as of successful people (ratings of +5) and half the experimenters were told that their subjects should rate the photos as being of unsuccessful people (ratings of −5). Results showed that experimenters expecting higher photo ratings obtained higher photo ratings than did experimenters expecting lower photo ratings. Subsequent studies tended to obtain generally similar results.

Animal Subjects.   Pfungst's work with Clever Hans and Pavlov's work on the inheritance of acquired characteristics had both suggested the possibility of experimenter expectancy effects with animal subjects (Gruenberg, 1929; Pfungst, 1911). In addition, Bertrand Russell (1927) had noted this possibility, adding that animal subjects take on the national character of the experimenter. As "Bertie" put it: "Animals studied by Americans rush about frantically, with an incredible display of hustle and pep, and at last achieve the desired result by chance. Animals observed by Germans sit still and think, and at last evolve the solution out of their inner consciousness" (pp. 29–30).

But it was not only the work of Pavlov, Pfungst, and Russell that made us test the generality of experimenter expectancy effects by working with animal subjects. It was also the reaction of my friends and colleagues who themselves worked with animal subjects. That reaction was: "Well of course you'd find expectancy effects and other artifacts when you work with human subjects; that's why we work with rats."

A good beginning might have been to replicate with a larger sample size Pfungst's research with Clever Hans; but with horses hard to come by, rats were made to do (Rosenthal & Fode, 1963a).

A class in experimental psychology had been performing experiments with human subjects for most of a semester. Now they were asked to perform one more experiment, the last in the course, and the first employing animal subjects. The experimenters were told of studies that had shown that maze-brightness and maze-dullness could be developed in strains of rats by successive inbreeding of the well and the poorly performing maze-runners. Sixty laboratory rats were equitably divided among the 12 experimenters. Half the experimenters were told that their rats were maze-bright while the other half were told their rats were maze-dull. The animal's task was to learn to run to the darker of two arms of an elevated T maze. The two arms of the maze, one white and one gray, were interchangeable; and the "correct" or rewarded arm was equally often on the right as on the left. Whenever animals ran to the correct side they obtained a food reward. Each rat was given 10 trials each day for 5 days to learn that the darker side of the maze was the one which led to the food.

Beginning with the first day and continuing on through the experiment, animals believed to be better performers became better performers. Animals believed to be bright showed a daily improvement in their performance, while those believed to be dull improved only to the third day and then showed a worsening of performance. Sometimes an animal refused to budge from the starting position. This happened 11% of the time among the allegedly bright rats; but among allegedly dull rats it happened 29% of the time. When animals did respond and correctly so, those believed to be brighter ran faster to the rewarded side of the maze than did even the correctly responding rats believed to be dull.

When the experiment was over, all experimenters made ratings of their rats and of their own attitudes and behavior vis-à-vis their animals. Those experimenters who had been led to expect better performance viewed their animals as brighter, more pleasant, and more likeable. These same experimenters felt more relaxed in their contacts with the animals and described their behavior toward them as more pleasant, friendly, enthusiastic, and less talkative. They also stated that they handled their rats more and also more gently than did the experimenters expecting poor performance.

The next experiment with animal subjects also employed rats, this time using not mazes but Skinner boxes (Rosenthal & Lawson, 1964). Because the experimenters (39) outnumbered the subjects (14), experimenters worked in teams of two or three. Once again about half the experimenters were led to believe that their subjects had been specially bred for excellence of performance. The experimenters who had been assigned the remaining rats were led to believe that their animals were genetically inferior.

The learning required of the animals in this experiment was more complex than that required in the maze learning study. This time the rats had to learn in sequence and over a period of a full academic quarter the following behaviors: to run to the food dispenser whenever a clicking sound occurred; to press a bar for a food reward; to learn that the feeder could be turned off and that sometimes it did not pay to press the bar; to learn new responses with only the clicking sound as a reinforcer (rather than the food); to bar-press only in the presence of a light and not in the absence of the light; and, finally, to pull on a loop which was followed by a light which informed the animal that a bar-press would be followed by a bit of food.

At the end of the experiment the performance of the animals believed to be superior was superior to that of the animals believed to be inferior and the difference in learning favored the allegedly brighter rats in all five of the laboratory sections in which the experiment was conducted.

Just as in the maze learning experiment, the experimenters of this study were asked to rate their animals and their own attitudes and behaviors toward them. Once again those experimenters who had expected excellence of performance judged their animals to be brighter, more pleasant, and more likeable. They also described their own behavior as more pleasant, friendly, enthusiastic, and less talkative, and they felt that they tended to watch their animals more closely, to handle them more, and to talk to them *less*. One wonders what was said to the animals by those experimenters who believed their rats to be inferior.

The absolute amount of handling of animals in this Skinner box experiment was considerably less than the handling of animals in the maze learning experiment. Nonetheless, those experimenters who believed their animals to be Skinner box bright handled them relatively more, or said they did, than did experimenters believing their animals to be dull. The extra handling of animals believed to be brighter may have contributed in both experiments to the superior learning shown by these animals.

In addition to the differences in handling reported by the experimenters of the

Skinner box study as a function of their beliefs about their subjects, there were differences in the reported intentness of their observation of their animals. Animals believed to be brighter were watched more carefully, and more careful observation of the rat's Skinner box behavior may very well have led to more rapid and appropriate reinforcement of the desired response. Thus, closer observation, perhaps due to the belief that there would be more promising responses to be seen, may have made more effective teachers of the experimenters expecting good performance.

Teacher Expectation Effects and an Essential Principal

If rats became brighter when expected to then it should not be farfetched to think that children could become brighter when expected to by their teachers. Indeed, Kenneth Clark (1963) had for years been saying that teachers' expectations could be very important determinants of intellectual performance. Clark's ideas and our research should have sent us right into the schools to study teacher expectations; but that's not what happened.

What did happen was that after our lab had completed about a dozen studies of experimenter expectancy effects (we no longer used the term unconscious experimenter bias), I summarized our results in a paper for the *American Scientist* (Rosenthal, 1963).[1] I concluded this paper by wondering whether the same interpersonal expectancy effects found in psychological experimenters might not also be found in physicians, psychotherapists, employers, and teachers. "when the master teacher tells his apprentice that a pupil appears to be a slow learner, is this prophecy then self-fulfilled?" (p. 280).

Among the reprint requests for this paper there was one from Lenore F. Jacobson, the principal of an elementary school in South San Francisco, CA. I also sent her a stack of unpublished papers and thought no more about it. On November 18, 1963, Lenore Jacobson wrote me a letter telling of her interest in the problem of teacher expectations. She ended her letter with the following line: "If you ever 'graduate' to classroom children, please let me know whether I can be of assistance". On November 27, 1963, I accepted Lenore's offer of assistance and asked whether she would consider collaborating on a project to investigate teacher expectancy effects. A tentative experimental design was suggested in this letter as well.

On December 3, 1963, Lenore replied, mainly to discuss concerns over the

---

[1]As an aside, I should note that although this research had begun in 1958, and although there had been more than a dozen papers, none of them had been able to find their way into an APA publication. I recall an especially "good news-bad news" type of day when a particular piece of work was simultaneously rejected by an APA journal and awarded the AAAS Socio-Psychological Prize for 1960. During these years of nonpublication there were three "psychological sponsors" who provided enormous intellectual stimulation and personal encouragement: Donald T. Campbell, Harold B. Pepinsky, and Henry W. Riecken. I owe them all a great deal.

ethical and organizational implications of creating false expectations for superior performance in teachers. If this problem could be solved, her school would be ideal, she felt, with children from primarily lower-class backgrounds. Lenore also suggested gently that I was "a bit naive" to think one could just *tell* teachers to expect some of their pupils to be "diamonds in the rough." We would have to administer some new test to the children, a test the teachers would not know.

Phone calls and letters followed, and in January of 1964, a trip to South San Francisco to settle on a final design and to meet with the school district's administrators to obtain their approval. This approval was forthcoming because of the leadership of the school superintendent, Dr. Paul Nielsen. Approval for this research had already been obtained from Robert L. Hall, Program Director for Sociology and Social Psychology for the National Science Foundation, which had been supporting much of the early work on experimenter expectancy effects.

The Pygmalion Experiment (Rosenthal & Jacobson, 1966; 1968).   All of the children in Lenore's school were administered a nonverbal test of intelligence, which was disguised as a test that would predict intellectual "blooming." The test was labeled as "The Harvard Test of Inflected Acquisition." There were 18 classrooms in the school, three at each of the six grade levels. Within each grade level the three classrooms were composed of children with above average ability, average ability, and below average ability, respectively. Within each of the 18 classrooms approximately 20% of the children were chosen at random to form the experimental group. Each teacher was given the names of the children from his or her class who were in the experimental condition. The teacher was told that these children had scored on the "Test of Inflected Acquisition" such that they would show surprising gains in intellectual competence during the next 8 months of school. The only difference between the experimental group and the control group children, then, was in the mind of the teacher.

At the end of the school year, 8 months later, all the children were retested with the same test of intelligence. Considering the school as a whole, the children from whom the teachers had been led to expect greater intellectual gain showed a significantly greater gain than did the children of the control group. The magnitude of this experimental effect was .30 standard deviation units, equivalent to a point biserial r of .15 (Cohen, 1977).

An Unexpected Finding in Pygmalion.   At the time the Pygmalion experiment was conducted there was already considerable evidence that interpersonal self-fulfilling prophecies could occur, at least in laboratory settings. It should not then have come as such a great surprise that teachers' expectations might affect pupils' intellectual development. For those well-acquainted with the prior research, the surprise value was, in fact, not all so great. There was, however, a surprise in the Pygmalion research. For this surprise there was no great prior probability, at least not in terms of many formal research studies.

At the end of the school year of the Pygmalion study, all teachers were asked to describe the classroom behavior of their pupils. Those children in whom intellectual growth was expected were described as having a significantly better chance of becoming successful in the future, as significantly more interesting, curious, and happy. There was a tendency, too, for these children to be seen as more appealing, adjusted, and affectionate, and as less in need of social approval. In short, the children in whom intellectual growth was expected became more intellectually alive and autonomous, or at least were so perceived by their teachers.

But we already know that the children of the experimental group gained more intellectually, so that perhaps it was the fact of such gaining that accounted for the more favorable ratings of these children's behavior and aptitude. But a great many of the control group children also gained in IQ during the course of the year. We might expect that those who gained more intellectually among these undesignated children would also be rated more favorably by their teachers. Such was not the case. The more the control group children gained in IQ the more they were regarded as *less* well-adjusted, as *less* interesting, and as *less* affectionate.

From these results it would seem that when children who are expected to grow intellectually do so, they are benefited in other ways as well. When children who are not specifically expected to develop intellectually do so, they seem either to show accompanying undesirable behavior, or at least are perceived by their teachers as showing such undesirable behavior. If children are to show intellectual gain, it seems to be better for their real or perceived intellectual vitality and for their real or perceived mental health if their teacher has been expecting them to grow intellectually. It appears worthwhile to investigate further the proposition that there may be hazards to unpredicted intellectual growth (Rosenthal, 1974).

Reactions to Pygmalion

Reactions to Pygmalion were extreme. Many were very favorable, many were very unfavorable. In this chapter we note only the best known of the negative criticisms, those written by very highly regarded, very well-qualified, and clearly talented workers.

The Jensen Critique.   In his famous article in the *Harvard Educational Review*, Arthur Jensen (1969) made three criticisms. The first criticism was that the child, rather than the classroom, had been the unit of analysis and that if the classroom had been the unit of analysis, results would have been negligible. Actually, classrooms *had* been employed as the unit of analysis, as well as children, with essentially the same results. That fact had, of course, been reported in Pygmalion (p. 95 and elsewhere).

Jensen's second criticism was that the same IQ test had been employed both pre and post so that practice effects were maximized. Jensen did not tell how practice effects could bias the results of a randomized experiment. If practice effects were so great as to drive everyone's performance up to the upper limit, or ceiling, of the test, then practice effects could operate to *diminish* the effects of the experimental manipulation but they could not operate to increase those effects.

Jensen's third criticism was that teachers themselves administered the group tests of IQ and that group tests are less reliable than individually administered tests. This was a two-pronged criticism so two points must be made. First, in the Pygmalion study when children were retested by testers who were blind to the experimental conditions, indeed to the existence of experimental conditions, the effects of teacher expectations actually increased rather than decreased. Second, Jensen implied that the unreliability of our group test might be responsible for our teacher expectancy effect. In fact, however, lower test reliability makes it harder, not easier, to obtain significant differences between conditions. Lowered reliability decreases power, increases Type II errors, and decreases Type I errors.

The Thorndike Critique.   Another critique of the Pygmalion experiment was by Robert L. Thorndike (1968). The general point was that the IQ of the youngest children was badly measured by the test employed and that, therefore, any inferences based on such measurement must be invalid. Since a detailed discussion is available elsewhere (Rosenthal, 1969a), we can give just the basic facts here. First, the validity coefficient of the reasoning IQ subtest, regarded as worthless by Thorndike, was .65, quite a bit higher than the validity coefficients often reported in support of the validity of IQ tests. Second, even if the IQ measure had been seriously unreliable, that could not have accounted for the significant results of Pygmalion. As we saw in our discussion of the Jensen critique, low reliability as a cause of spuriously significant results is a statistical non sequitur. Low reliability can lead to fewer significant results; it cannot lead to more significant results. Third, even if the reasoning IQ data for the youngest children, the results most suspect, had been omitted from the analysis, there would still have been a significant effect of teacher expectations for the remaining classrooms as measured by reasoning IQ ($p = .001$).

The Elashoff and Snow Critique.   The most ambitious critique of the Pygmalion experiment was published as a book by Janet D. Elashoff and Richard E. Snow (1971), and discussed in detail by Rosenthal and Rubin (1971).[2] Briefly, Elashoff and Snow transformed the original data of Pygmalion in eight different ways. Some of these transformations were seriously biased (e.g., discarding data unfavorable to the null hypothesis). Despite this, however, none of the transfor-

---

[2]Actually, the Rosenthal and Rubin (1971) discussion of the Elashoff and Snow volume was of an earlier draft than the one that was published in 1971. Rosenthal and Rubin were not permitted to respond to the published version, which included the deletion of information particularly damaging to the Elashoff and Snow position.

mations gave noticeably different results from those reported in the Pygmalion experiment. For total IQ, every transformation gave a significant result when one had been reported in the Pygmalion experiment. When verbal and reasoning IQ were also considered, the various transformations yielded *more* significant teacher expectancy effects than had been reported in Pygmalion. Despite these results, Elashoff and Snow concluded that the Pygmalion research did not demonstrate teacher expectancy effects.

The New Jensen Critique.   The criticisms of Pygmalion described so far were made shortly after the appearance of that research in the late 1960s. In a recent review of the literature on Pygmalion effects, Arthur Jensen (1980) again concluded that the Pygmalion effect was a myth. One experiment was admitted to be in support of the hypothesis of interpersonal expectancy effects. However, it was not viewed as in support of the Pygmalion hypothesis because it employed as a dependent variable an achievement test rather than an IQ test. Yet, three different studies showing no effect of teacher expectations were counted as evidence *against* the Pygmalion hypothesis although they too employed only achievement tests as dependent variables rather than IQ tests (Rosenthal, 1980a). In short, when achievement test results favored the hypothesis they were excluded from evidence bearing on the Pygmalion effect; when they went against the hypothesis they were included as evidence bearing on the Pygmalion effect.

Also singled out for comment was a study by Deitz and Purkey (1969) "as it revealed no expectancy effect based on pupil's race" (Jensen, 1980, p. 608). Indeed it did not, since that study was not a study of teacher expectancy effects at all! In that study, rather than manipulate teachers' expectations to determine the effects on pupils' performance, the investigators asked teachers to estimate the future academic performance of black or white boys. The finding of a non significant relationship between children's race and teachers' estimates of future academic success was interpreted as a failure to find an effect of teachers' expectation on pupils' IQ. This study had nothing to do with either IQ or achievement. Teacher expectation was not an independent variable at all but a dependent variable.

Of a total of 13 studies listed by Jensen (p. 608) as showing no "effects of teacher expectancy on children's IQs," four of the studies (or 31%) did not even employ IQ tests as dependent variables and one (or 8%) did not even employ teacher expectations as an independent variable. We expect a given degree of error in science (Rosenthal, 1978b); but Jensen's rate of making errors (31%), and his rate of making those errors in the direction of his hypothesis (100%), seems excessive. (Further evidence of biased reporting by Jensen is given in Rosenthal, 1980a).

Jensen also reported several studies of the expectancy effects of the examiner during the course of psychological testing. The study he singled out as "most powerful and most informative" (Samuel, 1977) was one that he felt provided no support for the expectancy hypothesis and that "only" 6.4% of the variance of that study was attributable to expectancy effects. The error here was in thinking that 6.4% of the variance was of little practical consequence. As Rosenthal and Rubin have pointed out elsewhere (1979b, 1982b) and as we shall see later in this chapter, accounting for 6.4% of the variance is equivalent to increasing the success rate of a new treatment procedure from 37% to 63%, a change that can hardly be considered trivial.

The Rosenthal Critique.   Now that we have had a look at some of the best known criticisms of Pygmalion, let me level two criticisms of my own at the Pygmalion research. My major criticism is that, for the most part, significance tests were employed unaccompanied by estimates of the sizes of the effects discussed. I now regard that as an unacceptable mode of reporting results of data analyses. My other criticism, a more technical one, is that there were instances in which omnibus F tests were performed, that is, where df in the numerator were greater than one. If those Fs had been computed at all, and there is a question as to whether they should have been, they should at least have been followed up by the linear trend contrasts (and perhaps by the quadratic trend contrasts) implied by the structure of the data. Thus grade level ($df = 5$) and ability track level ($df = 2$) imply an interest at least in the linear effects of grade and of ability track and the interaction of these linear effects with other factors such as experimental condition.

A Heuristic Note.   Before leaving the topic of negative criticisms of Pygmalion, one casual observation should be offered for any possible heuristic value it may hold. The bulk of the criticism of Pygmalion did not come from mathematical statisticians, nor from experimental social psychologists, nor from educators (though the president of a large teachers' union attacked Pygmalion bitterly as an affront to the good name of the teacher or the teachers' union). The bulk of the negative reactions came from workers in the field of educational psychology. Perhaps it was only they who would have been interested enough to respond. That seems unlikely, however, since many other kinds of psychologists regarded the Pygmalion effect with great interest. We leave the observation as just a curiosity, one that might be clarified by workers in the fields of the history, sociology, and psychology of science.

PYGMALION EFFECTS: WHERE TO?

Overview

There are several types of implications that flow from the research on Pygmalion effects, and, more generally, from research on interpersonal expectancy effects. Some of these implications are more methodological, some are more substantive. Within each of these two main types, some implications tend more to address

TABLE 3.2
Implications of Research on Interpersonal Expectancy Effects

Issues Addressed	Type of Implication	
	Methodological	Substantive
Process	Controls for experimenter effects in behavioral research	Processes of social influence, especially nonverbal processes
Generality	Meta-analytic procedures	Domains of application

issues of process, for example, how the research process can be modified to minimize experimenter effects (methodological), and how processes of social influence might operate to mediate interpersonal expectancy effects (substantive). Similarly, within each of the two main types some implications tend more to address issues of generality, for example, quantitative procedures for summarizing results of research domains (methodological) and a mapping of the domains of human interaction in which interpersonal expectancy effects have been shown or may yet be shown to operate (substantive). Table 3.2 shows the two by two table that results when the methodological and substantive types of implications are crossed by the major types of issues addressed; issues of process and issues of generality. We turn now to a consideration of each of the four cells of this two by two table.

Methodological Implications: Process

The many experiments that have investigated experimenter and other interpersonal expectancy effects have led to a number of suggestions as to how we might minimize the unintended effects of experimenters in behavioral research. These suggestions have been discussed elsewhere in great detail (Rosenthal, 1966; 1976), and can be summarized here briefly to give the flavor of the type of strategies that have been proposed. Table 3.3 summarizes 10 strategies for the reduction of experimenter expectancy effects; for each strategy some consequences of its employment are listed.

Methodological Implications: Generality

Even before the negative reactions to Pygmalion were published, a major critique of the earlier research on experimenter expectancy effects had been launched by Theodore X. Barber and Maurice J. Silver (1968). They concluded that since "only" 12 out of 31 experiments (i.e., 39%) apparently showed a significant expectancy effect, the effect was neither pervasive nor easy to demonstrate. The implication appeared to be that unless the vast majority of studies showed a

TABLE 3.3
Strategies for the Reduction of Experimenter Expectancy Effects

---

1. Increasing the number of experimenters
      decreases learning of influence techniques
      helps to maintain blindness
      minimizes effects of early data returns
      increases generality of results
      randomizes expectancies
      permits the method of collaborative disagreement
      permits statistical correction of expectancy effects
2. Observing the behavior of experimenters
      sometimes reduces expectancy effects
      permits correction for unprogrammed behavior
      facilitates greater standardization of experimenter behavior
3. Analyzing experiments for order effects
      permits inference about changes in experimenter behavior
4. Analyzing experiments for computational errors
      permits inference about expectancy effects
5. Developing selection procedures
      permits prediction of expectancy effects
6. Developing training procedures
      permits prediction of expectancy effects
7. Developing a new profession of psychological experimenter
      maximizes applicability of controls for expectancy effects
      reduces motivational bases for expectancy effects
8. Maintaining blind contact
      minimizes expectancy effects
9. Minimizing experimenter–subject contact
      minimizes expectancy effects
10. Employing Expectancy Control Groups
      permits assessment of expectancy effects

---

significant effect, the null hypothesis might really be true. Neither the actual p value nor the size of the effect obtained was to be considered in evaluating research results; only whether the study reached some critical level of significance. That didn't seem reasonable; as I noted in 1968: "If replications are really helpful, then there must be some way in which the results of replications have some cumulative bearing on what we think we should believe about the nature of some relationship" (p. 31).

I therefore owe my long-time interest in the quantitative summarizing of research domains (or meta-analysis as Gene V Glass has named it) to my controversy with Barber and Silver. I felt there must be some way to use the information in a study cumulatively with the information in other studies that tested the same hypothesis, but I didn't know how to do it. Luckily, Frederick Mosteller was a colleague in the then Harvard Department of Social Relations, and from him I learned some fundamental procedures he had described in his classic chapter with Robert R. Bush in the old *Handbook of Social Psychology* (1954). Finding 12 significant (at $p = .05$) results out of 31 studies yields a combined probability we would not often encounter if the null hypothesis were true. By my own reckoning, which includes some studies cited in the footnotes of the Barber and Silver paper, there were 14 significant studies (at $p = .05$) out of 35 total studies (40%), a figure which agrees very well with the Barber and Silver result of 12 out of 31 or 39%.

Table 3.4 shows the results of seven such meta-analyses, beginning with the one just described. The last column shows that the percentage of studies of interpersonal expectancy effects to reach $p \le .05$ has held remarkably steady from that first percentage of 40% based on only 35 studies to the current percentage of 36% based on over 10 times as many studies (388).

Beginning with the second entry of Table 3.4, that for 1969, the total number of studies is divided into those that were laboratory situations involving experimenters as ''expecters'' and those that were everyday life type of situations involving teachers, therapists, supervisors, friends, or acquaintances as ''expecters.'' Since 1969 there has been only a slight decrease in the percentage of significant studies conducted in laboratory settings from 35% to 33%. During that same period there has been some increase in the percentage of significant studies conducted in everyday life contexts from 36% to 42%. Since 1971, a slight majority of the total studies of interpersonal expectancy effects have been conducted in everyday life contexts rather than in laboratory contexts.

Before leaving Table 3.4 we want to note that in the 1971 entry by Rosenthal and Rubin, 38% of the 37 studies of everyday situations showed significant

TABLE 3.4
Summary of Seven Meta-analyses: Percentage of Studies of
Interpersonal Expectancy Effects Reaching Statistical Significance
$(p \le .05)$

		Laboratory Situations		Everyday Situations		Total	
Date	*Source*	*(N)*	*% Sig.*	*(N)*	*% Sig.*	*(N)*	*% Sig.*
1968	Rosenthal, 1968	(35)	40%[a]	(—)	—	(35)	40%[a]
1969	Rosenthal, 1969b	(94)	35%	(11)	36%	(105)	35%
1971	Rosenthal & Rubin, 1971	(162)	33%	(37)	38%[b]	(199)	34%
1974	Rosenthal, 1974	(185)	34%	(57)	37%	(242)	35%
1976	Rosenthal, 1976	(215)	34%	(96)	38%	(311)	35%
1978	Rosenthal & Rubin, 1978	(233)	34%	(112)	40%	(345)	36%
1982	Rosenthal, this chapter	(249)	33%	(139)	42%	(388)	36%

[a]The corresponding percentage based on a critique by Barber and Silver (1968) was 39%.

[b]The corresponding percentage based on a review by Baker and Crist (1971) published by Elashoff and Snow (1971) in their critique of Pygmalion was 37%.

expectancy effects. All of these 37 studies were studies of teacher expectancy effects. In that same year, in a critical review by Baker and Crist (1971) (published by Elashoff & Snow [1971] in their critique of Pygmalion) 19 studies of teacher expectancy effects were summarized of which seven or 37% were judged to show significant effects. Their finding of 37% agreed very closely, then, with our finding of 38% of the results reaching statistical significance.

The interest in meta-analysis, which grew out of my controversy with Barber and Silver (1968), was nurtured by the controversy with Elashoff and Snow (1971) and has developed into an area of research interest that now has functional autonomy for me, as Gordon Allport would have said (Allport, 1937). My special interests in meta-analysis have been in conceptualizing the process (Rosenthal, 1980b; 1982; 1983a,b), in combining and comparing significance levels and effect size estimates (Rosenthal, 1978a; Rosenthal & Rubin, 1979a, 1982a) and in the very special problem of the "file drawer" in which we try to estimate how many null results there must be in the file drawers of the world before our combined significant result would become nonsignificant (Rosenthal, 1968, p. 32; Rosenthal, 1969b, p. 208; Rosenthal, 1979a). Much of the quantitative work alluded to here has been at the mathematical level of high school algebra, that is, my level of mathematical sophistication. The more sophisticated work, in which I appear to have participated, has been due to the contributions of my friend and collaborator Donald B. Rubin.

Substantive Implications: Process

Among the most interesting and important implications of the research on interpersonal expectancy effects have been those for the study of subtle processes of unintended social influence. The early work on this area has been summarized in detail elsewhere (e.g., Rosenthal, 1966; 1969b). When we look more particularly at the mediation of teacher expectancy effects, we find early summaries by Brophy and Good (1974), workers whose contributions to this area have been enormous, and by Rosenthal (1974). The most recent and up-to-date summary of this domain is Jere Brophy's chapter in this volume (Chapter 12) on teacher–student interaction. There is space here only to be illustrative of the type of research results that have been accumulating. A preliminary four-factor "theory" of the communication of expectancy effects suggests that teachers (and perhaps clinicians, supervisors, and employers) who have been led to expect superior performance from some of their pupils (clients, trainees, or employees) tend to treat these "special" persons differently than they treat the remaining less-special persons in the four ways shown in Table 3.5 (Rosenthal 1971; 1973; 1974).

Careful reading of the several dozen studies on which the four factor "theory" is based has led to the development of a preliminary model that is useful in pointing out areas most in need of attention before we can understand (a) the

TABLE 3.5
Summary of a Four Factor "Theory" of the Mediation
of Teacher Expectancy Effects

Factor	Summary of the Evidence
Climate	Teachers appear to create a warmer socio-emotional climate for their "special" students. This warmth appears to be at least partially communicated by nonverbal cues.
Feedback	Teachers appear to give their "special" students more differentiated feedback, both verbal and nonverbal, as to how these students have been performing.
Input	Teachers appear to teach more material and more difficult material to their "special" students.
Output	Teachers appear to give their "special" students greater opportunities for responding. These opportunities are offered both verbally and nonverbally (e.g., giving a student more time in which to answer a teacher's question).

variables serving to moderate or alter the magnitude of interpersonal expectancy effects and (b) the variables serving to mediate the operation of interpersonal expectancy effects, including the role of various channels of nonverbal communication (Rosenthal, 1981).

The 10 Arrow Model for the Study of Interpersonal Expectancy Effects. The model utilizes an underlying dimension of time and therefore looks path analytic in form; it does not, however imply any particular data analytic method. The model makes explicit the classes of variables that must be examined in relation to one another before we can achieve any systematic understanding of the social psychology of interpersonal expectation effects. The basic elements of the model include (A) distal and (B) proximal independent variables, (C) mediating variables, and (D) proximal and (E) distal dependent variables.

Distal independent variables refer to such more stable attributes of the expecter (e.g., teacher, therapist, experimenter) or expectee (e.g., pupil, patient, subject) as gender, status, ethnicity, ability, and personality. (It should be emphasized that distal independent variables refer to stable attributes of the expectee as well as of the expecter. That increases the power of the model by allowing us to make use of expectee attributes as moderating variables.) The proximal independent variable in this model generally refers to the variable of interpersonal expectation—especially expectations that have been varied experimentally rather than those that have been allowed to vary naturally. When expectations are simply measured rather than varied experimentally, a correlation between distal and proximal variables is introduced; (e.g., teachers usually expect superior performance from brighter students) this correlation makes it virtually impossible to disentangle the effects of interpersonal expectations from the effects of attributes of the expectee, so that the effects of interpersonal expectations per se become virtually unassessable.

Mediating variables refer to the processes by which the expectation of the expecter is communicated to the expectee. These, then, are like the process variables of the psychotherapy research literature, and our focus is on the behavior of the expecter during interaction with the expectee. By constraining the nature of the verbal communication permitted between expecter and expectee, many studies have shown that these mediating variables must, to a great extent, be nonverbal in nature.

Proximal dependent variables refer to the behavior of the expectee after interaction with the expecter has occurred. A significant relationship between these variables and the experimentally varied proximal independent variables is what we mean by an interpersonal expectancy effect. We should note that the behavior of the expectee (D), including the nonverbal behavior, may have important feedback effects on the behavior of the expecter (C) and the expectation of the expecter (B). Distal dependent variables refer to longer term outcome variables such as those obtained in followup studies, for example, the 1 year followup testing in the Pygmalion research by Rosenthal and Jacobson (1968). We can present the model diagrammatically as in Figure 3.1.

The 10 arrows of the model summarize some of the types of relationships that are to be examined before any claim to a thorough understanding of interpersonal expectancy effects can reasonably be made. As will be shown, each of the arrows

Classes of Variables

Independent		Mediating	Dependent	
A	B	C	D	E
Distal	Proximal	Process	Proximal	Distal

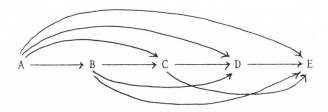

FIG. 3.1. Model for the Study of Interpersonal Expectancy Effects

is usually of social psychological significance, with the exception of arrow AB, which is often of only methodological significance. An overview of the meaning of the 10 arrows follows.

AB.   These relationships are often large in studies not manipulating interpersonal expectations. Thus, in studies in which teachers are asked to state their expectancies for pupils' intellectual performance, high correlations between teacher expectations (B) and pupil IQ (A) are inevitable. These high correlations make it difficult to conclude that it is the teacher's expectancy rather than the pupil's IQ that is "responsible" for subsequent pupil performance. Covariance analysis, cross-lagged panel analyses, and related procedures can be useful here, however, and have been creatively employed (e.g., Crano & Mellon, 1978). When expectancies are varied experimentally, the expected value of the AB correlations is zero, since neither the attributes of the expecter nor of the expectee should be correlated with the randomly assigned experimental conditions. A nonzero correlation under these circumstances serves as a methodological warning of a "failure" of the randomization procedure.

AC.   These relationships describe the "effects" on the expecter's interactional behavior of various characteristics of the expecter, the expectee, or both. The joint "effects" of teacher gender and pupil gender on the teacher's subsequent behavior toward the pupil serve as illustration.

AD.   These relationships describe the effects of (usually) the expecter's characteristics on the subsequent behavior of the expectee. A relationship between teacher attitude and pupil learning would be an illustration.

AE.   These relationships are like those of AD except that behavior E occurs at some time in the future relative to D.

BC.   These relationships describe the effects on the expecter's behavior toward the expectee of the expectation that has (usually) been induced experimentally in the expecter. An example is the four factor "theory" of the mediation of teacher expectancy effects that summarizes several dozen studies of BC relationships.

BD.   These relationships define the phenomenon of interpersonal expectancy effects when the expectancy has been experimentally manipulated. These relationships may be self-moderating over time as when expectee behavior (D) affects the subsequent expectation of the expecter (B).

BE.   These relationships define the longer term effects of interpersonal expectations. There are very few studies of this type available.

CD.   These relationships provide suggestive clues as to the type of expecter behavior that may have effects on expectee behavior. It is often assumed that CD relationships tell us how teachers, for example, should behave in order to have certain desirable effects on pupil behavior. Except in those very rare cases where mediating variables are manipulated experimentally, such assumptions are unwarranted. Finding certain teacher behaviors to correlate with certain types of pupil performance does not mean that teachers changing their behavior to emulate the behavior of the more successful teachers will show the same success with their pupils. These relationships may also be self-moderating over time as when expectee behavior (D) affects the subsequent behavior of the expecter (C).

CE.   These relationships are like the CD relationships except that the outcome variables are of the followup variety.

DE.   These relationships may merely assess the stability of the behavior of the expectee, as when the measures employed for D and E are identical. When these measures are not very similar, the DE relationship may yield an index of predictive validity that is of substantive interest.

Of the 10 arrows of the model, three are clearly most important and should ideally be included in most studies of interpersonal expectancy effects: BC, BD, and CD.

The BD relationship tells us the degree to which interpersonal expectancy effects occurred. The BC relationship tells us the degree to which the (usually experimental induction of) expectancy was a determinant of a particular type of behavior of the expecter toward the expectee. The CD relationship tells us the degree to which certain behaviors of the expecter are associated with changes in the behavior of the expectee. If the BC results show an increase in behavior X due to the induced expectations, and the CD results show that increases in behavior X by the expecter are associated with changes in the performance of the expectee, behavior X becomes implicated as a candidate to be regarded as a mediating variable. Among the most outstanding investigations of these relationships are the studies of Brophy and Good (1974), (AC or BC); Jones and Cooper (1971), (CD); Snyder, Tanke and Berscheid (1977) (BC, BD); and Word, Zanna, and Cooper (1974), (BC, CD).

Measuring Sensitivity to Nonverbal Cues.   Much of the research on interpersonal expectancies has suggested that mediation of these expectancies depends to some important degree on various processes of nonverbal communication. Moreover, there appear to be important differences among experimenters, teachers, and people generally, in the clarity of their communication through different channels of nonverbal communication. In addition, there appear to be important differences among research subjects, pupils, and people generally, in their sensitivity to nonverbal communications transmitted through different nonverbal channels. If we knew a great deal more about differential sending and receiving abilities we might be in a much better position to address the general question of what kind of person (in terms of sending abilities) can most effectively influence covertly what kind of other person (in terms of receiving abilities). Thus, for example, if those teachers who best communicate their expectations for children's intellectual performance in the auditory channel were assigned to children whose best channels of reception were also auditory, we would predict greater effects of teacher expectation than we would if those same teachers were assigned to children less sensitive to auditory nonverbal communications (Conn, Edwards, Rosenthal, & Crowne, 1968).

Ultimately, then, what we would want would be a series of accurate measurements for each person describing his or her relative ability to send and to receive in each of a variety of channels of nonverbal communication. It seems reasonable to suppose that if we had this information for two or more people we would be better able to predict the outcome of their interaction regardless of whether the focus of the analysis were on the mediation of interpersonal expectations or on some other interpersonal transaction.

Our model envisages people moving through their "social spaces" carrying two vectors or profiles of scores. One of these vectors describes the person's differential clarity in sending messages over various channels of nonverbal communication. The other vector describes the person's differential sensitivity in receiving messages in various channels of nonverbal communication. Table 3.6 illustrates this model.

In general, the better that persons A and B are as senders and as receivers, the more effective will be the communication between persons A and B. However, two dyads may have identical overall levels of skill in sending and receiving and may yet differ in the effectiveness of their nonverbal communication because in one dyad the sender's skill "fits" the receiver's skill better than in the other dyad. One way to assess the "fit" of skills in dyad members is to correlate the sending skills of A with the receiving skills of B and to correlate the sending skills of B with the receiving skills of A. Higher correlations reflect a greater potential for more accurate communication between the dyad members since the receiver is then better at receiving the channels which are the more accurately encoded channels of the sender.

The mean (arithmetic, geometric, or harmonic) of the two correlations (of A's sending with B's receiving and of B's sending with A's receiving) reflects how well the dyad members "understand" each other's communications. That mean correlation need not reflect how well the dyad members like each other, however, only that A and B should more quickly understand each other's intended and unintended messages, including how they feel about one another.

As a start toward the goal of more completely specifying accuracy of sending and receiving nonverbal cues in dyadic interaction, an instrument has been developed that was designed to measure sensitivity to various channels of non-

TABLE 3.6
Vectors of Skill in Sending and Receiving in Various Channels
of Nonverbal Communication

Examples of Channels of Nonverbal Communication	Vectors of Person A		Vectors of Person B	
	Sending	Receiving	Sending	Receiving
1. Face				
2. Body				
3. Tone				
4. etc.				
5. ---				
. . ---				
. . ---				
. . ---				
. . ---				
k. ---				

verbal communication: The Profile of Nonverbal Sensitivity, or PONS. We cannot describe the instrument here, but the details of the test, its development, and the results of the extensive research that has been conducted employing the PONS are given elsewhere (Rosenthal, 1979b; Rosenthal, Hall, DiMatteo, Rogers, & Archer, 1979).

Substantive Implications: Generality

In what spheres of social relationships are we likely to find the operation of interpersonal expectancy effects or self-fulfilling prophecies as Merton (1948) called them? In this chapter we have referred specifically only to the locales of the psychological laboratory and the classroom as the settings for research on interpersonal expectancy effects. Of the hundreds of experiments conducted on the interpersonal self-fulfilling prophecy, many have implications for their operation beyond the laboratory and the classroom. Here we can be only illustrative, however. Pygmalion in the gymnasium has been demonstrated recently by Babad, Inbar, and Rosenthal (1982) who found interpersonal expectations to affect the number of sit-ups or pushups performed, the number of feet and inches jumped, and the speed of running. Berman (1979) showed Pygmalion effects to operate in the psychotherapy relationship and King (1971) showed them to operate in the workplace. Snyder, Tanke, and Berscheid (1977) demonstrated interpersonal expectancy effects in more ordinary social situations while introducing a new terminology where the term "behavioral confirmation" is substituted for the term "interpersonal expectancy effect."

Although interpersonal expectancy effects have a well-established generality, further work on generality is still needed. For example, do judges' beliefs about a defendant's guilt or innocence or judges' expectations for how juries will find, actually affect the jury's verdict? Do physicians' expectations for the longevity of "terminal" patients actually affect such longevity? Do physicians' expectations for the course of a particular illness actually play a part in the course of that illness? The evidence available suggests that these hypotheses may not be so very farfetched.

PYGMALION EFFECTS: HOW IMPORTANT?

There seems to be little doubt that interpersonal expectancy effects occur. The combined p is much less than $1/10^{100}$ or a decimal point followed by over a hundred zeros before the first nonzero digit appears (i.e., combined $Z = 26.3$, Rosenthal & Rubin, 1978). However, to say that the null hypothesis is nearly certainly false is not to say that the effect in question is of any practical importance. To address the issue of the practical social and methodological importance of Pygmalion effects requires two steps: (a) estimating quantitatively the typical size of the effect of interpersonal expectations, and (b) evaluating usefully the practical meaning of the typical size of the effect obtained.

The Magnitude of Pygmalion Effects

Table 3.7 shows the ranges and medians of effect sizes (indexed in standard deviation units, that is, $(M_1 - M_2)/\sigma$) obtained in two meta-analyses. The more general meta-analysis tended to obtain larger effect sizes than did the more specific meta-analysis. This difference might be due to sampling differences, procedural differences, or to a lessened susceptibility to Pygmalion effects of measures of pupil ability and achievement. For each of the two meta-analyses, two alternative mean effect sizes, r^2 and r, are also provided.

Evaluating the Magnitude of Pygmalion Effects

The three estimated effect sizes of Table 3.7, d, r^2, and r, all suffer from a common problem. The typical use of these indices involves a widespread tendency to underestimate the practical importance of the effects of behavioral or biomedical interventions (Rosenthal & Rubin, 1979b, 1982b). We found this tendency to underestimate the importance of effects, not only among experienced behavioral researchers, but among experienced statisticians as well. Accordingly, we proposed an intuitively appealing general purpose effect size display whose interpretation is far more transparent: *The Binomial Effect Size Display (BESD)*.

TABLE 3.7
Summary of Estimated Magnitudes of Effects
of Interpersonal Expectations

	Type of Meta-Analysis	
	General: All Areas of Laboratory and Everyday Situations[a]	Specific: Pupil Ability and Achievement Only[b]
N of Studies	345	47
Range of ds for Sub-areas of Analysis[c]	.14–1.73	.16–.53
Weighted Mean d	.70	.33
Equivalent r^2	.11	.03
Equivalent r	.33	.16[d]

[a]From Rosenthal and Rubin (1978).
[b]From Smith (1980).
[c]d is defined as $(M_1-M_2)/\sigma$ by Cohen (1977).
[d]The corresponding r from the original Pygmalion experiment was .15.

The question addressed by BESD is: What is the effect on the success rate (e.g., survival rate, cure rate, improvement rate, selection rate, etc.) of the institution of a new treatment procedure? It therefore displays the change in outcome attributable to the new treatment procedure. The details of the BESD are given elsewhere (Rosenthal & Rubin, 1982b). Here we simply illustrate the BESD for the mean effect sizes estimated in the two meta-analyses of Table 3.7.

Table 3.8 shows the BESD's for rs of .33 and .16. Obviously, a treatment that reduces death rates from 66% to 34% or even from 58% to 42% is of substantial practical importance. Death rates are dramatic but so are failure rates, rejection rates, and error rates. To employ the BESD, we compute the effect size r for our experimental effect. Adding the quantity $r/2$ to .50 gives the experimental group success rate. Subtracting the quantity $r/2$ from .50 gives the control group success rate. When effect sizes are displayed as a BESD we get a better picture of the real world importance of any treatment effect. Even so "small" an effect as one accounting for "only" 3% of the variance, the BESD shows, has practical implications to a degree most psychologists and most statisticians find surprising.

PYGMALION EFFECTS: RETROPROSPECTIVE

It's been a long time since that 1956 doctoral dissertation showed a significant treatment effect before the treatment had been administered. Along the way there have been a lot of studies in laboratories and in schools to show that expectancy

TABLE 3.8
Binomial Effect Size Displays (BESD) for *r*s of .33 and .16 that
Account for "Only" 11% and 3% of the Variance, Respectively

		Treatment Result		
Effect Size	*Condition*	*Alive*	*Dead*	Σ
$r = .33$	Treatment	66.5	33.5	100
$(r^2 = .11)$	Control	33.5	66.5	100
	Σ	100	100	200
$r = .16$	Treatment	58	42	100
$(r^2 = .03)$	Control	42	58	100
	Σ	100	100	200

effects occur and there have been a lot of studies to investigate how they occur. We've learned something about that and about some related things as well; for example, about the quantitative summary of research domains and various processes of nonverbal communication. Most of what we really wanted to know is, unfortunately, still not known. But perhaps that's not too bad. It's true that finding the answer is the best outcome, but looking with energy and with fun, that's not bad either.

ACKNOWLEDGMENT

Preparation of this chapter and much of the research described was supported financially by the National Science Foundation and psychologically by Donald T. Campbell, Harold B. Pepinsky, and Henry W. Riecken. The chapter is based in part on an address "Distinguished Lecture in the History of Social Psychology" sponsored by Divisions 26 and 8 for presentation at the 90th Annual Convention of the American Psychological Association, Washington, D.C., August 24, 1982.

REFERENCES

Allport, G. W. *Personality*. New York: Holt, 1937.
Babad, E. Y., Inbar, J., & Rosenthal, R. Pygmalion, Galatea, and the Golem: Investigations of biased and unbiased teachers. *Journal of Educational Psychology*, 1982, *74*, 459–474.
Baker, J. P., & Crist, J. L. Teacher expectancies: A review of the literature. In J. D. Elashoff & R. E. Snow, *Pygmalion reconsidered*. Worthington, Ohio: Jones, 1971.
Barber, T. X., & Silver, M. J. Fact, fiction, and the experimenter bias effect. *Psychological Bulletin Monograph Supplement*, 1968, *70* (No. 6, part 2), 1–29.

Barr, A. S. A study of the amount of agreement found in the results of four experimenters employing the same experimental technique in a study of the effects of visual and auditory stimulation on learning. *Journal of Educational Research* 1932, *26*, 35–45.

Berman, J. S. Social bases of psychotherapy: Expectancy, attraction and the outcome of treatment. Doctoral dissertation, Harvard University, 1979.

Brophy, J. E., & Good, T. L. *Teacher–student relationships*. New York: Holt, Rinehart & Winston, 1974.

Clark, E. L. The value of student interviewers. *Journal of Personnel Research*, 1927, *5*, 204–207.

Clark, K. B. Educational stimulation of racially disadvantaged children. In A. H. Passow (Ed.), *Education in depressed areas*. New York: Bureau of Publications, Teachers College, Columbia University, 1963.

Cohen, J. *Statistical power analysis for the behavioral sciences*. New York: Academic Press, 1969; Rev. ed., 1977.

Conn, L. K., Edwards, C. N., Rosenthal, R., & Crowne, D. P. Perception of emotion and response to teachers' expectancy by elementary school children. *Psychological Reports*, 1968, *22*, 27–34.

Crano, W. D., & Mellon, P. M. Causal influence of teachers' expectations on children's academic performance: A cross-lagged panel analysis. *Journal of Educational Psychology*, 1978, *70*, 39–49.

Deitz, S. M., & Purkey, W. W. Teacher expectation of performance based on race of student. *Psychological Reports*, 1969, *24*, 694.

Ebbinghaus, H. *Memory*. New York: Teachers College, Columbia University, 1885. (Translated 1913).

Elashoff, J. D., & Snow, R. E. *Pygmalion reconsidered*. Worthington, Ohio: Jones, 1971.

Freud, S. *Collected papers. Vol. 4*. London: Hogarth, 1953.

Gruenberg, B. C. *The story of evolution*. Princeton, N.J.: Van Nostrand, 1929.

Jacobson, L. F. Personal communication. November 18, 1963.

Jensen, A. R. How much can we boost IQ and scholastic achievement? *Harvard Educational Review*, 1969, *39*, 1–123.

Jensen, A. R. *Bias in mental testing*. New York: Free Press, 1980.

Jones, R. A., & Cooper, J. Mediation of experimenter effects. *Journal of Personality and Social Psychology*, 1971, *20*, 70–74.

King, A. S. Self-fulfilling prophecies in training the hard-core: Supervisors' expectations and the underprivileged workers' performance. *Social Science Quarterly*, 1971, September, 369–378.

Marine, E. L. The effect of familiarity with the examiner upon Stanford-Binet test performance. *Teachers College Contributions to Education*, 1929, *381*, 42.

Merton, R. K. The self-fulfilling prophecy. *Antioch Review*, 1948, *8*, 193–210.

Moll, A. *Hypnotism*. (4th ed.) New York: Scribner, 1898.

Mosteller, F. M., & Bush, R. R. Selected quantitative techniques. In G. Lindzey (Ed.), *Handbook of social psychology. Volume 1: Theory and method*. Cambridge, Mass.: Addison-Wesley, 1954.

Murray, H. A. The effect of fear upon estimates of the maliciousness of other personalities. *Journal of Social Psychology*, 1933, *4*, 310–329.

Pavlov, I. (See Gruenberg, 1929)

Pfungst, O. *Clever Hans*. Translated by Rahn, C. L. New York: Holt, 1911; Holt, Rinehart & Winston, 1965.

Rice, S. A. Contagious bias in the interview: A methodological note. *American Journal of Sociology*, 1929, *35*, 420–423.

Rosenthal, R. An attempt at the experimental induction of the defense mechanism of projection. Doctoral dissertation, UCLA, 1956.

Rosenthal, R. On the social psychology of the psychological experiment: The experimenter's hypothesis as unintended determinant of experimental results. *American Scientist*, 1963, *51*, 268–283.

Rosenthal, R. *Experimenter effects in behavioral research.* New York: Appleton-Century-Crofts, 1966.

Rosenthal, R. Experimenter expectancy and the reassuring nature of the null hypothesis decision procedure. *Psychological Bulletin Monograph Supplement,* 1968, *70,* (No. 6, part 2), 30–47.

Rosenthal, R. Empirical vs. decreed validation of clocks and tests. *American Educational Research Journal,* 1969, *6,* 689–691. (a)

Rosenthal, R. Interpersonal expectations. In R. Rosenthal & R. L. Rosnow (Eds.), *Artifact in behavioral research.* New York: Academic Press, 1969. (b)

Rosenthal, R. The silent language of classrooms and laboratories. *Proceedings of the Parapsychological Association,* 1971, Number 8, 95–116.

Rosenthal, R. The mediation of Pygmalion effects: A four factor "theory." *Papua New Guinea Journal of Education,* 1973, *9,* 1–12.

Rosenthal, R. *On the social psychology of the self-fulfilling prophecy: Further evidence for Pygmalion effects and their mediating mechanisms.* MSS Modular Publications, New York, 1974, Module 53, pp. 1–28.

Rosenthal, R. *Experimenter effects in behavioral research: Enlarged edition.* New York: Irvington Publishers, Halsted Press Division of Wiley, 1976.

Rosenthal, R. Combining results of independent studies. *Psychological Bulletin,* 1978, *85,* 185–193. (a)

Rosenthal, R. How often are our numbers wrong? *American Psychologist,* 1978, *33,* 1005–1008. (b)

Rosenthal, R. The "file drawer problem" and tolerance for null results. *Psychological Bulletin,* 1979, *86,* 638–641. (a)

Rosenthal, R. (Ed.) *Skill in nonverbal communication.* Cambridge, Mass.: Oelgeschlager, Gunn & Hain, 1979. (b)

Rosenthal, R. Error and bias in the selection of data. *The Behavioral and Brain Sciences,* 1980, *3,* 352–353. (a)

Rosenthal, R. (Ed.) *Quantitative assessment of research domains.* San Francisco: Jossey-Bass, 1980. (b)

Rosenthal, R. Pavlov's mice, Pfungst's horse, and Pygmalion's PONS: Some models for the study of interpersonal expectancy effects. In T. A. Sebeok & R. Rosenthal (Eds.), *The Clever Hans phenomenon.* Annals of the New York Academy of Sciences, No. 364, 1981.

Rosenthal, R. Valid interpretation of quantitative research results. In D. Brinberg & L. H. Kidder (Eds.), *Forms of validity in research.* San Francisco: Jossey-Bass, 1982.

Rosenthal, R. Assessing the statistical and social importance of the effects of psychotherapy. *Journal of Consulting and Clinical Psychology,* 1983, *51,* 4–13. (a)

Rosenthal, R. Toward a more cumulative social science. In L. Bickman (Ed.) *Applied Social Psychology Annual* (Vol. 4). Beverly Hills, Calif.: Sage, 1983. (b)

Rosenthal, R., & Fode, K. L. The effect of experimenter bias on the performance of the albino rat. *Behavioral Science,* 1963, *8,* 183–189. (a)

Rosenthal, R., & Fode, K. L. Three experiments in experimenter bias. *Psychological Reports,* 1963, *12,* 491–511. (b)

Rosenthal, R., Hall, J. A., DiMatteo, M. R., Rogers, P. L., & Archer, D. *Sensitivity to nonverbal communication: The PONS test.* Baltimore, Md.: Johns Hopkins University Press, 1979.

Rosenthal, R., & Jacobson, L. Teachers' expectancies: Determinants of pupils' IQ gains. *Psychological Reports,* 1966, *19,* 115–118.

Rosenthal, R., & Jacobson, L. *Pygmalion in the classroom.* New York: Holt, Rinehart & Winston, 1968.

Rosenthal, R., & Lawson, R. A longitudinal study of the effects of experimenter bias on the operant learning of laboratory rats. *Journal of Psychiatric Research,* 1964, *2,* 61–72.

Rosenthal, R., & Rubin, D. B. Pygmalion reaffirmed. In J. D. Elashoff & R. E. Snow, *Pygmalion reconsidered*. Worthington, Ohio: Jones, 1971.

Rosenthal, R., & Rubin, D. B. Interpersonal expectancy effects: The first 345 studies. *The Behavioral and Brain Sciences*, 1978, *3*, 377–386.

Rosenthal, R., & Rubin, D. B. Comparing significance levels of independent studies. *Psychological Bulletin*, 1979, *86*, 1165–1168. (a)

Rosenthal, R., & Rubin, D. B. A note on percent variance explained as a measure of the importance of effects. *Journal of Applied Social Psychology*, 1979, *9*, 395–396. (b)

Rosenthal, R., & Rubin, D. B. Comparing effect sizes of independent studies. *Psychological Bulletin*, 1982, *92*, 500–504. (a)

Rosenthal, R., & Rubin, D. B. A simple general purpose display of magnitude of experimental effect. *Journal of Educational Psychology*, 1982, *74*, 166–169. (b)

Rosenzweig, S. The experimental situation as a psychological problem. *Psychological Review*, 1933, *40*, 337–354.

Rosnow, R. L. *Paradigms in transition*. New York: Oxford, 1981.

Russell, B. *Philosophy*. New York: Norton, 1927.

Samuel, W. Observed IQ as a function of test atmosphere, tester expectation, and race of tester: A replication for female subjects. *Journal of Educational Psychology*, 1977, *69*, 593–604.

Smith, M. L. Teacher expectations. *Evaluation in Education*, 1980, *4*, 53–55.

Snyder, M., Tanke, E. D., & Berscheid, E. Social perception and interpersonal behavior: On the self-fulfilling nature of social stereotypes. *Journal of Personality and Social Psychology*, 1977, *35*, 656–666.

Thorndike, R. L. Review of Pygmalion in the Classroom. *American Educational Research Journal*, 1968, *5*, 708–711.

Word, C. O., Zanna, M. P., & Cooper, J. The nonverbal mediation of self-fulfilling prophecies in interracial interaction. *Journal of Experimental Social Psychology*, 1974, *10*, 109–120.

4 Teacher Expectancy Effects and Educational Psychology

Vernon C. Hall
Stephen P. Merkel
Syracuse University

INTRODUCTION

As educational psychologists and teacher educators we are interested in the application of research findings to educational settings. Thus, it should come as no surprise that we have noticed the large number of teacher expectancy studies which have appeared in the journals during the past several years. Just as one would predict, the results of these studies have now begun to be included in educational psychology textbooks. Often such texts have reported general findings of this research without evaluating the procedures used or the extent to which the results of specific studies are directly applicable to classroom situations.

Because we have not been directly involved in teacher expectancy research, the invitation to write this chapter provided us with an opportunity, as educational psychologists, to become more familiar with specific studies in the area. We view educational psychology as a field containing psychologists interested in education. The areas of specialty which are most often developed include learning, motivation, development, measurement, and statistics. In some situations educational psychologists have been overzealous in attempting to make direct applications from other areas (e.g., making Piaget into an educator). In other situations they have been initiators of theories and research in the mainstream of psychology (e.g., the development of tests which led to theories of mental topography). Because they interpret psychological research for educators, as well as carry out basic and applied research, educational psychologists often find employment as teacher educators. It is as teacher educators that we have written this chapter. We have attempted to critically evaluate methods used, results reported, and applications recommended, in teacher expectancy research. In essence, we were interested in determining how important teacher expectancy research was for the field of educational psychology as it relates to teacher education.

The procedures we used consisted of several steps. First, we read several summaries of the literature. Second, we categorized individual studies under two general headings: research which provided teachers with student information; and research which included teacher interactions with students for whom they had varying naturally occurring expectations. While these two categories were not necessarily all encompassing, they did include the great bulk of research reports. We then selected several representative studies from each category. This selection was based on frequency and recency. That is, we selected studies which were cited most often and included some of the more recent reports. Presumably, the best studies will have remained in the literature as the most cited, while recent studies represent methodological advancements and newer findings. We must admit that no systematic procedure was specified and used. Nevertheless, we believe that these studies are representative of those available in the area of teacher expectancy. We then read these studies and attempted to specify (1) methodological strengths and/or weaknesses, (2) voids in questions explored, and (3) specific recommendations which could be made from this literature to professors in educational psychology courses.

In general, we found that teacher expectancy research has tended to (1) develop outside of the mainstream of the educational psychology literature and hence, often ignores knowledge and variables developed in other areas (e.g., measurement and development), (2) suffer from a number of methodological problems, and (3) not address what we would perceive as two extremely important questions for teacher education. These latter two questions are (a) How *should* teachers develop and modify accurate expectancies? and (b) How should these accurate expectancies be translated into appropriate teacher behaviors?

RESEARCH WHICH PROVIDED TEACHERS WITH STUDENT INFORMATION

Classroom Setting

In the original study dealing with teacher expectancies (Rosenthal & Jacobson, 1968) students from kindergarten through fifth grade were given Flanagan's (1960) Tests of General Ability (TOGA) in May. This test was presented to the classroom teachers as one that would predict which youngsters were most likely to show an academic spurt. The following fall, teachers were given a list of students (randomly selected) who they were told should show the spurt that year. A retest of the TOGA 1 year after the initial testing showed that in grades one and two there were significant differences in the mean gains in IQ (TOGA) between the experimental (spurt) students and the control students. There were no significant mean experimental-control differences in the other grades. The causal inferences made were that (1) the treatment influenced the teachers' expectancies (never measured) for the experimental group by setting the expectancies higher than they would have been which, in turn, (2) influenced the teacher behavior (never measured) which (3) influenced the students' capacity and thus the higher TOGA scores.

We believe that few results in educational research have had more intuitive appeal than those of the Rosenthal and Jacobson study. The possibility that teachers could actually *cause* children to become smarter by merely being told that these children should become smarter struck a responsive chord in American education. Since publication of this study there have been many researchers who have used this original design in an attempt to replicate and extend these findings. Such replication is always necessary, and in the present case, it was particularly important. This is because a number of methodological problems were raised with the original study (e.g. Snow, 1969; Thorndike, 1968, 1969).

In 1971, José and Cody represented a major attempt to replicate the Rosenthal and Jacobson (1968) study. They also made several additions in an attempt to extend the findings. In addition to the TOGA, they also gathered standardized reading and math achievement scores, grades, and observational data of the teachers' behaviors.

Nine first and nine second grade teachers were randomly selected from an unspecified number of teachers and schools. From each of these 18 classrooms, eight students were randomly selected. Half (balanced for sex) were designated as experimental and the remainder served as controls. No demographic data were provided for teachers or students.

Initially, observers who were ostensibly part of a separate study, tabulated teacher–student interactions in the study using the Interaction Analysis Scale, a modification of Bales (1950) scale. Next, the TOGA and the Metropolitan Achievement Tests were administered to all students. Teachers were then given the names of the experimental students who were identified as late bloomers. Teacher observations were continued every 4 weeks for 16 weeks. No observer reliabilities were reported for the three observers. Finally, the standardized tests were readministered and a posttest questionnaire was given to the teachers to determine the effectiveness of the expectancy manipulation.

The standardized test scores were submitted to separate 2 (treatment) × 2 (sex) × 2 (grade) analyses of variance. The only significant effects were for grade. In addition, t tests were computed on gain scores for arithmetic and reading grades. Again there were no significant effects.

For some reason only the raw scores on each of the 12 behavior categories were presented for each of the observation periods. It is clear, however, from observing these raw scores that overall the teachers did not treat experimental and control groups differently in the categories of behavior that one would expect as a result of more teacher attention (e.g., reward, information) over the time period observed.

Finally, on the teacher questionnaire only seven teachers reported that they had expected performance of the experimental students to improve. Of these, only four felt the predicted improvement had occurred. In reality, there were no significant differences between experimental and control children in these four classrooms on any measure.

Dusek and O'Connell (1973) also employed the Rosenthal and Jacobson design. Shortly before school opened, two second and two fourth grade teachers in a school serving lower-class children were told that the investigators were going to pilot a test designed to predict future academic performance in language and math. This test (really the Stanford Achievement Tests) was administered at the beginning, middle, and end of the year. Teachers were also told that as part of the validation procedure, school grades and teacher opinions would be acquired. Thus, during the initial testing, teachers ranked students based on their expectancy of the students' academic performance. These predictions were used to equalize initial expectancies of experimental and control children. One week later the names of eight students who would show large academic gains were given to the teachers.

The achievement test scores were analyzed using multiple regression. While there were no significant differences on any measure between experimental and control students, teacher rankings of expectancy (which teachers reported were based on work in previous grades, readiness tests, and written and oral classroom performance during the first few weeks of classes) were found to be quite accurate. The authors concluded that "it appears that the child's academic potential determined the teacher's expectation rather than the reverse" (p. 375). Finally, they indicated that "neither biasing statements nor false test scores given to teachers affect childrens' achievement test performance" (p. 376).

One year later O'Connell, Dusek, and Wheeler (1974) administered the SAT to the students who had been tested the first year and who remained in the same school. The initial results were replicated in that there were still no significant differences between experimental and control students and the original teacher predictions continued to be accurate. This time the authors were somewhat stronger in their conclusions. After suggesting that teachers base their expectations on "criteria relevant to academic performance" (p. 328) they conclude, "If this is the case, teachers do not bias the education of children (p. 328)."

The results of these last three studies were replicated in a number of other classroom studies (e.g., Anderson and Rosenthal, 1968; Claiborn, 1969; Conn, Edwards, Rosenthal, & Crowne, 1968). Thus, to the relief of the present authors, expectancy studies using this original design have failed to replicate the major finding. That is, no subsequent study has resulted in significantly higher intelligence test scores for the experimental group. We are relieved because such a replication would bring into question many accepted theories and vast amounts of empirical work concerning the nature of the construct being measured by standardized intelligence tests. More specifically, intelligence is conceived of as a relatively stable trait across age, and indeed, intelligence tests have proven to be some of the most stable measures developed by psychologists. It would be rather surprising to find that measures of intelligence are so fragile that student performance can be permanently increased in such an easy manner (i.e., tell the teacher the student should become smarter and the teacher somehow makes him/her smarter).

The present senior author was a researcher in Head Start, where large amounts of money and effort were spent designing and implementing programs to increase children's intelligence test scores. Not only were children specifically selected because they were at an age when intelligence was hypothesized to be malleable, but also because their present environment was actually preventing them from naturally developing their full cognitive capacities. The generally recognized failure of the Head Start program to permanently increase intelligence test scores is well-known. If it now turned out that teachers in elementary schools could raise intelligence test scores of randomly selected middle-class students at will, something would clearly be amiss.

Although Crano and Mellon (1978) did not manipulate information given to teachers, their study is mentioned here because they attempted to address the failure of others to replicate Rosenthal and Jacobson's (1968) results. In referring to these replication failures, Crano and Mellon indicated that ''these findings would not necessarily indicate that expectancies did not operate, but merely that the particular experimental treatments employed were not sufficient to counteract naturally occurring expectations'' (p. 40). In an attempt to determine the importance of these naturally occurring expectations Crano and Mellon acquired access to a large data base that included both teacher ratings (expectancies) and achievement test scores in four separate academic years. These data included 72 schools (36 streamed and 36 nonstreamed) with a total of 5200 students. The schools included primary grades and were located in England and Wales.

The teacher ratings included both academic questions (3 point scales rating reading and math ability and a 5 point scale rating global ability), which were available for the last three years, and questions labeled by the authors as social (4 point scales indicating the degree to which the student was a hard worker, obedient, and a pleasure to have in class), which were available for the entire four year period. We would suggest that these latter three items could also be called indicators of student motivation. The achievement tests (constructed by the original researcher Barker Lunn, 1970) and the rating scales were administered near the end of the school year.

The major contention was that through cross-lagged panel analysis they could assign causation of achievement to teacher ratings or causation of teacher ratings to achievement. More specifically, they argued that if the relationship between teacher ratings (expectancies) in one spring (E_1) and student achievement in the following spring (A_2) was significantly greater than the relationship between student achievement in one spring (A_1) and teacher ratings (expectancies) the following spring (E_2) we could say that teacher expectancy was operating causally on student achievement. If the reverse was true, they would make the opposite case (i.e., achievement causally operating on expectancy).

All correlations between achievement and teacher ratings were positive. Of the 84 comparisons between correlations, 26 were significant. Seven favored achievement causing expectancy and 19 favored expectancy causing achievement. All 19 significant differences favoring teacher ratings and 4 of the significant differences favoring achievement were on the social (motivation) questions. It should also be pointed out that 12 of these 23 significant differences (8 favoring expectancy) were on correlations on the first two grades where academic ratings were not available. Crano and Mellon believed these results favored the Rosenthal and Jacobson (1968) position, basing their conclusion on an overall data pattern which showed t differences (ignoring significance) in 62 of the 84 comparisons that favored expectancy causing achievement. According to Crano and Mellon (1978):

> While the results of this investigation provide some support for the causal implications of both of these competing explanations, the preponderant causal sequence observed in the cross-lagged panel correlational analyses of this research suggests that teachers' expectations caused children's performance to an extent appreciably exceeding that to which performance influenced expectations [p. 47].

While these are interesting findings, we do not believe they necessarily support the above contention. It must be realized that the teachers doing the ratings at E_1 were not the teachers teaching the material or interacting with the students during the year that the students were learning the material ostensibly covered on the test at A_2, and the achievement at A_1 was not the achievement observed by the teachers rating the students at E_2. Any effects from those teachers rating the students at E_1 would need to have been transmitted to the new teachers, who would in turn exert the behaviors which caused the expectancy effects. This is recognized by the authors, who suggest that it is possible that the effect operated between teachers. This would be much like the process described by Rosenthal and Jacobson (1968), with the former teachers instigating the expectancy effects.

We believe an equally plausible alternative explanation. There are indeed student behaviors (e.g., working hard or not working, following or ignoring teacher instructions) which tend to maximize or inhibit academic potential. Teachers are able to observe, report, and to some extent, influence, these behaviors. By the end of the school year these behaviors, if stable, would be predictive of future academic progress over and above the scores on achievement tests. Thus, the accuracy of such ratings could also be due to the teachers' knowledge about the students, rather than any bias they transmit to future teachers. The degree to which these two explanations are accurate could be determined by an experimental manipulation in which the amount of information transmitted from one teacher to the next was varied.

In addition the use of cross-lagged panel analysis has been criticized by some as being an inadequate procedure to use for inferring causation. Cook and Campbell (1979) warn that this procedure ought to be treated with extreme caution. Rogosa (1980) critiqued the cross-lagged correlation (CLC) procedure and concluded that it does not provide a basis for causal inferences. He states that: CLC may indicate that absence of direct causal influence when important causal influences, balanced or unbalanced, are present. Also, CLC may indicate a causal predominance when no causal effects are present. Moreover, CLC may indicate a causal predominance opposite to that of the actual structure of the data; that is, CLC may indicate that X causes Y when the reverse is true (p. 246).

Laboratory Setting

Besides the studies in real classrooms, there have also been a number of experimental studies in laboratory settings in which attempts have been made to manipulate expectancies. In such settings it is somewhat easier to observe experimental differences in both process and outcome. We questioned whether these studies were relevant to the real classroom setting. Detailed examination of two studies, in which experimenters manipulated expectancies and attempted to determine differences in instructor treatment, made us aware of problems in generalizing such findings to teacher behaviors in classrooms (particularly first and second grade).

In the first, (Smith & Luginbuhl, 1976), 80 male introductory psychology students were randomly assigned as observers (two per session), teachers (one per session), or students (two per session). Before instruction began, those assigned as teachers were told that, based on the results of a test of analytic ability, one student was "apparently quite bright" and the other "performed rather poorly". Half (eight) of these teachers (aware) were told that "research shows there is an unfortunate but apparently natural tendency for teachers to treat students of high or low ability differently. As a consequence, 'poor' students sometimes do even more poorly on later evaluations. In your role of teacher, use this knowledge based on scientific research to guard against differential treatment of your two students" (p. 267). The other half (unaware) did not receive this instruction.

The observers merely watched the 30 minute instruction period in which the instructors were helping the two students solve the "Joe Doodlebug Problem" (actually Denny Doodlebug) which was used by Rokeach (1960). Smith and Luginbuhl (1976) claim that the "teacher plays an interactive and supportive, but nondirective role as the student strives toward solution of the problem" (p. 271). In reality the problem can be solved quite rapidly if three hints are given or one states the solution. It is unclear how an interactive and supportive role would affect outcome. In addition, interactions between students and teachers may be influenced more by the student than the teacher. When describing a subject's reaction to this problem Rokeach (1960) stated, "There is also a basic emotional and motivational attitude of the thinker to be reckoned with. . . . [A] person who dislikes playing around with new ideas . . . would typically approach new problems with resistance and defensiveness. This he may reflect by rejecting the problem, or the experimenter, or the experimental situation" (p. 177).

Upon completion of 30 minutes, the observers and the students rated the teacher on 3 point scales for (a) overall attention, (b) encouragement, and (c) criticism by the teacher of each student. With regard to expectancy effects, analysis of the overall attention ratings of the naive raters (observers and students) resulted in a significant main effect for aware vs. unaware (aware teachers were rated as giving more attention). For student ratings only, a main effect for expectancy (teachers were rated as giving more attention to bright students) was significant. In another ANOVA, encouragement and criticism were entered as levels of an evaluative feedback (within subject) factor. The result of this analysis produced the major finding now being cited. There was a significant evaluative feedback × teacher awareness interaction (notice no main effects nor interactions involving levels in the evaluative feedback factor). Further post hoc analysis determined that unaware teachers were rated by observers as giving higher evaluative feedback scores (encouragement and criticism) to bright rather than dull students. In addition, aware teachers gave dull students more evaluative feedback than unaware teachers. Analysis of student ratings of teachers resulted in no significant differences. Finally, no performance measures on the Doodlebug problem were reported.

The second study (Swann & Snyder, 1980) also used male introductory psychology students as both teachers and students (half "competent" and half "moderately competent"). The famous Katona (1940) card trick was used as the task. Teachers were told that they had a total of 10 minutes to teach the students (one at a time) and needed to decide how to split the time between them. In addition, three methods of teaching the trick were presented. The first two (memory and intuition) were adequate for the eight card problem being taught but would not help with other numbers of cards. The third method (question mark) was the most effective, but also the most time consuming. Teachers were told "it was unlikely that one could teach the question mark method to both pupils in the time allotted" (p. 882). Finally, instructors were provided with a theory manipulation. Half (extrinsic) were told that "pupils learn best when the instructor adopts a 'directive' approach to teaching. Thus the more pupils were coaxed, nurtured, and reinforced, the better they would learn the trick" (p. 882). The other half (intrinsic) were told that "Since ability to perform the card trick was typically a function of the extent to which pupils developed their own personal understanding of the trick, . . . it was best to take a nondirective approach to teaching and encourage pupils to try to develop a solution to the trick on their own'' (p. 882).

Thus each instructor had two students (competent, moderately competent), 10 total minutes to teach them by one of three methods, and a theory about the nature of ability. The major dependent measures were (1) teaching strategy used, (2) performance on the trick using 13 cards, and (3) instructors' final impressions about the students.

One major finding was that instructors within the extrinsic theory condition used the question mark method more often (11 of 15) on the high-ability students while those within the intrinsic theory condition used the question mark method more often (13 of 15) with the low-ability students. What the authors do not explain is why they imposed the conditions that an instructor had only 10 minutes in which to teach one student at a time and did not have enough time to teach both by the best method. The effect of this manipulation was to force the naive instructors to choose how much time to allocate to each student (never reported) and what overall strategy to adopt to complete their task. W. B. Swann (personal communication May 17, 1982) has explained that "teachers were generally motivated to maximize the performances of pupils. Presumably, they believed that the best way to do this was to make sure that the gifted pupil performed well." Because of the highly unusual situation in which this manipulation places the instructor, it is difficult to understand how one can generalize from these results.

The other major finding involves the students' performances and the instructors' final impressions. Although performance on the eight card task was not reported, performance on the 13 card task was used in an analysis. As predicted, in the extrinsic condition, high-ability students outperformed low-ability students (behaviorally confirming the instructors' beliefs) and in the intrinsic conditions, low-ability students outperformed high-ability tudents (behaviorally disconfirming the instructors' beliefs). It was concluded that this was a direct consequence of the method of teaching employed (i.e., the question mark method led to superior performance in all conditions). Another analysis, however, showed that instructors' final impressions (from a 10 point scale measuring how easily students caught on to the task) were influenced only by the ability manipulation (i.e., high-ability students were rated as having caught on better than low-ability students in all conditions). Swann and Snyder (1980) concluded that ''Apparently, once instructors formed images of their pupils, their subsequent information processing activities were structured in ways that guaranteed the survival of these images'' (p. 886). Three important factors that the author seem to ignore are: (1) These were naive instructors. (2) Each instructor spent less than 10 minutes with each student. (3) The instructor did not view the students' performance on the 13 card task.

Aside from the methodological and interpretation problems, we would maintain that these latter two studies have little or no value in determining what happens in a real classroom (particularly first and second grade). The tasks are not similar to those used, procedures are not appropriate and teachers are not placed under special demand characteristics (e.g., only teach one way per student).

GENERAL COMMENTS

Inappropriate High Expectancies

Our major concern about this research is that the effects of increasing the level of a teacher's expectancy (telling the teacher that a particular student should spurt or do better) are all presumed to occur in the same manner. Teachers initially do not expect enough from a student and hence the student does not perform to capacity. Once the teacher expects more, or believes the student can perform at a higher level, the teacher instigates a more appropriate treatment and student performance improves. There has been little speculation about the problems that can result from teachers expecting too much. This is somewhat surprising when we realize that this is a primary concern in Rotter's (1954) social learning theory that was a relatively early and influential expectancy theory (see Chapter 2). In this theory, problem behavior occurs when reinforcement value of a reinforcer (e.g. a grade of A) is relatively high and expectancy for receiving the reinforcer is very low. Hence cheating, avoidance or more serious behaviors will occur when the reinforcement value of an A is high (it will lead to love from family, praise from the school, etc.) and the probability of acquiring the high grade is very low (e.g., the teacher only gives As to the top 10% of the class and the student cannot acquire an A even through extreme effort). Rotter uses the term Minimum Goal Level to refer to the minimum level on a continuum for which a student will receive a reward. If the minimum goal level is too high (e.g., parents only reward for an A and the student can only acquire a C with maximum effort) the student will suffer. Any experienced teacher will report cases where parents expect too much by insisting that their children could achieve any grade with effort. In the case of expectancy research, we would raise the possibility that some problems could arise if teachers are led to expect too much via the experimental manipulation (e.g, the student they are told should spurt does not). We would also urge researchers to begin investigating effects of teachers having unrealistically high expectancies.

In a recent study Covington and Omelich (1979) investigated a related problem which should be considered. In their discussion of self-worth theory they indicate that while teachers may reward students for effort even when they fail to succeed, students who try but are unsuccessful will be hesitant to continue trying because they realize it means they lack ability to accomplish the task.

Recommendations to Teacher Educators

What can we say to teacher educators about these studies? First, we believe they should caution prospective teachers against accepting the initial findings of any single study. It is always important to have replications of significant findings before they are accepted with a reasonable degree of certainty. Hopefully, teachers would keep informed about progress in their field by reading such replications. If findings of studies which are of interest or are relevant for them are not replicated they should know it. In the present case most texts or research reviews of teacher expectancy research rarely mention that the original results have not been replicated. At the very least, teachers should be told that the teacher expectancy findings concerning intelligence test scores are to be viewed with caution.

A second far more important finding of these studies was the failure of teachers in any of these studies to ever question the investigators' information. We have failed to find a report of even one instance in which teachers made reasonable inquiries about the false information presented to them. Why were researchers using the Rosenthal and Jacobson design not asked to present the reliability and validity data for the test scores which they provided? Why don't teachers routinely ask teacher expectancy researchers more penetrating questions?

We suspect that there are at least two answers which are directly traceable to, and thus can be modified by, teacher training. First, we have taught teachers to accept experimental findings and their interpretation from professors or other authorities rather than teaching them to develop the critical research evaluation skills that would make it possible for them to read and interpret research on their own. Educational psychology text books are often encyclopedias of findings and interpretations but seldom do they discuss limitations of the findings or ways of reading or critically evaluating research reports. We know of no undergraduate teacher training program which requires a course in how to read, interpret, and evaluate educational research. Unfortunately, these teachers are the same people we are depending on to train our youth to be questioners and seekers of knowledge, rather than rote memorizers. In essence, teachers should be taught how to be readers and critics of educational research, rather than passive consumers of information interpreted for them by textbooks and teacher educators.

A second reason is related to the first. We grant teachers access to standardized test scores and make it mandatory for them to create their own tests, which are used to evaluate student performance. Yet, seldom if ever, is a measurement course required for teacher certification. We maintain that if teachers were required to satisfactorily pass a carefully constructed course in evaluation, teachers would have questioned those researchers using the Rosenthal and Jacobson procedure. They would have asked how such tests of spurt potential had been validated and on whom. Teachers, before being given access to any standardized test scores, should understand how such tests are constructed, standardized, and validated. They should know what reliability and validity are and have some idea as to how they are computed. They should be able to read and understand test manuals. They should know the meaning of stanines, standard error of measurement, and regression of the mean. If this were done, teachers would no longer be victims of teacher expectancy researchers. This is because the researchers would have to provide clearcut data from their tests. In addition, teachers would be better able to develop reasonable expectancies of academic performance for their students. Finally, they would be better equipped to construct their own evaluation instruments so that teachers and students would have a more accurate picture of what students did and did not know.

RESEARCH WHICH INCLUDED TEACHER INTERACTIONS WITH STUDENTS FOR WHOM THEY HAD VARYING NATURALLY OCCURRING EXPECTANCIES

Seven Representative Studies

As early as 1971 (e.g., Rothbart, Dalfen, & Barrett, 1971) researchers were suggesting that we had probably learned as much as possible from using the Rosenthal and Jacobson paradigm and should move on to other designs. If teacher expectancy was a widespread antecedent of individual differences in student intelligence and/or achievement, then we should find that teachers do indeed treat students for which they have differing expectancies in a different manner. In effect, the high-expectancy students should be treated in a more pedagogically sound manner. The assumption was that teachers would decide which students they believed had the most learning potential and then teach them in a superior manner. The exact nature of the superior manner would be determined empirically.

At about this time, two studies appeared which did indeed use this design. These two studies have been quoted numerous times as examples of how expectancy influences teacher behavior.

The first was a study by Rist (1970) in which he reported the results of observing a single kindergarten classroom in an all black (students and teachers) school. Subsequently he observed some of these children in first and second grades. The observation technique used was a high inference transcribing system in which the observer kept a running account of what occurred in the classroom twice weekly for 1½ hour periods. In the first grade, a classroom was visited informally (no notes were taken) for four visits. Rist's basic contention was that the kindergarten teacher utilized expectancies of academic potential to group and teach her students. According to Rist, these expectancies were developed on the basis of the degree to which these students were similar to the teacher's own reference group (white and black middle-class) rather than any cognitive measures. Thus the seating in the kindergarten classroom was ostensibly based on ability to learn (higher ability students seated closer to the teacher) but according to Rist the real criteria were such things as physical appearance, leadership, use of Standard American English, and school and family conditions (e.g., SES). Once the seats had been assigned, the teacher began a program of differential treatment (later labeled polarization by others) in which she spent most of her time teaching or interacting with the students sitting close to her who were also ideal students. The most important contention of this report was that this treatment in kindergarten formed the basis for achievement at the end of kindergarten and thus achievement throughout these children's academic lives. In effect this kindergarten teacher (and hence the public school system) was perpetuating an American caste system.

The specific causal chain proceeded in the following manner: By the end of the eigth day the teacher had decided which students conformed to her idealized model and proceeded to teach these students, letting the remainder of the class rely on what they could pick up on their own or by listening to the teacher interact with the others (labeled secondary learning). This teaching of the favored students led to superior performance on readiness tests at the end of kindergarten and thus placement in a higher (translated as better) reading group in the first grade. This division was perpetuated in second grade and presumably throughout the children's school lives. Not only has Rist accounted for SES differences in intellect, he has also specified how differential rates of intellectual development occur. (If only differential rates of physical development could be handled as easily.)

As mentioned earlier, most of the data presented were of the high inference variety from what we must label a biased source. However, there were some data presented which we would agree were relatively reliable in nature. We believe these data were not all supportive of the major contentions. For instance, in second grade Rist tallied control, supportive, and neutral teacher behavior over 3 observational periods during reading instruction. The supportive behavior was roughly equivalent to what we would call positive reinforcement (e.g., "That's a very good job") while control was obviously punishment (e.g., "Lou, sit on that chair and shut up"). Since it appears that Rist was the only observer there was no index of observer reliability. There were two general findings which are often cited. First, a higher percentage of control statements were directed toward the lowest group and second, there were no differences across groups on percentage of support statements. This latter finding is in contrast to several other studies and earlier statements in the article concerning the teacher's attitude toward the low-expectancy child. It should also be noted that no statistical tests were computed on the above percentages and it is questionable whether the differences in control statements were significant.

In addition, not all evidence supported the hypothesis that the kindergarten teacher had relegated low children to permanent ignorance. By second grade all four of the children who had been in the lower kindergarten tables and had remained in the school were assigned to the second reading group (Cardinals) which the teacher saw as one containing students with adequate learning potential and more similar to the high reading group that the lower group. During the school year no students changed reading groups. Thus, these students identified as being low expectancy in kindergarten were indeed progressing at a satisfactory rate.

During the same year, another observation study appeared that was designed to investigate teacher expectancy effects. Brophy and Good (1970) reported an observational study using four first grade classrooms in a small integrated Texas school district (15% of the student body were Mexican-American). Teacher expectancy was operationalized by asking teachers to rank children in order of achievement. The six highest and six lowest ranked children were selected for observation (children who did not speak English or were suspected of having emotional or biological disturbances were excluded). In an unusual procedure alternates were chosen to be observed when the originally selected children were absent for observation. How often this happened is not reported. On a given day each observer (two per classroom) either observed all high- or all low-expectancy children in the class (another questionable procedure). We are not told how many observers were used or what their qualifications were. No observer reliability procedures or values were reported.

There were seven teacher–student interaction categories that the authors believed were related to communication of teacher expectations. Of these the authors believed that the results on five provided direct evidence that teachers were communicating differential expectations via their performance. These results were: (1) A higher percentage of correct answers were followed by priase for high achievers; (2) a higher percentage of wrong answers were followed by criticism for low achievers; (3) a higher percentage of wrong answers were followed by repetition or rephrasing for the high achievers; (4) a higher percentage of reading problems were followed by repetition or rephrasing of the question of giving a clue for high achievers; and (5) a higher percentage of answers were not followed by any feedback from the teacher for the low achievers. While, as mentioned earlier, these results have been widely cited by expectancy researchers as being important differences in how expectancy effects may operate, it should be noted that in three of the five behavior categories listed above (2, 4, and 5) there were significant class by expectancy interactions, indicating that these differences were not consistent across even these four classrooms. In addition, one of the remaining two categories (3) was significant at the $p<.10$ level rather than the usually accepted $p<.05$ level.

Since these two studies, there have been a large number of observational studies that have included teacher–student interactions with students differing in levels of achievement (i.e., expectancy). Several include specific hypotheses that were derived from the expectancy literature. We discuss five published studies we believe are representative and illustrate the procedures used and findings reported. The first three of these studies used variations of the observational instrument developed by Brophy and Good (1969).

Weinstein (1976) observed teacher–student interactions in three racially integrated heterogeneously assigned first grade classes during early fall (September and October) and winter (January). Although we are not told how many observers there were, or with whom the agreement was assessed, (e.g., a trainer, one other observer or all other observers) or for how long or how many periods of time (e.g., 1 hour) they do report high percentages of preobservation agreement (85% and 93%). They observed during periods when small group reading and teaching was occurring as well as during entire class academic work. Even though these were small classes (21, 21, 18) all seemed to have three reading groups. One of the purposes was to replicate both Rist (1970) and Brophy and Good (1970) by determining differences in teacher–student interactions between high, medium, and low reading (expectancy) groups.

It is difficult to directly compare exact replications of the Brophy and Good (1970) results because of the method of reporting but two categories were identical—(1) percentage of correct responses followed by teacher praise and (2) percentage of answers (correct or incorrect) not followed by any feedback from the teacher—to the original five categories in which significant expectancy differences were found. In both cases there were no significant reading group differences (for interactions occurring during reading groups) in fall, but by winter the means now favored the low groups (the reading group means were significant at $p<.01$ for the first category and at $p<.10$ for the second category with the class $\times$ reading group interaction significant at $p<.10$ for the first category and at $p<.01$ for the second category).

Overall the data did not indicate that the high reading group received preferential treatment. For the fall data, Weinstein says "In summary, although several kinds of teacher treatment, in particular, frequency of types of contact and amount of instructional time available, were differentially accorded the various reading group memberships (favoring the lows), a consistent teacher bias towards members of any reading group was not found during the second month of school" (p. 107). The midyear data continued to favor the low groups as she indicates "The results suggest that at midyear, the teachers continued to provide more response opportunities to members of the low reading group during the reading group itself as well as spending more time per student. Evaluative comments, particularly praise, were still most frequently directed toward low group members" (p. 108).

Of particular interest was the fact that the mean reading achievement gain was significantly greater for the high group than the low group. Thus, although the teachers were using what were hypothesized as being equally effective or even superior teaching for the low reading groups, the students in the high reaing groups were acquiring skills at a faster rate. Rather than rejecting the expectancy hypothesis, Weinstein suggests that the specific behaviors tabulated in the study were not the ones important for establishing the status system of the classroom. She says "Perhaps we look too minutely at classroom process when we focus on the transactions between the teacher and an individual child. The context of that transaction both within and outside the classroom may be the more powerful expression of expectations" (p. 116). She does not consider the possibility that student gains were a function of student cognitive ability or developmental rate differences.

Cooper and Baron (1977) reported another observation study utilizing the Brophy and Good instrument. They used eight volunteer teachers (six second grade classrooms, two classrooms combining first and second grade students). No demographic characteristics of the subjects were included. Again teacher ratings were used to designate academic expectations (a modified procedure using counselors was initiated but abandoned in favor of teacher rating after the observations had been completed). Eight undergraduates were used as observers who reached an 80% agreement rate before observation commenced. Nine students (three high, three medium and three low expectancy) were observed in each classroom.

The specific expectancy hypothesis being tested was one generated by Rosenthal (1974) to account for teacher expectancy effects. In this case it was predicted that high expectancy students would receive significantly more praise and criticism than other groups. Thus they would have more knowledge about correct and incorrect answers and would learn more than other groups. This hypothesis was not verified. High expectancy students received significantly more praise (a new index labeled praise per correct answer was generated in which praise— defined as being more than simply indicating a correct response—was divided by the number of correct answers given). But there were no significant group differences in criticism (defined as an expression of anger on the part of the teacher toward the student relating to an academic performance). Observation of group means clearly indicates that the high-expectancy females received much more praise and low-expectancy females received more criticism than other groups. There was no significant classroom by expectancy interaction reported. Of the six other interaction categories reported (public academic, teacher-initiated academic, child-initiated academic, teacher-initiated procedure, child-created procedure, negative behavior) only negative behavior resulted in a significant expectancy main effect with low-expectancy children having the highest mean while average and low-exectancy groups did not differ.

Finally, Good, Cooper and Blakey (1980) used the Brophy and Good instrument to observe students in seven third, four fourth, and five fifth grade classrooms in five schools (three city and one rural schools containing white middle-class students and one city school containing ⅔ white and ⅓ black students). The study was designed to test the "polarization" hypothesis attributed to Rist (1970). Namely, it was suggested that teachers tend to change their behavior over the year in favor of the high-expectancy students. From 60% of the students whose parents agreed to allow their children to participate (No distribution of those who did not agree is reported across classrooms.) Four high-expectancy, four average-expectancy and four low-expectancy students were drawn from teacher rankings of verbal and general academic potential. These students were observed in the fall, winter, and spring. It should also be mentioned that in the spring, observer reliability was below the 80% agreement recommended by Brophy and Good (1969).

The initial analyses were computed on five separate groups of measures representing different aspects of classroom interaction—(1) appropriateness, (2) academic instruction, (3) nonacademic interaction, (4) absolute feedback, and (5) residual feedback—using separate multivariate analyses of variance. Of the five groups, the first four resulted in significant effects. These four groups included a total of 12 observational measures for which separate ANOVAs resulted in seven significant effects. High-expectancy students exhibited (1) more appropriate responses, (2) fewer inappropriate responses, (3) more teacher public interaction and (4) more child public interaction, and received (5) more praise, (6) less criticism and (7) less public reprimand from the teacher. Contrary to the polarization hypothesis, only two behaviors involving expectancy changed significantly over the year. In both cases, (absolute praise and praise for correct responses) the change was toward more similarity in teacher behavior with praise decreasing for the high-expectancy group. Although no class by behavior interactions were computed Good, Cooper and Blakey (1980) do indicate "It must be stated, however, that differential elementary school teacher behavior toward high and low achievers is not a universal finding. This is illustrated by the fact that some classrooms in our sample did not display the general pattern" (p. 383).

In concluding this selected review of observation studies concerned with expectancy, we would like to mention two which changed the focus of interest. In the first, instead of simply reporting teacher–student interactions among students of varying achievement, ability, or expectancy (depending on the person's viewpoint) Alpert (1974) was concerned about appropriate teaching behaviors for students of differing ability. More specifically, Alpert began by developing an instrument to measure good nonverbal and verbal teaching behaviors for high and low reading groups. Interestingly the reading specialists decided that good teaching behaviors were the same for top and bottom reading groups (We will come back to this later.) In addition, several of the behaviors were included in other observation instruments (e.g., praise for reading, support, reinforce, encourage). There were also two methodological changes in the observation process. First, verbal behaviors were tape recorded and then these behaviors were tabulated by raters blind to reading group classification. Second, rater reliability was more carefully specified (percentage agreement on three consecutive tape recordings) than in other studies and reliability was checked while data were being gathered.

The results were analyzed using correlated t tests and a critical level for significance was determined. There were no significant mean differences for any good verbal behaviors nor the total mean number of good verbal behaviors. The only significant effect was for size of group (bottom groups were significantly smaller). She concluded that "the results indicate the need to consider reasons other than teacher discriminatory behavior for the relatively slow growth of low-ability pupils. An alternative explanation is that educators do not know how to instruct pupils of low ability" (p. 352).

This latter hypothesis is interesting because at the same time these studies were proceeding, other educational researchers were developing models in which treatments were being designed for students depending on individual differences. This procedure, which became known as Aptitude by Treatment Interaction (ATI) (Cronbach & Snow, 1977), had as its basic premise that specific treatments are more effective with students who have specific trait patterns. Obviously, one of the traits which should be considered is intelligence (and hence achievement). In other words, one interpretation of differential treatments that have been found in these observational studies is that teachers have found differential treatments to be more effective with students of differing ability. In fact, that is exactly the interpretation of the final observation study reported here.

Haskins, Walden and Ramey (1983) had two females observe top and bottom reading groups in 19 kindergarten and/or first grade heterogeneously grouped classrooms. They recorded three types of data. The setting codes included amount of individual, sub-group, and whole group work. The teacher behaviors included control (direct control, discipline, positive reinforcement), instructional (drill, subject matter, questions, correction), delay (transition, wait) and miscellaneous categories. Finally, student behaviors included talk (statement, question, modification), address teacher (request attention or help), negative (disrupt, off-task) and miscellaneous categories. Results of the observational data were analyzed using first multivariate and then univariate analyses. The unit of analysis was the classroom. It was found that teachers used significantly more direct control, positive reinforcement, direct instruction and error correction statements with the low group but no significant differences were found in transitional activities (i.e., time wasted). They found that while low students were more apt to interfere with their peers' work, they were equally responsive to control statements by teachers. Of greatest interest is the interpretation of the teacher behavior towards the low reading group. According to Haskins, Walden and Ramey (1983):

> On the other hand, we do wish to emphasize that these expectancies are very much in accord with the observed academic achievements and behavioral propensities of low ability students. Thus, faced with students of low academic achievement who also tend to disrupt the instructional process, teachers organize their instructional groups and behave toward low group students in ways that seem well designed to offset the deficiencies of such students. All in all, we find little reason to question

the use of intraclass grouping, and even less reason to offer this practice as an explanation of the poor academic development of low income and minority group students. [p. 875]

GENERAL COMMENTS

Differential Interpretations

Thus we have come full circle (See summary of studies and conclusions in Table 4.1) from suggesting that differential expectancies of students with different abilities were causing differential treatment, which in turn resulted in insufficient progress and perpetuating a caste system based on social class, to the conclusion that these differential treatments are actually beneficial to all concerned. It should be mentioned that this latter conclusion is not one suggested by only a single author. Brophy (1979) on a number of occasions and Good (1981) have suggested similar kinds of differences in teacher behavior when dealing with students of differing ability and/or social class.

Methodological Problems

Besides the final conclusion that differences in treatment of students are not necessarily bad, we should mention a number of methodological and conceptual problems with this type of study of which it is important that prospective teachers be aware.

First, in our description of studies we have continually included a number of study characteristics. These include the number and characteristics of observers and the indices of observer agreement. Unless one has participated in an observation study, it is difficult to describe the importance of and problems in acquiring acceptable observer reliability. Even with much experience, it is almost impossible to determine the initiator and intent (positive or negative) of teacher–student interactions. Although several authors (e.g., Frick & Semmel, 1978) have suggested types of observer reliability and procedures which should be followed in observation studies, few observational studies have included such procedures. We believe that there are several specific procedures which should be followed in carrying out observational studies. These include (1) report both percentage of agreement (the percentage of agreement should be reported by category rather than a mean agreement for all categories) and interclass correlations (e.g., Cohen's κ), (2) number of times or over how much time (e.g. two consecutives 1 hour sessions) the agreement has been reached should be stated, (3) with whom agreement was reached (one other observer or all with a trainer) should be reported, (4) observer reliability should be acquired during the observation period, (5) how many and who the observers were should be stated, and finally (6) some index of behavior reliability should be stated. An observed teacher may

TABLE 4.1
Summary of Observational Studies

	Classrooms Observed	Observers	Observer Reliability	Student Characteristics	Groups Observed	Conclusions
Rist, 1970	One K One 2nd	Author	Not applicable	lower-class Black	Entire class	Teachers preserve American class structure
Brophy and Good, 1970	Four 1st	?	?	75% White lower class 15% lower-class Blacks 10% Mexican-American	6 high achievers 6 low achievers per class-room	Teachers treat high and low expectancy students differently
Weinstein, 1976	Three 1st	?	M 85% pre fall M 93% pre spring	78% White working-class 22% Black working-class	All students (60)	Teachers do not treat reading group students differently except for some better treatment for low group
Cooper & Baron, 1977	Six 2nd Two 1st–2nd	8 female undergrads	M 80% pre	?	3 high 3 medium 3 low per class-room	High expectancy females receive more praise, Low expectancy females receive more criticism

Study	Grade	Observers	Reliability	Classroom composition	Groups per classroom[a]	Findings
Good, Cooper and Blakey, 1980	Seven 3rd Four 4th Five 5th	?	$\kappa = .84$ $r = .85$ from videotapes M 91% fall M 88% winter 74% Spring	3 White middle-class 1 rural classroom 1 classroom with 67% White middle-class 33% Black	4 high 4 medium 4 low	Teachers treat high, medium and low expectancy students differently on some behaviors but no support for the polarization effect was found
Alpert, 1974	Fifteen 2nd	15 undergrads	76% on 3 consecutive pre study 76% during study		Top and bottom reading groups	No differences in good teacher behaviors
Haskins, Walden & Raney (in press)	Three K Seven 1st Nine K-1st	2 females	$M = 80\%$ pre range 33–100% during study	Top group = 105 Whites 20 Blacks Low group = 50 Whites 44 Blacks	Top and bottom reading groups	Differences in teacher behaviors were found but it was decided they were appropriate for the groups

Note. None of the observational studies provided an index of behavior reliability.

[a]From 60% for whom consent forms were available

exhibit a high number of a specific behavior for only 1 day or a low number of a different behavior across all days. When behaviors are summed over days, both of the above would be looked on in a similar manner. None of the studies cited followed all of these procedures.

A second major problem with these studies is that the unit of interest is the teacher not the students. In the case of Rist (1970) only one teacher was observed at a time and in the Brophy and Good (1970) study only four were included. In fact, the total number of teachers used in all seven studies summarized in Table 4.1 was 67.

Third, other variables, which are obviously potential contributors to teacher expectancy behaviors, are seldom varied, controlled or discussed (e.g., sex, race, and SES of teachers or students, sizes of class, age, and/or grade level of students) in summaries of findings (e.g., Good & Brophy, 1977). It should be recalled that expectancy effects were originally found for first and second graders only, yet observational studies have utilized up to fifth graders to determine effects of teacher expectancy.

Recommendations to Teacher Educators

What can we say to teacher educators about these studies? First, they should caution prospective teachers against accepting the conclusions found in the study abstract and discussion sections without carefully reading the method and procedure sections. In particular one should look at observer agreement indices, number of teachers observed, and operational definitions used in the observational instrument before drawing any conclusions. This is particularly true when attempting to compare studies since different behaviors may have been given similar labels.

Second, teachers vary a great deal in the way they treat students of different characteristics (age, sex, ability, SES, etc.). Interestingly enough, Good (1981) has indicated that he believes there is far more variability in how teachers treat low-expectancy than high-expectancy students. This should be easily predictable if we accept the premise that there are relatively stable individual differences in student learning ability beyond rate of acquisition. Once the teacher determines that the high-ability children are progressing at a satisfactory rate there is no need to change or vary treatments. On the other hand, when the students in the lower groups do not progress at a satisfactory rate teachers begin to vary techniques and hence behaviors.

General Advice to Teacher Educators

It should be evident by now that we believe that teacher educators should recognize that there is wide disagreement among psychologists concerning the most basic of questions. In the areas of individual differences and cognitive development specific viewpoints have direct implications for educational practice. It is our contention that it is presently impossible for any teacher educator to tell students that one position has been proven correct. Rather, they should make students familiar with the more prevalent positions, current research findings and, as suggested earlier, provide them with the basic skills necessary to read and evaluate new research. The position eventually adopted is obviously up to them.

In this context the basic questions in expectancy research concern the nature of individual differences and how they should be treated. It should be recognized that strong advocates of teacher expectancy effects believe that the teacher is a major influence in determining individual differences in student achievement. In its ultimate form it suggests that perfect teaching leads to a general reduction in individual differences. Thus, much of teacher expectancy literature is designed to show how teachers are failing to provide the best educational experience for all students. It also seems to be assumed that teachers can improve all student performance if they desire and often consciously or unconsciously select particular students to receive the best or worst treatment. In short, teachers are not trying hard enough to educate all students, use their own value system to select both favored and unfavored students, and are responsible for wide individual difference variations in achievement.

From our reading of the literature the evidence in favor of such a position is less than convincing. Not only is there a failure to experimentally replicate the initial findings, but more importantly the evidence for the existence of the process necessary for these differences to occur is particluarly weak. The most cited evidence shows that some teachers treat high achieving students different than low achieving students. At least some researchers believe that this is as it should be. In this case the appropriate question to ask is not How *are* teachers teaching students of varying ability? but rather How *should* teachers vary their treatment across different ability groups?

An additional question concerns the nature and antecedents of individual differences. We believe schools have treated this problem in a cursory manner. More specifically, American educators generally conceive of individual differences in terms of rate of acquisition. Thus, it is assumed that everyone is capable and should be learning the same material in primary and secondary schools. Classes emphasizing individual differences are built around allowing students to proceed at their own rate, but toward identical goals.

There is, of course, another more developmental viewpoint which can be applied to interpret the teacher expectancy research. This view emphasizes the natural unfolding of student abilities as a major source of individual differences. In this case student abilities develop at different rates and at any given time (particularly during elementary years) some students spontaneously learn things teachers are unable to teach the others. In addition, the former students would continue to learn at an accelerated rate so that the most capable teaching may well increase, rather than decrease, individual differences. Finally, such a position recognizes that there are some students who cannot meet the standard demands of school (e.g., learn to read) even with great effort (or we do not yet know how to teach them). These students can learn many things but would need to be treated via alternative teaching techniques. In effect such a position would predict different developmental rates and demand vast differences in the way teachers treat individual students. This is a position consistent with much developmental theorizing (e.g., Piaget, 1952) and empirical results (e.g., Hall & Kaye, 1980) as well as many of the observational studies cited here.

It is also consistent with information processing viewpoints that differentiate between structural and control processes. This latter position retains the teacher as playing a central decision-making role. They must decide when students should be taught specific skills or tasks. We would suggest that this be done jointly with the student because it is important that the students know and accept their capabilities without diminishing self-esteem. In this light we are encouraged to learn that teacher assessment is often in agreement with other measures of student ability (e.g., Dusek & O'Connell, 1973) and assume such findings are the basis for Brophys' (1982) assertion that teacher expectancies are by and large accurate.

We would caution teacher educators, however, that the developmental views provided here have also supported the position that rapid cognitive changes appear to occur at crucial times (e.g., between 5 and 7 years of age and during early adolescence) during the course of development. It is possible that students may lack the abilities to comprehend very basic concepts at one point but several months later find that these same concepts are relatively easy. This being the case, teachers must continuously evaluate student progress and abilities (expectancies). In this context we must make teachers aware of errors in decision making. Here we would acquaint teachers with the literature developed by Tversky and Kahneman (1974) on judgment under uncertainty. Certainly the tendency to predict outcomes with insufficient regard for prior probability, the effect of sample size on sampling variability, and regression to the mean are all topics which should be taught in courses covering teacher decision making. It is important to note that such research has been initiated by Borko, Cone, Russor and Shavelson (1979). If teachers are constantly aware of student abilities, student progress should be maximized.

Finally, we should assure readers we are not against teachers demanding progress from their students. We are aware of and impressed with the correlational data of Rutter, Maughan, Mortimore, and Ouston (1979) showing that a demanding environment is related to superior progress. We hope experimental studies replicating this work will follow. Our primary message is that the emphasis should be in providing teachers with theories, techniques and empirical information that will lead to improved teaching, rather than showing how things are presently or emphasizing educational inadequacies.

REFERENCES

Alpert, J. L. Teacher behavior across ability groups: A consideration of the mediation of Pygmalion effects. *Journal of Educational Psychology*, 1974, *66*, 348–353.

Anderson, D. F., & Rosenthal, R. Some effects of interpersonal expectancy and social interaction on institutionalized retarded children. *Proceedings of the 76th Annual Convention of the American Psychological Association*, 1968, *3*, 479–480.

Bales, R. F. A set of categories for the analysis of small group interaction. *American Sociological Review*, 1950, *15*, 257–263.

Barker Lunn, J. *Streaming in the primary school*. Slough, England: National Foundation for Educational Research, 1970.

Borko, H., Cone, R., Russo, N. A., & Shavelson, R. J. Teachers' decision making. In P. Peterson and H. Walberg (Eds.), *Research on teaching: Concepts, findings, and implications*. Berkeley, California: McCutchan, 1979.

Brophy, J., & Good, T. *Teacher–child dyadic interactions: A manual for coding classroom behavior* (Report Series No. 27). Austin: University of Texas at Austin, Research and Development Center for Teacher Education, December, 1969.

Brophy, J. E. Teacher behavior and its effects. *Journal of Educational Psychology*, 1979, *71*, 733–750.

Brophy, J. E., & Good, T. L. Teachers' communication of differential expectations for children's classroom performance: Some behavioral data. *Journal of Educational Psychology*, 1970, *61*, 365–374.

Brophy, J. E. Research on the self-fulfilling prophecy and teacher expectations. In *The self-fulfilling prophecy: Its origins and consequences in research and practice*. Symposium presented at the annual meeting of the American Educational Research Association, New York, 1982.

Claiborn, W. L. Expectancy effects in the classroom: A failure to replicate. *Journal of Educational Psychology*, 1969, *60*, 377–383.

Conn, L., Edwards, C., Rosenthal, R., & Crowne, D. Perception of emotion and response to teachers' expectancy by elementary school children. *Psychological Reports*, 1968, *22*, 27–34.

Cook, T. D., & Campbell, D. T. *Quasi-experimentation: Design & analysis issues for field settings*. Boston: Houghton Mifflin, 1979.

Cooper, H. M., & Baron, R. M. Academic expectations and attributed responsibility as predictors of professional teachers' reinforcement behavior. *Journal of Educational Psychology*, 1977, *69*, 409–418.

Covington, M. V., & Omelich, C. L. Effort: The double-edged sword in school achievement. *Journal of Educational Psychology*, 1979, *71*, 169–182.

Crano, W. D., & Mellon, P. M. Causal influence of teachers' expectations on children's academic performance: A cross-lagged panel analysis. *Journal of Educational Psychology*, 1978, *70*, 39–49.

Cronbach, L. J., & Snow, R. E. *Aptitudes and instructional methods: A handbook for research on interactions*. New York: Irvington, 1977.

Dusek, J. B., & O'Connell, E. J. Teacher expectancy effects on the achievement test performance of elementary school children. *Journal of Educational Psychology*, 1973, *65*, 371–377.

Flanagan, J. C. *Tests of general ability: Preliminary technical report*. Chicago: Science Research Associates, Inc., 1960.

Frick, T., & Semmel, M. I. Observer agreement and reliabilities of classroom observational measures. *Review of Educational Research*, 1978, *48*, 157–184.

Good, T. L. Teacher expectations and student perceptions: A decade of research. *Educational Leadership*, 1981, *38*, 415–422.

Good, T. L., & Brophy, J. E. *Educational psychology A realistic approach*. New York: Holt, Rinehart & Winston, 1977.

Good, T. L., Cooper, H. M., & Blakey, S. L. Classroom interaction as a function of teacher expectations, student sex, and time of year. *Journal of Educational Psychology*, 1980, *72*, 378–385.

Hall, V. C., & Kaye, D. B. Early patterns of cognitive development. *Monographs of the Society for Research in Child Development*, 1980, *45*(2, Serial No. 184).

Haskins, R., Walden, T., & Ramey, C. T. Teacher and student behavior in high and low ability groups. *Journal of Educational Psychology*, 1983, *75*, 865–876.

José, J., & Cody, J. Teacher–pupil interaction as it relates to attempted changes in teacher expectancy of academic ability and achievement. *American Educational Research Journal*, 1971, *8*, 39–49.

Katona, G. *Organizing and memorizing*. New York: Columbia University Press, 1940.

O'Connell, E. J., Dusek, J. B., & Wheeler, R. J. A follow-up study of teacher expectancy effects. *Journal of Educational Psychology*, 1974, *66*, 325–328.

Piaget, J. *The origins of intelligence in children*. New York: International Universities Press, Inc., 1952.

Rist, R. C. Student social class and teacher expectations: The self-fulfilling prophecy in ghetto education. *Harvard Educational Review*, 1970, *40*, 411–451.

Rogosa, D. A critique of cross-lagged correlation. *Psychological Bulletin*, 1980, *88*, 245–258.

Rokeach, M. *The open and closed mind*. New York: Basic Books, 1960.

Rosenthal, R. *On the social psychology of the self-fulfilling prophecy: Further evidence for Pygmalion effects and their mediating mechanisms*. New York: MSS Modular Publications, 1974.

Rosenthal, R., & Jacobson, L. *Pygmalion in the classroom*. New York: Holt, Rinehart & Winston, 1968.

Rothbart, M., Dalfen, S., & Barrett, R. Effects of teacher's expectancy on student–teacher interaction. *Journal of Educational Psychology*, 1971, *62*, 49–54.

Rotter, J. *Social learning and clinical psychology*. Englewood Cliffs, N.J.: Prentice-Hall, 1954.

Rutter, M., Maughan, B., Mortimore, P., & Ouston, J. *Fifteen thousand hours: Secondary schools and their effects on children*. Cambridge: Harvard University Press, 1979.

Smith, F. J., & Luginbuhl, J. E. R. Inspecting expectancy: Some laboratory results of relevance for teacher training. *Journal of Educational Psychology*, 1976, *68*, 265–272.

Snow, R. E. Unfinished Pygmalion. *Contemporary Psychology*, 1969, *14*, 197–199.

Swann, W. B., Jr., & Snyder, M. On translating beliefs into action: Theories of ability and their application in an instructional setting. *Journal of Personality and Social Psychology*, 1980, *38*, 879–888.

Thorndike, R. L. Review of Pygmalion in the classroom. *American Educational Research Journal*, 1968, *5*, 708–711.

Thorndike, R. L. But you have to know how to tell time. *American Educational Research Journal*, 1969, *6*, 692.

Tversky, A., & Kahneman, D. Judgment under uncertainty: Heuristics and biases. *Science*, 1974, *185*, 1124–1131.

Weinstein, R. S. Reading group membership in first grade: Teacher behaviors and pupil experience over time. *Journal of Educational Psychology*, 1976, *68*, 103–116.

5 Logical and Methodological Problems in Teacher Expectancy Research

Alexis L. Mitman
Far West Laboratory for Educational Research and Development

Richard E. Snow
Stanford University

This chapter examines the logic and methodology of research on teacher expectancies. Because such research attempts to capture and explain both the processes and effects of teacher expectations as they occur in actual classrooms, it must face many of the same complex methodological and analytical problems that plague classroom research in general. Yet teacher expectation phenomena appear also to be uniquely complex. The difficulties involved in analyzing networks of relationships among the personal characteristics, interpersonal perceptions, and behavior of from two to dozens of individuals in transaction over time pose methodological problems rarely faced in educational research.

The first section provides an overview of the network of variables involved in classroom expectancy phenomena as it is currently conceptualized. Then, major sections address the problems of analyzing the causal linkages among these variables and improving their measurement. Within these sections the strengths and weaknesses of various approaches to these problems are discussed. Example studies are cited where appropriate, but no attempt at exhaustive review of each possible type of study is made. Suggestions for improved approaches to future research are then advanced. The chapter focuses on logical and methodological problems, not on the problems of statistical analysis or data processing. References to detailed discussions of statistical and methodological issues are given as appropriate for further reading.

THE NATURE OF NATURAL EXPECTANCIES

To introduce the complexities with which theory and research must ultimately cope, consider the diagram of Fig. 5.1. The figure is an elaboration of one designed by West and Anderson (1976) to illustrate alternative hypothesized

94

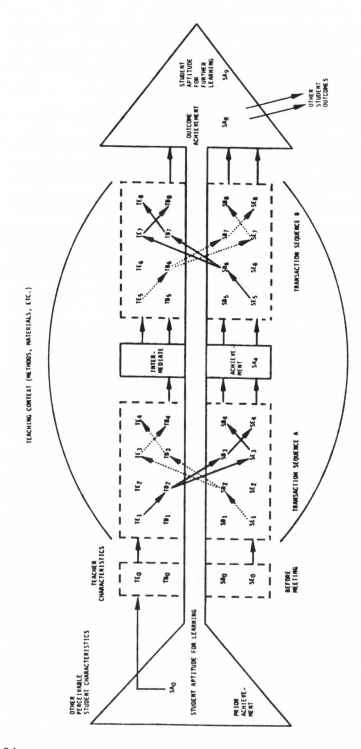

FIG. 5.1. Hypothetical elements and linkages in expectancy-outcome network.

linkages of elements in the expectancy-outcome network. Our version brings into view several additional variables of potential importance and some of the linkages between them.

Students come to instruction with certain aptitudes for learning, and they usually differ from one another in these aptitudes. Measures of such student differences, in relevant prior achievements or academic abilities for example, often predict learning outcome to a substantial extent regardless of the teachers, teaching methods, or topics studied. One issue for research, then, is to take those aptitude differences into account in ways that show their effects on learning processes and outcomes, and on teacher and student expectation processes. In particular, it is important to determine if, when, and how teachers and students use information about student aptitude differences to condition their approaches to teaching and learning.

Students differ also in other perceivable characteristics, some of which may be associated with variables such as ethnic background, gender, or socioeconomic status, for example. Some of these may be correlated with aptitude for learning for a variety of reasons, including the effects of teacher expectancies, if any, from previous classroom experiences. Both the aptitude differences and the other perceivable student characteristics, with which aptitudes may or may not be correlated in a given instance, can serve as sources of teacher or of student expectancies.

Teachers also differ in many characteristics relevant to teaching and to expectancies. Personality differences, and related aptitudes and attitudes, may affect not only classroom teaching behavior but also the degree to which attention is paid to student characteristics. Teachers differ in their use of information on prior student achievement and aptitude; they differ also in social skills and attitudes that can moderate interpersonal transactions. And students are not without similar differences in social skills and attitudes and in prior information they may have from parents, siblings, and peers, about the characteristics and habits of teachers to which they now find themselves assigned. Both teachers and students thus vary in the amount and kind of information about one another they bring to class.

A research problem of no small significance is to ferret out the sources of teacher and student expectancies in this network of prior information and to distinguish between valid and invalid expectancies based on it. Self-fulfilling prophecies that are based on invalid or misleading inferences from prior information are likely to be quite different phenomena, functionally, than prophecies based on valid inferences. And, valid inferences can be either functionally involved in the fulfillment of predictions, or only incidentally correlated with them.

Furthermore, both teachers and students come to their first meeting with a host of other habitual expectations and behavior patterns built up from prior experience that have implications for the effects of expectancies: One teacher feels inhibited by extra-large classes but persists in whole-class teaching; another routinely divides students into small groups; one student usually feels tired in any class following gym; another dislikes math. These variables too may be correlated with other teacher and student characteristics and enter into the mix of expectations relevant to performance, and thus relevant to research on expectancy effects.

In Fig. 5.1, the mixes of expectancies and behavior patterns held by teachers and students before meeting are signified by TE_0, TB_0, SB_0, and SE_0. Student aptitude, including measured prior achievement, is coded SA_0. Other perceivable student and teacher characteristics are identified in the figure but not coded.

Classroom transaction sequences follow from these bases. There may be any number of sequences and intermittant assessments of ongoing achievement. Fig. 5.1 is simplified, showing just two transaction sequences and one intermediate assessment, but many more would occur in the course of instruction at almost any grade level. In this stream of classroom events, a teacher expectancy (TE_1) about one or more students, based on some mix of information available from Time 0, may influence teacher behavior (TB_2) at Time 2. This, in turn, may influence subsequent student behavior (SB_3) and then student expectations (SE_4), or student expectations (SE_3) which then influence student behavior (SB_4). Either sequence may be hypothesized to result in temporary or long-lasting effects on student achievement (SA_4 or SA_8). The typical teacher expectancy hypothesis posits just this sort of effect, or more simply, a TE_1 - TB_2 - SB_3 - SA_4 or SA_8 sequence.

But competing hypotheses can be formulated that originate in student expectations (SE_0) such as the sequence SE_1 - SB_2 - TE_3 - TB_4 - SA_4. Student expectations and behavior can also be hypothesized to influence achievement directly. And, many other complex permutations of these sequences are possible. For a rich description of the many kinds of interactions possible between perceiver and target, in contexts beyond education, see Darley and Fazio (1980). It is reasonable to suppose, in the educational setting, for example, that information available to teachers and students from a first intermediate achievement assessment (SA_4), such as a unit test or quiz, can have the effect of creating new expectancies or of modifying substantially the expectancy-behavior patterns that might have operated prior to that assessment. Such information may strongly confirm or alter teacher or student expectancies since it reflects current criterion relevance rather than perceptions of distant past performances or correlates thereof. Some measures of intermediate or final achievement can themselves be substantially and directly influenced by teacher or student expectancies. Teacher grades might be expected to be more sensitive to teacher expectancies than would student test performance, while student anxieties might be expected to influence test performance directly and teacher grades only indirectly. Also, there are teaching and learning context variables that condition the functioning of all of the above. For example, teacher expectancies and behavior are moderated by the methods, materials, and grouping practices used. Student expectancies and behavior will be moderated by those of work mates and peers, and those associated with homework environments.

Finally, it is usually assumed that immediate achievement contributes to the development of student aptitude for further learning over the long haul. Where research considers this eventuality, some measure of intelligence or general academic ability is added at the end. The classical teacher expectancy hypothesis then becomes TE_1 - TB_2 - SB_3 - SA_9. This is in fact the hypothesis with which Rosenthal and Jacobson (1968) began.

The above account of hypothetical expectation processes, and their antecedents, concomitants, and consequences, brings out two general problems for research methodology. One is the measurement problem—How can each of the constituent variables in expectancy-outcome sequences best be measured? The other is the causal direction problem—How can the sequence of constituent variables best be analyzed to reach cause-effect inferences about their linkages? The second problem must be considered prior to the first problem, since the conditions needed to infer causal linkages may prescribe or proscribe certain kinds of measurements.

THE ANALYSIS OF CAUSATION

For centuries considerable philosophical debate has centered on questions about the nature of causality and the role of causal inferences in science. There is considerable debate today in social and behavioral science over just what view of the possibility and importance of causal inference will be most productive and how to judge the validity of research studies in this regard (Cook & Campbell, 1979; Cronbach, 1982a, 1982b). That debate need not be entered here. We can agree for the present that a theory of teacher expectancy will have to be subsumed under some general model of reciprocal determinism, such as that adopted by Bandura (1977, 1978) as the foundation for social learning theory, without abandoning the study of unidirectional causal hypotheses (see Phillips & Orton, in press). We can agree with West and Anderson (1976), that both theory and evidence exist to make plausible the hypothesis that, for each link in the expectancy-outcome chain, causal effects can run in a direction opposite to that posited by teacher expectancy hypotheses. That is, student aptitude and achievement may influence later student behavior and student expectations; student behavior can have marked effects on teacher behavior as well as vice versa; teacher behavior is more likely to influence teacher expectations than vice versa; and teacher expectations measured after a period of teacher–student interaction, or an intermediate student achievement, may primarily reflect valid teacher predictions of later student achievement based on observations and inferences about current achievement.

Given that plausible hypotheses suggest causal effects running in both directions in teacher–student transaction sequences, it is important to develop methodologies by which alternative causal hypotheses can be tested and compared. The traditional response to the problem of causality has been to say that formal experiments provide the only path to solution. There are, of course, both classroom experiments and nonclassroom experiments, however, and these have different strengths and weaknesses. There are also correlational methodologies by which researchers can test causal inferences. Constraints exist in each case; all studies are fallible. Only a careful examination of both the internal and external validity considerations in each particular case can show the degree to which proposed causal conclusions are tenable. In the long run, the different kinds of studies will need to be coordinated so that the strengths and weaknesses of each can be balanced in support of such conclusions. Our discussion can only highlight the most important considerations in each kind of research.

The Validity of Classroom Experiments

Certainly, the development of experimental work in educational research over recent decades has provided many significant advances. The movement was spurred by Campbell and Stanley's (1963) treatise on experimental and quasi-experimental design in educational research, which remains a central reference for researchers. Cook and Campbell (1979), Kerlinger (1973), and Kerlinger and Pedhazur (1973) have provided important updates and expansions. It is clear that the initial interest in teacher expectancies was fostered by formal experiments designed to demonstrate that the phenomenon existed. These were simple extensions into the classroom of experimental designs, used in the laboratory to study experimenter expectancy effects (Rosenthal, 1966; Rosenthal & Jacobson, 1968).

But classroom experiments taken alone can be extremely limited. As the complexity of the phenomena to be studied increases, such experiments can become cumbersome, and threats to their internal and external validity can multiply. There are often tradeoffs that strengthen experiments internally at the expense of their value in support of generalizations externally, and vice versa. There are also realms into which experimenters cannot, or dare not, tread. These problems become particularly acute with respect to the teacher expectancy hypothesis. Consider the following general constraints:

1. It would appear to be unethical to conduct classroom experiments in which teachers are given false negative expectations about particular students. One cannot risk harm in the interest of science. Thus, classroom experiments on the teacher expectancy hypothesis typically manipulate *only* positive teacher expectancies; teachers are given favorable predictions about some students and these are compared with "untreated" control students. But there is no evidence or

theoretical justification for assuming that negative expectancies function as mirror images of positive expectancies. In fact, it is plausible to hypothesize that the two functions are distinctly different psychologically. Investigators who generalize the results of experiments on positive teacher expectancies to make statements about the effects of negative teacher expectancies do so with no scientific justification.

2. Both teacher and student expectancy can be manipulated experimentally. It appears possible, therefore, to investigate the opposing unidirectional causal hypotheses by such means. But manipulating the reciprocal functions of teacher and student expectancies and behavior in regular classrooms appears to be nearly impossible (for examples in limited classroom settings, see Rappaport & Rappaport, 1975; Zanna, Sheras, Cooper & Shaw, 1975). Classroom experimental work has thus typically been limited to one or the other of the two unidirectional hypotheses; usually, the teacher expectation–student achievement direction has been the only focus, and this leaves out more than half the phenomena of interest.

3. In classrooms, experimental controls are difficult to maintain. Various breakdowns occur in ongoing teaching and normal school functioning that threaten the internal validity of the experiment as originally designed. The threats multiply as time in the experiment increases. Yet the phenomenon as hypothesized is potentially important primarily as its effects extend over time. Hence, the longer the experiment, the more important the conclusion, but the more the conclusion is likely to be compromised by threats to internal validity.

Classroom experiments have typically followed the procedure used by Rosenthal and Jacobson (1968), although many have broadened the range of variables measured and included in the analysis, and some have also included checks on validity omitted by Rosenthal and Jacobson. What all such studies share is that participating teachers receive information from the experimenter indicating that a certain subset of each teacher's students have obtained high scores on measures of academic skills or academic potential. Although most studies have attempted to manipulate such favorable expectations of teachers using a single, impersonal exposure to expectation information, a few have used more intense interventions, such as personal interviews or repeated mailings, to ensure that teachers are aware of the information—to increase the probability, in other words, that TE_1 includes the experimental variable. Students on the experimental list are randomly chosen or matched in such a way that the positive expectancy information is false. Other students in each teacher's class serve as a control group. Time is then allowed to pass. Dependent measures usually are achievement or intelligence test scores administered at semester or end-of-year breaks to represent SA_8 or SA_9. Pretest performance reflecting SA_0 may or may not be collected and used appropriately. Some studies have also been able to include measures of teacher behavior toward the experimental and control students.

Such designs have had great appeal in that they maintain the framework of formal experiments carried out in actual classroom environments. As such, they are considered to be internally valid and generalization of their results across similar classrooms has seemed straightforward. As noted above, their validity and generalizability can be challenged because such experiments concern only the effects of favorable teacher expectations, assumed to be operating as a unidirectional cause of student outcome differences, and because they do not document in any detail the myriad classroom events that intervene between TE_0 and SA_8 or SA_9. Several further challenges connect with these concerns.

Manipulation Validity.   One question concerns whether or not the expectation manipulation of the experimenter actually worked to produce the desired effect in teachers. In other words, is it reasonable to think that teachers will change their expectations for individual students based on an experimenter-provided list when the teacher's original expectations usually are based on several valued sources, including school records and behavioral observation? In the Rosenthal-Jacobson study, for example, teachers later could not remember, and reported hardly having glanced at, the names on the experimenter's list of high-expectancy students. Even extended experimental manipulations, designed to make the expectation information salient and believable for teachers, may not fully overcome this problem. Several studies have included teacher reports suggesting that most teachers do not shape or reshape their expectations according to the experimental manipulation (e.g., Henrikson, 1970; Jose & Cody, 1971; Mendels & Flanders, 1973).

Prediction Integration.   Another question follows from the above. If teachers rely on prior information from school records or their own or other teachers' experiences, a favorable bit of information provided by the experimenter will be consistent with experience for students who have done well academically in the past, and inconsistent with experience for those who have not done well in the past. Thus special attention need be given by the teacher only to the inconsistent information. The teacher will either dismiss the new information because of its inconsistency with what is known or revise what is known to incorporate the new message. As suggested by Fig. 5.2, less than half of the experimental students have a chance to have the valence of their expectation substantially influenced by the experimental intervention, and the fate of this intervention is unknown. Research has only now begun to investigate if and how teachers assimilate new positive information with previously existing negative information to make predictions about students (see Shavelson, Cadwell, & Izu, 1977; Shavelson & Stern, 1981), yet this is the only case in which experimental expectancy interventions in classrooms are likely to have marked effects. In such research also, the degree of favorableness or unfavorableness of the prior information could turn out to be a crucial variable.

Student	TE_0	Expectancy Intervention	TE_1
1	++	+	+++
2	++	0	++
3	+	+	++
4	+	0	+
5	0	+	+
6	0	0	0
7	-	+	?
8	-	0	-
9	--	+	?
10	--	0	--

FIG. 5.2. Possible resulting teacher expectancies (TE_1) based on combinations of favorable (+) or neutral (0) expectancy interventions with degree of favorable, neutral, or negative (−) teacher expectancies from prior information (TE_0) for ten hypothetical students in a classroom.

A futher implication of Fig. 5.2 should also be noted. If TE_0 is rectangularly distributed as shown, or normally distributed, and correlated with pretest as expected, then the effect of positive expectancy inductions might be seen primarily in the regressions of posttest on pretest, rather than in the posttest means, since the effect, if any, would increase as one goes up the favorableness scale of TE_0. In other words, the newly provided positive expectancies should primarily enhance valid predictions from previously held positive information. This suggests that the relation of pretested student aptitude and prior achievement to TE_0 and to TE_1 in experimental and control groups deserves careful study. These relationships should not be presumed to be linear, or equivalent in different treatment groups, or neutralized by randomization. In fact, little is known about the metric properties of a + imposed at different points on the TE_0 scale, since pre-post regressions have rarely been studied.

Effect Level.   The kinds of effects noted above can occur at the individual student level. But they can occur as well at the class level (e.g., Finn, Gaier, Peng, & Banks, 1975), and even at the level of the school (e.g., Brookover, Schweitzer, Schneider, Beady, Flood, & Wisenbaker, 1978). Most importantly, teachers often hold, or are given, expectancies regarding the functioning of whole class groups or subgroups within a class and these might well interact with expectancies held for individual students. What, for example, might the resultant prediction be for an experimental student with moderately high absolute TE_0 but who appeared relatively low in TE_0 because of inclusion in a class with very high average TE_0? Cronbach and Webb (1975; see also Cronbach, 1982b) have demonstrated how such class level effects, and interactions between class and individual level effects, can occur in research on aptitude. Aggregation effects of this sort have not been studied in relation to teacher expectancies either in classroom experiments or in correlational studies. In either case, however, their presence would alter interpretation of such effects significantly.

Teacher Action and Reaction.   Another set of problems concerns the many other events that naturally intervene, or that can be made to intervene by teachers and students in classrooms. Given the list of resultant expectations identified in Fig. 5.2 as TE_1, teachers proceed through complex transactions with these students (or subgroups or classes) over the course of months. Many events occur and accumulate that are unrelated to the expectancy induction and yet have positive, neutral, or negative implications for teacher and student expectancies. To the extent that these distribute in correlation with TE_0, as well they might if TE_0 is a valid predictor, then they augment the experimental expectancy intervention in the higher range of TE_1 and negate it in the lower range. The effect is to produce the appearance of a larger expectancy effect than would actually occur. This has been called the "history threat" (Cook & Campbell, 1979).

Suppose instead that teachers orchestrate the stream of events subsequent to TE_1, so as to compensate those students for whom no favorable expectation was provided by the experimenter. One might expect such compensatory behavior toward students for whom favorable expectations were available from past performance (at TE_0) but not from the experimenter. One might expect compensatory behavior also where the purposes of the experiment were transparent to teachers. The result would be a reduction in the expectancy effect obtained and this too might not be uniform across TE_0; regression analysis rather than means analysis would be indicated. This threat is related to those referred to as "compensatory equalization and rivalry" (Cook & Campbell, 1979).

Transitory Effects.   Such effects, including the basal expectancy effect itself, can change over time for several reasons. Reported findings in social science can have the effect of changing the phenomenon to which they pertain.

The example often cited concerns a report from personality research that females have been found to be more submissive, on average, than males. The effect of this report may be to cause females to react by behaving less submissively in later experiments or on later personality inventories. In teacher expectancy research, such reaction appears to be a major concern. There are probably few teachers who have not heard of the "Pygmalion" effect, because of the coverage given to early studies by the news media (see Snow, 1969) and its subsequent inclusion in many teacher education programs. Measures that inquire about, and particularly experiments that seek to manipulate, teacher expectancies are rendered increasingly transparent as the news spreads. The phenomenon may well be changed fundamentally as a result. Uncooperativeness in research and self-consciousness and overcompensation on the part of teachers in their daily classroom activities are only a few of the processes that may change the phenomenon.

Public broadcast and reaction is not even necessary for generalization to fail. Any natural phenomenon that is in transition as a function of passing conditions will be inadequately represented in a following era by experiments conducted in a preceding era. Causal generalizations will always be limited in such instances unless the change aspect of the phenomenon is explicitly included in the generalization. Teacher expectancy is likely to be just such a phenomenon in transition, because of changes in the roles of teachers and students, changes in the population of teachers and the teacher education programs through which they were trained, and changes in the social conditions of the schools.

The Validity of Nonclassroom Experiments

A common response of experimenters facing the problems outlined above is to move out of classrooms and into the laboratory, or other simulated settings. Here, the controls on internal validity can be more fully maintained and the ethical question can at times be circumvented, if negative interventions are relatively mild and shortlived, and proper debriefing of subjects is possible. Most importantly, the reciprocal functions, not just the unidirectional hypotheses, can be manipulated.

Nonclassroom experiments fall into two categories: laboratory studies and questionnaire studies. Teachers in the typical laboratory study receive information about students in the form of a manipulated profile of one or more student characteristics. Teachers then meet singly with one or more students and present the student(s) with a task or lesson. Individuals in the student roles may be experimenter confederates or naive participants. The teachers or the students, or both, are often college students. Dependent measures may include students' actual performance, teachers' perceptions of the students' performance, and teacher ratings of students. Measures of teacher behavior, derived from observer ratings, are often included to detect the processes that may communicate expectations. Examples of laboratory studies of teacher expectation effects include Carter (1969), Johnson (1970), Rubovits and Maehr (1971, 1973), and Smith and Luginbuhl (1976).

A rare laboratory study that manipulated both teacher expectations and student expectations was reported by Feldman and Theiss (1982). Female undergraduates were paired for a short lesson on learning a written passage; one was assigned to the role of teacher, the other to the role of student. Teachers' expectations were manipulated prior to the lesson by indicating that they would be paired with either a high-ability or low-ability student. Students' expectations were manipulated by indicating that they would be taught by either an excellent student teacher or a student teacher having great difficulties. The performance and attitudes of both teachers and students served as dependent measures.

Questionnaire studies are usually designed to determine what specific characteristics of students are important sources of expectation bias for teachers. The method provides an inexpensive and easily manipulted approach. Typically, the experimenter prepares a packet containing hypothetical student information and rating forms. Each packet or student profile is drawn from a facet design with crossed levels for the student characteristics (e.g., sex, race, achievement) to be studied; subjects in the experiment receive profiles with different facet combinations. The rating forms ask subjects to study the information and then to evaluate and make predictions about various aspects of student performance. The packets usually are mailed to a large sample of teachers or students or, less frequently, administered in a classroom situation. Sometimes, characteristics of the teacher are controlled as well. For examples of questionnaire studies, see Finn (1972), Rotter (1974), and Long and Henderson (1974).

While questionnaire and laboratory experiments can be made internally rigorous, their external validity is often severely compromised, and the compromises are rarely addressed directly. Concerns about external validity apply to both classroom and nonclassroom experiments, but they represent the most salient threats to the latter. These concerns are interwoven; they can best be introduced by first considering the nature of generalization from the laboratory (or its exportable, questionnaire form), and then examined in somewhat more detail under the headings of population and ecological representativeness, and the referent generality of measures and constructs.

Generalizations From Laboratory Research.   The great power of laboratory analysis lies in its controlled demonstration of the *possible* functional mechanisms involved in a natural phenomenon. The experimenter arranges conditions in such a way that a phenomenon can be demonstrated to exist and something of its etiology can be exposed and understood. Series of such experiments can be designed to follow each exposed clue toward an elaborated explanation of the phenomenon and an enumeration of the conditions that moderate its occurrence.

Certainly the pages of physical, biological, and psychological science are filled with examples of success attained using this strategy.

The term possible is emphasized above, however, because its implications are often overlooked. Systematic experiments conducted under ideal conditions show possibilities that may exist in nature but they do not guarantee that such possibilities actually occur in the same form or frequency in nature as they do in the laboratory. The artificialities of the laboratory may create behavior that may not generalize well to natural conditions, or may not generalize at all. This is the lesson to be learned from many examples in animal and human ethology. To paraphrase one ethologist, psychologists have tended to concentrate on what animals and humans *can do* in test and laboratory conditions, not on what they *actually do* in their natural habitats (Charlesworth, 1976). Human behavior, because of its adaptive and purposive character, may be particularly subject to distortion just by the act of participating in a laboratory experiment. Human beings perform in experiments for their own purposes; they may choose to adapt or not to adapt to what they think the experimenter's purposes are, and what they think in this regard may or may not be what the experimenter actually intended. Their behavior may be unrepresentative of natural behavior as a result.

In all science, the steps of generalization from laboratory conditions to natural conditions are nontrivial. In the mature sciences, the path between laboratory and field has been paved by a wealth of experience and intervening research devoted to each generalization in turn. Also, particularly in the physical sciences, these generalizations have a long halflife, so they can usually be counted upon to remain relatively constant over many years, if not over eons. The path between the physicist's bell jar and the engineer's bridge, for example, is so solid that a bridge's collapse is considered incredible. But even bridges occasionally collapse. The generalizations still do not always anticipate all possible local natural conditions to which they must be adapted; they are still to some degree unrepresentative.

In the social and behavioral sciences, however, there is little intervening experience and research on which to base generalizations. And the halflife of such generalizations may often be quite short. Social research tends to be time-slice work on phenomena that are in dynamic transition, if not entirely transitory (Cronbach, 1975, 1982a). There are even instances in social science, as noted above, where the statement of a generalization about a phenomenon may change the phenomenon. Again, natural conditions have not been fully represented or anticipated in the research.

Population Representativeness. Beyond the behavioral distortions that may be prompted in any person by participation in an experiment, the persons participating may or may not behave like teachers and students. In many cases, such persons are college students who may also be paid volunteers. Their characteristics and behavior in the role of teacher or student may well not be representative of the populations of teachers and students to whom the experimenter wishes to generalize.

There are two statistical steps involved in generalizing from any empirical data. One step generalizes from the sample studied to the accessible population from which it was drawn. A second step generalizes from the accessible population to the target population of interest. There is an assumption of representative random sampling at each step. Because in human behavioral research this assumption is virtually never met, the recourse is to include detailed descriptions of the target population, the accessible population, and the sample studied (Bracht & Glass, 1968; Snow, 1974). Such descriptions should at least contain measures of those variables that theory and prior research, or investigator intuition, suggest as relevant to the phenomena being studied. Then, in addition to informing comparisons between sample and various populations, such studies permit testing for interactions between person characteristics and the phenomena investigated and, as studies accumulate, between sample characteristics and the effects obtained.

As in many other areas of experimentation, both classroom and nonclassroom teacher expectancy research falls far short here. But the concern attaches doubly to nonclassroom studies because they typically combine reliance on volunteerism with use of nonteachers and relatively mature students as subjects. Rosenthal and Rosnow (1975) have provided an extensive summary of research on volunteerism in behavioral research, with suggestions on ways to meet some of the problems it poses. Research on teacher expectancy needs to mount a comparable effort if it is to detect the interactions that may severely limit generalizations.

Ecological Representativeness.   Generalization requires representative sampling of the situations studied, just as it requires representative sampling of the persons studied. Experimental treatments are sampled from an accessible universe of possible experimental treatments and, in turn, from a target universe of natural treatments, whether the experimenter recognizes this explicitly or not. Because such sampling is also difficult to achieve, again the recourse is to obtain and provide detailed descriptions of the universes and samples of treatments at hand, the measurement of relevant moderating variables, and the testing of interactions (see Snow, 1974).

Experiments are often expressly designed to control some of the complexities inherent in natural situations; that is a source of strength. But to do so without regard to the simulation of situational variables that are functional in the phenomenon studied is to risk substantial experimental invalidity. Teacher expectancy experiments especially, have paid little attention to ecological representativeness. The teacher subjects are often given little or no information about their student subjects, other than the expectancy manipulations being studied, and the two come together for a few brief moments, up to perhaps an hour; these conditions are unlikely to simulate those in which expectancy phenomena occur in natural classrooms. The conditions, furthermore, provide only for a tutoring or small-group teaching interaction, hardly a typical classroom situation. The tasks or lessons used to provide the medium for teaching (e.g., marble-dropping, word-sign association) often do not even vaguely resemble school tasks or lessons. Questionnaire studies are similarly limited to unrepresentative tasks and unrepresentative conditions for teacher response. The questionnaires call only for conscious verbal responses, when expectancies may be communicated behaviorally in nonconscious and subtle ways in classrooms. It can also be argued that this kind of experiment calls for the obvious; in the absence of the other information usually available to teachers, the questionnaire constrains them to be merely logical rather than naturally psychological—to give the experimenter, that is, the obvious prediction that the higher achieving students will receive the higher grades.

In short, while individual experiments can simulate some aspects of the natural environments in which teacher expectancies are expected to function, they must ignore many other potentially important aspects. Since series of experiments have not been systematically designed to detect the situational variables that may moderate effects, there is not yet a clear understanding of how best to do laboratory and questionnaire experiments in this field.

The Referent Generality of Measures and Constructs. Another aspect of generalization concerns both the construct validity and the range or pervasiveness of the experimental outcomes measured in a given study. When experiments show effects on narrow, short-term specialized, dependent variables, which have little or no relation to valued instructional outcome variables in education, their results are less generalizable to education. The more outcome variables an experimental manipulation is shown to affect and the more this effect is shown to influence fairly general, enduring, and pervasive characteristics of teachers and students, the more generalizable are the results.

A laboratory experiment that shows causal influence of expectancies on performance in a specialized game-like task is of little interest to education in its own right. But if performance on this task is known to correlate strongly with mathematics achievement, or more generally with the development of fluid-analytic reasoning ability, or better, if the same experimental manipulation can be shown to influence these more general outcome variables directly, then the referent generality of the experimental effect may be substantial.

The issue is a kind of double-edged sword, because the closer or more directly connected an outcome variable is to the source of the experimental manipulation, the more likely it is to show the experimental effect. but the less likely it is to reflect more generally important outcome variables, and vice versa. The spread of effect is probabilistic: It is likely to be stronger the closer an outcome variable is to the experimental intervention and weaker the further away it is from the intervention. In teacher expectancy experiments, an expectancy manipulation (of

TE$_1$) will likely show its most pronounced effect on observed teacher behavior (TB$_2$); its next largest effect on student behavior (SB$_3$); a somewhat weaker effect on immediate achievement (SA$_4$); and a still weaker effect on more general outcomes (SA$_8$ or SA$_9$), if any. This is exactly the sort of result one would expect if the causal influence of teacher expectancies operates as a probabilistic chain of events across a string of correlated variables. And this is essentially what the evidence on teacher expectancy shows. Of course, no one study can include outcome variables representing the whole range of referent generality. But a review of the early experiments on teacher expectancy by Baker and Crist (in Elashoff & Snow, 1971) provided an accumulation across studies to suggest that 11 of 14 experiments (79%) had shown effects on teacher behavior, two of six and three of nine (33%) had shown effects on student behavior or achievement, respectively, and zero of nine (0%) had shown effects on student intelligence (see also Snow, 1974). Mitman (1976) updated this table to confirm that the same trend still holds.

In short, to demonstrate important generalizable effects, classroom experiments and laboratory experiments alike need to attend to the referent generality of these effects. Classroom experiments can best do this by including measures that reflect effects all across the TE$_1$ to SA$_9$ range. Laboratory and questionnaire experiments are relatively limited in this respect, but they can at least be designed to show correlations between their experimental dependent measures and variables representing parts of the TE$_1$ to SA$_9$ range.

Correlational Studies

Correlational studies overcome some of the shortcomings of experiments. They are, in effect, attempts at unraveling nature's experiments. They describe the state of nature, rather than attempting to manipulate it, and thus can include measures of negative expectancies. When collection of measures is more or less routine for the classrooms involved, or can be made relatively unobtrusive, correlational studies can also be substantially more ecologically representative than experiments. The measurement of naturally existing expectancies eliminates the problems and uncertainties of experimental manipulations and allows the description of classroom processes over extended periods of time.

Studies in this group are difficult to characterize because a variety of correlational approaches have been taken. Perhaps the most common design is that used by Brophy and Good (1970a). In this study, teachers' rankings of students in order of achievement level were used to identify high- and low-expectation students within each class. Observers coded interactions between the teachers and their respective target students according to specific behavior categories. Each behavior category was then examined to determine whether high- or low-expectation students had significantly more of certain teacher acts directed toward them. This approach has been adopted in a great number of studies with various modifications. Some studies have focused on different grade levels and different racial and socioeconomic populations. Some studies have also observed target students from the middle-expectation band, or controlled for additional student and teacher characteristics. A few have focused on specific instructional settings, such as teacher behavior in reading groups of different levels (e.g., Alpert, 1974; Weinstein, 1976). Together, these studies present much evidence about teachers' differential instruction toward students for whom they hold different expectations. This differential instruction presumably represents an important way that teachers' expectations have an impact on student learning and performance.

Another approach has been to relate measures of teachers' natural expectations directly to student outcomes, making some adjustment for initial student performance. Studies by Doyle, Hancock, and Kifer (1972), Lockheed (1976), and Sutherland and Goldschmid (1974) provide examples. Here, the performance of all students in teachers' classes is usually examined, rather than that of extreme groups only. Sometimes additional analyses are performed for small subsets of students, who have been identified as being the object of notably inaccurate positive or negative expectations held by the teacher.

The Problem of Causal Inference.   The most severe and often noted weakness of correlational studies rests in the uncertainty of causal inference. Direction of causation in correlation is not obvious, and it is always possible that unobserved variables underlie the correlation among variables observed. In short, all alternative plausible hypotheses can rarely be ruled out. An example can serve to show this weakness clearly, while also illustrating some of the strengths of such studies.

Seaver (1973) used archival data to show the possible effects of natural teacher expectancies correlationally. From the records of two elementary schools, he identified 79 pairs of siblings and determined for each pair whether the siblings had been assigned to the same or a different teacher. Then the older of each sibling pair was judged to have been a good or bad student in first grade on the basis of intelligence and achievement test scores and grades. Within this fourfold classification, the younger siblings could be compared on *their* first grade achievement test scores. Results (for four of six achievement measures) showed that the younger siblings of those judged to be good students displayed higher achievement if assigned to the same teacher; younger siblings of those judged to be poor students showed higher achievement if assigned to a different teacher than their older siblings had. As shown in Fig. 5.3, the interaction was clear and compelling.

However, the interpretation is not clear. Correlational studies of this sort can be used to test causal hypotheses, since they provide opportunities for such hypotheses to be disconfirmed. In the case of Seaver's study, a causal hypothesis relating to teacher expectancies survived an opportunity to be disconfirmed. But competing hypotheses cannot be ruled out unless variables reflecting them are measured and included in the study, and no study is complete in this respect. One

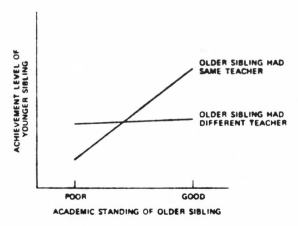

FIG. 5.3.   (From Baker & Crist, in Elashoff & Snow (Eds.), *Pygmalion Reconsidered*, 1971, Charles A. Jones)

alternative hypothesis, suggested by Reichardt (1975), is that of selection among teachers, such that the same teachers of the siblings of older good students were more effective instructors than the different teachers of these siblings. Likewise, the same teachers of the siblings of older bad students may have been less effective instructors than the different teachers of these siblings. In short, differences in the instructional effectiveness of teachers, rather than their expectations, conceivably could explain the outcome results. Another plausible alternative hypothesis is that expectancies were communicated from older to younger siblings, or from parents; teachers were the passive objects of student expectancies, not the active agents of their own expectancies. There is also, of course, the reciprocal hypothesis that would implicate both teacher and student expectancies. To rule out such alternatives, additional measures must be included. Even then, completeness of the possible causal networks cannot be assured.

   A study by Heines and Hawthorne (1978) sought to extend the Seaver finding by including classroom observation. They identified 30 students assigned to the same seventh grade English teacher as an older sibling had been and 73 students whose older sibling had a different teacher. They then divided these students into high-, middle-, and low-expectancy groups on the basis of the older sibling's grade point average. The results showed no achievement differences for high- and middle-expectancy students with the same versus different teachers, but did show achievement deficits for low-expectancy students with the same teachers, relative to those with different teachers. Teacher grades showed no effect. The observational data provided little evidence of differential treatment of high-, middle-, and low-expectancy students assigned to their siblings' teacher. It was noted that teacher praise following correct student answers was higher for high-expectancy students with their siblings' teachers than with different teachers, and lower for low-expectancy students with their siblings' teachers than with different teachers. However, this effect occurred in Spring but not Fall, and was accompanied by general increases in teacher praise following a teacher training workshop that had intervened.

These studies illustrate not only the inability to rule out alternative causal hypotheses in correlation work, but also the difficulty for both experimental and correlational studies in controlling or measuring the many variables that conceivably influence the expectancy network. Going back to Fig. 5.1, it can be seen that the Seaver study tapped limited aspects of three variables: student characteristics (the academic goodness or badness of an older sibling); teacher characteristics (whether the teacher was the same or different from the teacher of the older sibling); and student outcome achievement (as measured by standardized tests and grades). Heines and Hawthorne added classroom observation of selected teacher–student interactions at two points in time, but apparently not those substantially associated with the achievement deficit of low-expectancy students.

All classroom studies, and especially correlational studies, must necessarily contend with the problem that other variables exist that might equally or better account for variance in the dependent measures. There is also the related problem of ascertaining whether particular variables contribute uniquely to explanation or only work in interaction with other variables (Dunkin, 1978). In short, the difficulty of disentangling the roles that myriad variables may or may not play in accounting for outcome variance is another serious weakness of correlational studies that intertwines with the causality issue.

Further illustration of this second weakness is seen particularly in the Heines and Hawthorne study, but also in much other correlational work that follows the Brophy and Good (1970a) design, focusing on teachers' differential behavior toward students in different expectation groups. Such studies typically include measures of a wide range of specific instructional and managerial teacher behavior. In the analyses, these behavior variables are examined for the direction and size of relative difference between two or more expectation groups. There also exists a body of literature that examines whether or not these same (or similar) variables relate to student growth on cognitive outcomes. These are studies of teaching effectiveness (for reviews, see Berliner, 1980; Gage, 1978; Good, 1979), aimed at correlating the average levels displayed by different teachers on each behavior variable with the achievement of students in each teacher's class. In other words, the same teacher behavior measures are being used to study two kinds of effects—those associated with differences among student groups within a class and those associated with average levels of teacher performance.

To date, there has been virtually no integration of the teacher expectation and teacher effectiveness literature, despite substantial overlap in approach and instrumentation. Yet, one may expect distortions when teacher expectation studies attend only to within-class differences without taking the average level of occurrence into account. As suggested by Mitman (1981), it is quite possible that there are teachers whose behavior is differentiated so that low students receive fewer instructional opportunities than high students. Yet these same teachers may be highly effective on average, so that even lows receive a good number of opportunities. In contrast, there may be other teachers who treat highs and lows equally, yet who are ineffective on average; neither high students nor low students receive adequate instructional opportunities. Thus, even within the one variable category of teacher behavior, correlational studies may have difficulty disentangling the multiple aspects of teacher behavior, in which the differential behavior is embedded and in which it must be interpreted. The teacher's ability to structure course content, to communicate clearly, to manage the classroom, etc., can all moderate teacher expectancy behavior. Exclusive focus on teachers' relative distribution of attention among students leaves all of this out.

Cross-lagged Correlations and Path Analysis.   Special correlational studies can be designed to use the relative size of correlations among two (or more) variables measured at two (or more) points in time as a basis for causal inference. The cross-correlations of variables lagged across time are compared, hence the name cross-lagged. Under specified conditions, it is expected that a cause–effect correlation across time should be higher than an effect–cause correlation across time. It is also possible to investigate hypothesized causal paths through a network of variables, also usually measured across time, using systems of structured regression equations in a procedure generally called path analysis.

Since the West and Anderson (1976) summary on causal directions, there have been several attempts to use these special correlational analyses to resolve the causality problem. Williams (1976) reported a limited path analysis of data from over 10,000 Canadian high school students, concluding that teacher expectations influence teacher-assigned grades but not tested student achievement. Humphreys and Stubbs (1977) then conducted a study of cross-lagged correlations using the Williams data, arguing that the results supported a "grades cause teacher expectations" rather than a "teacher expectations cause grades" conclusion. Crano and Mellon (1978) also carried out an analysis of cross-lagged correlations, based on data from over 5000 U.S. elementary school students, to report that, of 84 possible comparisons among variables, 62 were in a direction consistent with the hypothesis that teacher expectancies influence student achievement. Unfortunately, as now demonstrated by Rogosa (1980), differences among cross-lagged correlations of the sort studied in this work really do not provide as sound a basis for causal inference as previously thought. Rogosa recommended that the cross-lagged correlation approach ". . . be set aside as a dead end" (p. 257).

It is conceivable that a path analytic approach based on structural regression models can still be formulated to support causal inferences from correlational data of the sort obtained in teacher expectancy research. Structural regression models have been developed successfully in various fields of sociology and econometrics following the procedures of Blalock (1961), Duncan, Featherman, and Duncan (1972), Goldberger and Duncan (1973), and several others. But such developments require strong theory: One must be ready to specify all of the variables entering into the causal paths of interest, and assume that no important variables have been omitted. For teacher expectancy research, this means that variables reflecting teacher and student expectancies will need to be embedded in the much larger network of variables influencing classroom interactions and outcomes suggested in Fig. 5.1. Research on classroom teaching generally has begun to take steps in this direction, in the work of Cooley and Lohnes (1976), Cooley and Leinhardt (1976), McDonald and Elias (1976) and Stayrook (1982). It will be some time to come, however, before this research is sufficiently developed to justify strong inferences about causal pathways and the role of expectancies in them.

Meta-Analysis.   Another form of correlational analysis has now been developed, aimed at reaching causal conclusions at the level of research summary rather than at the level of primary data within any one study. The approach first establishes a common metric for the outcome variable(s) of concern in a range of individual studies on a particular topic or question, and then obtains a statistical integration of research results across studies to reach an estimate of magnitude of effects, including the characteristics of studies that correlate with the effects obtained. The unit of analysis is usually the individual study or research report; where studies investigate multiple effects, it is the individual effect or effect size. For a presentation of initial ideas, methods, and results, see Glass (1976) and Glass, McGaw, and Smith (1981). The approach has now been applied to a variety of research questions in educational and psychological research, including the question of teacher expectancy effects.

Two meta-analyses of expectancy effects by Rosenthal and Rubin (1978) and Smith (1980) are now available. Smith provided a useful integration of 47 studies of teacher expectancy. Unfortunately, Rosenthal and Rubin lumped their teacher studies in with 345 studies on a variety of kinds of interpersonal expectancies, with a variety of dependent variables, indiscriminately.

The Smith (1980) analysis included both experimental and correlational studies of teacher expectancy and the general results were consistent with the probabilistic chain interpretation based on the earlier reviews by Baker and Crist (in Elashoff & Snow, 1971) and Mitman (1976) previously discussed. Strong effects were found for teacher expectancies in the form of labeling information on teacher ratings of student ability, achievement, and behavior; that is, teachers rated according to the information provided them. No effect was found on teacher ratings of student motivation, interest, or appeal, however. Teacher behavior toward students was found to be influenced to a modest degree by expectancies; teachers tended to provide more learning opportunities to high-expectancy students and to ignore low-expectancy students more often. Expectancy was unrelated to the amount of teacher feedback, encouragement, or positive reinforcement, however. Effects on student achievement of teacher expectancies were found to be significant, whereas effects on student intellectual ability were found to be negligible. Apparently, reading achievement showed more expectancy influence than did math achievement. Also, student participation and social competence were shown to be influenced, but not other affective outcome variables.

The Smith summary thus yields support for the hypothesized causal influence of teacher expectancies on teacher and student variables close to the expectancy source in time, and a gradient of declining effect on student variables as these move away from the expectancy source in time or in referent generality. It confirms the presence of effects on student achievement and the absence of effects on student intelligence in general. It presumably balances, the weaknesses of many kinds of studies, but it tests only the teacher-to-student unidirectional hypothesis. The rest of the causal network, and interactions embedded therein, remains to be understood.

THE IMPROVEMENT OF MEASUREMENT

Measurements in teacher expectancy research have usually represented one or more of three classes of variables: the expectations of teachers (TE); the behavior of teachers (TB); and the cognitive outcome performance of students (SA_8 or SA_9). As suggested in Fig. 5.1, however, there are several other classes of variables to be considered: student aptitudes (SA_0), student expectations (SE), student behavior (SB), and other possible intermediate or cumulative student outcomes. Measurement issues related to each of these kinds of variables are considered below, in categories for teachers, students, the classroom interactions between them, and instructional outcomes.

Characteristics and Expectations of Teachers

Teacher Characteristics.   It is plausible to hypothesize that teachers differ in characteristics likely to interact with expectancies. Because of personalities and habitual teaching styles, teachers may differ in the degree to which they seek out information about students on which to base predictions (TE_0) and they may be differentially susceptible to expectancy manipulation as well (the TE_0–TE_1 transformation). It also is possible that teacher characteristics may mediate the way in which teacher expectancies are communicated (e.g., the TE_1 to TB_2 link). Brophy and Good (1974) suggested some of the kinds of teacher personality characteristics that may be important, including the ability to deal constructively with failure, willingness to take personal responsibility for student progress, and beliefs about achievement and intelligence tests. Cooper (1979) suggested that teachers' differing perceptions of personal control may produce individual differences among teachers in their patterns of expectancy-linked behavior.

While only a few expectancy studies have included independent assessments of these kinds of teacher personality characteristics (e.g., Cooper & Baron, 1977; Rubovits & Maehr, 1973), this approach can prove fruitful given good theoretical justification for the selected characteristics. Brophy and Good (1974) also used classroom observations to categorize teachers who differ in style with respect to expectancy formation and use. For the near future, this approach may be more practical and theoretically appropriate than assessment of teacher personality characteristics; it is at least an important start toward measurement of this important class of moderators for both experimental and correlational studies. A useful step for classroom experiments, in particular, would be to conduct such observations of teachers in advance of expectancy interventions, either in classes involved in the study or in previous or parallel classes taught by the same teachers.

Teacher Expectations.   The measurement of teacher expectations is also an issue for both experimental and correlational studies. In experimental studies, independent measures of teacher expectations have not often been included; teachers are simply assumed to adopt the expectation-inducing information provided by the experimenter. However, because the correct interpretation of such experiments pivots on the question of whether or not teachers actually do adopt the expectations intended by the experimenter, a separate, follow-up measure of teacher expectations can serve the important function of certifying that the experimental manipulation actually worked. Teachers' grouping or ordering of students according to expected performance level should correspond closely to that of the experimenter.

The few experimental studies that have included such follow-up checks on teachers' actual expectations highlight the problem of achieving a successful experimental manipulation. Henrikson (1970), for example, had teachers rank their kindergarten students on reading readiness following the experimental manipulation and found that experimental-group students were not ranked higher than control-group students on average. Furthermore, there was a high correlation ($r = .93$) between teachers' rankings and students' actual performance on a reading readiness test that was given following the rankings, suggesting that teachers had developed fairly accurate perceptions (TE_0) of students' academic performance that outweighed the experimenter's manipulation in the transition to TE_1.

A post hoc but useful check on teachers' perceptions of students is to ask teachers to reproduce the list of experimental students at the conclusion of the study. When Mendels and Flanders (1973) asked teachers to recall the names of their "spurters," teachers identified 46% of the students from the experimental group and 33% of students from the control group. The Rosenthal and Jacobson (1968) report that teachers were unable to recall or recognize the names of experimental-group students in the school year following the experiment was not viewed by the authors as evidence challenging experimental treatment, but it was so viewed by reviewers; its availability was important in any event.

In short, checks on teachers' perceptions can verify the experimental manipulation. Teachers' groupings or rankings of students according to their own expectations can be even more revealing than indexing teachers' memory of the manipulation alone, since it provides more detailed information for use in the statistical analyses.

In correlational studies, teachers' natural expectations typically are measured by asking them to rank order their students on a presented list according to expected overall academic performance. The criterion for ranking usually is stated broadly to encourage teachers to base their rankings on global perceptions. These rankings are then used to identify groups of students with different levels of expectation. Expectation groups thus formed can be balanced for student gender, since this is an easily controllable variable that may be an important moderator of differential teacher perceptions. Potentially, other student moderator variables could be brought into the study in a similar way. There is no reason, furthermore, why classroom experiments could not similarly represent other TE_0 and SA_0 variables of interest.

The ranking method of measuring teachers' academic expectations for students appears to provide a useful measure on several counts. First, as a measure of social perception, the ranking procedure avoids many of the response bias problems inherent in alternative procedures, such as rating scales (see Hastorf, Schneider, & Polefka, 1970). Second, although it is difficult to judge the validity of the technique as a measure of academic expectations per se, there is a readily available criterion for judging the accuracy of teachers' rankings: students' actual scores on measures of academic performance. While there is no reason to think that all teachers' academic expectations for students will be accurate, the focus of most teaching is on increasing students' academic competencies, and teachers usually accumulate considerable amounts of formal and informal information about students' relative levels of performance. The evidence that there are strong correlations between teachers' rankings of students and students' actual scores (e.g., Dusek & O'Connell, 1973; Mitman, 1981; Willis, 1972) suggests that the ranking procedure taps an appropriate category of teacher perceptions. Finally, two or more rankings by the same teacher of the same students over the course of the school year are likely to be highly correlated (e.g., Willis, 1972). This suggests that the ranking procedure is reliable, tapping perceptions that are fairly stable across time.

Despite its strengths, there are some potential limitations to the ranking method of measuring teacher expectations and selecting expectation groups. The procedure forces students onto an ordinal scale, whereas teachers may perceive students as being grouped in a few categories. One can of course allow teachers to assign tied ranks or to identify groups of similar students on a reduced ordinal scale. The ranking may also be limited to measuring expectations about academic performance. As interest in expectation phenomena expands to other student dimensions (e.g., social competence, motivation) and additional audiences (e.g., administrators, parents, and students themselves), other procedures may need to be developed.

Another limitation may be teacher reaction to the procedure itself. As teachers become increasingly astute about the implications of labeling and their own perceptual biases, it can be anticipated that some may be reluctant to use such a procedure. Teachers may claim that ranking is impossible because students perform differently in different subject areas or change their relative positions frequently across time. Or it may be argued that students' strengths in nonacademic areas need to be reflected. Some teachers may feel that the act of ranking itself has detrimental effects on their efforts to avoid comparisons among students. Such reactions are of research interest in their own right. Nonetheless, investigators need to prepare to confront these reactions, to justify the procedure, or to propose more acceptable alternatives. Otherwise, nonrandom sample attrition, or even sabotage, can result.

Characteristics and Expectations of Students

Student Aptitudes.   Student aptitudes in the form of measures of intellectual ability or prior academic achievement usually are significant predictors of achievement outcome in instructional settings, regardless of what other variables are receiving research attention. They can be expected to correlate with teacher expectations and are also known to interact with instructional treatment variables representing variations in teaching methods (Cronbach & Snow, 1977), and may well interact, additionally, with variations in teacher expectancies. Research studies that use only student pretest measures to obtain some estimate of gain as a dependent variable miss an important opportunity to investigate the potentially complex, substantive relation of student aptitude to teacher and student expectancy phenomena. This is a deficiency in much past research.

But there may be student aptitudes other than conventional cognitive ability or prior achievement that are relevant to expectancy research in rather different ways. The Brophy-Good (1974) research mentioned previously not only identified categories of teachers who were differentially influenced by expectancies, but also suggested some categories of students who showed differential susceptibilities in this regard; expectancy effects seemed particularly problematic when certain types of teachers and students were matched. Brophy and Evertson (1981) have now substantially expanded the array of student characteristics that should be examined as potential aptitudes in different kinds of teaching.

Interactions between the personal characteristics of teachers and students, which moderate the effects of positive, and especially of negative, expectancies, deserve much more extended study in the future. Some kinds of relevant student

aptitudes may be measurable by conventional methods at pretest, while others may require assessment by observational procedures, such as those used by Brophy and Good. It is clear, however, that little will be gained by research that continues to ignore differential susceptibility hypotheses.

Other Student Characteristics.   Attributes such as gender, race, ethnicity, language, socioeconomic status, and the like, are often linked into hypotheses about teacher expectancies and may also be linked to hypotheses about student expectations. They may or may not be correlated with other student aptitudes. Such variables can and should be routinely indexed for study as moderators, even in research aimed at other aspects of expectancy phenomena.

Student Expectations.   Research on student expectations is a relatively recent interest, and thus, the methodological approaches in this area are less developed than are those aimed at teacher expectations. For the consideration of measurement issues, two kinds of student expectations should be distinguished: student expectations for self, especially as related to academic performance; and student expectations for teachers.

The strongest evidence on student expectations for self has appeared in studies devoted to empirical validation and elaboration of attribution theory, which posits that future expectations for success and failure performance are based on one's perceived determinants of success and failure (see Weiner, 1980; Chapter 7 of this book). Although much of the initial work was conducted with adults in laboratory settings, the study of students in achievement-related settings is becoming more common. Students typically are asked to indicate which of two or more causes or causal dimensions accounts for their own (or a peer's) success or failure on an actual or hypothetical academic task. Student responses may be solicited through open-ended questions (e.g., Nicholls, 1978), forced-choice questions (e.g., Johnson, 1981; Medway & Lowe, 1980), or through ratings of the importance of various causes (e.g., Arkin & Maruyanna, 1979; Bar-Tal, Raviv, Raviv, & Bar-Tal, 1982). Each of these measurement methods has its strengths and weaknesses. Open-ended questions have the advantage of avoiding imposition of preconceived categories on students, but they pose the problem of developing a priori or post hoc schema that both accommodate student responses and make sense theoretically. Forced-choice questions or ratings circumvent this problem but pose others. Some students may be resistant to completing forced-choice items if they feel that all or none of the responses are appropriate. Analysis of student ratings of the importance of any one cause may fail to take into account individual differences in patterns of responses across all the causes (Medway & Lowe, 1980). Clearly, these tradeoffs deserve further exploration in future research, especially in light of Nicholls' (1978) suggestion that different methodologies can produce quite divergent results.

Some studies of student self-expectations, including attribution studies, obtain direct student estimates of their own performance level. Nicholls (1976) for example, devised a measure in which students are shown a list of 30 circles (or faces) with the top circle representing the top student in the class and the bottom circle representing the bottom student in the class, and are then asked to identify which circle represents themselves. Stipek (1981) used a chart with columns of one to five stars, with five stars for the "smartest" person in the class and one star for the "dumbest." Students then are asked to select the number of stars they should have. Entwisle and Hayduk (1978) asked individual students to engage in the "game" of guessing their report card grades in reading, arithmetic, and conduct. Students select a card with their expected number (1 to 4) or letter (A to D) grade and place it on a chart designed to represent a report card. Establishing the validity of these kinds of self-ranking and self-rating instruments is a problem because studies often have found little correspondence between students' responses and more objective measures of their performance (e.g., Entwisle & Hayduck, 1978; Nicholls, 1978; Stipek, 1981). The measurement problem interacts with age; Blumenfeld, Pintrich, Meece and Wessels (1982) have reviewed evidence indicating that younger children are biased towards perceiving themselves as able.

What little research exists on students' expectations for their teachers has typically been conducted in the laboratory where student expectations are manipulated by the experimenter. Perry, Niemi, and Jones (1974) and Perry, Abrami, Leventhal and Check (1979), for example, gave students a written introduction containing either a positive or negative instructor evaluation adapted from an actual student guide to course selection. Feldman and Prohaska (1979) manipulated student expectations using a confederate, posing as another student who had just been instructed by the teacher. The confederate either described the teacher as competent or incompetent and asked the student to hand in a rating form completed in a manner consistent with the confederate's story.

Such manipulations probably work; students entering a laboratory-simulated classroom setting have little or no prior knowledge of the teacher and their exposure to the teacher during the experiment is brief (e.g., one lecture or lesson). Thus, the manipulation is likely to carry weight in the students' frame of reference about the teacher. However, because teachers are all assumed to possess some minimal competence, the range of good-to-bad teaching that a student expects to encounter may be truncated relative to the range a teacher expects between high and low students.

In sum, the new research on student expectations reflects a variety of measurement approaches. In the case of student expectations for self, there are obvious tradeoffs between approaches. All are worthy of continued exploration and refinement. If there is one major limitation, it pertains to age; young children do not appear capable of articulating or responding to a multifaceted conception of self-ability and performance. Because self-concepts and self-expectations are seen as developmental phenomena, changing with age, the problem becomes a theoretical, not just a measurement, issue. In the case of student expectations for teachers, research to date suggests that some process hypotheses can be gotten from the laboratory framework, but that measurement problems will become quite complex as this research moves into naturalistic settings.

Teacher and Student Behavior Interaction

The need to understand if and how teacher behavior mediates teacher expectation effects spurred the development of the Dyadic Interaction Observation System by Brophy and Good (1970b) that was substantially more sophisticated than most of its predecessors as a general approach for studies of effective teaching behavior (see Medley & Mitzel, 1963). Because most studies examining teacher expectation behavior have used this or a similar instrument, it serves as a good example of the problems entailed in capturing teacher expectation behavior.

Whereas earlier instruments focused observations on teacher behavior toward the class as a whole, ignoring the identities of different students, the Brophy-Good (1970b) instrument codes interactions between the teacher and particular students. The instrument also allows coding of teacher–student exchanges in a form that captures some of their sequential characteristics. For example, the quality of teacher feedback to a student's answer is coded in conjunction with the quality of the student's answer, thus permitting the calculation of which kinds of feedback followed which kinds of answers. In turn, these connections make possible the calculation of ratios of different behavior variables (e.g., percentage of correct answers receiving praise). These may be especially meaningful indicators of differential behavior because they control for differences among teachers and among students in absolute frequencies of behavior. Furthermore, the instrument includes important distinctions between classroom contexts. Codings for large-group instruction are kept separate from codings for seatwork. There are separate codings for behavior initiated by the teacher versus behavior initiated by students, and for academic versus behavioral versus personal contacts. The inclusion of these and other contextual factors allows controlled focus on specific dynamics of teacher differential behavior.

Use of this system by its authors and other colleagues has been quite successful in identifying a range of specific teacher acts that seem to distribute differentially among high- and low-expectation students (see Chapter 12 of this book). This and other similar observation instruments also have contributed to improved understanding of the occurrence and effectiveness of various kinds of teaching behavior. While the success of these recent instruments for classroom observation is heartening, cumulative experience suggests that there still are ways in which measures of teacher–student interaction need to be improved, and these improvements are applicable to studies of teacher expectation behavior as well as to general studies of teaching behavior. Brophy (1979, 1981) points out that the coding of a seemingly straightforward variable, such as teacher praise, often results in grouping together praise statements that have different meanings, for example, statements of genuine praise and statements of perfunctory praise.

In teacher expectation research, treating such praise statements as equivalent may be misleading to the extent that teachers give one group of students more of one kind of praise and another group of students more of another kind of praise. Many categories of teacher and student behavior are no doubt susceptible to this problem. In short, current classroom observation systems do not adequately distinguish between different and often subtle kinds of teacher behavior that are likely to have different meanings and effects for students. Solving this problem requires instruments that allow finer levels of distinction, as well as observers familiar enough with particular teachers and their classes to make judgments about the finer levels and intended meanings of observed behavior. Studies that analyze the actual verbal content of teacher–student dialogue represent still another potentially useful approach to the problem of verbal meaning (e.g., Cherry, 1978).

Another recognized problem with most available classroom observation instruments, also noted by Brophy (1979), is the failure to take into account a sufficient number of potentially important contextual factors. While instruments such as the Dyadic Interaction Observation System generate separate coding for some different contexts, the inclusion of additional context distinctions, such as subject matter or activity structure (Bossert, 1979), may prove valuable as well. The role of context factors in teacher expectation research seems worthy of further study because there is already some suggestion that teachers may display different patterns of behavior depending on the instructional task at hand (e.g., Leinhardt, Seewald, & Engel, 1979; Weinstein, 1976).

There are still other ways in which observational tools for examining the expectation network may be improved. The kind of instruments mentioned so far focus predominantly on the teacher, with students' behavior being coded only when it involves the teacher. Instruments that devote more attention to student behavior in all its aspects would also be informative. Second, there are many ways other than verbal behavior by which a teacher might communicate expectancies. While coding systems for nonverbal behavior have been developed in laboratory settings (e.g., Chaiken & Derlega, 1978), application to actual classroom settings is still forthcoming. Also, teachers may communicate their expectations through other dimensions, such as their grouping arrangements, the level of their task assignments, their room displays, and the amounts of time they devote to any one activity. These behavioral dimensions warrant inclusion in observation systems.

Suggestions for increasing the behavioral and contextual distinctions in classroom observation systems aim at increasing the validity of the instruments, that is, ensuring that the instruments capture behavior at the level of definition or analysis where the most meaningful variation occurs. As the behavior categories of such instruments become more refined and numerous, however, it becomes increasingly difficult to obtain reliable observation in each. The problem of adequate observation time is not new to teacher expectation research. Some prior studies of teacher expectation behavior have had to be based on as few as 2 hours of observation per teacher (e.g., Haigh, 1974), an amount not likely to provide useful estimates of instrument reliability.

There are ways to estimate minimally acceptable amounts of observation time, but these are seldom used. The generalizability theory and methods of Cronbach, Gleser, Nanda and Rajaratnam (1972), for example, make it possible to conduct studies to estimate the influence of occasion, observer, and any other facet of concern, on measurement error. A study by Erlich and Borich (1979) provides one of the few examples of this approach applied to an instrument commonly used in expectation research. Using data from the Dyadic Interaction System (Brophy & Evertson, 1976), they found that of 167 coded variables, only 35 reached their criterion of generalizability (a coefficient of at least .70 obtained by observation on 10 or fewer occasions, each 3 hours in length). Within these limits, their data further indicated that the number of required occasions fluctuated according to the particular observation variable, with some variables requiring as few as two occasions. These analyses used teacher and occasion as facets; assuring reliable data for subgroups of students or individual students on this already limited subset of variables would require even more observation occasions. And, as already noted, creating observation variables with greater levels of discrimination also requires more observation.

There are now ways to examine questions about stability of teacher and student behavior over time. These questions have been thorny problems for all research on teaching (Shavelson & Dempsey-Atwood, 1976). Rogosa, Floden, and Willett (1982) have reevaluated previously used methods and devised an array of new and improved approaches to various aspects of these questions. To the study of consistency of individual teacher behavior, they apply such devices as Bernoulli trials and the parameters of Poisson, as well as Gaussian distributions. For questions about the consistency of individual differences among teachers, they propose various indices of tracking over time, obtained from biometric research, as substitutes for the correlational measures usually used in research on teaching. Given that stability of behavior over time is an important issue for teacher expectancy research, in particular, it can be expected that the application of these new forms of measurement will sharpen the study of expectancy phenomena significantly.

In sum, moving from more global, summative categories of observed behavior to more specific, differentiated categories of behavior requires increased effort in instrument development, observer training, and the study of observation time and occasion variation per teacher and per student.

Instructional Outcomes

Instructional outcome is always multivariate, whether measured as such or not. And, although most research on expectancy has concentrated on cognitive instructional outcomes, there is reason to believe that social, motivational, and other affective outcomes may be influenced substantially by expectancy effects. The meta-analysis by Smith (1980) was noted above as one strong indication of this. The choice and evaluation of outcome measures ought to reflect the implications of past research and avoid the problems it has faced, wherever possible.

Cognitive Outcome Measures.   A variety of cognitive outcome measures have been used, representing a range along the referent generality continuum from specific laboratory tasks and unit quizzes, through intermediate achievement tests and teacher grades, to standardized achievement tests and generalized measures of intelligence. The specific, immediate, and informal measures can suffer from all the problems typically discussed in measurement textbooks (see, e.g., Cronbach, 1970; Ebel, 1972): We need not recite those here. The standardized instruments, on the other hand, are often chosen for use in research on the assumption that they are psychometrically adequate, and examined no further. However, to assess the soundness of any outcome measurements, it is usually necessary to consider the nature of the data actually obtained in a particular study and the manner in which it is used, regardless of the stature of the instrument. Elashoff and Snow (1971) illustrated how the instrument used by Rosenthal and Jacobson (1968), for example, fell short on several counts. The points made in that discussion serve as an outline of the kinds of measurement problems that can occur. First, the test was administered to students in grade levels for which it was not adequately normed. Many scores were in abnormally low or high ranges, an indication of poor norming. Second, the scores for quite a few students were unstable across four points in time, suggesting norm problems or reliability problems or both. Third, little evidence was presented to support the validity of the test as a measure of intelligence in the sample of students studied. Correlations between other measures of student performance and the test that would serve as indicators of construct validity were not reported. Fourth, the measure stood alone. Multitrait–multimethod measurement (Campbell & Fiske, 1959) of outcome constructs is as important for interpretation as is such measurement of constructs all along the many causal paths between SA_0 and SA_9. Fifth, the test was used only to produce a derived measure—a simple gain score—the properties of which were also not examined.

Other Outcome Measures.   Few nonlaboratory studies of teacher expectancies have included measures of other student outcomes of interest, such as self-esteem, attitudes, motivation, anxiety, and locus of control. The classroom experiments of Carter (1970), Keshock (1970), and Kester and Letchworth (1972) were first attempts to provide measures of student self-esteem, school motivation, and attitudes toward school, respectively. Mitman (1981) measured student self-esteem and attitudes, along with achievement and reasoning, in a correlational study of teacher expectancies. Given the increasing interest and improvement of measurement in noncognitive areas, the inclusion of such measures now appears feasible. There are distinct theoretical advantages in comparing results on multiple outcome measures within a single study.

Cumulative Effects.   While there may be consensus that teacher expectations can impact some aspects of student behavior, there is virtually no direct evidence indicating when this impact is greatest or how the expectations of the many teachers to whom a student is exposed in school life or beyond relate and interact. Most teacher expectation research conducted in classrooms has used samples of primary school children, where it is assumed that teacher expectations are most potent. Is it thus assumed that an individual's scholastic fate is determined after the first few years of school and that teachers' expectations in later grades do little to influence or alter students' academic development? To examine such questions, future research will need to take a longer view.

One aspect of this view would require a distinction between teacher expectation behavior that maintains the status quo versus teacher behavior that alters it. There is evidence, for example, that teachers do exhibit expectation-related patterns of differential behavior in the secondary school years (e.g., Cornbelth, Davis, & Button, 1974; Jones, 1971; Mendoza, Good, & Brophy, 1972). It is possible that this differential instruction simply reflects teacher adaptation to long established performance differences among students that serves to reinforce but not change historical trends. It is also possible that in these later years of schooling, students' academic self-concepts and learning styles have crystallized to a degree wherein they are virtually immune to teacher influence. The best evidence about the impact of teacher expectations may come from studies that focus on students for whom current (but not past) teachers hold inaccurate expectations to determine whether students' performance levels change accordingly.

Research on such cumulative effects of teacher expectations will also need to determine how the expectations of different teachers of the same students interact. In secondary school, when students move among different teachers for different subjects, each student may be exposed to approximately five to seven teachers per day. It is important to know if and how teachers communicate their expectations to one another; the extent of expectation agreement among teachers; and the degree to which students perform differently in classes where teachers hold atypical expectations for them.

Thus, student centered longitudinal research on the cumulative effect of teacher expectations will need to follow students throughout their school careers. While the logistics of this kind of research are complicated, scaled-down attempts (e.g., with small samples of students over limited time spans) may be extremely informative. Only with such longitudinal views can a sense be gained of the variation in teacher expectations and expectation-related behavior that an individual student encounters over time. To date, longitudinal work has been limited to studies of the relationship of one teacher's expectations to students' performance at points in time after the students had left that teacher (see Dusek & O'Connell, 1973; O'Connell, Dusek & Wheeler, 1974; Pedersen, Faucher & Eaton, 1978).

PROSPECTS FOR FUTURE RESEARCH

No one study, perhaps not even a string of carefully counterbalanced studies, can escape all of the threats, uncertainties, and plausible counterhypotheses that bear on teacher, or student, expectancy hypotheses. Yet research and research summary can and should go on. Classroom experiments will need to continue to seek manipulations and measures that validate and evaluate the network of variables, which carry and also moderate expectancy effects, in real classroom settings. Correlational studies will also need to continue to provide enriched descriptions of this network, attempting to identify in particular the variables that may result in negative expectancy effects. Laboratory experiments and questionnaire studies, too, will continue to be designed to open up to view the possible process mechanisms that may account for teacher and student expectancy effects, and particularly the reciprocal relations between them. Research on all these fronts may be expected to improve as investigators gain understanding of the phenomena and facility with the improved methodological and measurement techniques that are coming forward.

But quantum advances in future research may require combinations of the three major approaches reviewed here that will multiply the value of each kind of data. One can conceive of combinations of laboratory or questionnaire experiments with classroom experiments. And combinations of correlational modes of research with either of these is clearly possible. This chapter is best concluded, not with a recitation of past woes in summary, but with a brief sketch of some of the combinations possible for future research.

Suppose, for example, that a classroom experiment of the traditional Pygmalion design identified teachers and students for whom the positive expectancy intervention did and did not work as predicted. Suppose also that improved classroom observation measures could be used to identify teachers, positive expectancy students, and control students, for whom positive and negative behavioral interaction of certain sorts took place. A multifaceted classification of teachers and students would result, from which could be drawn several important contrasts using the observational and other measures available in classroom research.

Laboratory experiments might then be designed to use these contrasting persons as subjects, either in side-rooms at school or away from school. The laboratory arrangements might differ from those used in the past; they would be geared to provide analyses of certain kinds of interpersonal interactions and the implicit judgmental or design-making processes that operate in these interactions, not merely to manipulate expectancy effects. Such experiments would still demonstrate only some of the possible mechanisms in expectancy phenomena, but they would do so with substantially more population representativeness than the experiments of the past because the subjects would be persons who had already demonstrated certain expectancy-related behavioral phenomena in the classroom. In the laboratory one might imagine collecting questionnaire or introspective reports, or even video-tape-aided recall and interpretation of their own or other persons' laboratory or classroom behavior.

The Seaver or Heines and Hawthorne studies could be replicated in any school that serves a reasonably stable community and that can be induced to keep records of teacher–student assignments. Such replications could be substantially extended by more detailed data collection from the teachers and students, and even the siblings involved. Specially designed experiments with such teachers and students might be able to detect some of the negative aspect of expectancy-related behavior, even while prohibited from attempting to produce it.

The laboratory setting could also provide a context for teacher training aimed at reducing negative expectancy-related behavior in classrooms and promoting various other aspects of improved teaching style. Training experiments, in themselves, may provide a unique view of expectancy phenomena; an important way to gain understanding of behavior has always been to try to change it.

The combination of laboratory and classroom research can also be made to work in the other direction. Laboratory experiments using teachers or students can be followed by classroom observation of those same teachers and students, so that the generalizability and correlates of laboratory behavior can be explicated. The relative strengths of classroom and laboratory research might best be capitalized on in strings of alternating studies that feed one another.

As a final example, consider the correlational categories of expectancy-prone teachers and students identified by Brophy and Good (1974) or the much more extensive description of student characteristics in relation to teaching provided by Brophy and Evertson (1981). Here are identified important student aptitude variables, which should be expected to interact with natural differences in teacher characteristics and expectancies, and also with experimentally induced differences in teacher expectancies. If such student and teacher characteristics can be measured ahead of experimental interventions, they can be entered into analyses in the same ways that combinations of aptitude variables are entered into any other sort of evaluation of alternative teaching or instructional treatments (Cronbach & Snow, 1977; Snow, 1977). Classroom observation variables could also be added in. One could then test, in a powerful way, what kinds of students are susceptible to what kinds of positive and what kinds of negative expectancy-related teacher behavior. One could also relate these effects to the cognitive student aptitudes known to correlate with achievement outcome and known to be used by teachers as a source of expectations for adaptive teaching. From such research should come new conceptions of the complex of student and teacher variables that interact to produce the most important expectancy effects.

REFERENCES

Alpert, J. L. Teacher behavior across ability groups: A consideration of the mediation of Pygmalion effects. *Journal of Educational Psychology*, 1974, *66*, 348–353.

Arkin, R. M., & Maruyanna, G. M. Attribution, affect, and college exam performance. *Journal of Educational Psychology*, 1979, *71*, 85–93.

Bandura, A. The self system in reciprocal determinism. *American Psychologist*, 1978, *33*, 344–358.

Bandura, A. *Social learning theory*. Englewood Cliffs, N.J.: Prentice-Hall, 1977.

Bar-Tal, D., Raviv, A., Raviv, A., & Bar-Tal, Y. Consistency of pupils' attributions regarding success and failure. *Journal of Educational Psychology*, 1982, *74*, 104–110.

Berliner, D. C. Using research on teaching for the improvement of classroom practice. *Theory into Practice*, 1980, *19*, 302–308.

Blalock, H. M., Jr. *Causal inferences in nonexperimental research* (1st ed.). Chapel Hill, N.C.: The University of North Carolina, 1961.

Blumenfeld, P. C., Pintrich, P. R., Meece, J., & Wessels, K. The formation and role of self-perceptions of ability in elementary classrooms. *Elementary School Journal*, 1982, *82*, 401–420.

Bossert, S. T. *Tasks and social relationships in classrooms: A study of instructional organization and its consequences*. New York: Cambridge University, 1979.

Bracht, G. H., & Glass, G. V. The external validity of experiments. *American Educational Research Journal*, 1968, *5*, 437–74.

Brookover, W. B., Schweitzer, J. H., Schneider, J. M., Beady, C. H., Flood, P. K., & Wisenbaker, J. M. Elementary school social climate and school achievement. *American Educational Research Journal*, 1978, *15*, 301–318.

Brophy, J. E. Teacher behavior and its effects. *Journal of Educational Psychology*, 1979, *71*, 733–750.

Brophy, J. E. Teacher praise: A functional analysis. *Review of Educational Research*, 1981, *51*, 5–32.

Brophy, J. E., & Evertson, C. The Texas Teacher Effectiveness Study: Classroom coding manual (Research Report No. 76-2). Austin: Research and Development Center for Teacher Education, University of Texas, 1976.

Brophy, J. E., & Evertson, C. M. *Student characteristics and teaching*. New York: Longman, 1981.

Brophy, J. E., & Good, T. L. Teachers' communication of differential expectations for children's classroom performance: Some behavioral data. *Journal of Educational Psychology*, 1970(a), *61*, 365–374.

Brophy, J., & Good, T. Teacher–Child Dyadic Interaction System. In *Mirrors for behavior: An anthology of observation instruments continued, 1970 supplement, Volume A*. Philadelphia: Research for Better Schools, Inc., 1970(b).

Brophy, J. E., & Good, T. L. *Teacher–student relationships: Causes and consequences*. New York: Holt, Rinehart & Winston, 1974.

Campbell, D. T., & Fiske, D. W. Convergent and discriminant validation by the multitrait-multi-method matrix. *Psychological Bulletin*, 1959, *56*, 81–105.

Campbell, D. T., & Stanley, J. C. Experimental and quasi-experimental designs for research on teaching. In N. L. Gage (Ed.), *Handbook of research on teaching*. Chicago: Rand McNally, 1963.

Carter, D. L. The effect of teacher expectations on the self-esteem and academic performance of seventh grade students (Doctoral dissertation, University of Tennessee, 1970). *Dissertation Abstracts International,* 1971, *31*(9A), 4539. (University Microfilms No. 71-7612)

Carter, R. M. Locus of control and teacher expectancy as related to achievement of young school children (Doctoral dissertation, Indiana University, 1969). *Dissertation Abstracts International,* 1970, *30*(11A). (University Microfilms No. 70-7946).

Chaiken, A.L., & Derlega, V. J. Nonverbal mediators of expectancy effects in black and white children. *Journal of Applied Social Psychology,* 1978, *8,* 117–125.

Charlesworth, W. R. Human intelligence as adaptation: An ethological approach. In L. B. Resnick (Ed.), *The nature of intelligence.* Hillsdale, N.J.: Lawrence Erlbaum Associates, 1976.

Cherry, L. A sociolinguistic approach to the study of teacher expectations. *Discourse Processes,* 1978, *1,* 373–394.

Cook, T. D., & Campbell, D. T. *Quasi-experimentation: Design and analysis issues for field settings.* Chicago: Rand McNally, 1979.

Cooley, W., & Leinhardt, G. The application of a model for investigating classroom processes. University of Pittsburgh, Learning Research and Development Center, 1976.

Cooley, W. W., & Lohnes, P. R. *Evaluation research in education.* New York: Irvington Press, 1976.

Cooper, H. Pygmalion grows up: A model for teacher expectancy communication and performance influences. *Review of Educational Research,* 1979, *49,* 389–410.

Cooper, H. M., & Baron, R. M. Academic expectations and attributed responsibility as predictors of professional teachers' reinforcement behavior. *Journal of Educational Psychology,* 1977, *69,* 409–418.

Cornbleth, C., Davis, O. L., & Button, C. Expectations for pupil achievement and teacher-pupil interaction. *Social Education,* 1974, *38,* 54–58.

Crano, W. D., & Mellon, P. M. Causal influence of teachers' expectations on children's academic performance: A cross-lagged panel analysis. *Journal of Educational Psychology,* 1978, *69,* 761–772.

Cronbach, L. J. *Essentials of psychological testing (3rd ed.).* New York: Harper & Row, 1970.

Cronbach, L. J. Beyond the two disciplines of scientific psychology. *American Psychologist,* 1975, *30,* 116–127.

Cronbach, L. J. Prudent aspirations for social inquiry. In W. Kruskal (Ed.), *The state of the social sciences: Fifty years at Chicago.* Chicago: University of Chicago, 1982(a).

Cronbach, L. J. *Designing evaluations of educational and social programs.* San Francisco: Jossey-Bass, 1982(b).

Cronbach, L. J., Gleser, G. C., Nanda, H., & Rajaratnam, N. *The dependability of behavioral measurements: Theory of generalizability for scores and profiles.* New York: Wiley, 1972.

Cronbach, L. J., & Snow, R. E. *Aptitude and instructional methods: A handbook for research on interactions.* New York: Irvington, 1977.

Cronbach, L. J., & Webb, N. Between-class and within-class effects in a reported aptitude X treatment interaction: Reanalysis of a study by G. L. Anderson. *Journal of Educational Psychology,* 1975, *67,* 714–724.

Darley, J. M., & Fazio, R. H. Expectancy confirmation processes arising in the social interaction sequence. *American Psychologist,* 1980, *35,* 867–881.

Doyle, W., Hancock, G., & Kifer, E. Teachers' perceptions: Do they make a difference? *Journal of the Association for the Study of Perception,* 1972, *7,* 21–30.

Duncan, O. D., Featherman, D. L., & Duncan, B. *Socioeconomic background and achievement.* New York: Seminar, 1972.

Dunkin, M. J. Student characteristics, classroom processes, and student achievement. *Journal of Educational Psychology,* 1978, *70,* 998–1009.

Dusek, J. B., & O'Connell, E. J. Teacher expectancy effects on the achievement test performance of elementary school children. *Journal of Educational Psychology,* 1973, *65,* 371–377.

Ebel, R. L. *Essentials of educational measurement.* Englewood Cliffs, N.J.: Prentice-Hall, 1972.

Elashoff, J. D., & Snow, R. E. *Pygmalion reconsidered.* Worthington, Ohio: Jones, 1971.

Entwisle, D. R., & Hayduk, L. A. *Too great expectations.* Baltimore: Johns Hopkins University 1978.

Erlich, O., & Borich, G. Occurrence and generlizability of scores on a classroom interaction instrument. *Journal of Educational Measurement,* 1979, *16,* 11–18.

Feldman, R. S., & Prohaska, T. The student as Pygmalion: Effect of student expectation on the teacher. *Journal of Educational Psychology,* 1979, *71,* 485–493.

Feldman, R. S., & Theiss, A. J. The teacher and student as Pygmalions: Joint effects of teacher and student expectations. *Journal of Educational Psychology,* 1982, 74, 217–223.

Finn, J. D. Expectations and the educational environment. *Review of Educational Research,* 1972, *42,* 387–338.

Finn, J. D., Gaier, E. L., Peng, S. S. & Banks, R. E. Teacher expectations and pupil achievement: A naturalistic study. *Urban Education,* 1975, *10,* 175–197.

Gage, N. L. *The scientific basis of the art of teaching.* New York: Teachers College, 1978.

Glass, G. V. Primary, secondary, and meta-analysis of research. Presidential address presented at the annual meeting of the American Educational Research Association, 1976.

Glass, G. V., McGaw, B., & Smith, M. L. *Meta-analysis in social research.* Beverly Hills, Ca.: Sage, 1981.

Goldberger, A. S., & Duncan, O. D. (Eds.). *Structural equation models in the social sciences.* New York: Seminar, 1973.

Good, T. L. Teacher effectiveness in the elementary school. *Journal of Teacher Education,* 1979, *30,* 52–64.

Haigh, N. J. Teacher expectancy: Accuracy, change, and communication. *New Zealand Journal of Educational Studies,* 1974, *9,* 97–112.

Hastorf, A. H., Schneider, D. J., & Polefka, J. *Person perception.* Menlo Park, Ca.: Addison-Wesley, 1970.

Heines, B. A., & Hawthorne, R. D. Pygmalion's sisters and brothers: the influence of sibling-related teacher expectancies on classroom behaviors and student achievement. Paper presented at the annual meeting of the American Educational Research Association, Toronto, 1978.

Henrikson, H. A. An investigation of the influence of teacher expectation on the intellectual and achievement performance of disadvantaged kindergarten children (Doctoral dissertation, University of Illinois at Urbana-Champaign, 1970). *Dissertation Abstracts International,* 1971, *31*(12A), 6278. (University Microfilms No. 71-14,791)

Humphreys, L. G., & Stubbs, J. A longitudinal analysis of teacher expectation, student expectation, and student achievement. *Journal of Educational Measurement,* 1977, *14,* 261–270.

Johnson, D. S. Naturally acquired learned helplessness: The relationship of school failure to achievement behavior, attributions, and self-concept. *Journal of Educational Psychology,* 1981, *73,* 174–180.

Johnson, R. W. Subject performance as affected by experimenter expectancy, sex of experimenter, and verbal reinforcement. *Canadian Journal of Behavioral Science,* 1970, *2,* 60–66.

Jones, V. The influence of teacher-student introversion, achievement, and similarity on teacher-student dyadic classroom interactions (Doctoral dissertation, University of Texas at Austin, 1971). *Dissertation Abstracts International,* 1972, *35,* 6205A. (University Microfilms No. 72-15, 785)

Jose, J., & Cody, J. J. Teacher-pupil interaction as it relates to attempted changes in teacher expectancy of academic ability and achievement. *American Educational Research Journal,* 1971, *8,* 39–49.

Kerlinger, F. N. *Foundations of behavioral research (2nd ed.).* New York: Holt, Rinehart, & Winston, 1973.

Kerlinger, F. N., & Pedhazur, E. J. *Multiple regression and behavioral research.* New York: Holt, Rinehart, & Winston, 1973.

Keshock, J. D. An investigation of the effects of the expectancy phenomenon upon the intelligence, achievement and motivation of innercity elementary school children (Doctoral dissertation, Case Western Reserve University, 1970). *Dissertation Abstracts International,* 1971, *32*(1A), 243. (University Microfilms No. 71-19, 010)

Kester, S., & Letchworth, G. Communication of teacher expectations and their effects on achievement and attitudes of secondary school students. *The Journal of Educational Research,* 1972, *66,* 51–55.

Leinhardt, G., Seewald, A. M., & Engel, M. Learning what's taught: Sex differences in instruction. *Journal of Educational Psychology,* 1979, *71,* 432–439.

Lockheed, M. E. Beginning Teacher Evaluation Study: Phase II, 1973–1974, Final Report (Vol. V.2). Some determinants and consequences of teacher expectations concerning pupil performance. Sacramento: California State Commission for Teacher Preparations and Licensing, 1976. (ERIC Document No. ED 127 371)

Long, B. H., & Henderson, E. H. Certain determinants of academic expectancies among southern and non-southern teachers. *American Educational Research Journal,* 1974, *11,* 137–147.

McDonald, F., & Elias, P. *Beginning Teacher Evaluation Study: Phase II Technical Summary, Final Report.* Princeton, N.J.: Educational Testing Service, 1976.

Medley, D. M., & Mitzel, H. E. Measuring classroom behavior by systematic observation. In N. L. Gage (Ed.), *Handbook of Research on Teaching.* Chicago: Rand McNally, 1963.

Medway, F. J., & Lowe, C.A. Causal attribution for performance by cross-age tutors and tutees. *American Educational Research Journal,* 1980, *17,* 377–387.

Mendels, G. E., & Flanders, J. P. Teachers' expectations and pupil performance. *American Educational Research Journal,* 1973, *10,* 203–212.

Mendoza, S., Good, T., & Brophy, J. Who talks in junior high classrooms? (Research Report No. 68). Austin, Tx.: Research and Development Center for Teacher Education, University of Texas, 1972.

Mitman, A. L. A summary of studies on teacher expectancy. Unpublished paper, Stanford University, 1976.

Mitman, A. L. Effects of teachers' naturally occurring expectations and a feedback treatment on teachers and students (Doctoral dissertation, Stanford Univeristy, 1981). *Dissertation Abstracts International,* 1981, *42,* 618-A. (University Microfilms No. 81 15812)

Nicholls, J. G. The development of the concepts of effort and ability, perception of academic attainment, and the understanding that difficult tasks require more ability. *Child Development,* 1978, *49,* 800–814.

Nicholls, J. G. When a scale measures more than its name denotes: The case of the test anxiety scale for children. *Journal of Consulting and Clinical Psychology,* 1976, *44,* 976–985.

O'Connell, E. J., Dusek, J. B., & Wheeler, R. J. A follow-up study of teacher expectancy effects. *Journal of Educational Psychology,* 1974, *66,* 325–328.

Pedersen, E., Faucher, T. A., & Eaton, W. W. A new perspective on the effects of first-grade teachers on children's subsequent adult status. *Harvard Educational Review,* 1978, *48,* 1–31.

Perry, R. P., Abrami, P. E., Leventhal, L., & Check, J. Instructor reputation: An expectancy relationship involving student ratings and achievement. *Journal of Educational Psychology,* 1979, *71,* 776–787.

Perry, R. P., Niemi, R. R., & Jones, K. Effect of prior teaching evaluations and lecture presentation on ratings of teaching performance. *Journal of Educational Psychology,* 1974, *66,* 851–856.

Phillips, D. C., and Orton, R. The new metaphysics of cognitive learning theory: Perspectives on Bandura's "reciprocal determinism." *Psychological Review,* in press.

Rappaport, M. M. & Rappaport, H. The other half of the expectancy equation: Pygmalion. *Journal of Educational Psychology,* 1975, *67,* 531–536.

Reichardt, C. A plausible rival hypothesis for the Seaver study of teacher expectancies: A selection and regression artifact of teacher effectiveness. Unpublished document, Northwestern University, 1975.

Rogosa, D. A critique of cross-lagged correlations. *Psychological Bulletin,* 1980, *88,* 245–258.

Rogosa, D., Floden, R., & Willett, J. B. Assessing the stability of teacher behaviors. Unpublished manuscript, Stanford University, 1982.

Rosenthal, R. Experimenter effects in behavioral research. New York: Appleton-Century-Crofts, 1966.

Rosenthal, R., & Jacobson, L. Pygmalion in the classroom: Teacher expectation and pupils' intellectual development. New York: Holt, Rinehart, & Winston, 1968.

Rosenthal, R., & Rosnow, R. L. The volunteer subject. New York: Wiley, 1975.

Rosenthal, R., & Rubin, D. B. Interpersonal expectancy effects: The first 345 studies. The Behavioral and Brain Sciences, 1978, 3, 377–415.

Rotter, N. G. The influence of race and other variables on teachers' ratings of pupils (Doctoral dissertation, New York University, 1974). Dissertation Abstracts International, 1975, 35(11A). (University Microfilms No. 75-9694)

Rubovits, P. C., & Maehr, M. L. Pygmalion analyzed: Toward an explanation of the Rosenthal-Jacobson findings. Journal of Personality and Social Psychology, 1971, 19, 197–203.

Rubovits, P. C., & Maehr, M. L. Pygmalion black and white. Journal of Personality and Social Psychology, 1973, 25, 210–218.

Seaver, W. B. Effect of naturally induced teacher expectancies. Journal of Personality and Social Psychology, 1973, 28, 333–342.

Shavelson, R. J., Cadwell, J., & Izu, T. Teachers' sensitivity to the reliability of information in making pedagogical decisions. American Educational Research Journal, 1977, 14, 83–97.

Shavelson, R., & Dempsey-Atwood, N. Generalizability of measures of teaching behavior. Review of Educational Research, 1976, 46, 553–611.

Shavelson, R. J., & Stern, P. Research on teachers' pedagogical thoughts, judgments, decisions, and behavior. Review of Educational Research, 1981, 51, 455–498.

Smith, F. J., & Luginbuhl, J. E. Inspecting expectancy: Some laboratory results of relevance for teacher training. Journal of Educational Psychology, 1976, 68, 265–272.

Smith, M. L. Teacher expectations. Evaluation in Education, 1980, 4, 53–55.

Snow, R. E. Unfinished pygmalion. Contemporary Psychology, 1969, 14, 197–200.

Snow, R. E. Representative and quasi-representative designs for research on teaching. Review of Educational Research, 1974, 44, 265–291.

Snow, R. E. Research on aptitudes: A progress report. In L. S. Shulman (Ed.), Review of research in education, Vol. 4. Itasca, Ill.: Peacock, 1977.

Stayrook, N. A comparison of two causal models in elementary school reading. Unpublished doctoral dissertation, Stanford University, 1982.

Stipek, D. Children's perceptions of their own and their classmates' ability. Journal of Educational Psychology, 1981, 73, 404–410.

Sutherland, A., & Goldschmid, M. L. Negative teacher expectation and IQ change in children with superior intellectual potential. Child Development, 1974, 45, 852–856.

Weiner, B. Human motivation. New York: Holt, Rinehart & Winston, 1980.

Weinstein, R. S. Reading group membership in first grade: Teacher behaviors and pupil experience over time. Journal of Educational Psychology, 1976, 68, 103–116.

West, C. K., & Anderson, T. H. The question of preponderant causation in teacher expectancy research. Review of Educational Research, 1976, 46, 613–630.

Williams, T. Teacher prophecies and the inheritance of inequality. Sociology of Education, 1976, 49, 223–236.

Willis, S. Formation of teachers' expectations of students' academic and social behaviors of students (Doctoral dissertation, University of Texas at Austin, 1972). Dissertation Abstracts International, 1973, 33(9A), 4960. (University Microfilms No. 73-7678)

Zanna, M. P., Sheras, P. L., Cooper, J., & Shaw, C. Pygmalion and Galatea: The interactive effects of teacher and student expectancies. Journal of Experimental Social Psychology, 1975, 11, 279–287.

Section 2
Theoretical Formulations

The early research on teacher expectancies was conducted in what might be termed a theoretical vacuum. Although Rosenthal had conducted many studies of experimenter expectancy effects, the focus of the theoretical concerns was not directed specifically to the types of encounters that occur in the every day interactions between teacher and student in the typical classroom. Nor was the Rosenthal and Jacobson study based on theoretical propositions.

To a large degree, this was a result of the lack of a knowledge base. As further research began to accumulate, attempts at theory building were begun. The importance of these efforts, of course, is twofold. First, theories help us organize information and understand the processes operating in any given situation. This understanding, in turn, allows us to explain the phenomenon. Second, theories are very important for pointing to questions in need of further research. Hence, theories provoke the questions addressed by researchers. The three chapters comprising this section summarize the attempts to describe teacher expectancy effects and place them into productive theoretical contexts.

The most comprehensive theory of teacher expectancy effects on student achievement is Cooper's (Chapter 6). In his chapter, Cooper notes that teacher expectancies may act (a) to sustain current student levels of performance and (b) to alter student performance to bring it into closer agreement with the teacher's expectancies. Drawing on earlier work by Brophy and Good on the communication of teacher's expectancies and by Rosenthal on the general dimensions of teacher behaviors that are related to expectancies, Cooper has formulated a model of teacher expectancy effects that takes into account the formation of expectancies, the communication of expectancies, and the ultimate impact of expectancies on student achievement. As he notes, this model has served well in guiding research activities (and further theory development) by pointing out, for example, that expectancies may work differently in different grade levels, subject matters, and times of the school year.

As Cooper points out in his chapter, there are areas of theorizing in which further work needs to be done. One of these areas deals with describing how, and on what factors, teachers come to formulate expectancies. This subject is, in part, a topic discussed by Peterson and Barger (Chapter 7), who attempt to answer it by drawing on developments in attribution theories. A major focus of their contribution is a theoretical description of the formation of teacher expectancies. They note that teachers apparently use information from students' past performance in making expectancies on the basis of perceived attributes of the student or of the situation. Hence, successful performance by high-expectancy students is more likely to be attributed to ability, and successful performance by low-expectancy students is more likely to be attributed to external factors, such as luck. They also address the issue of other student individual difference characteristics, such as socioeconomic class and race, and their influence on the formation of expectancies. Peterson and Barger, then, present a more detailed analysis of one aspect of theorizing critical to understanding the import of teacher expectancy effects on student achievement.

The major theoretical efforts have been directed at either global descriptions of the influence of teacher expectancy effects or have focused on the role played by the teacher. A somewhat different perspective is offered by Eccles and Wigfield (Chapter 8). Their point of departure is the student; specifically the theoretical description of the impact of teacher expectancies on student motivation within the learning/performance aspects of the influence of teacher expectancy effects. They try to fill in theoretical concerns by describing how teacher expectancies translate into behaviors that facilitate or retard student motivation to perform and thereby affect student achievement. In so doing, they point to a variety of individual differences among students that may be related to teacher expectancy effects. This emphasis helps further theory development by taking into account the individual student, the person from whom criterion measures of expectancy effects are taken.

The theoretical perspectives described in this section have played a significant role in shaping the types of research conducted in the field. More importantly, they represent advances in our understanding of how teacher expectancies relate to student achievement. By focusing research efforts on various aspects of the entire chain of events, the theories have proved important from a heuristic sense. By examining the various theories offered by these contributors we are able to gain a reasonably veridical perspective of the complexity of teacher expectancy influences on student achievement.

6 Models of Teacher Expectation Communication

Harris M. Cooper
University of Missouri—Columbia

Rosenthal and Jacobson's study Pygmalion in the Classroom (1968) captured the interest of many segments of American society. Because so many took note, many also found fault. In retrospect, the criticism directed at Pygmalion seems to demonstrate its significance rather than its adequacy of method or conclusion. For instance, Pygmalion was criticized for not testing how teacher expectations were communicated (Elashoff & Snow, 1971). Some felt that Pygmalion neglected the process intervening between teacher expectations and student achievement. This perception indicated more about the critic's desire for fuller understanding than about the adequacy of Pygmalion itself.

Researchers who studied teacher expectations after Pygmalion were obligated to fill out the communication process. Gratifyingly, education psychologists took up the challenge of studying expectation communication, though public attention soon turned elsewhere. Today, 15 years later, the pieces of the puzzle framed by Pygmalion are still being fit—but not because our knowledge remains scant. Teacher expectations research still flourishes because the results of expectation studies have been complex and provocative in their own right.

It is my purpose to present models for how teacher expectations are communicated to students and ultimately affect student achievement. The word "model" is used in a loose path analytic, but nonmathematical, sense (Kerlinger & Pedhazur, 1973). That is, an attempt is made to present temporally-sequenced, assumedly casual sets of relations involved in the expectation communication process. The relations originate with the variable *teacher expectations* and terminate with the variable *student achievement*. In all cases, it is contended that the total affect of the indirect relations between these two variables is either (a) to sustain student performance at achievement levels accurately estimated by teachers, or (b) to alter student performance so that performance becomes more congruent with inaccurate teacher expectations. The models are simplified versions of nature (and rigorous path analyses) in that they do not incorporate feedback loops—or do not contain reciprocal influences among variables—and they do not claim to include all of the mechanisms through which expectations might be communicated—just those about which enough is known to justify declaratory presentation.

Multiple models of expectation communication are presented because the research findings to date strongly suggest that expectations affect teacher–student relations in different ways at different grade levels and at different times of the school year. Also, it appears that different models are needed to explain how teacher expectations affect (1) relative student performance within a single class and (2) classroom performance as a whole. Finally, researchers have used a variety of different operations to measure expectations and these correspond to two distinct conceptual definitions for the term "expectation effect."

In fact, it would not be possible, in the space provided, to present a separate expectation communication model for every schooling context that needs to be distinguished. Instead, the chapter begins with a listing of those schooling contexts that past research indicates cannot be ignored when the limiting conditions of a model are set. Then the chapter takes a detailed look at the model relevant to the most frequently studied context—primary school education. Using this model and its limiting conditions as a starting point, several other models are then briefly discussed.

Finally, there were three sources of input into the notions contained in this chapter. The first was a 2-year study of some 30 classrooms for which the author served as principal investigator. The results of this study are reported in detail under separate cover (Cooper & Good, 1983). The second source was parallel work by other interested researchers. Several recent and thorough reviews of individual findings concerning expectation communication already exist (e.g., Brophy & Good, 1974; Cooper, 1979a; Rosenthal, 1974) so no attempt has been made to exhaustively cite these studies. Finally, my wife has been an active elementary school teacher for several years and has, through anecdote and angst, often guided or refined my thinking.

FACTORS AFFECTING HOW EXPECTATIONS ARE COMMUNICATED

Definitions of Expectations and Expectation Effects

It is not surprising to find that numerous operational definitions of the term "teacher expectations" have been employed in the studies since Pygmalion. These definitions can be loosely categorized into four general classes.

Ability or Achievement Measures.   The first type of expectation measure asks teachers to rate (typically on Likert scales) or rank order students in their class according to (1) the student's general competencies (Brophy & Good, 1970), or (2) how adequately they perform in a particular achievement domain (Luce & Hoge, 1978). Achievement and performance expectations contain a large ability expectation component, so the two approaches should typically be well correlated. Achievement measures, however, should be more influenced by characteristics of the student that affect performance but are unrelated to ability. These would include the student's industriousness, study habits, and/or test anxiety.

Achievement and ability expectations are also similar in that they share what might be called a concurrent focus. Teachers are asked to describe students as they presently appear to be, not to extrapolate about future performance. In a "pure" sense then, these are not really expectation measures, though they are frequently used in studies meant to uncover expectation communication.

Expected Improvement.   This type of measure asks teachers to predict how much academic progress they anticipate their students will make over a specified period of time. Cooper, Findley and Good (1982) found this measure to be only weakly correlated with ability rankings (r = .19). Thus, teacher beliefs about a student's present competence appear to be relatively independent of their expectation for the future change in a student's competence. Expected improvement measures are also conceptually more similar to what is typically understood to be an "expectation."

Manipulated Expectations.   As in the original Pygmalion study, researchers often create variability in teacher expectations by presenting false information about student ability or potential improvement (Taylor, 1979). By design, these manipulations are independent of the student's actual ability or improvement so it is permissible to characterize manipulated expectations as having an identifiable erroneous component. Through false feedback, the experimenter hopes to create a known discrepancy between the teacher's perception and the student's actual corresponding ability or potential.

Natural Discrepancy Measures.   As a naturalistic analog to manipulated expectations, some researchers devise measures of how much a teacher over or underestimates a student's performance (McDonald & Elias, 1976). This is done by comparing teacher estimates of student ability or achievement to standardized test scores or some other more objective assessment. These measures circumvent the ethical difficulties involved in manipulation of teacher beliefs. However, they also raise some interpretive problems, including whether this discrepancy can legitimately be labeled error. Some might argue that standard measures of student ability are not perfectly valid and may themselves be in error. However, in most schooling situations standardized test results are synonymous with achievement, so their use as criteria is pragmatically justifiable, if not wholly justifiable for labeling the teacher's over or underestimate of them as error.

Defining Expectation Effects.   Along with the several expectation definitions, researchers have identified two kinds of effects that expectations may have on student performance. The first effect (and that which motivated Pygmalion) is the self-fulfilling prophecy. According to Merton (1957) a self-fulfilling prophecy occurs when "a false definition of the situation evok(es) a new behavior which makes the originally false conception come true" (p. 423). Clearly, the manipulated and natural discrepancy measures of expectations are the most appropriate independent variables for studying self-fulfilling prophecies.

Expected improvement measures might also be used to study self-fulfilling prophecies but, as with natural discrepancy measures, the accuracy (or veracity) of these judgments cannot be clearly assessed. If the teacher has accurately assessed the student's potential for improvement, then a confirmation of this belief would not contain the "initially false" component of the definition of a self-fulfilling prophecy.

In the case of manipulated expectations, the appropriate dependent variable for studying self-fulfilling prophecies would be student performance at some time after the manipulation. No adjustment to subsequent raw performance is needed if the manipulations have been randomly assigned to students. For natural discrepancy measures, the dependent variable must reflect performance change subsequent to the time the ratings were gathered. This typically means final performance is adjusted to remove performance differences that existed when the discrepancy measure was constructed. The change measure is most appropriate for use with the discrepancy ratings because final raw performance and the discrepancy measure itself are both correlated with initial performance (see Cooper, Findley & Good, in press).

The second type of expectation effect involves sustaining student performance at preexisting levels. Sustaining expectation effects, according to Cooper and Good (1983) "occur when teachers respond on the basis of their existing expectations for students rather than to changes in student performance caused by sources other than the teacher" (p. 6). (Also see Salomon, 1981). To study sustaining effects, the ability and achievement definitions of expectation seem to be most appropriate. They focus on the teacher's assessment of the student's performance history and do not address the notion of accuracy. In fact, while self-fulfilling prophecies must be preceded by inaccurate expectations, it might be suggested that sustaining expectation effects are only salient for students about whom teachers hold accurate expectations. The accuracy of the expectation may suggest whether a potential exists for the communication of self-fulfilling prophecies or sustaining effects. Cooper (1979a) argued that sustaining expectation effects may be more frequent than self-fulfilling prophecies, since markedly inaccurate expectations for students are probably rare in real classrooms.

The major research problem regarding sustaining expectation effects is how to demonstrate that one has occurred. Part of the problem is that the prediction is supported by a finding of no change in student performance level which is much like predicting a null hypothesis. Also, rather than manipulate teacher expectations, the researcher interested in sustaining effects would have to randomly manipulate student learning potentials. Obviously, this would present logistical and ethical problems too difficult to surmount. Natural changes in student potential could be monitored, but accurate measurement would be difficult, and the proper moments of changed potential (and the return to previous potential) would be exceptionally difficult to identify.

Most evidence for sustaining expectation effects will probably remain indirect. Researchers must argue that particular teacher behaviors related to ability or achievement expectations serve to maintain student performance levels by making indicators of student change difficult for the teacher to notice. It is certainly regrettable that the expectation effect which probably occurs most frequently is also most difficult to research.

In sum, then, four general conceptions of expectations are available and these relate to two distinct types of expectation effects. Until we know otherwise, it appears wise to specify whether an hypothesized model of expectation communication relates to inaccurate expectations thought to cause alterations in student performance or to accurate expectations thought to sustain performance.

Units of Analysis

The structures of schools and classrooms create another important distinction in how expectation effects must be studied. Specifically, a distinction must be made between how relative teacher expectations are communicated to the separate students in a single class and how general teacher expectations are communicated to the class as a whole (Cronbach, 1976; Burstein, 1980). For instance, Cooper, Hinkel and Good (1980) found that the total number of dyadic interactions initiated by the teacher in private settings was negatively related to the teacher's general sense of control over the students in a class ($r = -.50$). At the same time, however, no consistent relation was found between the variations in teacher's sense of control over individual students in the class and the frequency of teacher initiated private interactions with individual students. The average correlation within classrooms was $r = -.08$ for the same sample of classrooms that revealed the $r = -.50$ between-class correlations.

Cooper and Good (1983) have speculated that the difference between relations at the two levels of analysis may be a function of the differing influence of social comparison processes: . . . "expectations within classrooms are communicated by teachers not only through feedback contingencies used with students, but also through students' awareness of differences between feedback to themselves and other students in the class'' (p. 153).

Little is known about the role of social comparison in classrooms. Levine (1983) has summarized the existing theoretical approaches and research on social comparison in schools. He makes three points relevant to this discussion. First, classrooms are ideally suited for eliciting social comparison processes. They generate cognitive uncertainty in students, have strong evaluative atmospheres and provide relatively similar peers. Second, social comparison appears to occur most frequently when comparison others are visible (Richer, 1976), substantiating the notion that social comparison may affect within-class relations more than between-class relations. Finally, Levine (1983) notes several aspects of task performance that are affected by social comparison information, including attention, self-monitoring, persistence, speed, and quality of performance.

Thus, it is unlikely that much social comparison occurs between individual students in different classrooms. If social comparison processes affect the overall behavior of a teacher, these processes probably relate to the comparisons teachers make to other teachers, not those comparisons made among students.

The unit of analysis problem is complex—this entire chapter could be spent on it alone. Again, however, it must be sufficient to say that the present evidence indicates expectation communication models must state whether they pertain to within- or between-class processes or both, since the generality of a model across this dimension should be demonstrated, not assumed.

Level of Schooling

The basic nature of the teacher–student relationship is different at different grade levels, as is the classroom structure in which teachers and students interact. Generally, the influence of an individual teacher on a given student's achievement probably diminishes in higher grades. This should be due partly to a change in the student's choice of significant others (from adults to peers) and partly to a diminishing amount of time spent with any particular teacher.

While the influence of the teacher on performance should generally diminish as the level of schooling goes up, there is reason to believe teacher expectations reemerge as an important influence in graduate school training. Here, teachers again become significant others (their value as role models increases) and the teaching situation regains much of its personal, dyadic character.

Expectation effects in graduate school have rarely been the topic of research. It is important to mention them, however, because they demonstrate that expectation effects can occur at any point in the schooling process. The author's personal experience with graduate-level expectation effects derive from having students in statistics courses ask for suggestions about how to analyze data for masters or doctoral theses. Sometimes less than optimal (but legitimate) solutions would be offered when it was felt the capabilities of the student were limited (this is an input effect, according to Rosenthal, 1974'. On a few occasions the judgment proved wrong. Given the number of times these interactions took place, the laws of probability suggest that several unknown misjudgments must have occurred, rendering a thesis less elegant than the student's actual capabilities would have permitted.

In sum, although it is likely that expectation effects occur throughout the schooling process, it is also likely that their magnitude and/or form change considerably at different educational levels. Therefore, it is extremely important for theorists to specify the schooling level to which an expectation communication model pertains.

Time of Year

As with any social relation, the passage of time will affect how teachers and students interact. Teachers and students must go through periods of acquaintance, familiarity, and finally, separation. With regard to expectation effects, distinguishing among four periods of the school year may capture much of this variation.

First Week.   If expectation effects occur during the first week of school, they are probably very difficult to demonstrate. Teachers' expectations are probably unstable or ill-defined so they should still be receptive to information that modifies expectations. Even if expectations are firm, within-class expectation communication would be extremely rare, since a stable pattern of interaction between teacher and student would not have yet emerged. Some expectation effects may take root in the first week, however. Teachers might be familiar with a student's siblings (Seaver, 1971) or the impressions of previous teachers (Cooper, 1979b), and this might influence general classroom rules and/or how seating patterns are arranged.

By the end of the first week of school, expectations have probably grown fairly stable (Willis, 1972) and academic work should have begun in earnest.

Second Week Through Second Month.   This is probably the period during which expectations have their greatest impact on student performance. If an inaccurate expectation has lasted through the first or second week of school, it should have its greatest potential for changing the student on first being clearly communicated.

Third Through Eighth Month.   Sustaining expectation effects can probably occur throughout the school year, exclusive of the first week. Once a teacher's expectation has formed, its insulation from new information should be fairly constant and changes in student potential due to factors other than the teacher can occur at any time (i.e., changes in peer group, home environment, health). Self-fulfilling prophecies, however, should be less evident during the third through eighth months than earlier in the year. It is hard to imagine that inaccurate expectations could be maintained by the teacher for more than 2 or 3 months without something giving, that is, without the teacher altering the perception or the student changing his or her behavior.

Ninth or Final Month.   The last month of school needs to be distinguished because of a possible shift in the importance of the level of analysis. Cooper and Good (1983) reported diminishing within-class expectation effects as the year progressed, but some increase in between-class expectation effects. The within-class decrease in expectation communication might be due to several factors including (1) a diminution in the use of teacher feedback to socialize or control students; (2) an emotional disengagement between teachers and students; and/or (3) a decrease in the amount of academic activity that occurs. At the same time, however, the between-class effect of expectations may increase somewhat as the year draws to a close because teachers may begin to think about the class' general progress and how it will reflect on their own performance, relative to other teachers. Teachers who sense their students can accomplish more than they already have may quicken the pace of instruction (in light of their own pending evaluation) while lower expectations may lead teachers to coast through the final month.

Subject Matter

There is empirical evidence that the effect of expectations varies as a function of the achievement domain under study. Smith (1980) found that the average effect size (d index) over a sample of 44 estimates for the influence of expectations on reading achievement was $d = .48$. A d index of only $+.18$ was found for math achievement, however (over 17 estimates). The difference in expectation effects may lie in the amount of subjectivity that remains in the teaching of different subject matters. Mathematics curricula may be more structured than reading curricula and therefore may allow less variation in teacher behavior. To date, there has been scant research examining whether these subject matter differences represent a qualitative distinction in how teachers and students interact during different lessons or simply one of quantity, that is, the same expectation communication process occurs in all lessons but to different degrees.

Summary

Assuming six levels of schooling, the above list of factors potentially mediating how expectations are communicated (and how often) creates 192 separate sets of circumstances! Obviously, 192 separate models are not needed to present an exhaustive picture of expectation communication. Some combinations (i.e., the first week of graduate school) are ludicrous while others are relatively uninteresting. More positively, some models are probably applicable across several distinctions, with perhaps modification in strength rather than quality of communication.

The remainder of this chapter will focus on expectation effects that occur in early elementary school grades, when expectation effects are probably most frequent. This model has four significant theoretical benchmarks: the works of Brophy and Good (1974), Rosenthal (1974), Cooper (1979a) and Cooper and Good (1981). Since much of the research upon which the model is based involved naturalistic observation and ability or achievement measures of expectations, the model is probably most appropriate for considering sustaining expectation effects. Also, the model is probably most applicable to within-class expectation effects. Each of the qualifying conditions, however, will be assessed for its potential impact on the model's generality after the basic model has been fully explicated.

MODELS OF THE EXPECTATION COMMUNICATION PROCESS

The Brophy and Good (1974) Model

A good deal of the naturalistic research that examined how performance expectations influenced teacher interactions with students was based on the sequential model of events developed by Brophy and Good (1974). With an eye toward uncovering the mediators of expectation effects, Brophy and Good conceptualized the communication process in terms of observable behaviors.

The model involved four steps: (1) The teacher develops an expectation predicting specific behavior and achievement for each student; (2) because of these expectations, the teacher behaves differently toward each student; (3) this treatment informs each student about the behavior and achievement expected from him/her and affects the student's self-concept, achievement motivation, and level of aspiration; and finally, (4) if teacher treatment is consistent over time and the student is behaviorally compliant, the student's achievement will come to correspond, or remain correspondent, with the teacher's belief.

Among the theoretical advances contained in the Brophy and Good model were its recognition that (1) teacher expectations had to be translated into consistent patterns of behavior before they could change student performance and (2) students had to incorporate this information into their self-concepts before achievement would be affected.

Most of the research generated by the Brophy and Good model was atheoretical. That is, many researchers examined the behavioral correlates of teacher expectations (typically measured as ability or achievement perceptions), but few simultaneously speculated about or tested how the uncovered behaviors affected student self-perceptions or performance. Good and Brophy (1980) reviewed 12 of the more common ways teacher actions covary with expectations:

1. Seating low-expectation students far from the teacher and/or seating them in a group.
2. Paying less attention to lows in academic situations (smiling less often and maintaining less eye contact).
3. Calling on lows less often to answer classroom questions or to make public demonstrations.
4. Waiting less time for lows to answer questions.
5. Not staying with lows in failure situations (i.e., providing fewer clues, asking fewer follow-up questions).
6. Criticizing lows more frequently than highs for incorrect public responses.
7. Praising lows less frequently than highs after successful public responses.
8. Praising lows more frequently than highs for marginal or inadequate public responses.
9. Providing lows with less accurate and less detailed feedback than highs.
10. Failing to provide lows with feedback about their responses as often as highs.
11. Demanding less work and effort from lows than from highs.
12. Interrupting performance of lows more frequently than highs.

Brophy and Good were quick to point out that not all teachers treat high and low expectation students differently. Thus, even though teachers describe students as having high and low potential, these cognitions do not necessarily translate into differential behavior. Ultimately, it is the *expression* of expectations, not their existence, that is critical.

Brophy and Good also pointed out that many of the differences in teacher treatment are not necessarily signs of ineffective communication or inadequate teaching. For instance, demanding less work from lows may prevent lows from experiencing too much failure and frustration—the pace of learning must be tailored to the student's ability. In addition, not calling on lows as often in public recognizes that group situations involve the needs of many students and that public failures can be especially debilitating to motivation. However, the behavioral differences suggested by Brophy and Good strongly implied the existence of sustaining expectation effects. Although this evidence was indirect, nearly all the behavioral differences they suggested would make learning by lows relatively more difficult.

The Rosenthal (1974) Four-Factor Categorization

Brophy and Good provided a sequence of steps underlying expectation communication and stimulated research into observable differences in teacher behavior. Rosenthal (1974) suggested more general and abstract social dimensions of teacher behavior that might summarize the discrete behaviors involved in the sequence. He provided a four-factor typology: (1) climate, (2) output, (3) input and (4) feedback.

First, teachers appear to create warmer socioemotional atmospheres for brighter students. Videotapes of simulated tutorial sessions have found that teachers who believed they were interacting with high-expectation students leaned toward students and smiled and nodded their heads more often than teachers interacting with low-expectation students (Chaikin, Sigler & Derlega, 1974). Kester and Letchworth (1972) found that induced expectations in professional teachers lead to more supportive and friendly behavior toward high-expectation students. Thus, many nonverbal behaviors associated with positive emotional attachment are displayed by teachers most frequently in interactions with students believed to have more potential.

There is also evidence indicating that teachers' verbal input to students is dependent on performance expectations. Students labeled as low expectation have been found to receive fewer opportunities to learn new material and have less difficult material taught to them than students labeled as bright.

The third factor, verbal output, involves two teaching behaviors: (1) the teacher's persistence in pursuing interactions to a satisfactory conclusion, and (2) the frequency with which academic interactions take place. For instance, research indicates that teachers tend to stay with highs longer after they have failed to answer a question. Teachers pay closer attention to highs' responses, give them more clues and more often repeat or rephrase questions when highs answer incorrectly than when lows answer incorrectly. Teachers also sometimes allow highs longer to respond before redirecting unanswered questions to other class members.

Among the best researched behavioral correlates of performance expectations is the absolute frequency of interaction. The finding that high-expectation students will seek more academic contact with the teacher than low-expectation students is thus strongly supported by research. However, whether teachers equalize or accentuate this difference through their own initiation is not clear and appears to be a matter of varying teaching styles. A substantial number of studies can be found reporting that teachers initiated more contacts with highs, or more interactions with lows, or showed no initiation differences at all.

The final factor, feedback, involves the teacher's use of praise and criticism after an academic exchange. Teachers appear to praise high-expectation students more, and proportionately more per correct response, while lows are criticized more, and proportionately more per incorrect response. The conclusion seems to hold whether one simply counts positive and negative use of affect or whether one adjusts praise and criticism use by the number of correct and incorrect responses.

The measure of expectations employed (i.e., induced or naturally occurring) also does not appear to effect this result as long as professional teachers' behavior is under consideration.

The Cooper (1979a) Expectation Communication Model

The next advance in explaining expectation communication in the classroom involved applying basic social theory to the process. The expectation communication model proposed by Cooper (1979a) adopted concepts, findings and hypotheses from achievement attribution theory (Weiner, 1977), learned helplessness theory (Seligman, 1975) and locus of control research (Lefcourt, 1981). The model was especially notable for (1) its attention to the mechanisms through which teacher behavior affected student self-concepts (Step 3 in the Brophy and Good Model, largely neglected in pre 1979 research) and (2) its suggestion that the contingencies leading to teacher behavior might be a communication mechanism as important as the frequency with which a behavior occurred. A description of the Expectation Communication Model follows. The model is depicted in Fig. 6-1.

Teachers Form Expectations.   Cooper began his model by stating that variations in student background and ability lead teachers to form differential perceptions of how likely students are to succeed. This obvious point was made so that the fact that the expectation communication process involved many feedback relations was acknowledged, even though only one causal sequence among many was discussed. Also acknowledged was West and Anderson's (1976) point that performances were as likely to affect expectations as expectations were to affect performance.

Context and Expectations Influence Teacher Perceptions of Control.   Cooper next distinguished classroom contexts according to the amount of personal control they afforded the teacher. Control was defined as having at least three subdimensions all related to the parameters of dyadic interactions: teacher control over interaction content (what the interaction is about), timing (when it occurs), and duration (how long it lasts).

Two classroom context variables were offered as affecting teacher perceptions of control. These were the interaction initiator (teacher or student) and the setting (public or private). It was hypothesized (and later demonstrated by Cooper, Burger & Seymour, 1979) that when a teacher personally initiated a contact, the teacher perceived more control over the interaction than when a student was the initiator. Also, interactions in public were viewed by teachers as less controllable than private interactions. The setting effect was conjectured to be caused primarily by the number of individuals whose needs the teacher must simultaneously consider in public.

In addition to classroom contexts, teachers' performance expectations for students were also posited as having control implications. High expectations

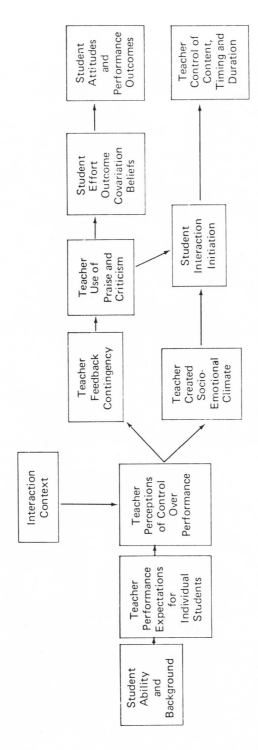

FIG. 6.1. A Model for Expectation Communication and Behavior Influence

were viewed to be associated with a greater range of potential content choices in an interaction. More importantly high success expectations were associated with appropriate responding by the student, giving the teacher more leeway in when to end an interaction and move on to other matters.

Cooper established the relevance of teacher control perception to expectations communication by suggesting that high-expectation students retain a high likelihood of success regardless of degree of control afforded by the setting. Low-expectation student success, on the other hand, was viewed as more dependent on the material, timing, and duration of an interaction. Therefore, the interaction context may be seen by the teacher as an important contributor to whether interactions with low expectation students end in success. The more control a context affords a teacher who is interacting with a slow student, the greater the likelihood that the teacher can end the interaction positively.

Teachers' Perceptions of Control Influence Climate and Feedback Contingencies. If teacher control over low-expectation student performance is important for lows to succeed, then high control contexts should be most desirable for interactions with lows. Cooper hypothesized that teachers may feed control over lows' performances could be maximized by inhibiting lows' initiations and seeking lows out in private settings. The teacher might, therefore, decrease initiations by low expectation students through (1) the creation of an unrewarding socioemotional environment and (2) the relatively infrequent use of praise and freer use of criticism with lows. Of course, these relations were already suggested in the literature reviews of both Brophy and Good (1974) and Rosenthal (1974). The perception that context contributed more to low than high expectation student successes creates a problem, however. If teachers use feedback and classroom climate in order to inhibit low-expectation students' initiations, it also means highs and lows may be evaluated using different criteria. Cooper wrote:

> Teachers will tend not to praise strong efforts from lows because praise may reduce future personal control by encouraging initiations. Teachers may tend to be more critical of weak efforts from lows since criticism increases control. In evaluating highs, teachers may dispense praise and criticism with greater dependence on exhibited effort, since future control of highs' behavior is not as necessary [p. 399].

As the Expectation Communication Model implied, reinforcement was used by some teachers first as an aid in classroom management and second, as an indicator of the student's efforts. More pertinently, the model suggested that as performance expectations for students decrease, the teacher may use climate and feedback to control future contexts and thereby reduce the contingency between rewards and expended student effort.

This differing contingency hypothesis predicts that the frequency of praise and criticism and the emotional climate produced by teachers are causally linked to rates of student interaction initiation. Several studies have indicated that this is, in fact, the case (Cooper, 1977; Entwisle & Webster, 1972; Sarbin & Allen, 1968).

Feedback Contingencies Influence Student Self-Efficacy Beliefs.   The sustaining of low-expectation student performance was not viewed as a direct result of the amount of feedback per se, but rather as a result of the contingencies upon which feedback was based. Cooper wrote:

> High expectation students may be criticized when the teacher perceives them as not having tried and may be praised when efforts are strong. Low expectation students, however, may be praised and criticized more often for reasons independent of their personal efforts, namely the teacher's desire to control interaction contexts. Greater use of feedback by teachers to control interactions may lead to less belief on the part of students that personal effort can bring about success [p. 401].

Student Self-Efficacy Beliefs Influence Student Performance.   Most of the research associated with learned helplessness phenomena supports the notion that if a person perceives that reinforcement is not contingent on personal behavior it leads to performance deterioration (e.g., Seligman, 1975). Other studies have found that a lesser belief in self-efficacy is also associated with less task persistence (Dweck & Reppucci, 1973) and negative affect (Riemer, 1975) and attitudes toward tasks presented.

Cooper was careful to specify three qualifications to the model. First, it was not concluded that teachers try to avoid low expectation students. Teachers may want to control when interactions that demand large personal efforts will occur, not make their environment free of effort or failure. Second, it was suggested that teachers were unaware of systematic differences in feedback contingency choices, since their reactions to student performance were frequently spontaneous. Finally, it was noted that teachers would vary in their tendency to communicate expectations, so the model would apply more or less to teachers with different personality types (see Badad, 1979).

The Cooper and Good (1983) Revision

In an effort to test the Expectation Communication Model, Cooper and Good (1983) undertook an exhaustive study of nearly every stage of the expectation communication process. Briefly, they performed a naturalistic investigation in 17 third through fifth grade classrooms. At three times of the school year (Fall, Winter, and Spring), teachers provided expectations, control perceptions, and causal attributions for the performance of students in their classes. Students provided self-efficacy ratings and perceptions of the frequency of teacher behaviors. Teacher–student dyadic interactions were observed simultaneously with all three test administrations.

The results of the study were largely consistent with the model's predictions but also suggested some revisions were necessary. For instance, the study was quite successful at replicating the relations between expectations and teacher behaviors which others had reported and which were taken as "givens" in the model's construction. Specifically, high teacher expectations for performance were associated with more frequent teacher and student initiations in public situations and more frequent teacher praise. Low teacher expectations were associated with more behavior problems and more academic criticism.

In addition, the study confirmed the predicted relations between expectations, interaction control perceptions, and causal attributions (Burger, Cooper & Good, 1982; Cooper, Hinkel & Good, 1980). However, only weak relations were uncovered when interaction control perceptions were correlated with teacher behaviors and these were largely inconsistent with the model's predictions.

Also, the model predicted that effort attributions by the teacher would be more strongly related to teacher praise and criticism for high- than low-expectation students. Instead of finding this relation, the Cooper and Good study revealed that academic praise to low-expectation students was more strongly related to the attribution of "following the teacher's directions and instructions" than was praise to highs. Finally, student self-efficacy beliefs were found to be related to perceptions of teacher behavior in much greater correspondence to the model's prediction than were observed frequencies of teacher behavior.

To accommodate the findings that were inconsistent with the original Expectation Communication Model, Cooper and Good suggested two conceptual revisions. First, the notion of teacher control was redefined to involve two types of control referents: (1) control over interaction parameters and (2) control over performance outcomes. The three earlier control subdimensions (timing, content, and duration) were recast as measuring separate aspects of interaction parameter control only. The teachers' use of the attribution category indicating that their own directions and instructions caused student success or failure was seen as measuring teacher beliefs about control over performance outcomes or personal involvement in success or failure. Cooper and Good speculated that these two control perceptions related to teacher behavior in a hierarchial fashion. That is, control over interaction parameters related to teacher reinforcement behavior until the teacher felt such control over the student was at a satisfactorily high level (with satisfactory being subjectively defined by the teacher). However, adequate control over the context of performance does not necessarily imply that outcomes can also be adequately controlled. In instances where parameter control is satisfactory but outcome control is not, control of outcomes becomes the operating variable. Finally, when the teacher feels outcome control is satisfactory then the teacher's perception of student effort becomes the dominant influence over rewards and punishments.

Cooper and Good contended this conceptualization was consistent with their findings, since teachers in their study expressed generally high interaction parameter control over even their lowest expectation students. They noted that had their sample been more diverse (i.e., their school district was largely middle-class with students of above average intelligence) they might have found a stronger relation to interaction parameter control perceptions.

As their second conceptual revision, Cooper and Good suggested that student perceptions needed to be given more of a role in the model. They noted that while students were only marginally accurate in assessing how frequently they received particular teacher behaviors relative to their classmates, these social comparison perceptions, accurate or not, were quite strongly related to self-efficacy beliefs and closely paralleled the model's predictions. Therefore, it was suggested that the translation of teacher behavior into student perceptions of teacher behavior should be given a formal link in the model's chain. This link would fall between the "teacher use of praise and criticism" and "student self-efficacy beliefs" boxes depicted in Fig. 6-1.

The Generality of the Revised Model

In addition to the conceptual revisions, Cooper and Good (1983) also made some restrictions on the generality of the Expectation Communication Model. The mediators discussed at the beginning of the chapter included those suggested by Cooper and Good, as well as several others. Below, the Expectation Communication Model is examined for the effect each of the aforementioned mediators has on its applicability. In this manner contexts to which the model does not apply can be singled out for needed attention.

Altering or Sustaining Effects.   Cooper (1979a) concluded that the Expectation Communication Model probably described how performance levels of students were sustained as a function of teacher expectations rather than how achievement might be dramatically altered. Indeed, it was suggested that the occurrence of self-fulfilling prophecies was probably very rare because "expectations inappropriate enough to bring about severe biasing cannot be maintained in real-life situations" (p. 392). Cooper also noted that the past research that had been most supportive of expectation effects had been nonmanipulative in nature (i.e., used student achievement or raw teacher rankings as measures of teacher expectation).

In retrospect, it appears this assessment may have been an overly conservative estimate of the occurrence of self-fulfilling prophecies (though it is probably safe to say that sustaining effects are more frequent). For instance, Cooper pointed out that two often cited studies supporting expectation effects (Crano & Mellon, 1978; McDonald & Elias, 1976) were nonmanipulative, quasi-experimental studies. However, the definitions of teacher expectation used in these studies fit into the category of "discrepancy measures" for studying achievement change. That is, Crano and Mellon (1978) used a cross-lagged panel analysis which, to oversimplify, tests whether discrepancies are resolved more often by changes in the teacher's expectations or changes in the student's achievement. McDonald and Elias (1976), on the other hand, identified students with similar achievement but different teacher expectation ratings and then examined achievement differences later in the school year. Thus, achievement change was at issue in both studies, though no manipulation took place. In addition, Cooper, Findley and Good (1982) have since reported a correlation of +.24 between a regression-based discrepancy measure and achievement change over a 6 month period.

If both sustaining and altering expectation effects occur with notable frequency, does the Expectation Communication Model explain them both? In order to answer this question, it must first be decided whether teachers might have separate ways of communicating accurate expectations and over or underestimates of performance. This is unlikely, especially in light of Cooper et als.'s (1982) finding that the amount of improvement a teacher expected a student to make was *not* associated with achievement change. Only measures involving perceived ability (in its raw form or as discrepant from test scores) were predictive of change in student achievement. To suggest that teachers are aware (even subconsciously) of their inaccurate expectancies seems somewhat farfetched. It is more likely, therefore, that teacher communications inform students only about the teacher's perception of their ability. Then, whether these communicated expectations produce altering and/or sustaining effects depends on the perception's accuracy. To be concrete, a teacher who holds some accurate and some inaccurate expectations for student performance can potentially produce both sustaining and altering expectation effects, if the expectations are communicated. However, a teacher who accurately perceives all students' ability might exhibit identical relations between expectations and behavior as the first teacher but, by definition, only produce sustaining effects.

In sum, the communication of teacher expectations probably depends on if and how much of a relation exists between teacher ability or achievement perceptions and teaching behaviors. Whether this communication produces sustaining or altering expectation effects probably depends on the accuracy of the teacher's perceptions. These speculations, of course, await empirical testing.

The Unit of Analysis.   The unit of analysis issue in relation to the Expectation Communication Model engenders two questions. The first question is whether the model explains how expectations affect (1) the relative performance of separate students within the same classroom and (2) the average performance of separate, whole classrooms. The second question is whether the within-classroom process of expectation communication is similar for all classrooms, regardless of between-class differences.

Cooper and Good (1983) expressed disappointment over the model's ability to predict between-class relations. While the model was a good predictor of within-class data, the general pattern of between-class relations did not fit the hypotheses. In suggesting how between-class expectation communication occurs, Cooper and Good wrote:

> The strongest expectation influence at the between-class level may involve Rosenthal's (1974) input factor. The teacher's general expectations for the class may influence the amount of material the teacher presents and the quality of response the teacher is willing to accept before moving on to new material. It is likely that teachers who hold lower expectations for their classrooms as a whole will teach easier lessons, spend less time on rigorous academic activity and accept less than perfect performance before moving on to new or different material [p. 152–153].

This assessment was based on the finding that most significant between-class relations that were uncovered in their study involved the frequency of initiations rather than feedback variables.

Specifically, Cooper and Good found that (1) higher average expectations for a classroom were associated with more frequent initiation of private interactions by students; (2) less perceived teacher control over a classroom was associated with more frequent teacher initiations in private; and (3) classrooms with students who had stronger self-efficacy beliefs also had more frequent teacher initiations in public, as well as generally more academic interactions of all kinds. Only one feedback variable showed a strong between-class relation: classrooms with high self-efficacy students also had less frequent instances of criticism.

Apparently then, whole class expectations are fairly directly communicated through their influence on how much is taught by the teacher and how much active student participation is permitted. Communication of general expectations through the use of feedback and climate is probably rare and probably produces expectation effects only in extreme cases, when a teacher clearly communicates a strong dislike or enthusiasm for a particular group of students. The Expectation Communication Model, then, with its emphasis on affective communications, probably explains the within-class process best. Input differences from the teacher to different students within the same classrooms should be relatively undramatic (compared to between-class differences) because all students are, at the least, exposed to the same lecture content and spend relatively equal amounts of time on academics. Feedback differences, on the other hand, should be heightened within classrooms because of the students' ability to compare the teacher's evaluation of themselves with that of other students.

Is the within-class Expectation Communication Model equally applicable to all classrooms? Cooper and Good (1983) suggested that as general expectations for a class increased the frequency of within-class expectation effects should decrease. This was based on the assumption that teacher perceptions of control over interactions and/or outcomes should become a less important contributor to teaching decisions in higher expectation classrooms. One result of the Cooper and Good study that supported this notion was the finding that low-expectation students received fewer teacher public initiations only in classrooms where expectations were generally low. In high-expectation classrooms the reverse was found.

It could also be suggested that within-class expectation effects may be more frequent in classes where teacher expectations show more variation, whether the expectations are accurate or not. Such classrooms probably allow students to more easily and accurately distinguish where they stand with the teacher. Finally, as noted earlier, teacher personality differences will affect expectation communication and teacher traits at the between-class level of analysis.

In sum, the frequency of within-class expectation effects probably varies as a function of the level and diversity of the expectations for the class as a whole. There is little evidence, however, that the within-class process itself is *qualitatively* affected by between-class distinctions.

Time of the School Year.   The waxing and waning of expectation effects as the school year progresses was discussed earlier in the chapter. Briefly, it was hypothesized that expectations have their greatest impact on student self-perceptions and potential achievement from the second week through the second month of the school year. Self-fulfilling prophecies should be most frequent during this period, but sustaining effects should be equally likely to occur at any time, except perhaps during the final month of school when academic interactions decrease.

While the strength of expectation communication may vary across the year, it is unlikely that the mechanisms through which expectations are communicated change very much. Good, Cooper and Blakey (1980) reported only two teacher behaviors whose frequency of occurrence were related to the time of the school year: As the year progressed teachers initiated fewer interactions in private, while students initiated more interactions in public. In addition, an interaction effect revealed that the positive relation between expectations and the teachers' use of praise diminished from Fall to Winter to Spring. Good et al. (1980) suggested that early in the year teachers may attempt to socialize students into expected patterns of behavior and subsequently ease-up direct efforts in this regard as students begin to fit the pattern. There was no evidence, however, that the early pattern of differential behavior toward highs and lows was replaced by a qualitatively different pattern of discrimination later in the school year.

Subject Matter.   The subject matter should have little impact on how teachers and students communicate, at least at the level of abstraction being dealt with here (i.e., initator, setting, feedback). Several structural variables often associated with subject matters, however, may markedly affect expectation communication. For instance, whether the subject matter is taught to the class as a whole or to smaller subgroups should influence communications. Thus, small homogeneous groups of students may minimize expectation effects within the groups by diminishing the differences students see when they compare themselves to other group members. At the same time, however, by creating between-group expectation differences, the creation of small homogeneous groups within a class may lead to accentuated input and output differences, as discussed earlier. As a case in point, then, if reading is taught in small groups but math is taught to the class as a whole, it might be speculated that reading expectations are communicated more through input and output differences between groups while math expectations are communicated more through affective reinforcements or socioemotional climate.

Two other aspects of subject matter may affect expectation communication. Curriculum materials that are less specific about how a subject should be taught probably leave more potential for expectation effects than instructional materials that are more detailed. Finally, when subject matters are taught through self-pacing or peer-tutoring techniques, teacher expectation effects should be minimized. These instructional techniques are intentionally designed to lessen the salience of teacher perceptions of control over students.

In sum, the instructional context of different subject matters also probably affects both the potential for expectation communication and how the communication occurs. Again, however, this is an area which has undergone scant research attention.

Level of Schooling.   The likelihood that expectation effects occur less frequently and are less dramatic in later levels of schooling was discussed earlier. Along with the unit of analysis and subject matter, however, it is also likely that expectations are communicated differently at different grade levels. This conjecture rests on the assumption that the meaning of affect (both feedback and climate) from the teacher changes as the student grows older. As noted earlier, in lower grades, a teacher's evaluation of a student probably translates fairly directly into the student's self-evaluation. As the child grows older, however, the importance of the teacher to a student's self-image diminishes. The impact that teacher evaluation does have is probably mediated by peer reaction. A teacher's praise or criticism can be either diminishing or enhancing to the student, dependent on the reaction of peers. In addition (and perhaps in recognition of the lessened role), the use of affect in classrooms appears to decrease substantially in grades beyond the primary level (Evertson & Veldman, 1981).

Expectation effects in junior and senior high school are probably more of the between-class variety, involving input and output factors. At these levels of schooling, classes typically represent strict ability groupings and more frequently use the lecture format. These aspects mean within-class effects are less likely and between-class effects are more likely to occur. Once again, however, much research is needed to substantiate these conjectures.

CONCLUSION

This chapter began with the claim that teacher expectation research had uncovered results of both a complex and provocative nature. Hopefully, the intervening pages have convinced skeptical readers that this is, in fact, the case. More importantly, it is hoped readers sense that progress toward understanding has been made over the last decade and a half, but also that much remains to be understood.

More than in most areas of research, findings concerning teacher expectation effects need multiple, systematic replications. The number of intervening variables, the questionable generality of controlled laboratory studies to natural classrooms, and the difficulties inherent in classroom observation all indicate that reliable patterns of relations will be difficult to uncover. Isolated findings must be viewed with skepticism and are best interpreted as generating hypotheses for further study, rather than as uncovering the "natural laws" of classroom life. It is important that expectation researchers value a well-conducted replication attempt as much as a novel study.

The generality of assertions about expectation effects must also be critically tested. In the previous section, many speculations were offered concerning how general the best developed expectation communication model might be. The safest conclusion appears to be that some knowledge of expectation communication in its most important context (early education) is in hand but little is known about if or how expectation effects extend beyond this context. The ruminations on these questions are primarily opinion at this time, but hopefully, they may provide a framework for future study.

Finally, while the focus of this chapter has been on theoretical models, future research must translate these ideas into practical interventions designed to make teacher expectation effects work for, not against, student self-actualization. Can teacher training be modified to inhibit detrimental expectation effects? Can classrooms be designed so that only positive expectations get communicated? What role might parents play in the process? It is the obvious tie between theory, practice, and intervention that gives teacher expectation research its unique character and that draws so many researchers to it.

REFERENCES

Babad, E. Personality correlates of susceptibility to biasing information. *Journal of Personality and Social Psychology*, 1979, *37*, 195–202.

Brophy, J. & Good, T. Teachers' communication of differential expectations for children's classroom performance: Some behavioral data. *Journal of Educational Psychology*, 1970, *61*, 365–374.

Brophy, J. & Good, T. *Teacher–student relationships: Causes and consequences.* New York: Holt, Rinehart & Winston, 1974.

Burger, J., Cooper, H. & Good, T. The effects of outcome on teacher attributions for student performance. *Personality and Social Psychology Bulletin*, 1982, *8*, 685–690.

Burstein, L. The analysis of multilevel data in educational research and evaluation. In D. Berliner (Ed.), *Review of Research in Education, Vol. 8*. Washington, D.C.: American Educational Research Association, 1980.

Chaikin, A., Sigler, E. & Derlega, V. Nonverbal mediators of teacher expectancy effects. *Journal of Personality and Social Psychology*, 1974, *30*(1), 144–149.

Cooper, H. Controlling personal rewards: Professional teachers differential use of feedback and the effects of feedback on the student's motivation to perform. *Journal of Educational Psychology*, 1977, *69*(4), 419–427.

Cooper, H. Pygmalion grows up: A model for teacher expectation communication and performance influence. *Review of Educational Research*, 1979(a), *49*, 389–410.

Cooper, H. Some effects of performance information on academic expectations. *Journal of Educational Psychology*, 1979(b), *71*, 375–380.

Cooper, H., Burger, J. & Seymour, G. Classroom context and student ability as influences on teacher personal and success expectations. *American Educational Research Journal*, 1979, *16*(2), 189–196.

Cooper, H., Findley, M. & Good, T. The relations between student achievement and various indices of teacher expectations. *Journal of Educational Psychology*, 1982, *74*, 577–579.

Cooper, H. & Good, T. *Pygmalion grows up: Studies in the expectation communication process*. New York: Longman, 1983.

Cooper, H., Hinkel, G. & Good, T. Teachers' beliefs about interaction control and their observed behavioral correlates. *Journal of Educational Psychology*, 1980, *72*(3), 345–354.

Crano, W. & Mellon, P. Causal influences of teacher's expectations on children's academic performance: A cross-lagged panel analysis. *Journal of Educational Psychology*, 1978, *70*(1), 39–49.

Cronbach, L. *Research on classrooms and schools: Formation of questions, design and analysis*. Stanford Evaluation Consortium, Stanford University, Stanford, Calif. 1976, ERIC Document No. ED 135 801.

Dweck, C. & Reppucci, D. Learned helplessness and reinforcement responsibility in children. *Journal of Personality and Social Psychology*, 1973, *25*(1), 109–116.

Elashoff, J. D. & Snow, R. E. (Eds.), *Pygmalion reconsidered*. Worthington, Oh.: Jones, 1971.

Entwisle, D. & Webster, M. Raising children's performance expectations. *Social Science Research*, 1972, *1*, 147–158.

Evertson, C. & Veldman, D. Changes over time in process measures of classroom behavior. *Journal of Educational Psychology*, 1981, *73*, 156–163.

Good, T., Cooper, H. & Blakey, S. Classroom interaction as a fonction of teacher expectations, student sex, and time of year. *Journal of Educational Psychology*, 1980, *72*, 378–385.

Good, T., & Brophy, T. *Educational Psychology: A realistic approach*. (2nd Ed.) New York: Holt, Rinehart, & Winston, 1980.

Kerlinger, F. & Pedhazur, E. *Multiple regression in behavioral research*. New York: Holt, Rinehart & Winston, 1973.

Kester, S. & Letchworth, G. Communication of teacher expectations and their effects on achievement and attitudes of secondary school students. *Journal of Educational Research*, 1972, *66*, 51–55.

Lefcourt, H. (Ed.), *Research with the locus of control construct*. New York: Academic Press, 1981.

Levine, J. M. Social comparison and education. In J. M. Levine & M. C. Wang (Eds.), *Teacher and student perceptions: Implications for learning*. Hillsdale, N.J.: Lawrence Erlbaum Associates, 1983.

Luce, S. & Hoge, R. Relations among teacher rankings, pupil–teacher interactions and academic achievement: A test of the teacher expectancy hypothesis. *American Educational Research Journal*, 1978, *15*(4), 489–500.

McDonald, F. & Elias, P. *The effects of teacher performance on pupil learning*. Beginning Teacher Evaluation Study: Phase II, final report: Vol. 1. Princeton, N.J.: Educational Testing Service, 1976.

Merton, R. K. *Social theory and social structure*. New York: Free Press, 1957.

Richer, S. Reference-group theory and ability grouping: A convergence of sociological theory and educational research. *Sociology of Education*, 1976, *49*, 65–71.

Riemer, B. Influence of causal beliefs on affect and expectancy. *Journal of Personality and Social Psychology*, 1975, *31*, 1163–1167.

Rosenthal, R. *On the social psychology of the self-fulfilling prophecy: Further evidence for Pygmalion effects and their mediating mechanisms*. New York: MSS Modular, 1974.

Rosenthal, R. & Jacobson, L. *Pygmalion in the classroom: Teacher expectation and pupils' intellectual development*. New York: Holt, Rinehart & Winston, 1968.

Salomon, G. Self-fulfilling and self-sustaining prophecies and the behaviors that realize them. *American Psychologist*, 1981, *36*, 1452–1453.

Sarbin, T. & Allen, V. Increasing participation in a natural group setting: A preliminary report. *Psychological Record*, 1968, *18*, 1–7.

Seaver, W. B., Jr. Effects of naturally induced teacher expectancies on the academic performance of pupils in primary grades. Unpublished doctoral dissertation, Northwestern University, 1971.

Seligman, M. *Helplessness: On depression, development and death*. New York: Freeman, 1975.

Smith, M. Meta-analysis of research on teacher expectations. *Evaluation in Education*, 1980, *4*, 53–55.

Taylor, M. Race, sex, and the expression of self-fulfilling prophecies in a laboratory teaching situation. *Journal of Personality and Social Psychology*, 1979, *37*, 897–912.

Weiner, B. An attributional approach for educational psychology. In L. Shulman (Ed.), *Review of research in education* (Vol. 4). Itasca, Ill.: Peacock, 1977.

West, C. & Anderson, T. The question of preponderant causation in teacher expectancy research. *Review of Educational Research*, 1976, *46*, 185–213.

Willis, S. Formation of teachers' expectations of students' academic performance. Unpublished doctoral dissertation, The University of Texas at Austin, 1972.

7

Attribution Theory and Teacher Expectancy

Penelope L. Peterson
Sharon A. Barger
University of Wisconsin-Madison

The previous chapters introduced the concept of teacher expectancy, discussed several methodological and analytical problems in investigating teacher expectancy effects and provided a review of the history of expectancy research. The purpose of this chapter is to discuss how attribution theory can be applied to the interpretation of teacher expectancy effects.

Darley and Fazio (1980) have presented a model showing how attributions play a significant role in the self-fulfilling prophecy and teacher expectancy effects. Discussion of this model requires an understanding of the nature of attribution theory. Thus, we begin this chapter with a brief overview of the history and development of attribution theory.

The History and Development of Attribution Theory

There is no single theory of attribution. However, attribution theories are generally concerned with investigating the antecedents and consequences of human perceptions of causality. One important contributor to the development of attribution theory was Fritz Heider. Heider (1958) theorized that the attributions that an individual makes concerning a behavior or an event depend upon factors within the person as well as factors within the environment. Heider stated that in order to determine the causes of an event or behavior, people conduct simple experiments. In these experiments, people investigate the causal factors that may covary with the specific event or behavior. The perceived cause of an event depends on which causal factors the individual perceives as consistently covarying with the event or behavior.

Kelley (1967) elaborated on Heider's ideas by systematizing the factors which individuals use in making causal attributions to either personal or environmental factors. Kelley developed a covariation principle. According to Kelley, the covariation of potential causal factors is examined across situations, persons, time, and modalities. Kelley defined three types of information that people use in trying to determine whether an outcome covaries with some aspect of the person, environmental stimulus or the specific present situation. The three types of information are distinctiveness, consensus, and consistency.

Kelley defined distinctiveness information as whether or not a response occurs in the presence of other entities. Consensus information refers to whether or not people in the presence of some entity, make a similar response. Consistency information refers to whether the same response occurs each and every time the same entity is present. Kelley's theory, therefore, predicts that under high consensus, high distinctiveness, and high consistency, a response is most likely to be attributed to the stimulus. In conditions where the information indicates low consensus, low distinctiveness, and high consistency, an attribution to the person is most likely to occur.

Kelley's predictions were tested by McArthur (1972). McArthur had subjects complete a questionnaire in which they rated 16 different responses made by other people. These responses were accompanied by varying degrees of consensus, distinctiveness, and consistency information. The results of the experiment confirmed Kelley's predictions. A study by Orvis, Cunningham and Kelley (1975) replicated McArthur's (1972) findings and also found that individuals were able to use partial evidence to reach logical causal inferences despite the incompleteness of the information they received.

Kelley (1972) offered an explanation for how individuals make causal attributions in the absence of sufficient information. Kelley hypothesized that through experiences individuals develop sets of rules which form causal schemata. When individuals are not provided with sufficient information, these general rules are used in conjunction with whatever information is provided.

Weiner's Attribution Theory

Weiner, Frieze, Kukla, Reed, Rest and Rosenbaum (1971) brought attribution theory into the educational realm by suggesting four attribution categories or the perceived causes of success and failure. These are ability, effort, task difficulty, and luck. According to Weiner (1980) an ability inference about a success or failure depends upon past information, and consistent past information is important. If an individual receives consistently high grades on most past mathematics exams, then success, such as a high grade on a current exam, is likely to be attributed to ability. Ability, therefore, is defined as the capability of an individual to perform a task.

Effort usually implies how hard one tries to perform a given task. Weiner (1980) stated that the pattern of a person's performance can lead to an effort attribution. A study by Jones, Rock, Shaver, Goethals and Ward (1968) showed that subjects felt that stimulus persons demonstrating an ascending pattern of success tried significantly harder on a task than stimulus persons demonstrating a descending or random pattern of successes. External signs, according to Weiner (1980), also play an important role in making effort attributions. If an individual works persistently on a task and perspires and tenses his/her muscles while working, observers are likely to attribute the individual's success on the task as due to effort.

An inference about task difficulty as the cause of success or failure usually depends upon the performance of others on that task. If an individual fails on a task that most of the other participants also failed, then the individual's failure is most likely to be seen as due to the task being very difficult.

Weiner hypothesized that luck inferences can be the result of task structure on the pattern of outcomes. If the task is perceived as involving chance, such as guessing a winning horse, then the outcome is likely to be attributed in part to luck. When a subject perceives the pattern of outcomes on a task to be random, such as the shaking of dice, then luck is also likely to be attributed cause of the outcome.

Classification by Stability, Locus, and Controllability

Weiner (1979) presented a three dimensional classification of causal attributions for success and failure. (See Table 7.1.) Weiner's classification is a summary of the dimensions which he and other attribution theorists have employed. It includes the following three dimensions: stable–unstable, internal–external, and controllable–uncontrollable.

TABLE 7.1
Causes of Success and Failure, Classified According to Locus,
Stability, and Controllability (From Weiner, 1979)

	Internal		External	
Controllability	Stable	Unstable	Stable	Unstable
Uncontrollable	Ability	Mood	Task Difficulty	Luck
Controllable	Typical Effort	Immediate Effort	Teacher Bias	Unusual Help From Others

The first dimension is stable–unstable. This dimension refers to whether the cause of an outcome is perceived as a variable or a constant characteristic. Ability is an example of a stable characteristic because it fluctuates very little, while luck and effort fluctuate a great deal.

The second dimension of Weiner's classification is internal–external or locus of control. This dimension refers to whether the cause of an outcome is perceived as internal or external to the individual. If an individual fails on exam due to lack of effort, then the cause would be classified as internal because effort is seen as a cause within the person. If an individual fails the exam due to task difficulty, then the cause would be classified as external because the cause is not within the individual. This second dimension can be considered together with the dimension of stability. An individual may consistently put forth effort whenever taking an exam and, therefore, perform well on exams. Effort is an internal characteristic of the individual and if the individual consistently trys hard, then typical effort can also be classified as stable. In this example, typical effort is both an internal and a stable cause of the outcome.

The third dimension, controllable–uncontrollable, pertains to whether the cause of an outcome is perceived as controllable. Effort would be an example of a controllable cause of an outcome. An individual determines how much work he or she puts into performing a task. Weiner (1979) suggested that the difficulty of a task is an uncontrollable cause of performance because the individual has no control over how difficult the teacher makes the exam. This last dimension can be considered in relation to the other two dimensions. An attribution to ability (aptitude) would be classified as stable, internal, and uncontrollable. An attribution to immediate effort would be classified as internal, unstable, and controllable. However, Weiner et al. (1971) presented only a two dimensional classification that included locus of control and stability/instability. Thus, in the absence of a distinction between "typical effort" and "immediate effort," researchers have considered effort attributions to be internal, unstable attributions.

Attributions influence behavior in many ways. The type of attribution an observer makes regarding the perceived cause of an event can potentially influence the observer's future behavior. Berkowitz (1980) stated that if a bystander observes that a person on the street needs help and attributes the person's need to an external factor, the bystander is more likely to aid the person than if the cause is perceived as due to an internal factor. Berkowitz argued that attributing need to an external cause makes the need appear more legitimate.

Similarly, the attributions that individuals make concerning the perceived causes of their own behavior may influence their future behavior. Attribution theorists have discussed the concept of learned helplessness. (See for example, Dweck, 1975). Learned helplessness occurs when individuals perceive that outcomes are not influenced by their own behavior. If a girl feels that regardless of what she does, she will not succeed at dancing because the dance instructor dislikes her, the girl is perceiving external, uncontrollable factors as responsible for her failure. In cases of learned helplessness, the individual tends to withdraw and discontinue trying to perform the task.

These two examples demonstrate the potential role that the perceived cause of an outcome can play in determining future behavior. Both an observer and a participant can be influenced by their perceptions of causality.

Conceptualizing the Role of Attributions in the Expectancy Process

Darley and Fazio (1980) have proposed a model for conceptualizing expectancy effects that recognizes the importance of causal attributions. Brophy (1982) has used this model to refer to the sequence of events that lead to teacher expectancy effects on students. This sequence of events may be summarized as follows:

1. The teacher forms an expectancy.
2. The teacher acts.
3. The student interprets the teacher's actions.
4. The student responds.
5. The teacher interprets the student's response.
6. The student perceives his or her own actions.

Step 1

In the first step of the sequence of events, the teacher forms an expectancy about the behavior of the student. As Darley and Fazio (1980) pointed out, these expectancies can be about specific behaviors that the teacher expects the student to engage in. However, attribution theories suggest that these expectancies are more likely to be about the intentions and dispositions of the student, from which the teacher would predict a general class of behavior. Thus, from observation of the student's behavior and from observation of the student's past performance, the teacher may make attributions about the student's disposition, for example, that the student is either high or low in ability.

In this chapter we argue that the important expectancies formed by the teacher are those that deal with the teacher's attributions for a student's successes and failures. Thus, there are several important questions that need to be addressed. How do teachers come to develop attributions for the cause of students' performance, particularly achievement? Second, what is the relationship between students' past performance (i.e., successes or failures) and teachers' attributions? Third, what is the relationship between student characteristics, such as race, socioeconomic status (SES), and sex, and teachers' attributions for the cause of students' performance?

Step 2

In the second step of the sequence, the teacher's expectancies cause the teacher to engage or not to engage in certain behaviors with the target student. Because the relationship between teacher expectancies and teacher behavior has been discussed extensively on other chapters (See for example, Chapter 12), it will not be discussed here. Suffice it to say that most research has demonstrated a significant relationship between teachers' expectancies and teachers' actions toward the students for whom the expectancies are held. The focus of concern in this chapter is on the relationship between teachers' attributions and teachers' actions. Thus, the question to be addressed in this chapter is "What is the relationship between teachers' attributions for causes of students' performance and teachers' actions or behavior toward those students in the classroom?"

Step 3

In step three of the sequence, the student interprets the teacher's action. As Darley and Fazio (1980) indicate, it is at this point in the sequence that the student's self-attributions come into play. In addition, the student may attribute the teacher's actions to dispositional characteristics of the teacher (e.g., the teacher is "tough"), or the student may attribute the teacher's actions to the situation. Finally, the student may attribute the teacher's actions to an interaction of the above three determinants namely, the student's self-attributions, the teacher's disposition, and the situation. Unfortunately, little research has been done on the target person's interpretation of a perceiver's action in an interaction setting. However, recent research on students' perceptions presented in Chapter 13 of this volume are relevant here.

Step 4

In step four of the sequence, the student reponds. If the student believes that the teacher's behavior was due to situational factors or due to the disposition of the teacher, then the student's response may be quite different than if the student believes that the teacher's actions were related in some way to attributes of the student himself or herself. If, for example, as a result of the teacher's actions, the student comes to believe that his or her failure in an academic situation is due to a lack of ability, then his or her future behavior may be affected. Because ability is viewed as a stable factor and, as such, is difficult to change, the student may come to view failure as inevitable and cease to put forth any effort in classroom work. This phenomena of "learned helplessness" has been shown to have particularly debilitating effects on a student's achievement and performance in the classroom. (See Chapter 8, this volume, for a complete discussion of learned helplessness).

Step 5

The student's response will then be interpreted by the teacher. The teacher's interpretation may confirm or disconfirm the teacher's original expectancy. Two previous research findings are relevant here. First, psychological research by Darley and Fazio (1980) suggests the existence of an "impression maintenance attributional bias" such that "the perceiver attributes expectation-consistent behavior to the dispositional qualities of the target and expectation-inconsistent behavior to situational forces" (p. 876). For example, if the student's response was consistent with the teacher's expectation, the teacher would be likely to attribute the behavior to the student's disposition while if the student's behavior was inconsistent with expectancy, the teacher would be likely to attribute the behavior to the situation. Take, for example, the case of a student viewed by the teacher as low in ability and whose past failures the teacher has attributed to the student's lack of ability. If this student were to respond by putting forth little effort and, as a result, not do well on his or her homework assignment, the teacher would interpret the student's response—namely, failure on the homework assignment—as consistent with the teacher's initial expectancy of the student as being lacking in ability. If, on the other hand, the student put forth a great deal of effort and succeeded on the homework assignment, the teacher would be likely not to consider this behavior as reflective of the student's true disposition but rather, as due to a particular aspect of the situation. The teacher might believe that the student succeeded because he or she received help on the homework from parents or friends. Thus, one insidious outcome of the impression-maintenance attribution bias is that even if a student works hard to dispel a teacher's misconception of his or her lack of ability, the student might not receive full credit from the teacher for his or her actions.

A second major research finding relevant to the teacher's interpretation of the student's response is the finding that a participant is likely to underestimate the role of his or her own earlier action in determining the target person's response. (See for example, Jones & Nisbett, 1971). Thus, a teacher may underestimate the role of his or her own initial action in determining the student's response and is likely to conclude the behavior is an accurate reflection of the student's disposition. Again, the result is that, in the teacher's own eyes, the student's response confirms the teacher's initial expectancy.

Step 6

Finally, the student's perceptions of his or her own actions are likely to lead to the maintenance and confirmation of the teacher's original impression of the student. Darley and Fazio (1980) indicated that the student's perception of his or her own actions may lead the student to have a new attitude toward the situation, the teacher, or himself/herself. All of these new attitudes would be likely to lead to similar expectancy-confirming behavior in the future.

In summary, teachers' attributions come into play in steps one, two, and five of the model while students' attributions are important in steps three and six. In the remainder of this chapter, we discuss how teachers' attributions play a role in these steps of the teacher expectancy process. Because students' attributions are considered extensively in Chapters 8 and 13 of this volume, our discussion focuses only on the role of teacher's attributions in the expectancy process.

FACTORS AFFECTING THE FORMATION OF TEACHERS' ATTRIBUTIONS

As described above, an important question that needs to be considered is how teachers come to hold attributions for the causes of a given student's successes and failures. We will consider three major factors that may affect the formation of teachers' attributions: (a) the student's past performance; (b) characteristics of the student including race, SES, and sex; and (c) the effect on teachers' attributions of being an "actor" or participant in the student–teacher interaction process.

Student's Past Performance and Present Performance: The "Consistency Hypothesis"

The past performance of the student is likely to have a profound influence on the development of a teacher's attributions. Thus, the student's past history of successes and failures will undoubtedly influence the teacher's attributions for the student's present and future performance. Consistent with the "impression-maintenance attributional bias" described above, Weiner (1979) has noted that the perceived causes of successes and failures are related to the initial expectancy of success. Unexpected outcomes lead to unstable attributions, particularly luck, and expected outcomes lead to stable attributions. Thus, one would hypothesize that this pattern would hold true for teachers' attributions for the cause of students' successes and failures.

Research on teachers' attributions has tended to support the above "consistency hypothesis." In a study by Borko and Shavelson (1978), teachers were given scenarios describing a fictitious student and were asked to rate the extent to which a student's academic success was due to ability, effort, exam difficulty, and luck. Borko and Shavelson (1978) found that if a teacher received negative information about the student and if the student were presently succeeding, (i.e., an inconsistent pattern), the teacher was most likely to attribute the student's present success to luck. Moreover, when teachers were given positive information on a student, who was presently succeeding, the teachers were likely to attribute the student's present success to ability and/or effort. These results suggest that background information provided to teachers can influence the degree to which a student's success or failure is "expected" or "unexpected" by the teacher. Thus, background information may interact with student's performance to determine the formation of teachers' attributions.

One source or background information available to teachers is diagnostic labels. Such labels may lead the teacher to form different attributions for the causes of a student's performance depending on the label given the student.

Palmer (1979) provided elementary teachers with background information describing a student as normal achieving (NA), educationally handicapped (EH) or educable mentally retarded (EMR). Teachers were then given the student's current level of performance which was described as above or below grade-level. Results indicated that diagnostic labels affected teachers' attributions for below grade-level performance but not teachers' attributions for grade-level performance. Teachers judged lack of student ability as being more of a factor in determining the below grade-level performance of EMR students than of either NA or EH students. These findings support the above hypothesis that if a student's past and current performance are consistent (e.g., EMR student's below grade-level performance), the student's present performance is attributed to internal, stable factors, such as student ability.

Hanes (1979) also looked at the influence of background information on teachers' attributions for success or failure. Teacher trainees were given descriptions of students who were labeled either normal or gifted and were described as succeeding or failing. The teacher trainees then rated the extent to which they attributed the student's performance to each of the following factors: ability, effort, ease/difficulty of the task, or guessing. Results indicated that teachers' attributions depended on the student's performance (success or failure) as well as the background information (gifted or normal) provided about the students. Teachers were more likely to attribute a successful performance by gifted students to ability rather than to other factors. Teachers were likely to attribute a successful performance by normal students to effort rather than to other factors. Teachers attributed a failing performance by normal students to the difficulty of the task while they attributed a failing performance by gifted students to lack of ability and unlucky guessing. Again, these findings support the above hypothesis that unexpected outcomes lead to unstable attributions. In the Hanes (1979) study, the teacher trainees were instructed that they would be reading descriptions about either gifted or normal students. Thus, in comparison to gifted students, teacher trainees would expect normal students to fail more often than gifted students and gifted students to succeed more often than they would fail. Success by a normal student in this study would have been unexpected and was attributed to an unstable attribution, namely effort. Failure, on the other hand, would have been expected for these students and thus was attributed to a stable outcome, namely task difficulty. In contrast, success was expected of the gifted students and was attributed to a stable attribution—ability. Failure by gifted students would be an unexpected outcome, which was attributed to an unstable factor—unlucky guessing. The one puzzling finding is why failure by gifted students was equally as often attributed to their lack of ability as to their unlucky guessing.

The consistency hypothesis is also supported by the findings of a study by Rejeski and McCook (1980). Elementary school teachers completed a questionnaire in which both students' ability and performance outcomes (success or failure) were manipulated as variables. When teachers were told that a student was high in ability, the teachers were more likely to attribute the student's success (an expected event) to ability (a stable factor) and the student's failure (an unexpected event) to task difficulty and lack of effort (unstable factors). In contrast, when teachers were told that a student was low in ability, they attributed success (an unexpected event) to the student's effort (an unstable factor) and failure (an expected event) to task difficulty and lack of ability (stable factors).

Finally, results of a study by Cooper and Burger (1980) provide further support for the "consistency hypothesis." Cooper and Burger asked 43 teachers to list the initials of three students in their most recent classes whom they expected to do well academically and three whom they expected to do poorly. The teachers were then given four pages, each referring to a success or failure by a student group, and they were asked to list causal attributions for the successes and failures of both high- and low-expectancy students. Cooper and Burger hypothesized that unexpected events, that is, high-expectancy failure and low-expectancy success, would lead to less stable attributions than expected events. The results supported their hypothesis. Expected events led to greater use by teachers of internal stable attributions, while unexpected events led to greater use by teachers of internal unstable attributions. Teachers cited external causes more frequently for unexpected events.

In summary, research findings suggest that teachers use information about a student's past performance to make attributions for the causes of a student's present performance. Moreover, teachers tend to use information about past and present performance to form attributions that maintain a "consistent" picture of the causes of a student's performance.

We now examine a second factor that may affect teachers' attributions—student characteristics. Characteristics to be considered include the race, social class, and sex of the student.

Race, Social Class, and Sex of Student

Four studies have examined the effect of race of student on the kinds of attributions made by teachers. In all four studies, teachers were given a questionnaire describing students who varied in characteristics such as race, social class, and sex, and teachers were asked to make attributions for the causes of the student's performance.

In a study by Cooper, Baron, and Lowe (1975), preservice elementary education majors and introductory psychology majors were asked to complete a locus of control measure (The Intellectual Achievement Responsibility Scale) for a student who had been described. Results indicated that introductory psychology students and elementary education majors did not differ significantly in the locus of control scores they assigned to the student. Thus, the respondent types are merged in the subsequent discussion, and we discuss them as attributions of "teacher trainees". Teacher trainees attributed failure to internal causes (ability or effort) rather than external causes (task difficulty or luck) significantly more often for white middle-class students than for white lower-class students, black lower-class students, or black middle-class students. In other words, the failure of the latter three types of students was attributed to external causes rather than internal causes significantly more often for these students than for white middle-class students. Teachers trainees' attributions for success did not differ for each of the four types of students.

Similar results were obtained by Wiley and Eskilson (1978). Elementary school teachers were asked to rate a fictional record file of an elementary child who was presented either as performing well in the classroom and scoring well above average on a standardized achievement test or as performing poorly in school and scoring below average on a standardized achievement test. Teachers were asked to rate the probable importance of each of the following factors in influencing the student's past performance: teachers, parental encouragement, the child's own efforts, and chance. They were also asked to list additional likely causes for the student's previous academic performance. Results indicated that internal factors rather than external factors were mentioned significantly more often as causes for the performance of black students than for the performance of white students. Unfortunately, Wiley and Eskilson (1978) did not investigate social class as a variable. However, taken together with the findings of the Cooper, Baron, and Lowe (1975) study, these findings suggest a tendency for teachers to attribute the performance of black students to external factors and the performance of white students to internal factors. Unfortunately, neither study differentiated internal and external attributions further to identify whether internal attributions were more often to ability or effort and whether external attributions were more often to task difficulty or luck. From the previous discussion of the consistency hypothesis we have seen that the stability of attributions has been found to be an important dimension that is not taken into account by the internal/external classification.

In support of this position, two studies found the picture to be slightly more complex when teachers' internal and external attributions for black and white students were broken down into specific attributions. Domingo-Llacuna (1976) found that the social class of the student did not significantly affect preservice teachers' attributions for a student's performance. Race of the student, on the other hand, did have a significant effect on teacher trainees' attributions. As in the Cooper et al. (1975) study, Domingo-Llacuna had preservice teachers complete the Intellectual Achievement Responsibility Scale, but she broke down the internal score from that scale into average effort and average ability scores. She found that teacher trainees attributed students' successes and failures to effort significantly more often for black students than for white students. On the other hand, they attributed successes and failures to ability significantly more often for white students than for black students.

Finally, Feuquay (1979) had preservice teachers rate descriptions of six fictitious students, two students from each of three races (black, white, Indian). Within each race, one student was described as succeeding and one as failing. Feuquay found that teacher trainees did not make significantly different attributions between the races for students who had succeeded, but they did make significantly different attributions for students who failed. Teacher trainees attributed failure to bad luck significantly more frequently for black students and Indians than for white students. Preservice teachers' attributions to luck did not differ significantly for black students and Indians.

A potential problem with the Feuquay study is that teacher trainees were provided with more than one stimulus student to rate. This situation is different from the situation in the studies by Cooper et al. (1975), Wiley and Eskilson (1978), and Domingo-Llacuna (1976), where teachers were given only one stimulus child to rate. When given more than one stimulus student, the teachers may have engaged in a comparison process between the students which significantly altered their attributional patterns. Moreover, providing the teacher trainees with more than one student to rate would make it more likely that the trainee would guess that race was a variable of interest in the research study.

In summary, these four studies do not provide a clear picture of how race and social class affect teachers' attributions. Although it is reasonable to hypothesize that teachers perceive that black students have less control over their successes and failures than white students and that black students' failures are due to bad luck rather than lack of ability, this hypothesis appears to be unnecessarily simplistic. The effect of race of student seems to be mediated by social class of the student. In addition, teachers' attributions must be described more specifically than on only the internal/external continuum.

In contrast to the findings for race and social class, sex of student has not been shown to be a significant factor affecting teachers' attributions. For example, Wiley and Eskilson (1978) investigated sex of student as one of the variables in the study described above. They found that sex of the stimulus student in the description had no significant effect on the causal attributions of teachers for students' performance. Similar nonsignificant effects of sex were reported by Hanes (1979). On the other hand, Dweck, Davidson, Nelson, and Enna, 1978, reported significant sex differences in the attributional statements that teachers made to boys and girls in their classrooms. They found that teachers were more likely to make statements attributing failure to a lack of effort for boys than for girls. However, a subsequent study by Heller and Parsons (1981) failed to replicate the findings of Dweck et al. (1978). Heller and Parsons found no sex differences in the attributional statements that teachers made to students following unsuccessful classroom performance by the student.

The Effect of Being an "Actor" Rather than an "Observer"

Attribution theorists have hypothesized that a person's causal attributions will be affected by whether the person is an actor in the situation (i.e., one of the participants in the social interaction) or an observer (i.e., an onlooker who is uninvolved in the social interaction). (See for example, Jones & Nisbett, 1971). Thus in the classroom, because they are active participants in the social interaction process that leads to students' successes and failures, teachers' attributions for the performance of students might be systematically affected or biased by their role as actor rather than observer. The teacher's role in the situation may lead to two different patterns of teachers attributions: (a) ego-enhancing attributions or (b) counter-defensive attributions. Ego-enhancing or self-serving attributions occur when, as the result of being a participant in the social interaction, teachers attribute a student's successful performance to themselves as teachers and a student's failure to factors other than the teacher (i.e. characteristics of the student or the situation). Thus, teachers enhance their egos by accepting responsibility for students' successes while blaming the students for their failures. In contrast, the teachers' role as actor may lead them to form counter-defensive attributions in which teachers accept responsibility for students' failures and give credit to the students themselves for successes.

Four studies have found that being an actor in the situation leads the teacher to form ego-enhancing attributions for the student's performance. In the earliest study, Johnson, Feigenbaum, and Weiby (1964) had preservice teachers enrolled in an educational psychology course teach a mathematics lesson to two fictitious fourth-grade boys. The teacher "taught" these students via a one-way microphone system. Results indicated that teachers attributed an improvement in the student's performance to themselves as teachers. They attributed a lack of improvement to the student himself (ego-enhancing attribution).

The results of a study by Beckman (1970) also showed ego-enhancing attributions by the teacher. Preservice teachers were the *teachers,* and undergraduate psychology students were the *observers.* The task was to teach mathematics to two fictitious elementary school children via the same kind of one-way microphone system as was used in the Johnson et al. (1964) study. Beckman (1970) found that teachers attributed a student's successful performance to themselves as teachers, and a student's failure to factors other than the teacher (i.e., characteristics of the student or the situation). Observers attributions, on the other hand, were not affected by the student's performance. An obvious problem with the Beckman (1970) study is that the role of teacher versus observer was confounded with teaching experience of the undergraduate subjects—the teachers had actually had some teaching experience while the observers had not.

A similar problem exists in a study by Brandt, Hayden, and Brophy (1975) which employed a teaching task similar to the tasks used by Johnson et al. (1964) and Beckman (1970). The teachers were undergraduate students in introductory psychology who had had no previous experience in teaching. The task was teaching government to a fictitious fourth-grade student in four 4 minute lectures. As in the Johnson et al. (1964) and Beckman (1970) studies, Brandt et al. (1975) found that teachers made ego-enhancing attributions. Teachers who taught successful students assigned more responsibility to themselves rather than to the student than did teachers who taught unsuccessful students.

A fourth study by Wiley and Eskilson (1978) used a questionnaire rather than the stimulated teaching situation described in the previous three studies. In the Wiley and Eskilson (1978) study, 126 elementary school teachers completed an attribution questionnaire after reviewing the file of a fictitious student who was one of a number of a pool of students who varied systematically in sex, race, and past performance. Wiley and Eskilson found that teachers were rated as playing a more important role in the successful performance of a student than in the unsuccessful performance of a student (i.e., ego-enhancing attributions).

In contrast to the above support for a self-serving or ego-enhancing bias in teachers' attributions, three studies have found support for a counter-defensive bias in teachers' attributions. Beckman (1973) assigned preservice and in-service teachers at random to be either a teacher or an observer. Thus, the earlier problem of confounding of teacher role with teaching experience noted in the Beckman (1970) study was remedied in this study. The task was a simulated teaching task in which the teacher taught mathematics to a fictitious fifth grade student via a one-way microphone. In contrast to her previous results, Beckman (1973) found that teachers attributed any change in the student's performance to themselves more often than did observers. In particular, teachers were more likely to attribute a student's decreasing performance to themselves (i.e., counter-defensive attributions) more often than did observers.

In contrast to the previous studies in which fictitious students were used, Ross, Bierbrauer, and Polly (1974) and Ames (1975) used a teaching task in which the student was an actual student confederate of the experimenter. In both studies the results indicated that teachers tended to make counter—defensive attributions. Ross et al. (1974) had preservice teachers, in-service teachers, and undergraduate students teach spelling to a sixth grade confederate of the experimenter. Additional undergraduate students served as observers. Results indicated that teachers attributed the student's failure more often to themselves than to the student and attributed the student's success more often to the student than to the teacher. This effect was more pronounced for actual preservice and in-service teachers than for undergraduate teachers. Undergraduate observers and teachers did not differ significantly in their attributions. Ames (1975) had undergraduate students in educational psychology teach a concept classification task to a 10 year old male confederate. He found that teachers attributed a student's failure significantly more often to themselves than to the student or the situation. They attributed the student's success significantly more often to the student himself (i.e., counter-defensive attributions).

On the one hand, these latter studies, which showed that teachers tend to form counter-defensive attributions, seem to conflict with the results of the previous studies, which indicated a self-serving or ego-enhancing bias in teachers' attributions. On the other hand, the results of the studies may be interpreted as indicating that teachers are less self-serving in their attributions in more naturalistic situations. In the two studies (Ross et al., 1974; Ames, 1975) that employed an actual student confederate and permitted the teacher to interact during teaching with the actual student, the results indicated that teachers were counter-defensive in their attributions rather than self-serving. Thus, one might reasonably argue from the results of the Ross et al. (1974) and Ames (1975) studies (which are more similar to the situation a teacher faces in an actual classroom than the previous experimental studies by Johnson et al., 1964; Beckman, 1970; and Beckman, 1973) that actual teachers in real-world classroom settings are more likely to be counter-defensive than self-serving in their attributions for the causes of students' performance.

Why might teachers be more likely to make counter-defensive attributions than self-serving attributions? Tetlock (1980) hypothesized that teachers' counter-defensive attributions are "self presentations" designed to create favorable impressions in others. To investigate this hypothesis, Tetlock had undergraduate students in introductory psychology serve as observers. The observers read simulated materials from the study by Ross et al. (1974). These materials included descriptions of the teachers' attributions for the causes of the student's performance in the simulated teaching situation. Tetlock varied the teachers' attributions systematically from highly ego-enhancing to highly counter-defensive. After reading the simulated materials, the observers rated the competence of the teachers in the study. Consistent with the self-presentation hypothesis, Tetlock found that observers rated moderately counter-defensive teachers (like those in the Ross et al. study) as significantly more competent than the moderately or highly defensive (ego-enhancing) teacher. An obvious implication of this finding is that in a naturalistic setting, teachers would be more likely to be concerned about the impression that they are making on persons that they come into contact with on a daily and regular basis including students, parents of students, fellow teachers, and the principal. Thus, teachers would tend to make counter-defensive attributions in order to enhance their perceived competence.

Although the data suggest that teachers in an actual classroom setting would tend to be counter-defensive, only one study has investigated teachers' attributions for the performance of their students in an actual classroom setting with the intent of investigating whether teachers are self-serving or counter-defensive. Beckman (1976) asked nine teachers of fourth, fifth, and sixth grade students to identify high, medium, and low performing students in their classes. Each teacher then assigned attributions for the performance of the students in his or her class. In addition, one parent of each student was asked to make attributions for his or her child's performance. Unfortunately, only nine teachers were included in the study with 49 parents. An additional problem was that parents rated only their own children, while teachers rated all students in their classes thereby introducing the possibility of teachers making normative comparisons in their attributions and parents not making such comparisons. In addition, 40% of the students in the study were from minority groups, but race was not analyzed as a factor. As described above, race has been shown to affect teachers' attributions and thus may have been a confounding variable in the study.

Perhaps because of these problems, Beckman's (1976) results do not correspond to previous studies. She found neither a counter-defensive nor a self-serving bias, but rather a "humility" bias. On open-ended questions, parents of successful students were more likely to mention teaching as an important factor in determining students' performance than did teachers. In fact, Beckman noted that teachers *never* mentioned teaching as a factor on open-ended questions. On structured questions, parents attributed performance at all levels to teacher factors as often as to child factors (i.e., ability and effort), while teachers attributed performance more often to child factors than to their own teaching. Thus, the results of this study indicated that teachers assigned less responsibility to themselves for students' performance than did parents, and that teachers tended to assign greater responsibility to students for their performance than to themselves as teachers. These results differ from the results of studies described above. They suggest that perhaps in a situation in which teachers know their students well and in which they are concerned about creating a favorable impression, teachers are likely to make attributions that reflect their own humility. In other words, perhaps teachers never mentioned themselves as a factor on the openended questions because they were being humble about their own effects on students' performance. In this study, teachers obviously knew that parents were making attributions for performance of students in their class, and they also knew that experimenters would be looking at the attributions that both teachers and parents had made. A desire to create a favorable impression may have led to this "humility-bias" in teachers' attributions.

Thus far, we have examined the factors that seem to affect the formation of teachers' attributions. However, for teachers' attributions to play a role in the expectancy process, there must be a relationship between teachers' attributions and their behavior or actions toward students. We now review research that has investigated the link between teachers' attributions and their behavior toward students.

The Relationship Between Teachers' Attributions and Teachers' Behavior

Attribution theorists have argued that there is a significant relationship between teachers' attributions for the causes of a student's performance and the feedback that the teacher gives to the student. An initial study by Weiner and Kukla (1970) showed that the greater the student's success, the more positive the teacher's feedback. Students who were perceived as expending effort were rewarded more and punished less than students perceived as not trying. However, regardless of the attributed effort, low ability students were rewarded more and punished less by teachers than high ability students. Effort was a far more important determinant of reward and punishment than ability. In a recent review of attribution studies, Weiner (1979) has reiterated that: "The data from these investigations conclusively demonstrated that effort is of greater importance than ability in determining reward and punishment. High effort was rewarded more than high ability given success, and lack of effort was punished more than lack of ability given failure (p. 17)."

Most research on the relationship between teachers' attributions and teachers' behavior has tended to support the above statement that teachers' attributions to effort are highly predictive of the teachers' feedback to the student. Research in support of this position includes studies by Covington, Spratt, and Omelich (1980), Cooper and Burger (1980), Medway (1979), Meyer (1979), and Silverstein (1978).

Research Supporting the Relationship Between Teachers' Attributions to Effort and Teachers' Feedback

In the most experimental and least ecologically valid of these studies, Covington, Spratt, and Omelich (1980) asked introductory psychology students to read and rate fictitious students in eight failure situations. The failure situations varied in terms of overall effort by the student, stability of effort expenditure, and the direction of the unstable low effort (increasing or decreasing effort). Half of the introductory psychology students were randomly assigned to play teachers and to dispense feedback to each of the fictitious students. Thus, this study lacked ecological validity both in that a questionnaire method was employed and also that the teachers had had no prior experience as teachers. In spite of these limitations, the results supported the position of Weiner (1979) previously described. Results showed that low student effort, regardless of stability, led to more negative teacher feedback than did high effort. In addition, low effort pupils were seen by teachers as less conscientious, less motivated, less persistent, lazier, and more likely to procrastinate. Indeed, punishment by the teachers did *not* depend on teachers' inferences about student ability but rather on teachers' inferences about students' effort.

Similar findings were reported by Silverstein (1979), who also used a questionnaire methodology, in which 24 fictitious students were described who varied in ability, effort, and performance. This study was slightly more valid because Silverstein employed actual teachers in grades 1–12. The design was a within-subjects design in which each teacher evaluated all 24 fictitious students. Again, a significant main effect of attributions to effort appeared. Students who were perceived by teachers as putting forth greater effort were evaluated more positively regardless of their ability or their performance than students perceived as expending less effort. In fact, attributions to student ability were not a significant predictor of teachers' evaluations.

Cooper and Burger (1980) employed a methodology similar to that of Silverstein. They asked 62 preservice teachers to read a questionnaire in which a successful or unsuccessful student was described. Teachers were then presented with 12 causal attributions for the students' performance. For each attribution, the teachers stated how strongly they would praise or criticize the student and whether they would work more or less with the student. Unfortunately, Cooper and Burger analyzed the results by grouping attributions into categories that differed in stability-instability, internality-externality, and perceived teacher efficacy-inefficacy. Teachers showed a greater intention to criticize a student's failure when it was perceived as due to causes that were internal, unstable, and under little teacher influence. These causes included students' lack of attention and immediate effort. Teachers showed the greatest intention to praise success by students when it was perceived as caused by factors under the teacher's influence including students' attention, immediate effort, and interest. Thus, although the results here are confused by the authors' grouping of attributions, a close inspection of the results seems to suggest that the predominant factor in affecting teachers' use of praise and criticism is the teacher's perception of the student's effort, here defined as including what the authors called "attention", "immediate effort", and "interest".

Further support for the importance of teachers' attributions to effort in determining teachers' use of feedback is provided by a study by Medway (1979). Of the studies reviewed thus far, this study is the most ecologically valid because the teachers were 24 elementary school teachers and the students were actual students in the teachers' classes who had been referred by the teachers for special education. Each teacher was asked to rate the importance of six factors in contributing to the student's major problems. These factors included ability, effort, adjustment or personality, home situation, educational preparation, and teaching. In addition, each teacher was observed interacting with the target child in the classroom. Results indicated that although teachers' attributions were not related to their use of praise with the target student in the classroom, they were related to the teacher's use of criticism. In fact, effort attributions were the only attributions that significantly predicted the teacher's use of criticism with the target student. Attributions to effort or lack of effort accounted for approximately 32% of the variance in teachers' use of criticism with the target students. Teachers gave significantly more criticism to students whose learning problems they perceived as being due to low rather than high effort.

Research Not Finding a Relationship Between Teachers' Attributions and Teachers' Use of Feedback

The only contrary findings have been reported by Cooper and Baron (1977). Their methodology was similar to that of Medway in that they employed actual teachers and students. Eight elementary teachers participated in the study. Within each teacher's class, nine target students were selected for whom the teacher had high, medium, or low expectations, respectively. Teachers were asked to assign responsibility for each student's performance to either (a) personal factors or (b) environmental factors. The teacher's behavior toward the nine target students in the classroom was then observed. Results indicated that teachers' attributions for students' performance did not predict either teachers' use of praise to target students or teachers' use of criticism. On the other hand, teachers' expectations for the students' performance was significant predictors of teachers' use of feedback. Cooper and Baron (1977) did find, however, that teachers' attributions did predict the number of negative teacher–student interactions as well as the frequency of child-created interactions with the target student. As perceived responsibility for success increased, the number of negative interactions decreased and the frequency of child-created interactions decreased. As perceived responsibility for failure increased, so did the child-created procedural interactions between the target student and the teacher. Cooper and Baron interpreted their results to mean that teachers' attributions were not significantly related to teachers' behavior and that the important relationship was between teachers' expectations and teachers' behavior.

The study by Cooper and Baron (1977) has been criticized by Meyer (1979) on the grounds that the attribution questionnaire used by Cooper and Baron did not look specifically at the ability versus effort distinction. Meyer argued that attribution studies have shown that outcomes attributed to high effort will receive more praise than outcomes attributed to low effort. Moreover, outcomes attributed to low ability receive more praise than outcomes attributed to high ability. By merging ability and effort attributions in the same category (personal causation rather than environmental causation), Cooper and Burger (1977) guaranteed that they would not find a significant relationship between teachers' attributions and teachers' use of feedback. In other words, high personal causation due to high effort would lead to the teacher giving more praise, while high personal causation due to high ability would lead to the teacher giving less praise. Thus, the effect of effort attributions would cancel out the effect of ability attributions on teachers' use of feedback. Meyer also presented his own data, which showed a significant positive relationship between attributions to student effort and teachers' use of reward. In contrast, his data on the relationship between attributions to student ability and teachers' use of reward were shown to vary according to the correlation between ability and effort attributions.

In response to Meyer (1979), Cooper and Baron (1979) presented three counterarguments. First, they argued that they did not distinguish between teachers' attributions to effort and ability because these attributions are not orthogonal in real life. In other words, there tends to be a positive relationship between teachers' attributions to effort as a cause of students' performance and their attributions to ability. Second, they argued that laboratory studies such as those done by Meyer (1979) and other attribution theorists show different results from naturalistic studies conducted in the classroom. They suggested that results of laboratory studies should be disregarded in favor of results of naturalistic studies. Finally, they argued that Meyer's own data showed a positive relationship between attributions to student ability and teachers' use of reward such that when student performance was perceived as due to low ability, teachers gave students *less* not *more* reward. Thus, Meyer's own results are contrary to the prediction that he made.

Resolving the Controversy: In Support of a Relationship Between Teachers' Attributions and Teachers' Feedback

In considering the counter arguments of Cooper and Baron (1979), only one of the counter arguments appears to be partially justified. This argument is that Meyer's own data on teachers' attribution to ability do appear to go against Meyer's own hypothesis. However, Meyer's data *do* support the significant relationship between teachers' attributions to student effort and teachers' reward. Moreover, the other two counter arguments do not appear to be tenable. First, although attributions to effort and ability are not orthogonal in real life, this does not prevent one from examining them and making them orthogonal in actual experimental situations. In fact, this is the only way that one can ever separate out what effects are due to teachers' attributions to ability and what affects are due to teachers' attributions to effort. As long as the two are permitted to covary, one can never determine whether effort or ability is the more important factor in affecting teachers' behavior. Cooper and Baron's (1979) argument that laboratory studies show different results than naturalistic studies does not appear to be tenable. Although the majority of the studies described above are experimental or laboratory studies, the one study by Medway (1979) is a naturalistic study that employed methodology similar to that of Cooper and Baron (1977). However, in contrast to the Cooper and Baron (1977) findings, Medway (1979) found that teachers' attributions to student effort were the best predictor of teachers' use of criticism.

Cooper (1979) has gone on to argue that teachers' use of feedback is influenced most by teachers' perceptions of personal control. He has asserted that high- and low-expectation students who exhibit equal effort on a task may not receive identical feedback from the teacher. He has suggested that teachers will not praise strong effort from low students because praise will reduce the future personal control of the teacher by encouraging initiations. In evaluating high students, on the other hand, teachers will dispense praise and criticism with greater dependence on exhibited effort because future control by the teacher of the high student's behavior is not necessary.

Cooper's (1979) explanation does not seem either to be plausible or to be supported by the data for several reasons. First, Cooper's high and low expectancy students appear to be similar to high ability and low ability students. Thus, although Cooper previously argued that ability and effort covary, he himself seems to be making a distinction between ability and effort here. But more importantly, the research described above has shown that when attributions to ability are considered separately from attributions to effort, the important relationship between teachers' attributions and teachers' feedback behavior *is between teachers' attributions to effort and teachers' feedback,* not between teachers' attributions to students' ability and teachers' feedback. Not only is Cooper's (1979) explanation inconsistent with the majority of previous research, but it is also inconsistent with recent findings of a study by Prawat, Byers, and Anderson (1983) who conducted an attributional analysis of teachers' affective reactions to students' successes and failures. This recent study is important because, in the latest formulation of attribution theory by Weiner (1979), affect plays an essential role, serving as the key mediating link between thought (i.e., the attribution) and action. Thus, the study of Prawat et al. (1983) is important because it is a promising new direction for research on the relationship between teachers' attributions and their affective reactions to students' successes and failures.

New Directions for Research on Teachers' Attributions and Teachers' Behavior

Prawat et al. (1983) presented 58 elementary school teachers with 16 different scenarios describing students succeeding or failing on an important exam. Teachers were then asked to rate their own feelings or emotions about the students' success or failure. Prawat et al. (1983) found that "in the only unequivocal main affect, a lack of student effort made teachers angry" (p. 20). Teachers were angry when they perceived that a student had failed due to lack of effort. Also, teachers felt relatively more anger when bright students failed than when less bright students failed. Prawat et al. summarized the findings as follows:

> High ability students who failed through lack of effort, especially if their low motivation represents a consistent pattern, are thus in double jeopardy; First, high ability students *ought* to do well (one teacher wrote the comment "What a waste!" by the scenarios that described this sort of occurrence); teachers are angry when these children do poorly because this seems so unnecessary; Second, teachers are angry when any child fails to put forth effort. The combination of these factors may be more than teachers can stand [p. 20].

These findings underscore the fact that teachers place a high premium on student effort. Thus, these findings further support the statement by Weiner (1979) that teachers' attributions to effort are of greater importance than teachers' attributions to ability in determining teachers' feedback. The study by Prawat et al. (1983) also suggests that the study of teachers' affect may help to elucidate the relationship between teachers' attributions for the cause of students' performance and teachers' behavior toward those students.

In addition to examining the role of teachers' affect or emotions as a mediator between teachers' attributions and behavior, future research should also examine the effect of teachers' attributions on teacher behavior other than feedback. Presumably other kinds of teacher behavior may have an important effect on the social interaction process described by Darley and Fazio (1980).

A study by King (1980), although severely limited in sample size, illustrates the potential importance of other kinds of teacher behavior. King conducted a case study of one sixth grade teacher and two "successful students" in that teacher's class and two "unsuccessful students". The methodology involved interviews with and observations of the students and the teacher. King concluded that the teacher's behavior toward a student depended on whether the student was perceived by the teacher as being successful or unsuccessful and also whether the teacher perceived the student's performance as due to ability or effort. For example, the successful student whose success was attributed to ability by the teacher, was often called on by the teacher when she wanted to change the pace or direction of the lesson. In other words, interactions with this target student were often used by the teacher to steer the class discussion in the direction desired by the teacher. In contrast, the second student, whose success was perceived by the teacher as due to effort, was treated somewhat differently by the teacher. When this student requested help, the teacher expected the student's problem to be minor. She expected that the student would "catch on" by giving the student the merest of clues. The third student, whose lack of success was perceived by the teacher as due to lack of ability, was often provided additional academic support by the teacher. For example, the teacher helped the student to understand a task requirement by working through a problem with the student.

Also, the teacher had frequent interactions with this student. Finally, the fourth student was one whose lack of success was perceived by the teacher as due to lack of effort. The teacher seldom interacted with this student. When interactions did occur with the student, the teacher was mainly engaged in checking on the student's progress or checking to see whether the student had been paying attention.

In a recent study, Brophy and Rohrkemper (1981) also identified teacher behavior patterns that were importantly related to teachers' attributions. These included the types of goals that the teacher set for students, the way in which the teacher controlled and managed the student's behavior, the helping behavior of the teacher, and the type of education that the teacher employed with the student.

In sum, although these findings are suggestive rather than conclusive, they do identify teacher behaviors that might be investigated in future large-scale studies of the relationship of teachers' attributions and teachers' behavior. Such studies might lead to the discovery of teacher behaviors that are even more important in the expectancy sequence of events than is teachers' feedback to students.

SUMMARY AND CONCLUSIONS

In this chapter we attempted to show how teachers' attributions for the causes of a student's performance are influential in the process that leads to teacher expectancy effects on students. To describe the role of teachers' attributions we employed a model of the expectancy process by Darley and Fazio (1980). Using this model, we identified two important questions that needed to be addressed: (a) What factors affect the formation of teachers' attributions for the causes of students' performance? and (b) What is the relationship between teachers' attributions for the causes of students' performance and teachers' behavior toward those students in the classroom?

In reviewing research findings related to the first question, we found evidence for three major factors affecting the formation of teachers' attributions. First, teachers use information on a student's past performance in making attributions about the student's present performance so as to maintain a consistent picture. Thus, an expected outcome, such as success by a student perceived as high in ability, is likely to be attributed by the teacher to a stable factor, such as ability. On the other hand, an unexpected outcome, such as success by a student perceived as low in ability, is likely to be attributed to an unstable factor, such as luck. Second, teachers' attributions seem to be affected by the students' race and socioeconomic status. However, the effect is a complex one, and the research findings are not consistent. Third, teachers' attributions do appear to be affected by the fact that the teacher is an actor rather than an observer in the social interaction process that leads to the student's performance for which the teacher makes causal attributions. Some early research suggested that the teacher's role as actor led to the formation of self-serving or ego-enhancing attributions in which teachers attributed students' successes to themselves and students' failures to the students or to the situation. However, a review of the research to date suggests that in actual classroom situations the teachers' role as actor may lead to the formation of counter-defensive attributions rather than self-serving attributions for the causes of students' performance. Thus, in an actual classroom situation teachers tend to accept responsibility for students' failures and give credit to the student themselves for successes.

After reviewing research on the relationship between teachers' attributions and teachers' behavior toward students, we concluded that there is a significant relationship between teachers' attributions to effort as the cause of a student's performance and the teacher's feedback to that student. Thus, students who are perceived by teachers as expending effort are rewarded more and punished less than students who are perceived as not really trying. In addition, recent research is investigating some promising new leads in attempting to elucidate the relationship between teachers' attributions and teachers' behavior toward students.

ACKNOWLEDGMENT

Work on this chapter was funded by the Wisconsin Center for Education Research which is supported in part by a grant from the National Institute of Education (Grant No. NIE-G-81-0009). The opinions expressed in this chapter do not necessarily reflect the position, policy, or endorsement of the National Institute of Education.

We thank Susan Wescott-Trentadue for her assistance in locating the reference material for this chapter.

REFERENCES

Ames, R. Teachers' attributions of responsibility: Some unexpected nondefensive effects. *Journal of Educational Psychology*, 1975, *67*, 668–676.

Beckman, L. Effects of students' performance on teachers' and observers' attributions of causality. *Journal of Educational Psychology*, 1970, *61*, 76–82.

Beckman, L. Teachers' and observers' perceptions of causality for a child's performance. *Journal of Educational Psychology*, 1973, *65*, 198–204.

Beckman, L. J. Causal attributions of teachers and parents regarding children's performance. *Psychology in the Schools*, 1976, *13*, 212–218.

Berkowitz, L. *A Survey of Social Psychology* (2nd ed.). New York: Holt, Rinehart & Winston, 1980.

Borko, H., & Shavelson, R. J. Teacher' sensitivity to the reliability of information in making causal attributions in an achievement situation. *Journal of Educational Psychology*, 1978, *70*, 271–279.

Brandt, L. J., Hayden, M. E., & Brophy, J. E. Teachers' attitudes and ascription of causation. *Journal of Educational Psychology*, 1975, *67*, 677–682.

Brophy, J. E. *Research on the self-fulfilling prophecy and teacher expectations.* Paper presented at the annual meeting of the American Educational Research Association, New York City, March, 1982.

Brophy, J. E., & Rohrkemper, M. M. The influence of problem ownership on teachers' perceptions of and strategies for coping with problem students. *Journal of Educational Psychology,* 1981, *73,* 295–311.

Cooper, H. M. Pygmalion grows up: A model for teacher expectation, communication, and performance influence. *Review of Educational Research,* 1979, *49,* 389–410.

Cooper, H. M., & Baron, R. M. Academic expectations and attributed responsibility as predictors of professional teachers' reinforcement behavior. *Journal of Educational Psychology,* 1977, *69,* 409–418.

Cooper, H. M., & Baron, R. M. Academic expectations, attributed responsibility, and teachers' reinforcement behavior: A suggested integration of conflicting literatures. *Journal of Educational Psychology,* 1979, *71,* 274–277.

Cooper, H. M., Baron, R. M., & Lowe, C. A. The importance of race and social class information in the formation of expectancies about academic performance. *Journal of Educational Psychology,* 1975, *67,* 312–319.

Cooper, H. M., & Burger, J. M. How teachers explain students' academic performance: A categorization of free response academic attributions. *American Educational Research Journal,* 1980, *17,* 95–109.

Cooper, H. M., & Lowe, C. A. Task information and attributions for academic performance by professional teachers and roleplayers. *Journal of Personality,* 1977, *45,* 469–483.

Covington, M. V., Spratt, M. F., & Omelich, C. L. Is effort enough, or does diligence count too? Student and teacher reactions to effort stability in failure. *Journal of Educational Psychology,* 1980, *72,* 717–729.

Darley, J. M., & Fazio, R. H. Expectancy confirmation processes arising in the social interaction sequence. *American Psychologist,* 1980, *35,* 867–881.

Domingo-Llacuna, E. A. The effect of pupil race, social class, speech and ability on teacher stereotypes and attributions. (Doctoral dissertation, University of Illinois at Urbana-Champaign, 1976). *Dissertation Abstracts International,* 1976, *37,* 2737–2738. (University Microfilms No. 76-24, 072).

Dweck, C. S. The role of expectations and attributions in the alleviation of learned helplessness. *Journal of Personality and Social Psychology,* 1975, *31,* 674–685.

Dweck, C. S., Davidson, W., Nelson, S., & Enna, B. Sex differences in learned helplessness, II: The contingencies of evaluative feedback in the classroom, and III: An experimental analysis. *Developmental Psychology,* 1978, *14,* 268–276.

Feuquay, J. P. Teachers' self-attributions and their projections of student attributions under varying conditions. (Doctoral dissertation, Oklahoma State University, 1979). *Dissertation Abstracts International,* 1979, *40,* 4487. (University Microfilm No. 8003570).

Hanes, B. F. Causal attributions by teacher-trainees for success and failure outcomes of elementary students labeled normal and gifted. (Doctoral dissertation, Oklahoma State University, 1979). *Dissertation Abstracts International,* 1979, *40,* 3198–31995S. (University Microfilms No. 7928212).

Heider, F. *The psychology of interpersonal relations.* New York: Wiley, 1958.

Heller, K. A., & Parsons, J. E. Sex differences in teachers' evaluative feedback and students' expectancies for success in mathematics. *Child Development,* 1981, *52,* 1015–1019.

Johnson, T. J., Feigenbaum, R., & Weiby, M. Some determinants and consequences of the teacher's perception of causation. *Journal of Educational Psychology,* 1964, *55,* 237–246.

Jones, E. E., & Nisbett, R. E. *The actor and observer: Divergent perceptions of the causes of behavior.* Morristown, N.J.: General Learning Press, 1971.

Jones, E. E., Rock, L., Shaver, K. G., Goethals, G. R., & Ward, L. M. Pattern of performance and ability attribution: An unexpected primacy effect. *Journal of Personality and Social Psychology*, 1968, *10*, 317–340.

Kelley, H. H. Attribution theory in social psychology. *Nebraska Symposium on Motivation*, 1967, *15*, 192–238.

Kelley, H. H. *Causal schemata and the attribution process.* Morristown, N.J.: General Learning Press, 1972.

King, L. H. *Student thought processes and the expectancy effect.* (Research report 80-1-8). Perth, Australia: Churchlands College of Advanced Education, 1980.

McArthur, L. A. The how and what of why: Some determinants and consequences of causal attributions. *Journal of Personality and Social Psychology*, 1972, *22*, 171–193.

Medway, F. J. Causal attributions for school-related problems: Teacher perceptions and teacher feedback. *Journal of Educational Psychology*, 1979, *71*, 809–818.

Meyer, W. U. Academic expectations, attributed responsibility, and teacher's reinforcement behavior: A comment on Cooper and Baron, with some additional data. *Journal of Educational Psychology*, 1979, *71*, 269–273.

Orvis, B. R., Cunningham, J. D., & Kelley, H. H. A closer examination of causal inference: The roles of consensus, distinctiveness, and consistency information. *Journal of Personality and Social Psychology*, 1975, *32*, 605–615.

Palmer, D. J. Regular-classroom teachers' attributions and instructional prescriptions for handicapped and nonhandicapped pupils. *Journal of Special Education*, 1979, *13*, 325–337.

Prawat, R. S., Byers, J. L., & Anderson, A. H. An attributional analysis of teachers' affective reactions to student success and failure. *American Educational Research Journal*, 1983, *20*, 137–152.

Rejeski, W. J., & McCook, W. Individual differences in professional teachers' attributions for children's performance outcomes. *Psychological Reports*, 1980, *46*, 1159–1163.

Ross, L., Bierbrauer, G., & Polly, S. Attribution of educational outcomes by professional and nonprofessional instructors. *Journal of Personality and Social Psychology*, 1974, *29*, 609–618.

Silverstein, M. An attributional analysis of teachers' evaluative judgments. (Doctoral dissertation, University of Rhode Island, 1978). *Dissertation Abstracts International*, *39*, 1055–1056C. (University Microfilm No. 7813272).

Tetlock, P. E. Explaining teacher explanations of pupil performance: A self-presentation interpretation. *Social Psychology Quarterly*, 1980, *43*, 283–290.

Weiner, B. A theory of motivation for some classroom experiences. *Journal of Educational Psychology*, 1979, *71*, 3–25.

Weiner, B. *Human Motivation.* New York: Holt, Rinehart & Winston, 1980.

Weiner, B., & Kukla, A. An attributional analysis of achievement motivation. *Journal of Personality and Social Psychology*, 1970, *15*, 1–20.

Weiner, B., Frieze, I. H., Kukla, A., Reed, L., Rest, S., & Rosenbaum, R. M. *Perceiving the causes of success and failure.* Morristown, N.J.: General Learning Press, 1971.

Wiley, M. G., & Eskilson, A. Why did you learn in school today? Teachers' perceptions of causality. *Sociology of Education*, 1978, *51*, 261–269.

8 Teacher Expectations and Student Motivation

Jacquelynne Eccles
Allan Wigfield
University of Michigan

Models of teacher expectancy effects, several of which are reviewed in this volume, suggest that student motivation is an important link between teacher behavior and student achievement. But rarely have teacher expectancy models actually specified how motivation influences student achievement behaviors. Instead, these models have tended to focus on the link between teacher expectancies and teacher behavior, and have treated student motivation as a rather global, ill-defined construct. In this chapter we explore the nature of student motivation and its relationship to achievement. In addition, we suggest specific ways in which teacher behavior either facilitates or retards student motivation. However, since we are most concerned with the debilitating effects of low motivation, our discussion will focus primarily on the dynamics associated with underachievement, or with what Bahad, Jacinto, and Rosenthal (1982) have labeled the ''Golem'' effects of low teacher expectancy.

The link between motivation and school achievement has generated consistent interest over the years among both developmental and educational psychologists. This work is quite complex and has often yielded conflicting findings. Therefore we begin the chapter with some general comments on the relations between motivation and achievement in the classroom. We also suggest a general framework for thinking about student motivation. This framework, based on the students' perspective of school work, will provide the structure for the remaining sections of our chapter.

MOTIVATION AND ACHIEVEMENT IN THE CLASSROOM: A GENERAL OVERVIEW

It is now widely accepted that motivation influences achievement. It is also the case, however, that achievement influences motivation (Uguroglu & Walberg,

1979). Therefore, the link between motivation and achievement can best be characterized as a feedback system; that is, positive motivation facilitates achievement, which, in turn, facilitates continued positive motivation. Or high achievement facilitates the development of positive motivation, which, in turn, facilitates continued high levels of achievement.

Since both of these causal sequences exist, it is difficult to determine how or when the low motivation–low achievement cycle is set into motion. In addition, the optimal point for intervention is not clear. This problem becomes even more complex when we consider that the optimal point may vary depending on the age and sex of the child, and on the nature of the child's motivational problem. The relation between motivation and achievement is different for children of different ages. Not only does the strength of the relationship change with age (it is stronger for older children), but the very nature of the relationship may change with age. Young children appear to be less susceptible to the negative impact of failure on motivation. Negative feedback does not seem to deter their optimism about future success. In addition, their motivational system is relatively simple. In contrast, older children are more susceptible to the negative effects of failure. Furthermore, since the motivational system of older children is more complex than that of the younger child, the magnitude and nature of the effects of failure on motivation depend on characteristics of both the child and the situation. Given these developmental differences, the optimal teaching strategies to avoid negative teacher expectancy effects may be quite different for children of various ages.

The situation is further complicated by the fact that an individual's achievement motivation varies across domains of achievement. One person will like math and hate English; another will like English but hate math. While global measures of motivational constructs (like need achievement, or general self-esteem, or locus of control) exhibit some cross-situational consistency, by far the strongest relations between motivation and achievement emerge for motivational constructs that are specific to the achievement domain being studied, for example, between measures such as confidence in one's math ability and performance on math tests. These results suggest two important points: a) We need to think about the processes that lead to differential motivation across domains, and b) we should pay more attention to intraindividual variations in motivation in developing broad models of the link between motivation and achievement.

Finally, achievement in a school setting has some unique properties that make the relationship between motivation and achievement (especially for low academic skill students) different in the school setting than in the laboratory or nonschool settings. Children have to attend school until they are 16 and have to take a prescribed set of courses at least until high school. They can not escape the situation by choice. This fact has some important implications for our understanding of the link between motivation and achievement in school settings. For example, most motivational theories suggest that one strategy for dealing with low expectations of success and high anxiety is to avoid the situations that elicit these reactions and to focus one's achievement efforts on activities and tasks for which one has reasonably high expectations for success. In fact, in nonschool settings, low expectancies have an adaptive function. They help individuals select tasks of the appropriate level of difficulty. However, for the student doing poorly in school, this option is often not available. Students typically do not have a choice of the tasks they will perform in school. In addition, certain school practices, such as the use of norm referenced grading procedures, whole class instruction, and lockstep curricula, exacerbate this problem because they force low skill-level children into intolerable situations from a motivational perspective. These children are stuck in a situation in which success is really out of their control. They can not select tasks of appropriate difficulty, and so they are essentially doomed to failure or very low level success. This characteristic of the school setting may be responsible for most of the counterproductive academic behaviors we find among low skill-level children (see Covington & Beery, 1976; Eccles, Midgley, & Adler, 1984; Nicholls, 1979).

Having made these general introductory comments, let us turn to the issue of student motivation. What exactly is student motivation and how does it influence achievement? Psychologists have described many motivational constructs and have suggested a variety of hypotheses relating motivation to achievement. Motivation is presumed to impact on achievement behavior in a variety of ways, influencing a wide range of behaviors including persistence in the face of difficulty, the decision to try or not to try a new achievement task, selection of which courses to study and which to avoid, help seeking, test-taking strategies, attention during the learning phase of achievement, etc. Consequently, as we think about the impact of classroom processes on motivation, we have to keep in mind the complexity of this concept called student motivation.

For the student, motivational influences on achievement behaviors can be summarized with three basic questions: Can I succeed at this task?, Do I want to succeed at this task?, and What do I need to do in order to succeed at this task? Achievement is optimized when students' perceive that they can master the material (i.e., when self-concept, expectations, and sense of personal efficacy are high), when they think that mastering the task is important, (i.e., when subjective task value is high), and when their attention is focused on task mastery rather than on the evaluation of their ability (i.e., when mastery orientation is high and test anxiety is low). Conversely, students' efforts to achieve will be lowest when they think they can't master the material; when they think that mastering the material is not very important, very fun or very useful; or when they do not know what they need to do in order to move onto the next step of task mastery. This schema is summarized in Table 8.1.

The remainder of our chapter is organized around these three motivational questions. As we discuss each question, we explore the impact of teacher/student interaction patterns on student motivation, reviewing both the sparse literature

TABLE 8.1
Motivation: The Actor's View

Can I Succeed?	Do I Want to Succeed?	What Do I Need to Do (or Know) in Order to Succeed?
Self-Concept of Ability	Subjective Task Value	Attention
Expectations for Success	Attainment Value	Task Analysis
	Intrinsic Value	
Perceived Control	Utility Value	Mastery Orientation
Learned Helplessness	Personal Needs	Ego-Involved Orientation
Personal Efficacy		
Effectance Motivation	Self-Schemata	Anxiety
	Perceived Cost of Success	
	and Failure	
	Effort Needed to Succeed	
	Loss of Valued Alter-	
	native Opportunities	
	Cost of Failure	
	Affective Experiences	
	Objective Events	
	Psychological Events	

assessing the impact of within-class student/teacher interaction patterns on student motivation and the broader research literature linking general classroom processes to student motivation. We argue that the effects emerging in both of these literatures can be related to teachers' answers to the same questions; that is, Can I succeed at teaching these children? Do I want to put out the effort necessary to teach them? and What do I need to do in order to teach them successfully? More specifically, we argue that teachers' influences on student motivation are mediated by teachers' confidence in their ability to teach *all* students (teachers' sense of personal efficacy) and by the teachers' knowledge of effective teaching practices for children of various ability levels. In other words, we argue that low teacher expectancies have a debilitating effect (a Golem effect) on children's motivation to learn when the teacher believes that low expectancy children can't improve their performance and when the teacher doesn't know effective teaching practices for low skill-level children—that is, when teachers believe that they can not succeed at teaching low skill-level children.

COGNITIVE–MOTIVATIONAL CONSTRUCTS: CAN I SUCCEED?

One of the most important motivational questions facing a student is Can I succeed at this task if I choose to try? Both educators and psychologists have argued that the answer to this question is critical to a student's motivation. If the answer is yes, then a student will, at least, move onto next question—Do I want to? If the answer is no, then the student will, in all likelihood, give up. In this section we discuss the motivational constructs linked to this question; in particular, self-concept of ability and expectations of success, perceived control, and personal efficacy.

The current work assumes that individual differences in these constructs are due mostly to students' interpretations of their own achievement experiences. While objective reality certainly does play a critical role, theorists argue that reality's impact is mediated by causal attributions and by other interpretative processes. They also argue that these interpretative processes are subject to socialization influences. Teachers and parents provide children with interpretations of their achievement experiences. For instance, by responding differently to the failures of high expectancy and low expectancy children, teachers provide the children with (or reinforce) different interpretations of the event. Golem effects are created, it is argued, when the teacher leads low expectancy children to conclude that (or reinforces their conclusion that) their failures are due to lack of ability and that there is little that can be done to turn future failures into future successes. Golem effects can be avoided if the teacher provides these children with a different interpretation; namely, that their failures are due to insufficient skill and that they can achieve success in the future. Basic to this perspective is the assumption that individual differences on these congnitive—motivational variables do, in fact, influence achievement behaviors. Evidence regarding this assumption is discussed below.

SELF-CONCEPT OF ABILITY/EXPECTATIONS FOR FUTURE SUCCESS

Most directly related to teacher expectancy effects are student expectancy effects. Student expectations have been studied under two labels–self-concept of ability and expectations for future success. Since we have found that these two constructs are part of the same factor (Eccles [Parsons], Adler, Futterman, Goff, Kaczala, Meece, & Midgley, 1983), we discuss them together.

Many psychologists have hypothesized a relationship of self-concept of ability and future expectations for success to achievement (e.g., Atkinson, 1964; Brookover & Erickson, 1975; Covington & Beery, 1976; Eccles [Parsons] et al., 1983; Lewin, 1938; Nicholls, 1976, Purkey, 1970; Weiner Frieze, Kukla, Reed, Rest & Rosenbaum 1971). A meta-analysis has confirmed this relationship (Hansford & Hattie, 1982); the average correlation between indices of these two constructs is approximately .24. But the strength of the relationship varies across ethnic groups (highest for whites), age of child (highest for secondary school students), socioeconomic status (highest for middle and high SES children), and the ability level of the child (highest for middle and high ability children). The relationship also varies with the measures used. The relationship goes up as the measures get more specific. For example, the highest correlations exist between expectations for success in a particular subject and both grade point average and the teacher's rating of work/study habits for that particular subject. Conversely, the relationship is quite low between global measures of self-esteem and global IQ scores.

The link between self-concept of ability and achievement is of interest primarily because motivational psychologists believe that variations in self-concept of ability can cause variations in achievement behavior. They argue that self-concept of ability influences students' motivation to study and work hard, especially in the face of difficulty. Motivation to study, in turn, influences level of achievement. Because students with positive or high self-concepts and high expectations for success have faith in their ability to master academic tasks, they respond to difficulty or failure with increased persistence. In contrast, because students with low self-concepts and low expectations for success have little faith in their ability to master academic tasks, they give up when confronted with difficult tasks. By increasing their efforts in the face of difficulty, high self-concept children increase the probability of success at the task. Their success, in turn, confirms their high self-concept, creating a success-prone expectancy cycle. In contrast, by giving up in the same situation, low self-concept children condemn themselves to failure. Their failures, in turn, confirm their low self-concept, creating a failure-prone cycle.

Research assessing this series of predictions has yielded somewhat mixed results. The impact of achievement on self-concept and expectations for success has been established. High achievement (success) leads to high self-concept and high expectancies; low achievement (failure) leads to low self-concept and low expectancies (e.g., Calsyn & Kenny, 1977; Crandall, 1969; Eccles, Adler & Meece, 1984; Parsons & Ruble, 1977). In contrast, the impact of self-concept on subsequent achievement is less clear. On the one hand, laboratory studies have fairly consistently demonstrated that students with higher expectancies and higher estimates of their ability persist longer, do better on difficult tasks, and have higher subsequent expectations than students with low initial expectations and low estimates of their ability (Butkowsky & Willows, 1980; Crandall, 1969; Eccles, Adler, & Meece, 1984). These beneficial effects of high expectations are particularly evident on difficult tasks. On the other hand, field studies using *both* cross-lagged correlational procedures and structural modeling procedures have yielded a very mixed pattern of results.

Of the most comprehensive recently published studies we could locate, two found no evidence of a causal impact of self-concept of ability on subsequent achievement (Calsyn & Kenny, 1977; Harter & Connell, 1984). The results of these two studies, one using cross-lagged panel correlations and one using structural modeling, suggest that the relationship between achievement and self-concept is totally accounted for by the causal impact of achievement on self-concept. A recent dissertation provides additional support for this conclusion. Using panel data from a longitudinal study of attitudes and achievement, Newman (1982) evaluated the causal relationship between self-concept of math ability and math performance over a 3-year (second to fifth grade) and 5-year (fifth to tenth grade) time span. His results, based on structural modeling procedures, indicated that variations in level of achievement caused subsequent changes in self-concept during both time periods. Variations in self-concept of math ability had no effect on subsequent math achievement across either time period.

In contrast, two other studies found support for the causal impact of self-concept on subsequent achievement. Using structural modeling procedures, Shavelson and Bolus (1982) found clear evidence of the self-concept to achievement link for three different subject areas (math, English, and science). Using path analytic procedures, we have also found evidence of a small but significant effect of self-concept of math ability on subsequent math grades (Eccles [Parsons] et al., 1983).

Intervention studies have yielded equally conflicting results. Even when a significant effect emerges, it is typically quite small and difficult to interpret because the interventions are so general. In reviewing these studies, Scheiner and Kraut (1979) concluded that there was no support for the proposition that changes in self-concept cause changes in achievement. They argued that the "self-concept change evident in these intervention studies is likely to be an outcome of increased achievements with accompanying social approval, rather than an intervening variable necessary to occur" (p. 144).

What can we conclude? The laboratory studies provide sufficiently consistent and sufficiently strong evidence to conclude: (1) That low self-concept can lead to the failure-prone expectancy pattern predicted by motivational psychologists, and (2) that variations in self-concept have their impact primarily on students' reactions to failure. Variations in self-concept and expectations have less influence on students' responses to success. The field studies suggest that self-concept of ability is not, on the average, a very powerful determinant of achievement, in and of itself. In part, these weak relationships may reflect the fact that the relationships between self-concept of ability and performance is cyclic by its very nature. As a consequence the question of which causes which may be a pseudo-issue.

In part, these weak relationships may also be due to the fact that most measures of self-concept of ability reflect an assessment of past or current ability level and not of potential future ability level. Unfortunately, most people in this culture think of lack of ability as a stable construct—If I'm not able today, I won't be able tomorrow. In addition, future expectations are very closely related to assessments of one's current ability level (Eccles, [Parsons] et al., 1983). This need not, however, be the case. We could think of lack of ability as an unstable condition—a condition modifiable with appropriate experience. We could, in other words, dissociate our expectations for future success from our assessments of our current level of performance. There is, in fact, some data suggesting that is exactly what young children do (see Eccles, Midgley, & Adler, 1984). If students conceive of lack of ability as a modifiable characteristic, then their motivation to continue trying despite difficulty might be higher.

Of course we are not arguing that students develop unrealistic expectations for task mastery. Knowing when to give up is a very important skill. Some tasks will clearly be beyond the ability level of some students and they should be able to assess this reality with accuracy. We are arguing that some students may assume too soon that their low performance reflects lack of ability and that their difficulties reflect a stable, unmodifiable state. They may be attributing their difficulty with school material to lack of sufficient ability, when, in fact, more accurate attributions might be lack of sufficient skills and/or knowledge, inadequate teaching, or insufficient effort. Furthermore, some teachers, the teachers most likely to produce the Golem effect, may be reinforcing these inferences. In our opinion this mistaken attributional bias on the part of both the student and the teacher contributes to underachievement and to the failure of some students to progress at a rate commensurate with their ability level.

This line of reasoning suggests four conclusions: (1) Beliefs regarding the degree to which we can control future ability/skill and performance levels will have a stronger causal influence on subsequent achievement behaviors than beliefs regarding one's current ability level. The relationship of perceived control to achievement is discussed later. (2) Teachers who believe in ''late bloomers'' and who see lack of ability/skill as an unstable trait, subject to modification either through continued development or through active intervention, will be less likely to produce Golem teacher expectancy effects than teachers who see lack of ability as a stable state and attribute poor academic performance to lack of ability. In support of this prediction, Swann and Snyder (1980) demonstrated that subjects who were trained to believe in late bloomers were less likely to produce the Golem teacher expectancy effect than subjects allowed to believe that ability is a stable characteristic. (3) The variations across studies on the effects of self-concept of ability and expectancies on achievement may reflect the degree to which the measure used elicited a past orientation versus a future orientation. (4) Interventions should be designed which will help children to dissociate their assessments of their current level of performance from their future expectations or which will allow the children to use their assessments of their current level of performance in selecting academic tasks of the appropriate level of difficulty to insure success.

Perceived Control

The individual's perception of control over achievement outcomes has been shown to have an impact on self-concept and achievement motivation (see Stipek & Weisz, 1981). Perception of personal or internal control of outcomes, especially successful outcomes, has a positive influence (Bandura, 1977, 1979; Harter, 1978; Weiner et al., 1971). Bandura has labeled this perception of control personal efficacy. Perceptions that outcomes are not under personal control create difficulties (Abramson, Seligman & Teasdale, 1978; Dweck, 1975; Dweck & Goetz, 1978). This perception of lack of control has been termed learned helplessness. We begin our discussion of the influence of control with the construct of learned helplessness.

Learned Helplessness.   Seligman (1975) coined the term learned help-lessness to explain the reaction of laboratory animals to a particular conditioning program. The animals were first administered electric shocks in a situation where escape was not allowed. When conditions were changed so that escape was possible, the animals made no attempt to escape; the animals were said to be exhibiting learned helplessness. Abramson et al. (1978) reformulated the construct to make it more applicable to humans. They defined learned helplessness as the state in which a person believes she or he can not control the events in his or her life. They argued that perceptions of lack of control result in giving up and depression.

Attributions for success and failure are given a central role in Abramson et al.'s formulation of helplessness. In the achievement attribution model (Weiner, 1979; Weiner et al., 1971), certain kinds of attributions are associated with positive achievement motivation, whereas others are linked with negative achievement motivation. For instance, attributing success to ability and failure to lack of effort is associated with positive motivation, whereas attributing failure to lack of ability and success to external causes is associated with negative achievement motivation (see Weiner, 1979; Wigfield & Eccles-Parsons, 1982, for a more complete description of this model). Abramson et al. (1978) discussed how different attributions for failure relate to learned helplessness. Attributing failure to an internal factor, especially lack of ability, leads to loss of self-esteem. Attributing failure to a stable factor (again, ability is the best example) leads to the conclusion that the problem will be long lasting. Thus, helplessness, according to Abramson et al. (1978), results from attributions of failure to lack of ability.

Dweck and her colleagues have used the learned helplessness model to explain children's response to failure experiences in school. They suggested that children who give up when faced with difficult tasks may do so because they attribute their difficulty to lack of ability—a characteristic over which they have no control. In contrast, they suggested that children who persist do so because they attribute their difficulties to a more controllable cause, in particular, lack of sufficient effort. To test these hypotheses, Dweck and Reppucci (1973) compared the attributional patterns of two groups of upper elementary school children: One group had given up on a task after a series of failures; the other group had increased their efforts following the failures. The children who persisted emphasized motivational factors, like lack of effort, in explaining their failures. In contrast, the children who gave up emphasized lack of ability in explaining their failures.

In a subsequent study, Diener and Dweck (1978) asked children to verbalize their thoughts as they were doing difficult problems. Learned-helpless children began attributing their performance to lack of ability as soon as they ran into difficulty. In contrast, other children (called "mastery oriented" by Diener and Dweck) made few attributions, focusing instead on the strategies they were going to try next. Thus, there are differences not only in the kinds, but the extent to which learned-helpless and mastery-oriented children make attributions. Mastery-oriented children respond to difficulty with a task-analytic strategy—What should they do next in order to change their outcome? In contrast, learned-helpless children respond to difficulty with decreased persistence and attributions of low ability. Apparently, they do not think they can change the outcome by changing their strategy; they appear to attribute their difficulties to an unmodifiable deficit instead.

When does learned helplessness in response to failure develop? Rholes, Blackwell, Jordan and Walters (1980) found that first and third grade children did not show the helpless pattern, but by fifth grade some children did. Other studies assessing expectations and response to failure confirm this developmental pattern. Behaviors characteristic of learned helplessness are rare among young children, emerging with any frequency only after the third or fourth grade (see Eccles, Midgley, & Adler, 1984). Apparently, early failure experiences do not undermine children's motivation. Instead, it is only as failures mount and as the child incorporates a stable view of failure that some children develop the helpless pattern. These two processes appear to converge in the middle elementary school grades. Interventions may be most appropriate at this point in a child's school career. Attributional retraining programs with fourth and fifth graders have been particularly successful (Dweck, 1975).

But how does the learned helpless pattern develop? Dweck and Goetz (1978) suggested that the kinds of feedback children receive from different evaluative agents (parents, peers, teachers) influence whether they will develop learned helplessness or not. Dweck, Davidson, Nelson and Enna (1978) conducted an observational study in order to analyze the kinds of feedback children receive from teachers in elementary school. Since they were particularly concerned with the socialization of sex differences in learned helplessness, they focused on the differential treatment of boys and girls. They found, like others (see Brophy & Good, 1974 and Good, this volume), that boys receive more negative feedback than girls. In addition, however, they found that the patterns associated with both negative and positive feedback directed toward boys focused on conduct rather than the intellectual quality of their work. In contrast, because the girls received so little criticism for conduct, most of the criticism directed toward girls focused on the intellectual quality of their work. When the teachers in this study criticized children for the quality of their work (which was very rare), they were eight times more likely to attribute the boys' problems to lack of effort than they were to make such attributions for the girls' academic problems. Typically, they made no overt attribution for the girls' performance. It should be noted, however, that overt teacher attributions were rare for both boys and girls.

Dweck et al. (1978) suggested that these differences in teacher feedback patterns and in the teacher's attributions might predispose boys and girls to develop different attributional patterns for themselves. The boy pattern of diffuse criticism, they argued, should lead boys to ignore negative teacher feedback. If boys receive more criticism than girls and if the criticism usually focuses on their conduct rather than their competence, then, boys should come to view the teacher's negative feedback as reflecting the teacher's attitude toward them and not their academic potential. In addition, if teachers emphasize lack of effort when criticizing the boys for poor academic performance, then, Dweck et al. suggested, boys should learn to blame their failures on lack of effort.

In contrast, if the teachers praise girls more than boys, then girls should be less likely to attribute the teacher's criticism, when it occurs, to teacher bias. Furthermore, if teachers, in general, think that girls are hard workers, the girls should be less likely to learn to attribute their failures to lack of effort. Thus, girls should be more likely than boys to attribute their failures to lack of ability. In support of these predictions, Dweck and Reppucci (1973) found that girls were slightly more likely to attribute their failures to lack of ability than boys. But, the boys and girls in this same study were equally likely to attribute their failures to lack of effort. As a further test of their predictions, Dweck et al. (1978) manipulated teacher feedback patterns in a laboratory simulation. One group of children were given the boy-type pattern; the other group of children were given the girl-type pattern. As predicted, the children who had received the boy-type pattern had higher expectations for success and attributed their failures to external factors and lack of effort to a greater extent than did the children who had received the girl-type pattern. These data suggest that the pattern of teacher feedback can influence children's attributional patterns and expectations for success. They also suggest that these effects are quite subtle, depending on the context in which the feedback occurs.

Several recent studies, however, have yielded results that raise serious questions concerning both the results and interpretations made by Dweck et al. (1978). In particular, these studies raise questions regarding: (1) the sex differences in learned helplessness, (2) the sex difference in the patterns of teacher feedback, and (3) the predicted relationships between teacher feedback patterns and students' expectations (Blumenfeld, Hamilton, Bossert, Wessels, & Meece, 1982; Cooper, Burger, & Good, 1981; Eccles, Moses, & Yulish-Muzynski, 1982; Eccles et al., 1983; Frieze, Whitley, Hanusa & McHugh, 1982; Good, Cooper, & Blakey, 1980; Parsons, Meece, Adler, & Kaczala, 1982). For example, we have not found that girls are more prone to learned-helpless behaviors than boys. A similar conclusion has been reached by both Cooper et al. (1981) and Frieze et al. (1982).

In addition, observation studies have not replicated several aspects of the findings reported by Dweck et al. (1978). For example, in Parsons, Kaczala et al. (1982), teachers gave more work-related criticism to boys rather than to girls. There were no differences in the amount of criticism teachers gave to boys and girls for the nonintellectual aspects of their work, such as neatness, and the proportion of criticism given to work versus conduct was the same for boys and girls. The patterns of teacher praise were also similar for boys and girls. Finally, teachers' attributions for students' behavior and performance were made so infrequently that assessing their impact on student motivation was impossible. In addition, there were no sex differences in the patterns of these attributions. Failures were almost universally attributed to lack of effort. Furthermore, in a direct test of the hypothesis that teacher feedback patterns influence children's attitudes toward achievement, Parsons, Kaczala et al., found only very weak relationships in general between teacher feedback patterns and student attitudes toward math and found no support for the specific predictions made by Dweck et al. (1978). Furthermore, the effects of teacher expectations on student motivation had completely disappeared 1 year later when the children had moved on to a new teacher. Hence Dweck's notion that teacher feedback is a major determinant of student attributional patterns was not supported.

In a similar study, Blumenfeld et al. (1982) observed teacher–student interactions in first and fifth grade classrooms. They coded the kinds of attributions teachers gave concerning student performance. As in the Parsons, Kaczala et al. (1982) study, teachers did not make frequent attributions about their students' performance. Of the attributions made for students' academic performance, more were positive than negative. Teachers gave very few lack of ability attributions for poor performance; lack of effort was used most frequently for both boys and girls. Girls received more work-related attributions than did boys. Contrary to the results reported by Dweck et al. (1978), teachers attributed girls' failures more often to lack of effort than they did boy's failures, and they attributed boys' failures to lack of ability more often than they did the girls'. It should be noted, however, that teacher attributions were relatively infrequent, occurring in only 13% (with girls) and 8% (with boys) of the interactions.

It is clear then that other observational studies have produced results quite different from those reported in Dweck et al. (1978). Further work is needed to determine why such differences have occurred. But, at the very least, the discrepancies across studies indicate that teacher feedback varies greatly across classrooms, and that the kinds of attributions teachers give to boys and girls vary in type and frequency. It also does not appear that learned helplessness is a general phenomenon that is more common in girls than in boys. The Parsons, Kaczala et al.'s finding that teacher feedback patterns and teacher's overt causal attributions for the children's performance are only weak predictors of student's attitudes toward achievement further runs counter to the notion that teacher feedback is a major determinant of children's attributions and expectations for success. This is not to say that teachers do not or cannot affect children's motivation. We discuss some specific ways that teachers do affect children's motivation later. But we now believe that the typical experiences most children have with affective feedback and teacher attributions are not powerful determinants of their classroom motivation. On the average, these experiences are not that frequent and are probably not very salient in the stream of classroom interaction. When these experiences become salient, either because the teacher is making a special effort to make them salient or because they occur in a particularly affect-laden moment, then, we expect, they will have a strong impact on the students' motivation. But such experiences are rare and are difficult to uncover in normative studies of classroom life.

While teachers' overt attributions about their students' performance may not play a major role in the socialization of learned helplessness, the way they control students' success and failure experiences may. For instance, Cooper's (1977, 1979) work on teacher–student interactions suggests that teachers attempt to minimize public interactions with low expectancy students by praising them less and criticizing them more. Teachers encourage high expectancy students to interact with them publicly. Cooper argues that these teacher feedback patterns will lead low expectancy students to interact less with teachers, and to perceive that their efforts do not result in positive outcomes. These patterns can also result in the low expectancy children getting less instruction time and less engaged work time. While teacher attributions, especially covert attributions, may play some role in shaping the teacher's behavior, Cooper's work suggests that it is the way in which the teachers control opportunities for interaction that is the more important influence on the children's motivation and performance.

Though there is controversy over the origins of learned helplessness, most researchers agree that helplessness is a problem for some children in school. What can be done about this problem? Based on the relationship of attributions to learned helplessness, Dweck (1975) conducted an attribution retraining study with upper elementary school students to try to change the learned helpless children's attributions for failure. In one condition, the children had success experiences. In the attribution retraining condition, the children experienced success on most problems, and failure on a few. When failure occurred, the experimenter attributed it to lack of effort ("You can do better, try harder"). Following training, only the attribution retraining groups improved. They no longer gave up when they encountered failure, and they had learned to attribute failure to lack of effort rather than to lack of ability. These results show how children's attributions can affect performance, and indicate that one way to improve performance is to change children's attributions.

Other researchers have extended this work. Both Andrews and Debus (1978) and Fowler and Peterson (1981) investigated how various combinations of success and failure experiences, and attribution retraining experiences affect children's responses to failure. Dweck's (1975) study confounded the effects of success and failure with attribution retraining, since she did not include a group that received success and failure experiences without attribution retraining; these other studies corrected this confound. Results of both studies showed that the combination of attribution retraining and success–failure experiences was the most effective way of improving children's persistence, but it was not significantly better than the success–failure condition in which failure was interspersed with success. These results qualify Dweck's findings that attribution retraining is the way to overcome helplessness. What seems to be critical is that students learn that increased effort can lead to success and that failures are under one's control.

One other problem with attribution retraining should be mentioned here. Covington and Beery (1976) have argued that people maintain feelings of self-worth by maintaining high self-concepts of ability. When people experience failure, one way to maintain a high self-concept of ability is to attribute failure to lack of effort. In support of this view, Covington and Omelich (1979a,b) have shown that attributing failure to lack of effort is the preferred attribution among college students. This is a reasonable strategy as long as individuals believe they are not trying hard. Attribution retraining helps individuals overcome failure by getting them to try harder; feelings of self-worth can be maintained if success is attained. However, if individuals try harder and still fail, the only conclusion they can draw is that they lack ability. Covington and Beery (1976) argued that many individuals do not try hard in potential failure situations in order to avoid this very thing. Attributing failure to lack of effort is all right, *if* additional effort allows one to succeed. The implication is that individuals may need more than attribution retraining to do well; they may also need skill training. Without this skill training, increased efforts will not lead to an enhanced sense of competence because increased efforts will not lead to the increased incidence of success. This brings us to our next motivational constructs—personal efficacy and effectance motivation.

Personal Efficacy.   According to Bandura (1977, 1979), personal efficacy is the perception of how well one can do on various tasks. It is the belief that one can succeed at a task. Efficacy perceptions have been shown to influence various achievement behaviors, including the selection of easy or difficult tasks, and persistence on an achievement task. According to Bandura, individuals generally attempt those things they think they can do. He also argued that a sense of personal efficacy is created by observing how one's actions affect the environment. In the achievement domain, this means that personal efficacy is enhanced when one's efforts produce successful results. As is true of all these self-concept linked beliefs, self-efficacy beliefs can be enhanced or undermined by the interpretations and experiences provided by both parents and teachers.

While Bandura's (1977, 1979) analysis seems quite similar to Weiner et al.'s (1971, 1978) attribution analysis, with efficacy beliefs corresponding to attributing success to ability, Bandura maintains the two views are not the same. Both theories stress the importance of perceived control. But, because efficacy perceptions are concerned with the question "Can I do this task?", Bandura stresses the importance of skill training rather than attribution retraining. Indeed, Schunk (1981) tested the effectiveness of attribution retraining and efficacy training in improving slow-learning children's math performance. Children received one of two efficacy training procedures, either a modeling procedure or a practice procedure. Half the children in each training group also received attribution retraining like that used by Dweck (1975). While both training conditions improved children's persistence, accuracy, and perceived efficacy, there were no differences between the children who received attribution retraining and those who did not. Apparently, the critical aspect of training is that the children learn that increased efforts, using appropriate skills, can lead to increased success.

Effectance Motivation.   Harter's (1978) work on effectance motivation theory points out yet another construct related to perceived control. As originally formulated by White, (1959) effectance motivation is the motive to affect one's environment. Building on White's (1959) model, Harter has spent the last several years elaborating effectance motivation theory. Her work has focused on the following issues: (1) Distinguishing the components of effectance motivation; (2) looking at the impact of both success and failure experiences on effectance motivation; (3) examining the role of socialization agents in shaping effectance motivation; and (4) assessing developmental changes in effectance motivation. A major premise of Harter's view is that perceptions of internal control are a critical part of positive effectance motivation, and perceptions that events are externally controlled are an aspect of weak effectance motivation.

Harter's (1981b, 1982) recent empirical work has addressed primarily the first of these issues (i.e., the components of effectance motivation). She has developed a scale to assess children's perceptions of their competence in different skill domains, focusing on cognitive, social, and physical skills. Initial results of her investigations show that children (third through ninth graders) distinguish among these domains.

Harter and Connell (1984) have also assessed the relationships between actual and perceived competence, perceived control over achievement outcomes (either internal, external, or unknown), and motivational orientation (internal or external) of elementary and junior high school students. They used structural modeling procedures to derive best fitting models for the relationships obtained among these variables and between these variables and school achievement. (It should be noted that the statistics necessary to judge goodness of fit of the different models were not presented in the materials we obtained; hence it was impossible for us to determine how well the best fitting model actually fit the data.) Four models were assessed, each specifying different predictive links among the variables (e.g., achievement predicts perceived control versus perceived control predicts achievement, etc.). Though there were some differences between elementary and junior high school students, for both groups the model that best fit the data emphasized the perceived control variable as the primary predictor of the other variables. More particularly, the known/unknown distinction emerged as most critical; children who reported that they knew why academic outcomes occurred and, in fact, gave a reason, which was codable as either external or internal, were higher achievers than children who could not provide a codable reason for their academic outcomes. This finding supports the view that perceived control, in general, is an important determinant of achievement; however, the known/unknown distinction has not appeared in previous control theories, and will have to be assessed further. It collapses across the internal and external dimensions typically kept separate in attribution and efficacy models; instead, it compares children who can provide reasons for academic outcomes with children who can not provide such reasons. Thus, its exact theoretical status is not yet clear. In addition, since the study was cross sectional in design rather than longitudinal, the causal links are still unclear.

Thus, both Harter and Bandura, in their different but related perspectives, pay particular attention to perceived control over events, as does Dweck in her discussion of learned helplessness and mastery orientation. As summarized here, the perception that events are not personally controlled is a bad situation, and perceived personal control over events is a better one. Recently, some social psychologists (e.g., Janof-Bulman & Brickman, 1981; Rothbaum, Weisz, & Snyder, 1982) have argued that the importance of control perceptions has been overemphasized. While this may be true for adults in some situations, we believe that in the school situation, children have so little control over most events that it is quite important that they perceive some control over their achievement outcomes. This is particularly true in school settings because the children can *not* leave the situation and because they typically have so little control over the tasks assigned to them. Without such perceptions, the school situation will appear to be totally driven by external or uncontrollable forces, which, as we have shown, will have a negative influence on the children's motivation to achieve in the school setting.

Summary of Cognitive–Motivational Variables

In this section we have reviewed the impact on student achievement of a cluster of motivational variables that are related to the students' assessment of their abilities and to their interpretation of their academic successes and failures. These variables share a large cognitive component—the interpretation of events—and, as such, are related most directly to the question Can I succeed at or master this task? While not all children ask themselves this question, many children do act as though they do, especially when they are confronted with failure or with a very difficult task. Their answer to the question does affect their response to the difficulty.

We want to stress that it is the interpretation of failure that seems most critical. If failure is interpreted as stable and due to *enduring* characteristics of the individual such as lack of ability, then the student is likely to give up. If, in contrast, the failure is seen as surmountable and due to lack of effort, or lack of skill, or lack of specific knowledge, then the student is less likely to give up, more likely to persist, and, if necessary, to seek the help necessary to acquire the requisite skills.

Interestingly, the teacher expectancy literature also suggests that it is perceived control over future outcomes, or personal efficacy in the face of difficulty, that may be the critical mediator of teacher expectancy effects when they occur. As Brophy (Chapter 12) concludes, the major teacher expectancy effects are Golem rather than Galatea effects. Even these effects are only produced by some teachers. Evidence from several different sources suggests that one set of characteristics that distinguishes the teachers who produce the Golem effects from those who do not are the teachers' efficacy-related beliefs. These beliefs include (1) confidence in their own ability to help the low expectancy students to master the material, (2) confidence in the low expectancies students' ability to master the material, and (3) conviction that the material can and should be mastered by everyone (Ashton, Webb, & Doda, 1982; Brookover, Beady, Flood, Schweitzer, & Wisenbaker, 1979; Clauset & Gaynor, 1982; Weiner, 1979). In other words, teachers who enable low expectancy children to progress in their learning perceive themselves to have control over the students' progress, perceive the students as capable of learning the material, and consider it to be part of their responsibility to ensure that the low expectancy children do in fact learn. What seems to be critical is that teachers not interpret the students' failures as stable and predictive of continued failure and incompetence. Instead, it is important that teachers believe they can intervene to stop the failure cycle.

SUBJECTIVE TASK VALUE: DO I WANT TO SUCCEED?

The motivational constructs discussed up to this point have all been related to the basic questions of Can I do the work?, and Can I succeed on this task if I want to? Expectancy-value models of motivation stress the importance of another cluster of constructs in mediating achievement—namely, a cluster linked to the individual's assessment of the value or importance of the activity. This cluster is linked to the questions Do I want to do the work? and Do I want to succeed?''

Atkinson (1964) included one aspect of this construct in his original model of achievement behavior. He called this variable incentive value and defined it in terms of the reward value for succeeding. He assumed that the reward value of succeeding was directly related to the probability of success; success at harder tasks was assumed to have greater value than success at easier tasks. Since 1964, it has become clear that Atkinson's conceptualization of subjective task value does not capture the richness of the construct. Several theorists have elaborated broader models of task value (e.g., Crandall, 1969; Eccles et al., 1983; Eccles, 1984; Parsons & Goff; 1980; Raynor, 1974; Spenner & Featherman, 1978). Our own model proposes that the value or importance of engaging in a specific achievement task is determined both by the characteristics of the task and by the needs, goals, and values of the person. The degree to which the task is able to fulfill needs, to facilitate reaching goals, or to affirm personal values, determines the value a person attaches to engaging in that task. Activities that fulfill these needs will be seen as important and the individual will be motivated to work at mastering them. Activities that do not fulfill these needs will be seen as unimportant and the individual will not be motivated to work at them. Finally, activities that threaten the individual's self-concept will take on a negative value and the individual will be motivated to avoid them.

In our model, we assume that subjective task value (the value an individual places on the task) is comprised of three major components: attainment value, intrinsic value or interest, and utility value. Attainment value is the importance of doing well on a task. This component incorporates a variety of dimensions, including perceptions of the task's ability to affirm or disaffirm salient and valued characteristics of the self (e.g., masculinity, femininity, competence), to provide a challenge, and to offer either a forum for fulfilling achievement, power, and social needs, or a forum for failure and shame. We assume that the perceived qualities of the task interact with an individual's needs and self-perceptions in determining a task's attainment value. Consider, for example, a child who thinks that doing well is one characteristic of smart people and who wants to be a smart person. This child will place great value on doing well in school because doing well in school will affirm a critical component of his or her self-concept. Consider, in contrast, the child who doesn't think doing well in school is particularly important. This child will be less motivated to work hard in order to succeed at school, especially if he or she isn't sure of success anyway.

This component of subjective task value may be especially critical to our understanding of differences in motivation that are related to socioeconomic class, gender, and ethnic group membership. As several reviewers have concluded (e.g., Wigfield & Asher, 1984), middle-class children, especially girls, are more likely to believe that doing well in school is important. This makes the teacher's job much easier. In contrast, lower SES children and children from some ethnic groups are less likely to endorse the value of school performance. Consequently, teachers will need to do more to increase the motivation of these children, especially if they begin to associate school with failure and negative affective experiences. Providing these children with additional incentives to master material has been found to increase both their motivation and their achievement level (see Thomas, 1980).

Intrinsic or interest value, the second component of task value, is the inherent enjoyment one gets from engaging in an activity. Some people just enjoy doing school work. They gain great satisfaction from completing assignments and doing well. For example, they may find mathematics aesthetically pleasing, or science exciting, or reading pleasant and calming. For such people the value of school and related activities should be very high; they should be highly motivated to do their school work.

Psychologists concerned with intrinsically motivated learning (e.g., Covington & Beery, 1976; Deci, 1975; Harter, 1981a; Kruglanski, 1975; Lepper & Green, 1978; Maehr, 1983; Nicholls, 1979; White, 1959) have been most interested in this component of subjective task value. They argue that all children are intrinsically motivated to learn and to master their environment, but that schools, through evaluative procedures, teacher-controlled learning, and lock-step pacing of tasks, undercut this motivation in most children, but particularly in low ability children. Harter (1981b) has confirmed this developmental prediction. Older children are more likely to cite extrinsic reasons for doing school work than are younger children. This developmental change in intrinsic motivation suggests two conclusions: (1) Schools ought to consider ways to maintain intrinsic motivation. (2) Teachers should pay more attention to the other influences on subjective task value as children grow older. For example, utility value may become an especially important component of subjective task value as students move into high school.

Finally, apart from any feeling of interest or enjoyment, tasks also have utility value and are undertaken as a means of reaching a variety of long- and short-range goals. For example, a high school student may want to be a veterinarian and may need to take a particular course (e.g., calculus or advanced algebra) in order to gain entry into the appropriate college program. Consequently, the student may take advanced mathematics classes, even though he or she has little or no interest in math itself. In this case, the instrumentality of mathematics in helping to achieve a career goal outweighs an otherwise negative or neutral attitude toward the subject matter itself. The utility value of math in this case is high because of its long range usefulness.

As suggested above, utility value should increase in importance as students enter junior and senior high school. It is not until the adolescent years that students develop stable long-range goals and start to think about planning for these future goals. It is also the time in their educational careers when students start getting some options regarding what they take, and when absenteeism and truancy become a major problem. Given these age-related changes in the nature of students' school experiences, it is undoubtedly very important that schools and teachers begin to provide students with accurate information regarding the value of staying in school and in taking college track courses, lest teacher expectancy effects and underachievement patterns manifest themselves in dropout rates and inadequate preparation for adult employment. While these efforts may not be universally successful even in high school, they stand a better chance of being effective motivators among older students than among younger students, who do not yet have a future orientation. Unfortunately, in over 300 hours of observations in junior high school math classes, we rarely saw a teacher use this strategy.

In sum, we are proposing that task value is a function of both perceived qualities of the task and the individual's needs, goals, and self-perceptions. Individual differences in these factors are created by the experiences individuals have had with similar tasks in the past; by social stereotypes (e.g., girls can't do math; poor kids are dumb; Blacks are better at sports than math); by the kinds of information provided by parents, teachers, and/or peers about the importance of, or the difficulty involved in, doing well. We have been most interested in three particular influences on perceived task value: (a) personal needs, values, and self-schemata, (b) perceived cost of success and failure, and (c) affective experiences.

Personal Needs, Values, and Self-Schemata

A sizable portion of the literature related to the processes of socialization suggests that a variety of needs and values influence achievement behavior (Mortimer & Simmons, 1978; Parsons & Goff, 1980; Spenner & Featherman, 1978; Stein & Bailey, 1973; Veroff, 1969, 1977). For example, Parsons and Goff (1980) have argued that individuals develop an image of who and what they are as they grow up. This image is made up of many component parts including (a) conceptions of one's personality, (b) long range goals and plans related to anticipated adult roles, (c) schema regarding the proper roles of mothers and fathers, (d) instrumental and terminal values (Rokeach, 1973), (e) motivational sets, and (f) social scripts regarding proper behavior in a variety of situations.

Some parts of an individual's image are very central or critical to his/her self-definition. According to Markus (1980) these are the parts of one's self-image that exert the most influence on behavior. For example, if being a good student is a central part of an individual's self-image, then it is to be expected that this individual will work at being a good student and at projecting an image to others of being a good student. The degree of influence wielded by the values and needs is determined by their centrality to an individual's self-definition. Specifically, personal needs and values operate in ways that both reduce the probability of engaging in those roles or activities that are perceived as being inconsistent with one's central values and increase the probability of engaging in roles or activities perceived as being consistent with one's definition of self.

The impact of sex role on achievement behavior is a good example of this process. Males and females excel and have difficulty in different achievement domains. Males do better in math and science courses; females do better in

English and foreign language courses. Why is this true? While a full discussion is beyond the scope of this paper, a few comments are in order. One explanation for the difference relies on the mediating role of the motivation variables linked to expectations for success discussed earlier. The other explanation focuses more on subjective task value. We have argued elsewhere that sex roles influence behavior primarily through the mediating role of incentive value. In particular, we have argued that sex labeling of tasks influences the value children attach to these tasks, and that the value, in turn, influences achievement behaviors, such as persistence in the face of difficulty and task choice. Supporting this argument, both boys and girls attach higher attainment value to sex appropriate achievement activities (Stein & Smithells, 1969). Additionally, subjective value of math has emerged in several studies as the most important attitudinal influence on students' enrollment decisions and math-related career choice (Eccles, 1984). Finally, in a path analytic study of students' motivation to study math and English, we have found subjective task value (rather than self-concept of ability) to be the attitudinal variable that accounts for the sex differences in students' motivation to continue studying math (Eccles, Adler, & Meece, 1984).

Several of the other chapters in this volume discuss the impact of teacher expectancies on sex differences in achievement. In these chapters, it is argued that sex-related stereotypes of achievement abilities influence teacher expectations, which, in turn, influence teachers' behavior. The boys and girls incorporate the teachers' expectations into their own expectations for success and, as a consequence, perform differently. In other words, girls perform more poorly in math than boys because they have acquired lower expectations for success from their teachers. While it is true that some teachers treat boys and girls differently, especially in math classes, and that high school teachers expect boys to be better at math than girls, it is also true that high school teachers think math is more useful for boys than for girls and that boys enjoy math more than girls (see Eccles, 1984). Therefore it is possible that teachers may be influencing girls' and boys' achievement patterns by the messages they convey about the importance and value of math and by the affective support they give to high ability girls rather than by the messages they convey regarding expectations for success. Very little work has been done to assess this hypothesis.

Perceived Cost of Success and Failure

The value of a task to an individual is also affected by a set of variables that can best be conceptualized as the cost of success or failure. Borrowing from exchange theorists (e.g., Thibaut & Kelley, 1959), we conceptualize the influence of cost on the value of an activity in terms of a cost/benefit ratio. Assuming that individuals have a conception of both the cost and benefits of engaging in a variety of activities, then the value of each activity ought to be inversely related to this cost/benefit ratio. Variables influencing the benefit of an activity were discussed in previous sections. Variables influencing the cost of an activity include the amount of effort needed to succeed, the loss of time that could be used to engage in other valued activities, and the psychological meaning of failure.

Effort.   Kukla (1972, 1978) suggested that the amount of effort assumed to be needed for success may be a key determinant of achievement behavior. He argued that individuals calculate the minimal amount of effort needed to succeed on a task (i.e., to do as well as one considers essential) based on their estimates of their own ability and the difficulty of the task. Each individual will then exert that minimal effort. If we assume that individuals have a sense of how much effort they think is worthwhile for various activities, then we can extend Kukla's argument to the following prediction: As the anticipated amount of effort increases in relation to the amount of effort considered worthwhile, then the value of the task to the individual should decrease. That is, as the cost/benefit ratio in terms of amount of effort needed to do well increases, the value of the task to the individual should decrease.

Loss of Valued Alternative.   Closely related conceptually to the cost of effort involved in doing well is the cost of a task in terms of the time lost from other valued activities. Students have limited time and energy. If they spend 1 hour on task A, they have 1 hour less available for task B. They must make choices between various activities. For example, imagine a girl who likes math, knows it's hard, but also wants to be popular. To do as well in math as she feels she should, she thinks she'll have to do homework every night. She also believes that she can optimize her chance of being popular by spending a lot of time with her friends. Clearly, these two needs are in conflict. She can cope with the conflict by lowering the value she attaches to math, lowering her achievement standards for math, and, thereby, reducing the amount of time she will need to spend on it.

This analysis highlights the necessity of thinking about various achievement-related behaviors within the broad social array of behavioral options available to children. For example, the decisions to try or not to try hard in math, or to spend time with your buddies instead of studying, are not made in isolation of other very salient life decisions that directly affect the perceived value of all the available options. We should not underestimate the importance of these other goals for any student. But they may be especially important for children who are uncertain they can succeed in the academic domain of school even if they decide to work hard.

Psychological Cost of Failure.   Both the cost of success and the loss of valued alternatives are based on the assumption of anticipated success. But what if a student is unsure of success or is certain of failure? How might this uncertainty affect the perceived value of the task? The common practice of avoiding courses that might lower one's grade point average is a prime example of what can happen even to the most able students. For example, students planning to attend college or graduate school know they need high GPAs in order to compete. Therefore, they often avoid courses that will add even a B to their academic record.

As another example, consider those students who view themselves as competent, have strong achievement needs, yet are unsure of their mathematical abilities and feel as though they will have to try exceptionally hard to do well in their next math course. For these students, the cost of failure in math is high, precisely because failing to do well has important implications for their self-concept. In addition, these students are also unsure of success and may believe that the amount of effort needed to do well is excessively high. Consequently, the perceived value of math should be lower for these students than for students who are either certain of success or who do not find the prospect of failing particularly costly.

What do children do when faced with these negative beliefs? If the option is available, they can avoid the activity altogether. This option, however, is available only to older students who are provided with some choice over their courses and with increased opportunity for involvement in extracurricular activities. But what if they are forced to engage in the activity, as is often the case in American elementary and junior high schools? This is the situation given recent theoretical and empirical attention by Covington and Beery (1976), Covington and Omelich (1979a, 1979b), and Nicholls (1976). These theorists have suggested, and empirically demonstrated, that children adapt to this situation by exerting the minimal level of effort necessary to get by. This strategy has two advantages. First, it prevents out and out failure. Second, it provides the children with a face-saving attribution for their lack of success; namely, I didn't do better because I didn't try as hard as I could have. These theorists have argued that this attribution is psychologically less costly than attributing one's difficulties to lack of ability. Furthermore, they argue that students are forced to attribute their academic failures to lack of ability if they have tried as hard as they can and still have not succeeded. Unfortunately, the strategy of low effort puts children in a double bind because teachers often punish low effort, especially when it occurs in conjunction with poor performance. As a consequence, these students are basically damned if they try and damned if they don't. Their situation can be improved only by changing either the tasks they must complete or their repertoire of skills, in order to insure that increased efforts will lead to increased success.

Teacher expectancy can feed into this dynamic in two ways. First, if the teacher believes that the low-expectancy children can not succeed with increased effort, then the teacher may actually reinforce these children's coping strategy by letting low effort go unnoticed, or by focusing their criticisms of these children on misconduct rather than low achievement efforts. This teacher strategy allows both the teacher and the student to save face, provided the student doesn't create a discipline problem for the teacher.

Teachers who believe that the low-expectancy children can succeed can also perpetuate this low effort dynamic. If a teacher believes that low expectancy children can succeed with increased effort, the teacher may try to control the students' academic efforts through insincere praise of trivial success and punishment of low effort. If the teacher does not also diagnose each child's deficits and design programs to build their skill levels, then the children will not be provided with a strategy to improve. Increases in their efforts will not necessarily produce successful outcomes. And, to the extent that increased efforts do not produce increased success, these children will probably continue to opt for the low effort–low achievement coping strategy. It is only the teacher who both believes these children can do better and has the knowledge and skills to help them do better, who can help these children break out of the failure-prone cycle.

Affective Experiences

Achievement activities elicit a wide range of emotional responses. Previous affect-laden experiences can influence one's responses to similar situations in the present or future. For example, if one has had bad experiences with a math teacher in the past, one may be less positive in general toward current mathematics courses and mathematics teachers. To understand the subjective value attached to various achievement activities it is important to consider variations in the affective experiences children have had with different achievement activities. We discuss how children's affective experiences vary as a function of: (a) overt, objective events such as success and failure, and the behaviors of parents and teachers, and (b) more subjective or psychological events, such as causal attributions, and individual differences in confidence.

Objective Events.   Past successes and failures have been shown to elicit characteristic affective responses (e.g., Weiner, Russell, & Lerman, 1978). Success, especially on challenging tasks, leads to positive feelings, and failure, especially on easy tasks, leads to negative feelings (Harter, 1981a; Ruble, Parsons, & Ross, 1976). Other things being equal, these affective responses should influence the enjoyment or intrinsic value attached to related activities. One should like activities that have been associated with positive feelings in the past more than activities that have been associated with negative feelings. Both affect-laden behaviors of teachers and parents (e.g., praise, criticism, public ostracism, rejection) and more general experiences in school (e.g., test taking procedures, curriculum variations) have similar effects (see Covington & Beery, 1976; Hill, 1977; Nicholls, 1979; Eccles [Parsons] et al., 1983; Ruble & Boggiano, 1980, for reviews). And, as is documented in several chapters in this book, teacher expectancies clearly relate to the affective reactions teachers have toward children. Low-expectancy boys get an especially heavy dose of negative affective experiences throughout their schooling career. Therefore, it is quite reasonable that they turn off to (or lower the value they attach to) school and academic activities.

Psychological Events.   Weiner (1972) proposed that attributions of success and failure influence one's affective responses to achievement tasks as well as one's interpretation of the meaning of success or failure for one's self-concept. He has argued that attributing success and failure internally magnifies the associated affect. Thus, we should feel best about successes attributed to our abilities and efforts and feel worst about failures attributed to a lack of effort and/or ability. Evidence has supported this prediction (Ruble et al., 1976; Weiner, 1974). In more recent work, Weiner, Russell, and Lerman (1978, 1979) have identified a broader link between attributions and affective responses. They found that attributing one's successes internally leads to feelings of pride, satisfaction, and competence, while attributing them externally leads to feelings of gratitude and surprise. Attributing one's failure to internal causes leads to feelings of guilt, resignation, and regret. Attributing failures to external causes leads to feelings of anger and surprise. Thus, contrary to Weiner's earlier predictions, attributions to both internal and external factors can produce strong, albeit different, affective responses.

As previously discussed in more detail, Covington and his colleagues have also extended Weiner's original argument. Building on self-worth theory, they suggested two important affective dynamics: (1) Attributions of failure to lack of ability (not lack of effort) lead to the most ego-debilitating affective response, and (2) while lack of effort will lead to negative affective reactions from the teachers, these reactions are preferable to the ego-deflating affective reactions which accompany attributions to lack of ability. Covington, Spratt, and Omelich (1980) found support for these predictions.

These dynamics put low ability children in a particular bind. If the tasks at school are designed such that increasing their level of effort does not produce success, then increasing their level of effort is counterproductive for three reasons: (1) It doesn't work; (2) High effort coupled with low outcome increases the salience of a low ability attribution especially if other children in the class are succeeding with equivalent levels of effort; and (3) Failures attributed to low ability are especially painful. To cope, Covington, Spratt and Omelich (1980) predict that the student will stop trying. We predict that the child will also devalue the importance of the activity as a means of coping with the inevitable negative response of the teacher.

Summary of Subjective Task Value Variables

In this section we have argued that subjective task value is an important motivational mediator of achievement behavior. We have pointed out ways that children of different ability levels will come to attach different values to academic activities. And we have discussed ways in which teacher expectancies and teacher behavior might influence the value children attach to various achievement activities.

We have also tried to point out how values and expectancies interact in shaping achievement behavior. This analysis emphasizes the complex interplay of the psychological needs of students, their interpretation of their academic experiences, and the structure of the learning environment they are in. It should be clear from this analysis that there are many ways in which children's ability or skill levels on entering a class can interact with their experiences in the class to influence their achievement behaviors.

TASK FOCUS AND MASTERY ORIENTATION: WHAT DO I NEED TO DO IN ORDER TO SUCCEED?

We now come to the third and final motivational question: What do I need to do in order to succeed? The answer to this question depends on at least two different dynamics. First, at the most basic level, knowing what must be done in order to succeed involves the students' ability to play the student role. Being able to maintain attention and to focus one's attention on academic tasks are the cornerstones of this role. If students can not or do not attend carefully to their teacher's directions and instructions, they will not know what to do in order to succeed. The second dynamic associated with this question involves the response students make to difficulty. Students may confront difficulties either in their daily assignments or on evaluative tests. When faced with difficulty on daily tasks, some students (the mastery oriented students) try to analyze the source of their difficulty and to seek help if necessary. Other students become anxious and respond with behaviors more characteristic of learned-helpless children (Diener & Dweck, 1978). These children have great difficulty answering the question What do I need to do in order to succeed? In fact, their defense strategy appears to prevent them even asking this question in the face of difficulty. A similar dichotomy of student responses has been discovered for test-taking situations. Each of these dynamics is discussed below.

Attention and the Student Role

One consequence of perceived control over academic outcomes is that children will work hard and attempt to master the assigned school tasks. But before they can succeed at the task, they must know what the task is, understand the teachers' instructions, and be able to focus their energy on the task. All three of these require attention. Theorists from a variety of perspectives have discussed the importance of children maintaining their attention on the task at hand. For instance, those interested in teaching effectiveness have stressed the importance of increasing academic engaged time, mostly through direct instruction (see Brophy, 1979; Rosenshine & Berliner, 1978; Stallings, 1980; Stallings & Kaskowitz, 1974). Academic engaged time is said to be important because, during engaged time, children are focusing their attention on their work, and should be learning more. In support of this hypothesis, individual differences in attentiveness do predict school achievement. Samuels and Turnure (1974) found that attentiveness during reading instruction is positively related to performance on a word recognition test. Soli and Devine (1976), in an observational study of third and fourth grade classrooms, found not attending school to be one of the best predictors of low achievement. Camp and Zimet (1975) found that poor readers are less attentive during reading instruction. Lambert and Nicholl (1977) analyzed teacher ratings of their first grade pupils. They found that the teachers' ratings of children's problems in maintaining attentiveness in school is one of the strongest predictors of low reading achievement. Finally, Cobb and Hops (1973), Hops and Cobb (1974), and Walker and Hops (1976) have shown that training children in the early elementary grades to attend consistently, follow directions, and work hard (skills called "academic survival skills") significantly improves the children's reading performance.

If low expectancy students are having trouble focusing their attention on the task or on the teacher's instructions, then they will not be able to successfully complete, or master, the school tasks assigned to them. Teachers may misdiagnose their problem as one of lack of sufficient intellectual capacity, rather than inadequate attention monitoring skills. If this happens, or if the teacher has no strategy for helping students improve their attention monitoring skills, then Golem teacher expectancy effects are likely to occur.

Mastery Orientation Versus Self-focus

The second set of responses relevant to our third question is a set of responses that have been discussed under the labels of mastery orientation (Diener & Dweck, 1978) and task versus self-focus (Nicholls, 1979). Broadly defined, these responses reflect children's reaction to failure and/or difficulty. As discussed previously, some children give up when faced with difficulty while others try to surmount the difficulty. Diener & Dweck (1978) have argued that one critical distinction between these two types of children is their interpretation of the meaning of difficulty. Learned-helpless children appear to conclude that having difficulty on academic tasks reflects low ability while mastery-oriented children conclude that having difficulty reflects the use of an inappropriate strategy.

Nicholls (1979, 1980) has elaborated on this distinction, suggesting that children may differ in their basic orientations toward achievement. Some children, he suggests, have an ego-involved orientation toward achievement; others have a more task-involved orientation. Individuals with an ego-involved orientation define achievement tasks as those that can be used to demonstrate one's abilities. What is valued is demonstrating ability. Mastering the task in not seen as the end in itself, but rather is seen as a means of demonstrating that one has high ability relative to others. Individuals with a task-involved orientation define achievement tasks in terms of task mastery; what is valued is the opportunity to gain understanding and to master the task. Task mastery is seen as an end in itself rather than as a means to an end.

Nicholls argues that the ego-involved orientation has negative consequences for all but those who can demonstrate high ability. Those who do not demonstrate high ability will perceive they have failed, even if they have acquired new skills. Thus, when children with an ego-involved orientation start having difficulty with an academic task, they will begin to doubt their abilities and may shift to the low effort strategy we discussed earlier in order to save face.

While there may be fairly stable individual differences in ego-involved versus task involved orientations, Nicholls (1979), as well as others, has also argued that the situation can affect the likelihood of either of these orientations governing students' academic behaviors. Some situations, by their very nature, focus children's attention on self-evaluation; other situations minimize the salience of self-evaluation, thus increasing the salience of task mastery goals. Nicholls has suggested that schools which emphasize social comparison and competition among students, and learning as a means to another end, foster the ego-involved orientation. As a consequence, many students in such schools perceive themselves as failures. (See also, Johnson & Johnson, 1974; and Slavin, 1977, on differences between competitive and cooperative learning environments.)

Under conditions of task involvement, Nicholls asserts that all individuals can feel involved if tasks of different difficulty level are provided so that all can increase their skills (see Bloom, 1976, on mastery learning). With task involvement, individuals judge their performance in terms of skills gained, rather than in terms of their performance relative to that of others. Thus, relative ability standing becomes less important. Nicholls believes that task involvement can lead all individuals to be optimally motivated in educational settings, since what is valued is task mastery rather than doing better than others. Given the work on attentional focus and achievement, and Nicholls' discussion of the benefits of a task-involved orientation, the implication for teachers is to foster task focus, and to minimize competition, social comparison, and an ego-involved orientation toward academic tasks. Unfortunately, many widely used school practices, such as tracking, foster the very things that Nicholls and Eccles, Midgley, and Adler (1984) have argued increase the salience of ego involvement; namely, competition and social comparison.

Anxiety in Evaluative Contexts

The final set of responses relevant to the question What do I need to do in order to succeed? relate to the general topic of test anxiety. There has been a long tradition of work on the debilitating effects of test anxiety on children's performance on evaluative tasks, such as exams. This research indicates that the debilitating effects of test anxiety emerge gradually over the elementary school years (Hill & Sarason, 1966). The level of anxiety increases through the elementary school years. In addition, while there is essentially no relationship between reported anxiety and school performance in the early elementary school years, by the middle elementary years modest negative correlations between anxiety and school performance begin to emerge. By the end of elementary school, this negative relationship has reached an average correlation of $r = -.4$. Furthermore, by the end of elementary school, high anxious children are over a year behind low anxious children on tests of basic skills.

The increases in anxiety through the elementary school years suggest that teacher–student interactions, as well as parent–child interactions, have an important influence on the development of anxiety. Some studies have shown that high anxious children do better and are less anxious in more traditional, controlled classrooms than in open classrooms (see Cronbach, 1977), perhaps because they need more direction. Other studies (Brophy & Evertson, 1981; Cooper, 1977; see also Brophy, 1981) have shown that teacher praise may help lessen student anxiety. Still other studies have established a link between testing practices and the debilitating effects of anxiety on performance (Hill, 1977). Thus, it is clear that classroom practices do influence anxiety; and, while no one has assessed the role of teacher expectancy effects on anxiety directly, test anxiety does interfere with some children's test performance and learning and thus may be one reason some children enter a class with deficient skills.

But why are we including this discussion of test anxiety under the general question of What do I need to do in order to succeed? Several theorist (Liebert & Morris, 1967; Sarason, 1972, 1975a; Wine, 1971, 1980) have suggested that the lowered performance of high anxious individuals is due to the difficulty they have in attending to relevant task information, because of their preoccupation with doing poorly. Wine (1971, 1980) reviewed numerous studies documenting the fact that high anxious persons are more self-preoccupied as they do various tasks (e.g., Doris & Sarason, 1955; Sarason & Ganzer, 1962; Sarason & Koenig, 1965), and the fact that they have more task-irrelevant thoughts than do low-anxious persons. These studies suggest that test anxiety is similar to the construct of mastery orientation versus self-focus discussed previously. It differs primarily in its specificity because it is evident primarily in testing situations. But, like mastery orientation, it appears to be influenced by the definition of the task. If a task is described as a test of ability, high-anxious individuals do less well than low anxious individuals (Wine, 1971). When instructions emphasize that the task is nonevaluative, or that the most important thing is to focus on the task, high-anxious individuals often do better than low-anxious individuals. (In fact, low anxious individuals' performance sometimes declines somewhat relative to their performance in highly evaluative situations). In situations in which there are optimal task instructions, high and low anxious individuals often perform at similar levels (see Sarason, 1972).

These results suggest that attentional focus may be a critical component of test anxiety, just as it is a critical component of mastery orientation. Unfortunately, most of the studies on anxiety and attentional focus have been conducted with adults. But the few developmental studies that exist support this point of view. For example, Nottelmann and Hill (1977) observed fourth and fifth grade children as they did an anagrams task. As expected, high anxious children performed more poorly than did the low anxious children. Furthermore, the high anxious children were off task more often than the low anxious children, and asked fewer task-related questions. Dusek, Kermis, and Mergler (1975) and Dusek, Mergler, and Kermis (1976) found that high anxious children have difficulty attending to relevant information in a learning situation, and thus perform more poorly than low anxious children. Providing the high anxious children with an attentional encoding strategy improved their performance. Dusek et al. (1975, 1976) also found that high anxious children have increasing difficulty focusing on the task-relevant information as they get older. These studies clearly show that high anxious children, like high anxious adults, do not attend well to relevant task demands and, as a result, may not be very efficient at analyzing what is needed in order to succeed.

What can be done about the problem of anxiety in evaluative situations? Work with both adults and children (Dusek et al., 1976; Meichenbaum, 1972, 1977; Sarason, 1973, 1975b) indicates that directing high anxious persons' attention more toward the task and away from their own self-preoccupation improves their performance. Changing task instructions from evaluative to nonevaluative also improves the performance of both high anxious adults and children (Sarason, 1973, 1975b; Williams, 1976).

Hill and his colleagues have examined the impact of testing conditions on children's test performance. Hill and Eaton (1977) studied the impact of time limits on the performance of high and low anxious, upper elementary school children. They found that time limits adversely affected the performance of the high anxious children. When no time limits were set, the high anxious children performed quite similarly to the low anxious children in terms of both speed and accuracy. Similar results were reported by Plass and Hill (1979).

Wigfield, Hill, and Plass (1980) extended this research program by investigating how changing the testing conditions used for school-wide achievement tests would influence the performance of junior high school students. They found an interaction between anxiety, testing condition, and grade on the math subtest. Under standard conditions, the low anxious children performed much better than the high anxious children. The seventh grade high anxious children did best in the relaxed time limits condition. The eighth grade high-anxious children did best in the condition that combined the relaxed time limits and special instructions; in fact, they performed as well as low anxious children in this condition.

While the interaction did not reach significance on the reading measure, the pattern of means was quite similar, especially for the eighth graders.

These studies clearly demonstrate how negative motivational dynamics can lower many children's test performance. They also demonstrate how these effects can be minimized. The results are especially compelling because both laboratory and field-based procedures were used. Because changing testing dynamics allows high anxious children to perform as well as low anxious children, Hill (1980) has argued that anxiety is the causal agent in the anxiety–performance relationship. While we believe this conclusion is somewhat premature, we do believe that the work clearly shows that high anxious children's performance can be improved by modifying the testing situation.

Based on these results, Hill (1980) and Wigfield (1981) have made several suggestions for changing testing conditions in schools to help high anxious children perform better. One is to provide dual testing programs, in which children take tests under standard conditions and under optimizing conditions with relaxed time limits, changed instructions, etc. A student's score would be the higher of the two sets of scores. Another suggestion is to gauge tests more closely to children's performance levels, rather than giving the same test to children in several different grades. With this procedure, children would not be faced with as many overly difficult problems. Finally, classroom teachers could introduce activities to help children become familiar with testing and other forms of evaluations. In one such program at the elementary school level (see Hartman, 1981), children were given practice working problems under time limits, answering questions in test-like format, and dealing with computer answer sheets, and were allowed to discuss the purposes of testing with their teacher. Initial results of these experiences have been encouraging, especially for highly anxious children.

With regard to the more general perspective of teacher expectancy effects on children's motivation, of importance here is that teachers tailor their teaching to student characteristics. Children identified as having test-taking problems could be helped through programs like those just summarized. Less anxious students may not need such programs. Structuring classrooms in this way will avoid expectancy effects like "This student never does well in evaluative situations." Rather, positive steps will be taken to overcome the problem.

IMPLICATIONS FOR TEACHER EXPECTANCY THEORY

Our analysis highlights the complexity of the relationship between motivation and achievement in the classroom. We have tried to stress the importance of an ecological perspective on motivation in the classroom. As Bronfenbrenner (1977) has pointed out, both teacher and student behaviors are better understood when we consider the social and psychological context in which these behaviors occur. In this section, we summarize the implications of our analysis for teacher expectancy theory.

First, it is important to consider the role of ego-defensive strategies as well as more approach–oriented learning strategies in shaping children's classroom behaviors. Both students and teachers have a need to defend their self-esteem. Unfortunately, the strategies adopted by both low achieving students and teachers faced with low achieving students are often counter productive in terms of the students' continued educational progress. Behaviors designed to maintain self-worth are a prime example of this process. Covington and Beery (1976) have argued this case quite eloquently. Our only additional suggestion is that the Golem effect may result from these ego-defensive strategies. Furthermore, since these strategies have evolved within the traditional classroom structure and appear to serve an adaptive function in that environment, it may be difficult to avoid these effects within the traditional structure.

Second, again taking an ecological perspective, it is important to note that beliefs regarding the meaning of failure and lack of ability are part of the cultural context in which teacher expectancy effects occur. It is our contention that the belief that lack of ability reflects a stable learning deficit, rather than a skill deficit, is a widely held cultural myth (cf. Ashton & Webb, 1982; and Lewis, 1978 for a similar discussion). Furthermore, it is a belief held by both students regarding their own performance and by teachers regarding the learning potential of their students, especially if there has been a history of poor performance (Beckman, 1970). Recent cross-cultural data gathered by Harold Stevenson and his colleagues provide some support for our hypothesis that these beliefs are cultural myths. When asked to make an attribution for poor performance in mathematics, Japanese parents give a very different response than American parents; Japanese parents attribute poor performance to lack of effort, while American parents attribute it to lack of ability. Informal discussions with teachers have suggested a similar cross-cultural difference in belief structures (H. Stevenson, personal communication, March, 1982).

Because the belief in the stability of lack of ability is so widespread and because it has such a strong impact on behavior, we think this belief underlies much of the Golem effect. Specifically, we believe that both students' and teachers' beliefs regarding their abilities to control and change future performances are the critical mediators between past and future performance. This analysis suggests that teacher expectancy researchers ought to focus on this belief structure rather than on the teachers' assessments of the students' current ability levels. Too often teacher expectancy is operationally defined in terms of the teacher's assessment of the children's current ability level or in terms of test scores provided to the teacher by the investigator. If we are correct, it is really the teacher's expectancy regarding the children's potential for future learning that is the critical mediator of teacher expectancy effects. This belief ought to be tested or manipulated directly.

The final theoretical point we'd like to emphasize is the need for a developmental perspective on teacher expectancy effects. We have stressed throughout this chapter that the link between motivation and achievement varies depending on the children's ages. Consequently, the processes mediating teacher expectancy effects should also vary across grade level. Practices such as tracking or ability grouping may have a strong negative effect in some grades and minimal effects in other grades. A developmental perspective is also critical to the design of intervention programs because the optimal intervention strategies may also depend on grade level.

IMPLICATIONS FOR TEACHER EXPECTANCY
RESEARCH AND PRACTICE

While most models of teacher expectancy effects posit a motivational mediator, very few studies have actually tested these hypotheses. Most of the teacher expectancy studies have assessed or manipulated teacher expectancy (defined in terms of perceived student ability level) and then measured either teacher/student interaction patterns or student achievement. In one of the few studies to actually test the links between teacher expectancy, teacher/student interaction patterns, student perceptions of teacher expectancy, and student motivational beliefs, we found the interrelations to be very weak and highly context dependent (Parsons, Kaczala, & Meece, 1982). We found very little overlap between the interaction variables that were related to the students' perceptions of their teacher's expectancy; the interaction variables that were actually related to the teachers' expectancies; and the interaction variables that were related to the students' beliefs. Despite these rather weak results, teacher expectancies themselves were related to student expectancies, even after the effects of the students' past history of achievement had been partialled out. These results indicate that teacher expectancies do influence student beliefs but that these effects are not being mediated to any great extent by everyday student/teacher interaction patterns or by students' perception of the teachers' expectancies (see Eccles [Parsons] et al., 1983). A similar conclusion has been reached by Asbury (1982) and by Weinstein and her colleagues (see Chapter 13, this volume). Therefore, the motivational links mediating teacher expectancy and student achievement still need to be studied.

Stronger evidence for the link between teacher behavior and student motivation has come out of the literature on effective teaching, classroom climate, and tracking. Reviewing this literature is beyond the scope of this paper. We have already referred to the teacher effectiveness literature; the other literatures have been reviewed adequately elsewhere (see Brophy [Chapter 12, this volume], for an overview of the teaching and teacher effectiveness literature; Thomas [1980] and Eccles, Midgley, & Adler, [1984] for reviews of the classroom structure and classroom climate literatures; and Eccles, Midgley, & Adler [1984] for a review of the tracking literature). Several conclusions can be drawn from these reviews. First, class structure and teaching styles do affect student motivation. Motivation, especially in terms of personal efficacy, perceived control, and subjective task value, is highest when students are given some responsibility over their learning, when instruction is based on individualized mastery goals rather than on norm-referenced achievement-standards, and when the focus of attention is placed on task mastery rather than on ability level evaluation. According to Thomas (1980) learning environments characterized by external ''rewards, norm-referenced achievement standards, competitiveness, uniform goals, and an emphasis on achievement rather than effort'' can result in ''a cumulative depression of the affective and motivational prerequisites of academic achievement, at least for some students'' (p. 234). Therefore, it is possible to avoid the Golem effects associated with low teacher expectancies.

Second, different teaching strategies are needed to effectively motivate children of different skill levels. Low skill-level children are especially likely to be demoralized by the traditional classroom practices discussed in the previous paragraph. These children are in particular need of strategies that minimize the probability of failure; that tailor learning goals to the students' current skill level; that teach the students skills to insure success; that base reinforcements on effort and improvement rather than norm-referenced achievement level; and that provide sufficient guidance and structure to keep the student on-task. Therefore, teachers wishing to avoid the Golem effects will have to make a special effort to motivate low skill-level children.

Third, these effective teaching strategies are most likely to occur when the teacher believes that students can master the material and that teachers can and should help the students accomplish this goal; in other words, when belief in teacher and student efficacy is high. It is important to note, however, that these beliefs are not sufficient to insure effective teaching with low skill-level children. The teachers must also have the knowledge and administrative support to implement effective teaching practices.

Fourth, tracking students by skill level does not appear to an effective strategy of insuring an appropriate teaching environment for low skill-level students. If anything, the Golem effects associated with low teacher expectancy are likely to emerge in tracked classrooms as in nontracked classrooms. Tracking is typically justified with the following rationale; Students learn best when the material is adjusted to their level of understanding. The most efficient way to teach to a student's level of understanding is to group the students by ability and plan the entire group's curriculum at that level. Use of this teaching strategy is presumed to help the students' progress by avoiding a mismatch between the cognitive level of the lesson and the cognitive level of the student. In addition, the argument is often made that lower ability students' self-esteem suffers in a heterogeneous classroom where they will be compared to brighter students. Unfortunately, tracking within this culture has three basic characteristics: (a) It functions to stratify the population it is grouping. (b) It ranks the strata it creates. It is generally accepted, for example, that college prep tracks are better than vocational tracks and that high ability tracks are better than low ability tracks. (c) Due to our cultural myth regarding the meaning of low ability, it provides students and teachers with an explanation for the students' low skill level that absolves both the student and teacher of responsibility for continued learning.

As a consequence of these characteristics, the learning environment in many low-tracked classrooms is very poor, especially for low skill-level students (see Brophy, Chapter 12). In part, this is a consequence of student characteristics. These classes are harder to manage and traditional teaching techniques are not likely to be very successful. But the poor environment can also be exacerbated by the teacher's efficacy beliefs. Because they think that low-skill children can not learn, or do not want to learn, some teachers essentially stop teaching in their low-tracked classes (Ashton & Webb, 1982; Prawat, Lanier, & Byers, undated). Not surprisingly, little learning occurs in these classrooms.

Student motivation is also undermined by these tracking practices in the low-tracked classes. Placement in low tracks is related, for example, to lower levels of aspiration (Metz, 1978; Oakes, 1981), to feelings of worthlessness and rejection (Byers, 1961), to low self-esteem (Oakes, 1981; Prawat, Lanier, & Byers, undated), low self-concept of ability (Mann, 1960), lowered involvement in class activity (Metz, 1978), and greater test anxiety (Cox, 1962, Levy, Gooch, & Kellmer-Pringle, 1969). Apparently, students in the lower tracks accept the notion that they are to blame for their placement (Oakes, 1981) and that there is little reason to keep trying.

This situation is indeed unfortunate given the somewhat arbitrary nature of student placement in tracks (Rist, 1970; Rosenbaum, 1976) and the results of studies on the effects of being moved up in track placement. For example, Tuckman and Bierman (1971) found that both teacher expectations for low skill-level students and the students' actual performance on standardized tests improved significantly when these students were moved up in their track placement. In addition, the teachers in this study recommended that most of the students remain in the higher track the following year. These results suggest that the achievement level differences between tracks is as much a consequence of teacher and student attitudes as it is of true ability differences. In addition, they suggest that the same mechanisms underlying teacher expectancy effects within classrooms may underlie the Golem effects associated with tracking.

In conclusion, let us reiterate our main themes. First, we believe that the motivational variables underlying teacher expectancy effects are basically similar, whether one is focusing on the teacher or the student. These variables, we have argued, can best be summarized in the form of three questions: Can I succeed at this task?, Do I want to succeed at this task?, and What do I need to do to succeed at this task?. For the student these questions become Can I learn this material?, Do I want to complete the assignment?, and What do I need to do in order to complete the assignment? For the teacher these questions become Can I teach this child the material?, Do I want to teach this child the material?, and What do I need to do in order to teach this child the material? If both students and teachers can answer those questions positively, then Golem effects can be avoided, or at least minimized. We believe this outcome would be especially beneficial for low achieving students.

ACKNOWLEDGMENT

Research for this chapter was supported in part by a Spencer Fellowship awarded to the first author by The National Academy of Education and by a Public Health Service postdoctoral fellowship awarded to the second author by the Developmental Psychology Training Program at the University of Michigan. We wish to express our appreciation to the following individuals for their assistance and editorial comments: Steven Asher, Phyllis Blumenfeld, Jere Brophy, Harris Cooper, Jerome Dusek, and Diane Ruble.

REFERENCES

Abramson, L. Y., Seligman, M. E. P., & Teasdale, J. D. Learned helplessness in humans: Critique and reformulation. *Journal of Abnormal Psychology,* 1978, *87,* 49–74.

Andrews, G., & Debus, R. Persistence and the causal perception of failure: Modifying cognitive attributions. *Journal of Educational Psychology,* 1978, *70,* 154–166.

Asbury, J. E. *Student's perceptions of teachers' expectations.* Paper presented at the annual meeting of the American Educational Research Association. New York, 1982.

Ashton, P., & webb, R. *Teacher's sense of efficacy: Toward an ecological model.* Paper presented at the annual meeting of the *American Educational Research Association.* New York, 1982.

Ashton, P. T., Webb, R. B., & Doda, N. *A study of teachers' sense of efficacy: Final report.* Report to National institute of Education. Gainesville, Fl: University of Florida, 1982.

Atkinson, J. W. *An introduction to motivation.* Princeton, N.J.: Van Nostrand, 1964.

Bahad, E. Y., Jacinto, I, & Rosenthal, R. Pygmalion, Galatea, and the Golem: Investigations of biased and unbiased teachers. *Journal of Educational Psychology,* 1982, *74,* 459–474.

Bandura, A. Self-efficacy: Toward a unifying theory of behavioral change. *Psychological Review,* 1977, *84,* 191–215.

Bandura, A. Self-referent thought: The development of self-efficacy. In J. H. Flavell & L. D. Ross (Eds.), *Development of social cognition.* Hillsdale, NJ: Lawrence Erlbaum Associates, 1979.

Beckman, L. Effects of students' performance on teachers' and observers' attributions of causality. *Journal of Educational Psychology,* 1970, *61,* 76–82.

Bloom, B. S. *Human characteristics and school learning.* New York: McGraw-Hill, 1976.

Blumenfeld, P. C., Hamilton, V. I., Bossert, S. T., Wessels, K., & Meece, J. *Teacher talk and student thought: Socialization into the student role.* In J. M. Levine & M. C. Wang (Eds.), *Teacher and student perceptions: Implications for teaching.* Hillsdale, N.J.: Lawrence Erlbaum Associates, 1983.

Bronfenbrenner, U. Toward an experimental ecology of human development. *American Psychologist,* 1977, *32,* 513–531.

Brookover, W., Beady, C., Flood, P., Schweitzer, J., Wisenbaker, J. *School social systems and student achievement: Schools can make a difference.* New York: Praeger Publishers, 1979.

Brookover, W. B., & Erickson, E. L. *Sociology of education.* Illinois: Dorsey Press, 1975

Brophy, J. Teacher behavior and its effects. *Journal of Educational Psychology,* 1979, *71,* 733–750.

Brophy, J. Teacher praise: A functional analysis. *Review of Educational Research,* 1981, *51,* 5–32.

Brophy, J., & Evertson, C. M. *Student characteristics and teaching.* New York: Longman, 1981.

Brophy, J. E., & Good, T. *Teacher-student relationships: Causes and consequences.* New York: Holt, Rinehart & Winston, 1974.

Butkowsky, I. S., & Willows, D. M. Cognitive-motivational characteristics of children varying in reading ability: Evidence of learned helplessness in poor readers., *Journal of Educational Psychology,* 1980, *72,* 408–422.

Byers, L. Ability-grouping: Help or hindrance to social and emotional growth? *The School Review,* 1961, *69,* 449–456.

Calsyn, R., & Kenny, D. Self-concept of ability and perceived dvaluation of others: Cause or effect of academic achievement? *Journal of Educational Psychology,* 1977, *69,* 136–145.

Camp, B. W., & Zimet, S. G. Classroom behavior during reading instruction. *Exceptional Children,* 1975, *42,* 109–110.

Clauset, K. H., & Gaynor, A. K. *Improving schools for low achieving children: A system dynamics policy study.* Paper presented at the Annual Meeting of the American Educational Research Association, New York, 1982.

Cobb, J. A., & Hops, H. Effects of academic survival skill training on low achieving first graders. *Journal of Educational Research,* 1973, *67,* 108–113.

Cooper, H. Controlling personal rewards: Professional teachers' differential use of feedback and the effects of feedback on the student's motivation. *Journal of Educational Psychology,* 1977, *69,* 419–427.

Cooper, H. Pygmalion grows up: A model for teacher expectation communication and performance influence. *Review of Educational Research,* 1979, *49,* 389–410.

Cooper, J. M., Burger, J. M., & Good, T. L. Gender differences in the academic locus of control beliefs of young children. *Journal of Personality and Social Psychology,* 1981, *40,* 562–572.

Covington, M., & Beery, R. *Self-worth and school learning.* New York: Holt, Rinehart & Winston, 1976.

Covington, M., & Omelich, C. Effort: The double-edged sword in school achievement. *Journal of Educational Psychology,* 1979, *71,* 169–182. (a)

Covington, M., & Omelich, C. It's best to be able and virtuous too: Student and teacher evaluative responses to successful effort. *Journal of Educational Psychology,* 1979, *71,* 688–700. (b)

Covington, M., Spratt, M., & Omelich, C. Is effort enough, or does diligence count too? *Journal of Educational Psychology,* 1980, *72,* 717–729.

Cox, F. N. Educational streaming and general test anxiety. *Child Development,* 1962, *33,* 381–390.

Crandall, V. C. Sex differences in expectancy of intellectual and academic reinforcement. In C. P. Smith (Ed.), *Achievement-related motives in children.* New York: Russell Sage Foundation, 1969.

Cronbach, L. J. *Educational psychology* (3rd Edition). New York: Harcourt, Brace, Jovanovich, 1977.

Deci, E. S. *Intrinsic motivation.* New York: Plenum Press, 1975.

Diener, C. I., & Dweck C. S. An analysis of learned helplessness: Continuous change in performance, strategy, and achievement cognitions following failure. *Journal of Personality and Social Psychology,* 1978, *36,* 451–462.

Doris, J., & Sarason, S. B. Test anxiety and blame assignment in a failure situation. *Journal of Abnormal and Social Psychology,* 1955, *50,* 335–338.

Dusek, J. B., Kermis, M. D., & Mergler, N. L. Information processing in low- and high-test anxious children as a function of grade level and verbal labeling. *Developmental Psychology*, 1975, *11*, 651–652.

Dusek, J. B., Mergler, N. L., & Kermis, M. D. Attention, encoding, and information processing in low- and high-test anxious children. *Child Development*, 1976, *47*, 201–207.

Dweck, C. S. The role of expectations and attributions in the alleviation of learned helplessness. *Journal of Personality and Social Psychology*, 1975, *31*, 674–685.

Dweck, C. S., Davidson, W., Nelson, S., & Enna, B. Sex differences in learned helplessness. II. The contingencies of evaluative feedback in the classroom; III. An experimental analysis. *Developmental Psychology*, 1978, *14*, 268–276.

Dweck, C. S., & Goetz, T. E. Attributions and learned helplessness. In J. H. Harvey, W. Ickes, & R. F. Kidd (Eds.), *New directions in attribution research*, Vol. 2. Hillsdale, N.J.: Lawrence Erlbaum Associates, 1978.

Dweck, C. S., & Reppucci, N. D. Learned helplessness and reinforcement responsibility in children. *Journal of Personality and Social Psychology*, 1973, *25*, 109–116.

Eccles, J. Sex differences in mathematics participation. In M. Steinkamp & M. Maehr (Eds.), *Women in science*, Greenwich, Conn.: JAI Press, Inc., 1984.

Eccles (Parsons), J., Adler, T. F., Futterman, R., Goff, S. B., Kaczala, C. M., Meece, J. L., & Midgley, C. Expectancies, values, and academic behaviors. In J. T. Spence (Ed.), *Achievement and achievement motivation*. San Francisco: W. H. Freeman, 1983.

Eccles, J., Adler, T. F., & Meece, J. L. Sex differences in achievement: A test of alternate theories. *Journal of Personality and Social Psychology*, 1984, *46*, 26–43.

Eccles, J., Midgley, C., & Adler, T. F. Age-related changes in the school environment: Effects on achievement motivation. In J. G. Nicholls (Ed.), *The development of achievement motivation*. Greenwich, Conn.: JAI press, 1984.

Eccles, J., Moses, L., & Yulish-Muzynski, S. *The development of attributions, self and task perceptions, expectations, and persistence*. Developmental Reprints, University of Michigan, Ann Arbor, 1982.

Fowler, J. W., & Peterson, P. L. Increasing reading persistence and altering attributional style of learned helpless children. *Journal of Educational Psychology*. 1981, *73*, 251–260.

Frieze, I. H., Whitley, B. E., Hanusa, B. H., & McHugh, M. C. Assessing the theoretical models for sex differences in causal attributions for success and failure. *Sex Roles*, 1982, *8*, 333–343.

Good, T., Cooper, H., & Blakey, S. Classroom interaction as a function of teacher expectations, student sex, and time of year. *Journal of Educational Psychology*, 1980, *72*, 378–385.

Hansford, B. C., & Hattie, J. A. The relationship between self and achievement/performance measures. *Review of Educational Research*, 1982, *52*, 123–142.

Harter, S. Effectance motivation reconsidered: Toward a developmental model. *Human Development*, 1978, *1*, 34–64.

Harter, S. A model of intrinsic mastery motivation in children: Individual differences and developmental change. *Minnesota Symposium on Child Psychology*, Vol. 14, Hillsdale, N.J.: Lawrence Erlbaum Associates, 1981. (a)

Harter, S. A new self-report scale of intrinsic versus extrinsic orientation in the classroom: Motivational and informational components. *Developmental Psychology*, 1981, *17*, 300–312. (b)

Harter, S. The Perceived Competence Scale for Children. *Child Development*, 1982, *53*, 87–97.

Harter, S., & Connell, J. P. A model of the relationships among children's academic achievement and their self-perceptions of competence, control, and motivational orientation. In J. Nicholls (Ed.), *The development of achievement motivation*. Greenwich, Conn.: JAI Press, 1984.

Hartman, A. *Teaching test-taking skills and developing positive test motivation in the classroom*. Paper presented as part of a symposium entitled "Eliminating motivational test bias in educational testing" (K. T. Hill, organizer), presented at the Annual Meeting of the American Educational Research Association, Los Angeles, 1981.

Hill, K. T. The relation of evaluative practices to test anxiety and achievement motivation. *Educator*, 1977, *19*, 15–22.

Hill, K. T. Motivation, evaluation and educational testing policy. In L. J. Fyans (Ed.), *Achievement motivation: Recent trends in theory and research*. New York: Plenum, 1980.

Hill, K. T., & Eaton, W. O. The interaction of text anxiety and success/failure experiences in determining children's arithmetic performance. *Developmental Psychology*, 1977, *13*, 205–211.

Hill, K. T., & Sarason, S. B. The relation of test anxiety and defensiveness to test and school performance over the elementary school years: A further longitudinal study. *Monographs of the Society for Research in Child Development*, Serial No. 104, 1966, *31*(Whole No. 2).

Hops, H., & Cobb, J. A. Initial investigations into academic survival-skill training, direct instruction and first grade achievement. *Journal of Educational Psychology*, 1974, *66*, 548–553.

Janof-Bulman, R., & Brickman, P. Expectations and what people learn from failure. In N. T. Feather (Ed.), *Expectations and actions*. Hillsdale, N.J.: Lawrence Erlbaum Associates, 1981.

Johnson, D. W., & Johnson, R. T. Instructional goal structure: Cooperative, competitive or individualistic. *Review of Educational Research*, 1974, *44*, 213–240.

Kruglanski, A. W. The endogenous-exogenous partition in attribution theory. *Psychological Review*, 1975, *82*, 387–406.

Kukla, A. Foundations of an attributional theory of performance. *Psychological Review*, 1972, *79*, 454–470.

Kukla, A. An attributional theory of choice. In L. Berkowitz (Ed.), *Advances in experimental social psychology*, Vol. II. New York: Academic Press, 1978.

Lambert, N. M., & Nicholl, R. C. Conceptual model for nonintellectual behavior and its relationship to reading achievement. *Journal of Educational Psychology*, 1977, *69*, 481–496.

Lepper, M. R., & Greene, D. (Eds.), *The hidden costs of reward: New perspectives on the psychology of human motivation*. Hillsdale, N.J.: Lawrence Erlbaum Associates, 1978.

Levy, P., Gooch, S., & Kellmer-Pringle, M. L. A longitudinal study of the relationship between anxiety and streaming in a progressive and a traditional junior school. *British Journal of Educational Psychology*, 1969, *39*, 166–173.

Lewin, K. *The conceptual representation and the measurement of psychological forces*. Durham, N.C.: Duke University Press, 1938.

Lewis, M. *The culture of inequality*. New York: New American Literary, 1978.

Liebert, R. M., & Morris, L. W. Cognitive and emotional components of test anxiety: A distinction and some initial data. *Psychological Reports*, 1967, *20*, 975–978.

Maehr, M. L. On doing well in science: Why Johnny no longer excels: Why Sara never did. In S. Paris, G. Olson & H. Stevenson (Eds.), *Learning and motivation in the classroom*. Hillsdale, N.J.: Lawrence Erlbaum Associates, 1983.

Mann, M. What does ability grouping do to the self-concept? *Childhood Education*, 1960, *36*, 356–360.

Markus, H., The self in thought and memory. In D. M. Wegner & R. R. Vallacher (Eds.), *The self in social psychology*. New York: Oxford University Press, 1980.

Meichenbaum, D. Cognitive modification of test anxious college students. *Journal of Consulting and Clinical Psychology*, 1972, *39*, 370–380.

Meichenbaum, D. *Cognitive-behavior modification: An integrative approach*. New York: Plenum Press, 1977.

Metz, M. H. *Classrooms and corridors*. Berkeley, Calif.: University of California Press, 1978.

Mortimer, J. T., & Simmons, R. G. Adult socialization. *Annual Review of Sociology*, Palo Alto: Annual Reviews, 1978.

Newman, R. *The development of children's skills in mathematics*. Unpublished doctoral dissertation, University of Michigan, 1982.

Nicholls, J. G. Effort is virtuous, but it's better to have ability: Evaluative responses to perceptions of effort and ability. *Journal of Research in Personality*, 1976, *10*, 306–315.

Nicholls, J. G. Quality and equality in intellectual development: The role of motivation in education. *American Psychologist*, 1979, *34*, 1071–1084.

Nicholls, J. G. *Motivation for intellectual development and performance*. Paper presented at the Annual Meeting of the American Educational Research Association, Boston, 1980.

Nottelmann, E. D., & Hill, K. T. Test anxiety and off-task behavior in evaluative situations. *Child Development*, 1977, *48*, 225–231.

Oakes, J. O. *A question of access: Tracking and curriculum differentiation in a national sample of English and mathematics classes* (Tech. Rep. No. 24) Los Angeles: University of California, Graduate School of Education, 1981.

Parsons, J. E., & Goff, S. B. Achievement motivation: A dual modality. In L. J. Fyans (Ed.) *Recent trends in achievement motivation: Theory and research*. Englewood Cliffs, N.J.: Plenum, 1980.

Parsons, J. E., Kaczala, C. M., & Meece, J. L. Socialization of achievement attitudes and beliefs: Classroom influences. *Child Development*, 1982, *53*, 322–339.

Parsons, J. E., Meece, J. L., Adler, T. F., & Kaczala, C. M. Sex differences in attributions and learned helplessness? *Sex Roles*, 1982, *8*, 421–432.

Parsons, J. E., & Ruble, D. N. The development of achievement-related expectancies. *Child Development*, 1977, *48*, 1075–1079.

Plass, J., & Hill, K. T. *Optimizing children's achievement test performance: The role of time pressure, evaluation anxiety, and sex*. Paper presented at the Biennial Meeting of the Society for Research in Child Development, San Francisco, March, 1979.

Prawat, R. S., Lanier, P. E., & Byers, J. L. *Attitudinal differences between students in general mathematics and algebra classes*. Unpublished manuscript, Michigan State University, undated.

Purkey, W. W. *Self-concept and school achievement*. Englewood Cliffs, N.J.: Prentice-Hall, 1970.

Raynor, J. O. Future orientation in the study of achievement motivation. In J. W. Atkinson, & J. O. Raynor (Eds.), *Motivation and achievement*. Washington, D.C.: Winston, 1974.

Rholes, W. S., Blackwell, J., Jordan C., & Walters, C. A developmental study of learned helplessness. *Developmental Psychology*, 1980, *16*, 616–624.

Rist, R. C. Student social class and teacher expectations: The self-fulfilling prophecy in ghetto education. *Harvard Educational Review*, 1970, *40*, 411–451.

Rokeach, M. *The nature of human values*. New York: The Free Press, 1973.

Rosenbaum, J. E. *Making inequality: The hidden curriculum of high school tracking*. New York: Wiley, 1976.

Rosenshine, B. V., & Berliner, D. C. Academic engaged time. *British Journal of Teacher Education*, 1978, *4*, 3–16.

Rothbaum, F., Weisz, J. R., & Snyder, S. S. Changing the world and changing the self: A two-process model of perceived control. *Journal of Personality and Social Psychology*, 1982, *42*, 5–37.

Ruble, D., & Boggiano, A. Optimizing motivation in an achievement context. In B. Keogh (Ed.), *Advances in Special Education*, Vol. 1. Greenwich, Conn.: JAI Press, 1980.

Ruble, D. N., Parsons, J. E., & Ross, self-evaluative responses of children in an achievement setting. *Child Development*, 1976, *47*, 990–997.

Samuels, S. J., & Turnure, J. E. Attention and reading achievement in first-grade boys and girls. *Journal of Educational Psychology*, 1974, *66*, 29–32.

Sarason, I. G. Experimental approaches to test anxiety: Attention and the uses of information. In C. D. Spielberger (Ed.), *Anxiety: Current trends in theory and research*, Vol. 2. New York: Academic Press, 1972.

Sarason, I. G. Test anxiety and cognitive modeling. *Journal of Personality and Social Psychology*, 1973, *28*, 58–61.

Sarason, I. G. Test anxiety, attention and the general problem of anxiety. In C. D. Spielberger & I. G. Sarason (Eds.), *Stress and anxiety* (Vol. 1). Washington, D.C.: Hemisphere, 1975. (a)

Sarason, I. G. Test anxiety and the self-disclosing coping model. *Journal of Consulting and Clinical Psychology*, 1975, *43*, 148–153. (b)

Sarason, I. G., & Ganzer, V. J. Anxiety, reinforcement and experimental instructions in a free verbalization situation. *Journal of Abnormal and Social Psychology*, 1962, *65*, 301–307.

Sarason, I. G., & Koenig, K. P. The relationship of text anxiety and hostility to description of self and parents. *Journal of Personality and Social Psychology*, 1965, *2*, 617–621.

Scheiner, M. A., & Kraut, R. E. Increased educational achievement via self-concept change. *Review of Educational Research*, 1979, *49*, 131–150.

Schunk, D. H. Modeling and attributional effects on children's achievement: A self-efficacy analysis. *Journal of Educational Psychology*, 1981, *73*, 93–105.

Seligman, M. E. P. *Helplessness: Depression, development, and death.* San Francisco: Freeman, 1975.

Shavelson, R. J., & Bolus, R. Self-concept: The interplay of theory and method. *Journal of Educational Psychology*, 1982, *74*, 3–17.

Slavin, R. E. Classroom reward structure: An analytic and practical review. *Review of Educational Research*, 1977, *47*, 633–650.

Soli, S. D., & Devine, V. T. Behavioral correlates of achievement: A look at high and low achievers. *Journal of Educational Psychology*, 1976, *68*, 335–341.

Spenner, K., & Featherman, D. L. Achievement ambitions. *Annual Review of Sociology*, 1978, *4*, 373–420.

Stallings, J. Allocated academic learning time revisited, or beyond time on task. *Educational Researcher*, 1980, *9*, 11–16.

Stallings, J., & Kaskowitz, D. *Follow-through classroom observation evaluation, 1972–1973.* Menlo Park, Calif.: Stanford Research Institute, 1974.

Stein, A. H., & Bailey, M. M. The socialization of achievement orientation in females. *Psychological Bulletin*, 1973, *80*, 345–366.

Stein, A. H., & Smithells, T. Age and sex differences in children's sex role standards about achievement. *Developmental Psychology*, 1969, *1*, 252–259.

Stipek, D. J., & Weisz, J. R. Perceived personal control and academic achievement. *Review of Educational Research*, 1981, 51, 101–137.

Swann, W., & Snyder, M. On translating beliefs into action: Theories of ability and their application in an instructional setting. *Journal of Personality and Social Psychology*, 1980, *38*, 879–888.

Thibaut, J. W., & Kelley, H. H. *The social psychology of groups.* New York: Wiley, 1959.

Thomas, J. W. Agency and achievement: Self-management and self-reward. *Review of Educational Research*, 1980, *50*, 213–240.

Tuckman, B. W., & Bierman, M. L. *Beyond Pygmalion: Galatea in the schools.* Paper presented at the meeting of the American Educational Research Association, New York, 1971.

Uguroglu, M. E., & Walberg, H. J. Motivation and achievement: A quantitative synthesis. *American Educational Research Journal*, 1979, *16*, 375–389.

Veroff, J. Social comparison and the development of achievement motivation. In C. P. Smith (Ed.), *Achievement-related motives in children.* New York: Russell Sage Foundation, 1969.

Veroff, J. Process vs. impact in men's and women's motivation. *Psychology of Women Quarterly*, 1977, *1*, 283–292.

Walker, H. M., & Hops, H. Increasing academic achievement by reinforcing direct academic performance and/or facilitative nonacademic response. *Journal of Educational Psychology*, 1976, *68*, 218–225.

Weiner, B. *Theories of motivation: From mechanism to cognition.* Chicago: Markham Publishing Co., 1972.

Weiner, B. *Achievement motivation and attribution theory.* Morristown, N.J.: General Learning Press, 1974.

Weiner, B. A theory of motivation for some classroom experiences. *Journal of Educational Psychology*, 1979, *71*, 3–25.

Weiner, B., Frieze, I., Kukla, A., Reed, L., Rest, S., & Rosenbaum, R. M. *Perceiving the causes of success and failure*. New York: General Learning Press, 1971.

Weiner, B., Russell, D., & Lerman, D. Affective consequences of causal ascriptions. In J. H. Harvey, W. Ickes, & R. F. Kidd (Eds.), *New directions in attribution research*, Vol. 2. Hillsdale, N.J.: Lawrence Erlbaum Associates, 1978.

Weiner, B., Russell, D., & Lerman, D. The cognition-emotion process in achievement-related contexts. *Journal of Personality and Social Psychology*, 1979, *37*, 1211–1221.

White, R. W. Motivation reconsidered: The concept of competence. *Psychological Review*, 1959, *66*, 297–333.

Wigfield, A. *Eliminating motivational test bias with children: A report on two intervention studies*. Paper presented as part of a symposium entitled "Eliminating motivational test bias in educational testing", presented at the annual meeting of the American Educational Research Association, Los Angeles, 1981.

Wigfield, A., & Asher, S. R. The social and motivational context of reading. In P. D. Pearson (Ed.), *Handbook of reading research*. New York: Longman, 1984.

Wigfield, A., & Eccles, J. *The development of attributions and expectations: A critical review*. Unpublished manuscript, University of Michigan, 1982.

Wigfield, A., Hill, K. T., & Plass, J. *Effects of different kinds of optimizing instructions on seventh and eighth grade children's achievement test performance*. Paper presented at the annual meeting of the American Educational Research Association, Boston, April 1980.

Williams, J. P. *Individual differences in achievement test presentation and evaluation anxiety*. Unpublished doctoral dissertation, University of Illinois at Urbana-Champaign, 1976.

Wine, J. Test anxiety and direction of attention. *Psychological Bulletin*, 1971, *76*, 92–104.

Wine, J. D. Cognitive-attentional theory of test anxiety. In I. G. Sarason (Ed.), *Test anxiety: Theory, research and applications*. Hillsdale, N.J.: Lawrence Erlbaum Associates, 1980.

Section 3
Individual Differences and
Teacher Expectancies

The three chapters comprising this section are addressed to the issue of how teachers form expectancies for an individual student. Of course, this issue is at the heart of the study of teacher expectancies.

Dusek and Joseph (Chapter 9) present a meta-analysis of research aimed at discovering the characteristics to which teachers attend when forming expectancies. Research addressing this question is of two types: in-classroom studies, which are very rare, and analog studies in which some subjects act as teachers and judge the likely success of fictitious students. The authors review research investigating the degree to which student gender, physical appearance, family situation, sibling's performance, sex-role stereotypes, cumulative folder information, classroom conduct, name stereotypes, race, and social class relate to the expectancies the teacher has for the child's performance. In so doing, Dusek and Joseph note a number of deficiencies in the existing literature, most motable being the lack of research with classroom teachers and their own students.

Baron, Tom and Cooper (Chapter 10) focus their meta-analysis specifically on the issue of social class and race being determinants of teacher expectancies. In examining the main effect of each student characteristic, Baron et al. also look at the interactive effects of student social class and race in the determination of teacher expectancies. Furthermore, they have begun the examination of mediating factors involved in the influence of social class and race on teacher expectancies. In concluding their review, they note that social learning and social cognitive theories might prove useful in delineating basic processes underlying the impact of race and social class on teachers' beliefs about student performance.

Good and Findley (Chapter 11) discuss one type of information pertinent to the Baron et al. suggestion. The departure point for Good and Findley's review is the well established sex difference in student performance in mathematics and other subjects. In their review, they include information bearing on the question of teachers' differential behavior toward boys and girls as a function of beliefs about which gender might perform at higher levels. The material reviewed in this chapter, then, relates individual differences among teachers to individual differences among students. It also details evidence linking teacher expectations within the broad confines of sex roles to teacher behavior and student achievement in the classroom. As a result, Good and Findley's integration rounds out the importance of considering individual differences, in both teachers and students, in the understanding of teacher expectancy effects.

The chapters in this section point out the complexities involved in the study of teacher expectancies. Teachers form expectancies for students not only on the basis of individual differences among students, but also as a result of individual teacher characteristics, based in part on general social expectations.

9 The Bases of Teacher Expectancies

Jerome B. Dusek
Gail Joseph
Syracuse University

As is evident from previous chapters, it is now widely accepted that teachers form expectancies about student academic ability and social skills (cf. Braun, 1976; Cooper, 1979a; Dusek, 1975). Evidence indicates that teacher expectancies are correlated with student achievement test performance (e.g., Dusek & O'Connell, 1973; O'Connell, Dusek, & Wheeler, 1974) and student–teacher interactions in the classroom (cf. Brophy & Good, 1974). There can be but little doubt that understanding teacher expectancies is an important part of comprehending the nature of teacher evaluation of students.

Although we now have well-developed models of the communication of expectancy effects (cf. Cooper, Chapter 6; Brophy & Good, 1974; Chapter 12), knowledge in other areas is lacking. The purpose of this chapter is to provide a review of one of these areas of deficiency, namely, the bases on which teachers form expectancies for students' performance. In some instances (for example, student gender and student social class and race) we present only summary statements because extensive reviews are presented in other chapters in this book. In other instances, such as physical attractiveness and cumulative folder information, we present detailed reviews.

Meta-Analysis

In the present review, a meta-analysis was conducted of research aimed at determining the bases of teacher expectancies. Glass (1976, 1977) has defined meta-analysis as the combining of results of independent experiments for the purpose of integrating their findings. A meta-analysis is conducted on a group of studies having a common conceptual hypothesis or operational definition of independent or dependent variables. One result of a meta-analysis is a significance level that gives the probability that a set of studies exhibiting the reported

229

results could have been generated if no real relationship existed. In addition, a meta-analysis allows the description of the degree of overlap between experimental conditions on a normal curve. As a result, meta-analyses yield information about the effect size for differences between conditions.

Rosenthal (1978) has discussed the relative advantages and disadvantages of various meta-analytic techniques. The counting (Rosenthal, 1978) or voting (Johnson, Maruyama, Johnson, Nelson, & Skon, 1981) method is a simple categorization of findings into one of three types: significantly positive, significantly negative, or no difference (not statistically different). Rosenthal (1978) and Johnson et al. (1981) point out that this method has flaws, including low power to detect relationships, the ignoring of strength of effects (effect size), and the failure to account for sample size (larger samples result in a greater number of significant effects than do smaller samples). This approach is, in effect, a formalized model of the typical literature review. Given the disadvantages of this method it was not employed in this review.

The method of adding zs was developed by Stouffer (1949). All it requires is an accurate probability level for the effect of interest. Pertinent p levels are changed to z scores, added, and the sum divided by the square root of the number of studies included (Rosenthal, 1978). The resulting z score is referred back to the table and the probability level calculated. This probability level describes the likelihood that the results of all studies were generated by chance. Mosteller and Bush (1954) have suggested weighting each of the above standard normal deviates by the size of the sample on which it is based, by its degrees of freedom, or by any other positive weighting that is desirable. The weighted zs are summed and the sum is divided by the square root of the sum of the squared weights. The advantage of weighting lies in the reviewer's ability to make adjustments based on important criteria (e.g., sample size, methodological rigor). The weighting method will lead to a lower probability level when larger studies produce larger z scores and a higher probability level when smaller studies produce larger z scores. In the present review, only the method of adding zs was used. As others (e.g., Rosenthal, 1978) have noted, differences in conclusions based on the method of adding zs and adding weighted zs are minimal.

The meta-analytic review procedures have several additional advantages over the traditional literary review. First, estimates of effect size may be obtained. In the present review, effect size was estimated by Cohen's (1977) d statistic, which is a "scale free" measure of the degree of departure of the alternative hypothesis from the null hypothesis. In the case of two means an estimate of d is given by the following formula:

$$d = 2t/\sqrt{df}.$$

A second advantage of using meta-analysis procedures is the ability to calculate a failsafe N, the number of studies totaling a null hypothesis confirmation necessary to reverse a conclusion that a relationship exists. In effect, the question is "How many studies showing a summed z score total of zero would be necessary to raise the overall probability level to a nonsignificant level?'' Rosenthal (1979) has referred to this as the ''file drawer problem.'' The failsafe N is an estimate of the number of studies showing null results and, therefore, not published but sitting in file drawers. For the $p<.05$ criterion, the failsafe N is given by the formula

$$N_{fs.05} = (Z_{s1} + Z_{s2} + \ldots + Z_{sn} / 1.645)^2 - (N_s)$$

where $N_{fs.05}$ is the number of studies needed to increase the meta-analysis p level above .05, 1.645 is the z score for the $p < .05$ significance level, N_s is the sum number of the studies, and the Zs are the z scores from the existing studies (Cooper, 1979c).

Finally, Cohen (1977) has described a useful statistic, U_3, the percentage of distribution nonoverlap. The U_3 statistic denotes the percentage of the group with the smaller mean that is exceeded by 50% of the group with the larger mean. The U_3 statistic, then, represents the percentage of the smaller-meaned group that is exceeded by the average person in the larger-meaned group.

Scope of This Review

The focus of this review centers around the identification of the types of information teachers use in forming expectancies for students' academic potential. The general hypothesis tested was that teachers would hold differential expectancies for students varying in social class, race, attractiveness, etc. Specific directions for each hypothesis are spelled out in each section of the review. Only those studies bearing directly on the major question are included. Moreover, whenever feasible and appropriate, the meta-analysis is supplemented by discussions of research not directly translatable into the format. Finally, some areas of research include so few studies that to do a meta-analysis would be inappropriate. These areas are discussed in the more typical literary style.

The review is organized into sections based on student physical or intellectual characteristics (e.g., evidence regarding previous performance or scores on standardized tests) that have been hypothesized to be related to the formation of teacher expectancies. This organization is based on the kinds of factors to which teachers are presumed to attend when forming expectancies for student performance (Braun, 1976; Cooper, 1979b). Hence, it facilitates assessing previous claims regarding the bases of teachers' expectancies.

METHOD

Search Procedure

The major sources for the search were *Psychological Abstracts, Dissertation Abstracts International,* and *ERIC (Educational Research Information Center).* In order to have an intentionally broad initial search we scrutinized titles and abstracts for the key words "teacher expec...," "teacher bias," "teacher bases," etc. Reference to specific bases were excluded because we wished to obtain the largest number of studies possible for inclusion in the review. Abstracts were read and obviously irrelevant studies were eliminated. Full reports for all remaining studies, except those in *Dissertation Abstracts International,* were read, and any other irrelevant studies were eliminated. Finally, the titles of references in published studies were used to further search for relevant research. This procedure resulted in the identification of the 77 studies reviewed below.

Criteria for Relevant Studies

A study was considered for inclusion if it contained a measure of teacher expectancies, a measure of some student characteristic that could be viewed as a potential basis for forming expectancies, and a test of the relationship between the two measures.

Teacher expectancy was broadly operationally defined in two ways. *Academic expectations* dealt with teacher expectations for academic achievement, student ability, future academic attainment, and the like. *Social/personality expectations* dealt with perceptions of general social development, peer relations, personality attributions, adult relations, and the like. Specific measures are listed in each section of the review.

Analysis

The basic analytic procedures were outlined above. The method of adding z scores was used. Effect size was estimated by Cohen's d score. When significant effects were found, a failsafe N was calculated.

RESULTS

Results are presented for specific student characteristics presumed to be the bases of teacher expectancies.

Physical Attractiveness

The influence of physical attractiveness on human interactions has a long history of investigation in social psychology (cf. Berscheid & Walster, 1974). The majority of studies have been concerned with attractiveness to the opposite sex, attributions of personality traits, and judgments of transgressions. Recent research on the importance of physical attractiveness as a determinant of teacher expectancies has led some (e.g., Braun, 1976) to conclude that teachers have higher expectancies for more attractive children. This is the hypothesis that was tested.

A total of 14 studies in which physical attractiveness was related to a measure of teacher expectancy were identified. In 10 studies attractiveness was related to expectancies for both academic and social characteristics of students. In three studies attractiveness was related to expectancies for social development, and in one attractiveness was related to a measure of academic expectancies. Given the substantial number of studies in each domain, the data were analyzed separately for the academic (Table 9.1a) and social/personality (Table 9.1b) measures.

In general, the procedure employed involved providing teachers with information (e.g., achievement test performance) about a fictitious child and a picture of the child. Half the teacher sample received pictures previously rated as unattractive. Half received pictures previously rated as attractive. In all studies pictures of both male and female students were employed.

A variety of measures of teacher expectancy were obtained, including estimates of the child's future academic success, of parental concern about school, of the child's social relations with peers, of the child's IQ, and of the child's interest in school.

As may be seen in Table 9.1a, for the academic measures teachers were subjects in nine studies and college students were subjects in two. No significant difference was found in four studies, but more attractive children were expected to outperform less attractive children in seven studies. The Z was 5.43 (p = .0000001). The d value was .30 and the failsafe N was 109. The average attractive student was expected to perform better than about 61% of the less attractive students. These data leave little doubt that physical attractiveness is an important basis of teacher expectancies for academic achievement. However, as is noted below, the veridicality of this conclusion with regard to in-classroom teachers is open to question.

TABLE 9.1a
Physical Attractiveness

Academic Expectations

Author	*Year*	*Subjects*	*Expectation Favored*
Clifford & Walster	1973	Teachers	Attractive
Adams & LaVoie	1974	Teachers	Attractive
LaVoie & Adams	1974	Teachers	No Difference
Kehle et al.	1974	Teachers	No Difference
Ross & Salvia	1975	Teachers	Attractive
Adams & Cohen	1976a	Teachers	Attractive
Roland	1977	Teachers	No Difference
Salvia et al.	1977	Students	Attractive
Adams	1978	Teachers	Attractive
DeMeis & Turner	1978	Teachers	Attractive
Tompkins & Boor	1980	Students	No Difference

TABLE 9.1b

Social/Personality Expectations

Author	Year	Subjects	Expectation Favored
Clifford & Walster	1973	Teachers	Attractive
Adams & LaVoie	1974	Teachers	No Difference
LaVoie & Adams	1974	Teachers	No Difference
Kehle et al.	1974	Teachers	No Difference
Rich	1975	Teachers	Attractive
Ross & Salvia	1975	Teachers	Attractive
Adams & Cohen	1976b	Teachers	Attractive
Roland	1977	Teachers	Attractive
Adams	1978	Teachers	Attractive
DeMeis & Turner	1978	Teachers	Attractive
Marwit et al.	1978	Students	No Difference
Marwit et al.	1978	Teachers	Unattractive
Tompkins & Boor	1980	Students	Attractive

The relationship between student attractiveness and teacher expectancies for social/personality measures was assessed in 13 studies. In 11 studies teachers were the subjects, in one student teachers, and in one college students. Inspection of Table 9.1b shows a reversal in one study (less attractive students were given higher expectancies), null results in five studies, and results favoring attractive students in seven studies. The statistical analysis was significant ($Z = 3.84$, $p = .000065$, $d = .19$). The failsafe N was 58. The average attractive student was expected to have better social relations and personality development than 57% of the less attractive students. Again, then, the research leads to the conclusion that attractiveness is an important basis of teacher expectancies.

Some researchers have concluded that student attractiveness is actually only a transient basis of teacher expectancies. Adams and LaVoie (1974) and LaVoie and Adams (1974) argue that, at best, attractiveness may be important in the absence of other more academically relevant information (see also Cooper, 1979b; Kehle, Bramble, & Mason, 1974). Willis (1972; see also Willis & Brophy, 1974) reported that teachers' ratings of their students' physical attractiveness correlated significantly with expected achievment only during the initial part of the school year. The correlations for the midsemester and end-of-semester ratings were not statistically significant. Moreover, other teacher ratings, such as classroom attentiveness, self-confidence, and ability to work independently, showed larger and more enduring correlations with achievement. As LaVoie and Adams (1974) note, physical attractiveness may be important for initial expectancies but other, more academically pertinent information, gleaned after interacting with children for some time, become more important for expectancy formation.

Student Gender

The relationship between student gender and teacher expectancies has been of considerable interest, in part because of gender differences in measures of learning (cf. Bank, Biddle, & Good, 1980; Palardy, 1969), and, in part, because of the different types of interactions boys and girls have with teachers (cf. Brophy & Good, 1970, 1974). The general conception, which has some research support (cf. Bank et al., 1980; Brophy & Good, 1974), is that girls are favored during the elementary school years. Hence, one may well expect that girls will have an advantage over boys on measures of teacher expectancies. The major concerns in this domain are discussed in detail in Chapter 11. Therefore, we simply summarize our analyses (cf. Dusek & Joseph, 1983). The hypothesis tested was that teacher expectancies would be higher for girls than boys.

As may be seen in Chapter 11 by Good and Findley, student gender appears to be an important characteristic in determining teacher expectancies. However, research by Willis (1972) suggests the relationship may not be straightforward. Willis reported few relationships between student gender and teacher expectancies for measures of academic performance. Much stronger and enduring relationships were obtained between gender as a basis of expectancies and measures of student social/personality development.

This distinction is confirmed, to a degree, in the meta-analysis (cf. Dusek & Joseph, 1983 for a detailed review). A total of 20 studies were identified in which student gender was related to a measure of teacher expectancy. In 16 studies the dependent measure was an expectancy for student academic performance. In 12 studies expectancies for student social relations or personality development were assessed.

The meta-analysis for expectancies related to academic performance was not significant ($Z = .80$, $p = .21$, $d = .20$, $U_3 = 51.2$).

The results were somewhat different when teacher expectancies as a function of gender were related to a measure of social/personality development. A total of 12 pertinent studies were identified. The statistical analysis resulted in a borderline significant effect ($Z = 1.47$, $p = .071$) of low strength ($d = .07$). Approximately 53% of females were expected to perform better than the average male.

These results indicate that teacher expectancies as a function of gender are not related to academic measures but are at least weakly related to measures of social/personality development. Measures of social/personality development included getting along with others, having good self-control, being helpful to other children, being neat and careful, and having many friends. In the elementary school this is more likely to be the female than the male. Hence, it is not surprising that social/personality expectancies favor girls. The picture one gets is that the student who is easy to manage and who follows the classroom rules is in the more favorable position.

The issue of the relation of student gender to teacher expectancies, then, is a complex one, no doubt related to other student gender effects, such as student–teacher interactions, that occur in the classroom. In a global sense, student gender is not related to teacher expectancies. More specifically, it is not related to expectancies related to academic achievement. However, it may be related to expectancies regarding social/personality development. The latter relationship is not strong, but suggestive. Further research, such as that of Willis, with teachers rating their own students is clearly called for.

Cumulative Folder Information

The research reviewed in this section is a direct extension of Rosenthal and Jacobson's (1968) original study. Although the procedural aspects of the research make for some difficulty in grouping and discussing relevant studies, the researchers have in common an interest in assessing the influence of prior information—both objective and subjective—on the teacher's expectancies for academic potential. This is an especially important area of research because the varieties of information to which teachers are exposed may lead them to form expectancies for a student before they have had any personal contact with the student. The teacher may then act in a way to cause the child to fulfill the expectancy. The potential for information in student cumulative records to have this effect was shown by Willis (1972). Strong relationships existed between teacher expectancies and information found in student folders, for example, attentiveness, obedience, industriousness, work habits.

The general procedure followed in the studies reviewed in this section involved providing subjects with written descriptions, either positive or negative, of a fictitious student. Characteristics included in the description were study habits, general behavior, information on academic achievement, grades, IQ, in some instances a diagnostic label, such as EMR, and in some instances, information on family background. In general, the information was presented as if the subject were reading a cumulative folder for a real student. Because it was not possible to determine the specific aspect(s) of the information to which the subjects attended, no attempt was made to form subcategories of the retrieved studies. Because teachers no doubt read varieties of information in student folders this was not seen as a difficulty.

A total of 24 studies were identified. Teachers were subjects in 18 and graduate and undergraduate students were subjects in six. In 14 studies sufficient information was included to allow a meta-analysis. These are listed in Table 9.2 As will become apparent, were it possible to include the remaining 10 studies in the meta-analysis the conclusions would have been even stronger.

The meta-analysis resulted in a significant Z (6.22, $p = .00000001$) that reflected a strong relationship ($d = .852$) between cumulative folder information and teacher expectancies. The U_3 value was 71.5, indicating that over 70% of the more favorably described students were expected to perform better than the average less favorably described student. The failsafe N was 186. There can be

TABLE 9.2
Cumulative Folder Information

Author	Year	Subjects	Expectation Favored
Mason	1973	Teachers	Positive
Kehle et al.	1974	Teachers	No Difference
Mason & Larimore	1974	Teachers	Positive
Foster et al.	1975	Teachers	Positive
Yoshida & Meyers	1975	Teachers	No Difference
Adams & Cohen	1976a	Teachers	No Difference
Adams & Cohen	1976b	Teachers	No Difference
Mertens	1976	Students	Positive
Cooper & Lowe[1]	1977	Students	No Difference
	1977	Teachers	Positive
Helton & Oakland	1977	Teachers	Positive
Wiley & Eskilson	1978	Teachers	Positive
Cooper & Burger[2]	1980	Students	No Difference
Foster et al.	1980	Teachers	Positive

[1]Cooper and Lowe report two studies, each done with separate samples. They are treated separately here.

[2]Cooper and Burger report three studies, each done with a separate sample. Only the third is pertinent and reported here.

no doubt that information in student folders is a powerful determinant of teacher expectancies. This conclusion is strengthened by the findings of the remaining 10 studies. Herson (1974) reported that including a label (e.g., marginally retarded) with a behavioral description resulted in stronger expectancy effects than the behavioral description alone. Rich (1975) found that student personal and academic descriptions were related to teachers' judgments of the likelihood a child committed a transgression and the severity of punishment that should be given the child. Foster and Ysseldyke (1976) and Reschly and Lamprecht (1979) reported that deviancy labels resulted in negative expectancies on referral forms.

In several studies attempts have been made to provide a more pointed description of the relationship between information in cumulative folders and teachers' expectancies. Porter (1979), for example, found that the relationship between teacher expectancies and information about students depended on the area of expectancy. Information about student ability was a stronger predictor of academic achievement, and information about student personality was the stronger predictor of expectancies for student social behavior.

Algozzine (1981) and Algozzine and Stoller (1981) presented teachers with both labels (LD or ED) and statements of competence (high or low) for fictitious students. Statements of competence were related to expectations for academic success but labeling was not.

These latter three studies lend some insight into the types of information teachers use in forming expectancies. Clearly, further research to disentangle the relationship of student folder information to teacher expectancies is needed.

In yet another caveat, several researchers have examined the question of the relationship between teacher perception of the accuracy of folder information and teacher expectancies. Shavelson, Cadwell and Izu (1977) reported that both teachers and teachers in training attended more to information perceived as being more accurate (parent report), with the information perceived as less accurate (peer report) having a much lower influence on expectations for future grades. Borko and Shavelson (1978) extended this work to teacher attributions for student performance. Attributions to ability were greater when information was from a reliable source. Reliability of information was not related to attributions, to luck, or task difficulty. Finally, any information, reliable or less reliable, indicating the student had tried led the teachers to rate effort as an important determinant of student success.

Cooper (1979b) has gone a step further and tried to identify the sources of information teachers viewed as reliable. The subjects, college students in education classes, rank orderd various types of information. The following order (in descending perceived accuracy) resulted: standardized test scores, what previous teachers say, family background, and physical characteristics. Initial expectancies for performance on a spelling test were higher when based on standardized tests than when based on any other information, including reports from previous teachers. After being given information about performance on a similar spelling test a second estimate was obtained. The second expectancy was influenced by *both* the previous estimate and by the performance information. As quality of performance increased expectancies for future performance increased. In this study, then, the most reliable information, test scores and performance, were related much more strongly to expectancies than less reliable information. If these findings were replicated with teachers rating their own students it would strengthen the conclusion that teachers perceive differences in reliability of information and rely primarily on information that is seen as reliable.

Several conclusions are warranted on the basis of the information reviewed in this section. First, cumulative folder information clearly is an important source of information for teachers' expectancy formation. Academic or social/personal information in student folders, or acquired in conversations with others, is used to form expectancies for student academic and social behavior. Second, it appears that teachers are selective in the information they use, judging the reliability of it and attending more to information perceived as reliable.

Social Class and Race

Social class and race effects related to teacher expectancy are reviewed in Chapter 10. As Baron, Tom and Cooper note, both race and social class may be significant determinants of teacher expectancies. Because they thoroughly review the relevant literature, we present only a brief summary of some major points, drawing on our earlier meta-analysis (Dusek & Joseph, 1983).

That social class and race stereotypes might be influential in teacher expectancies was suggested by Clark (1963) and subsequently dramatically illustrated by Rist (1970, 1973), who reported that the expectations of the child's initial teacher, in this case the kindergarten teacher, resulted in the child remaining in the same expectancy group in grades one and two. Once grouped by the kindergarten teacher, the child had little chance of moving up to a higher expectancy group. Hence, children initially placed in the low-expectancy group remained in that group for at least 2 more years, despite their being with different teachers. Rist (1970) suggested that in part this was a result of the type of teacher attention these children received. For example, children in the low-expectancy group often were placed in a disadvantageous physical position in the room. Most of these children came from very poor families of the lower social and economic strata. Both Rist and Clark suggest that social class was an important determinant of group assignment.

Some other research (Friedman, 1976; Weinstein & Middlestadt, 1979) leads to the conclusion that teachers treat students differentially as a function of social class. In effect, teachers may give more and higher quality interaction to middle-than lower-class students. And, students are aware that teachers differentially interact with and reinforce students. More specifically, Weinstein and Middlestadt (1979) have shown that students are aware that high achieving students are expected by the teacher to perform better and get reinforced more for high levels of performance.

Taken together, these studies support the contention that teachers use social class information to form expectancies. As a result, the nature of teacher–student interaction, which differs for students as a function of level of teacher expectancy, differs for students in the various social classes.

Separate meta-analyses were conducted for assessing the influence of student social class and race on teacher expectancies. A total of 20 studies were identified in which student social class was related to a measure of teacher expectancies. Teachers were subjects in 15 studies, students in four, and psychologists in one. Seventeen studies could be included in the meta-analysis. The resulting Z was 5.29 ($p = .0000003$), reflecting an effect of moderate magnitude ($d = .47$). Approximately 64% of the middle-class students were expected to perform better than the average lower-class student. The failsafe N was 155.

A total of 29 studies in which teacher expectancies were assessed as a function of race of child were retrieved. In 24 studies comparisons were for black versus white students, in one the comparison involved black, white and chicano students, in one white vs. Asian students, and in three white vs. Mexican students. Only the 24 studies involving white and black students were included in the meta-analysis. The resulting Z was 4.90 ($p = .0000024$). The d value, however, was low (.11), as was the U_3 value (54%). The failsafe N was 168.

This meta-analysis, and that described in Chapter 10, make it clear that social class and race of student are important sources of information to teachers and relate to their expectancies. The mechanisms are detailed in Chapter 10.

Other Possible Bases

There are several other potential bases of teacher expectancies for which data are too limited for a meta-analysis. These areas are reviewed briefly below.

Student Conduct.   An obvious potential basis for teacher expectancies is the student's conduct in school. Students who follow rules, use their time wisely, and in general behave well, are likely to impress the teacher more positively than students who do not behave as well.

Some evidence supports this contention. Willis (1972; see also Willis & Brophy, 1974) reported a number of positive correlations between aspects of classroom conduct and teacher expectancies. Expectations were higher for students who were more attentive, more obedient, possessed good solf-control, were helpful, and were careful.

The experimental work of Adams and LaVoie (1974) and LaVoie and Adams (1974) lends further support for the importance of student conduct as a basis for teacher expectancies. Teachers who read descriptions of students who exhibited good conduct had higher expectations for their IQ, work habits, peer relations, etc. than did teachers who read descriptions of poor conduct students. More recently, Purgess (1979) replicated these findings and found that for a variety of academic measures of expectancy good conduct students received higher expectancies than poor conduct students.

La Voie and Adams (1974) suggest the influence of conduct rests on classroom management issues. Specifically, they argue that problem children make classroom management difficult. Hence, these children are viewed as having lower levels of aspiration but also are seen as having less ability than good conduct students. As a result, poor conduct students may be subject to a "self-fulfilling prophecy."

Sex-Role Behaviors.   Bernard (1979) has suggested that student sex-role behaviors may be related to teacher expectancies. After reading descriptions of a fictitious male or female student who was characterized as behaving in either a typically masculine or typically feminine way, male and female teachers rated the student on a variety of traits. Students with masculine descriptions were rated higher than those with feminine descriptions on intelligence, masculinity, independence, and logic. Students with feminine descriptions were rated as warmer, more concerned with others, and more likely to encounter difficulty in subsequent study. Moreover, students with masculine sex-role descriptions were rated higher in ability to express a point of view, in having understood the question about which they were to write an essay, in overall writing ability, in knowledge and use of grammatical rules, and in overall quality of answer. Bernard explains these findings by noting that sex-role behaviors represent not only complex behavioral predispositions, but also a coding scheme for expected behaviors. He argues that teachers use this coding scheme in evaluating students, apparently believing the male role is more suited to success in the academic environment.

Phillips (1980) reported similar findings. Elementary school teachers viewed boys as more aggressive and as more interested in science and math than girls. Girls were viewed as more emotional and more interested in art and literature than boys.

Such stereotypes may well relate to the advising functions of teachers and to teacher–student interaction. In turn, then, they may form the basis of teacher expectancies. Of course, further research is needed in order to assess the validity of these results and speculations.

Previously Taught Siblings.   Several researchers have investigated the possibility that teacher expectancies may in part be based on experiences with previously taught siblings. Seaver (1973) suggested that teachers may have a tendency to expect younger siblings to be more like older siblings than they actually are. As a result, bright students may lead teachers to expect younger siblings to perform well, and less bright students may lead teachers to expect poorer performance from younger siblings. He reported data indicating that when the older sibling had performed at a high level the younger sibling scored higher if taught by the same as opposed to a different teacher. The reverse also was the case. However, Heines (1982) and Rivers (1980), who used essentially the same procedure, failed to replicate Seaver's (1973) findings.

Richey (1981a,b) carried these investigational strategies a step further by asking elementary school teachers for their academic, social, and behavioral expectations for the siblings of previously taught LD and non LD children. The teachers' expectancies were higher for the sibs of non LD children. Sibs of LD children were expected to perform less well academically and socially, and were expected to need more support services.

The findings of these studies are not only interesting in their own right— particularly because of the novel and naturalistic approach used—but provide some evidence of the bases of teacher expectancies. The results of Seaver (1973) and Rivers (1980) indicate that in the early elementary school years an older sibling's previous performance *may* create expectancies for a younger sibling's performance. This was true for both positive and negative expectancies.

Name Stereotypes.   Harari and McDavid (1973) hypothesized that teachers may make more favorable judgments of work samples linked with students having common or frequent names and less favorable judgments of work samples linked with students having unusual names. They suggest that name stereotypes carry with them expectations for performance. The teachers and college students in their study read and scored essays identified by a first name that was either male or female and either common or uncommon. Essays attributed to students with common names tended to be scored higher than essays attributed to students with less common, or undersirable, names.

Garwood (1976) has presented evidence indicating that teacher interactions with students differ as a function of first name stereotypes. She reported that students with more common or desirable names scored higher on the Children's Self-Concept of Achievement Test scale and on the Tennessee Self-Concept Scale. Moreover, these same students scored higher on the IOWA achievement tests, presumable because they received a higher quality of student–teacher interaction.

Some evidence indicates that the degree of name stereotype effects may depend on teaching experience. Experienced teachers show the effect but college students do not (Harari & McDavid, 1973; Tompkins & Boor, 1980). Apparently, experience with students strengthens, or initiates, stereotypes.

Clearly, it would be premature to conclude that name stereotypes are a well-documented basis of teacher expectancies. Nonetheless, the findings of these studies are interesting and deserving of further investigation.

One- vs. Two-Parent Home.   Several researchers (e.g., Santrock, 1975; Santrock & Tracy, 1978; Levine, 1981) have investigated the effect of coming from a one-parent home on teacher expectancies. The most informative of these studies was conducted by Levine (1981), who had 100 teachers rate both psycho-social and academic attributes for children from one- versus two-parent homes. Analyses revealed the teachers expected the children from one-parent homes to have lower academic achievement and more psycho-social problems than children from intact families. At present it is not possible to determine, objectively, if this is in reality the case. That is, it may be that children experiencing the death of a parent or parental divorce may experience academic and social problems that are apparent to teachers. Until further research is conducted, however, it is not possible to determine if this factor is, indeed, a veridical determinant of teacher expectancies.

CONCLUSIONS

The purpose of a review such as this one, of course, is to provide an objective summary of our knowledge of a field of research. Through such reviews it is hoped that misconceptions will be corrected and solid knowledge bases will be established. In addition, critical reviews help identify shortcomings in the existing literature, which aids interpretation and theory building.

Misconceptions/Shortcomings

The research reviewed above, and the procedures employed in the review, allow an objective assessment of the types of information to which teachers attend when forming expectancies for student academic performance, social relations, and personality development. The conclusions drawn from the literature review are summarized in Table 9.3. As may be seen, five student characteristics were related significantly to teacher expectancies, two were not, and the data were equivocal for three.

Of the five bases related to teacher expectancies two, cumulative folder information and student conduct, provide objective, academically relevant information that may be useful in program planning for students and may help the teacher better understand individual student's needs. Moreover, these types of information are perceived as highly reliable (Cooper, 1979b). These results are consistent with other studies (cf. Brophy & Good, 1974) relating teacher–student interactions to student classroom behavior and characteristics.

Two of the remaining three positively identified bases, SES and race, likely reflect stereotypic (perhaps prejudicial) expectancies for social behaviors. In the absence of more academically relevant information teachers may rely on this type of knowledge, imperfect though it may be, about students when forming initial impressions and expectations.

The significant physical attractiveness effect is perhaps most readily explained as due to the procedures employed in the conduct of the research. Having subjects give expectancy information for a student based only on a picture and no interaction may result in an artificial finding. Willis (1972) reported that for teachers and their own students there was a positive effect between attractiveness and expectancies early in the school year but not later. In the research reviewed above we may be seeing an initial reaction equivalent to that reported by Willis. As Adams and LaVoie (1974) and LaVoie and Adams (1974) note, physical attractiveness may be important initially but not later, when other more academically pertinent information becomes available.

TABLE 9.3
Summary of Bases of Teacher
Expectancies

Related:
Attractiveness (academic and social/personality)
Student Classroom Conduct
Cumulative Folder Information
Race
Social Class
Not Related:
Gender (academic and social/personality)
One-Parent Family Situation
Questionable:
Older Sibling's Previous Performance
Sex-Role Behavior
Name Stereotypes

Two types of information, student gender and number of parents in the home, were not related to teacher expectancies. The failure of student gender to relate to expectancies was unexpected given the gender differences in student–teacher interactions (cf. Bank et al., 1980; Brophy & Good, 1974). Apparently, differential behaviors to male and female students in the classroom do not reflect to a significant degree differential expectancies for student academic or social development.

The failure of living in a one-parent family to relate to teacher expectancies is not entirely unexpected. Although the trauma of divorce or death of a parent may disrupt the child's classroom performance, teachers may be able to alleviate some of the difficulties by careful attention to the student and by understanding. Moreover, such disruption of the student's performance may be viewed as temporary, unlike other bases of expectancies. Hence, its transciency may lead to it being a weak overall predictor of teacher expectancy.

Three potential bases of expectancies, namely, previously taught siblings, sex-role behavior, and name stereotypes, were at best weakly associated with teacher expectancies. Further research is necessary before it can be determined if these types of information are predictive of teacher expectancy effects.

Although a number of criticisms may be leveled against some of the research presented above, the most critical statement lies in the artificial nature of most of the designs employed. Although teachers were subjects in many studies, they were asked to make judgments about students with whom they had no direct contact. Research in which teachers made judgments about their own students resulted in stronger findings and, at times, findings different from similar research in which teachers made judgments about unfamiliar students. Teachers do not form expectancies in the void of other information. Daily interactions with students help shape and even change expectancies, an issue addressed most directly by Willis (1972). Clearly, this must temper findings because of issues related to external validity of the results.

Implications for Future Research

Consideration of the findings reviewed in this paper leads to a number of suggestions for future research. First, and most important, is the necessity of conducting research with classroom teachers and their own students. The findings reported above, when compared with research cited by others (e.g., Braun, 1976; Cooper, 1979a), support the contention that a more veridical picture of the bases of teacher expectancies will be gained by studying intact classrooms. A number of examples make it clear that data collected from nonteachers do not necessarily lead to the same set of conclusions as data collected from classroom teachers. Although research in allied fields, such as social psychology, may provide pertinent leads to research with classroom teachers, one must carefully evaluate the translation of such research to the classroom situation.

One reason for the disparity of the findings may rest in the artificiality of the procedures used in the majority of the studies. One must seriously question the degree to which even teacher ratings in such experiments are valid indices of how teachers form expectancies about the students in their class.

It also appears that the context of teacher expectancies is an important consideration. Some research leads to the conclusion that teachers' expectancies are not unitary, that is that teacher expectancies may have different bases depending upon the area of expectancy, for example, academic versus social behavior. A prime example of this differential may be found in the literature relating student gender to teacher expectancies. Future research should be directed at examining the importance of these differential effects of student characteristics for teacher expectancies.

Third, the majority of research has been directed at a single potential influence on teacher expectancies. Although there is some research on multiple/interactive influences, much more research needs to be done.

Fourth, existing research is largely cross-sectional in design. When this research is done in classrooms little attention is paid to the experience the teacher has had with the class, that is, time of the year (Palardy, 1969). Since experience with the students no doubt will lead to expectancies with different bases than the expectancies after but little interaction with the class, longitudinal research, such as that done by Willis (1972), is called for. Longitudinal studies will allow for estimates of the importance of class contact time and will allow measurement of *changes* in expectancies and their bases. This is an area of research that is completely neglected. We know virtually nothing about whether, how, or why teachers change expectancies for students' performance.

Of course, the real crux of the concerns expressed above is the lack of research with teachers and their own students. By conducting research with intact classrooms (that is, teachers and their own students) a more ecologically valid understanding of the bases of teacher expectancies will be obtained. Research such as that conducted by Willis (1972), Cooper and Lowe (1977), Friedman (1976), Palardy (1969), Salvia Algozzine & Sheare (1977), and Seaver (1973) demonstrate the benefit of ecologically valid research.

An important question is the degree to which expectations are formed on the basis of information that is steeped in what occurs in the real world. For example, Clifford and Walster (1973) found that teachers expected attractive children to have better relations with peers than unattractive children. This may in fact be the case, indicating the expectancy is not a bias (cf. Dusek, 1975). However, it would seem to be difficult to justify teachers' expecting better or poorer academic performance because of the student's name. This expectation may be a biasing influence, causing some children to obtain a poor education. Expectations may be based on reasonable and appropriate information, and may lead to teacher behaviors that will benefit the student. Or, expectancies may be founded on inappropriate or extraneous information, leading to a biased (positive or negative) education (Dusek, 1975). Research should be done to clarify this issue.

Finally, although broad-based underpinnings of expectancies have been investigated, a number of specific potential bases of teachers' expectancies have not yet been investigated, for example, academic and nonacademic behavior in the classroom, verbal and written reports by previous teachers and the principal, and meetings with parents. In addition, most of the research reported above has been for a single grade level. The bases of expectancies may well be different for different grade levels. These, and other, questions must be answered in a satisfactory manner before statements about the bases of teacher expectancies may be made with any significant degree of accuracy. Given the importance of the concerns, this is not an issue to be taken lightly.

REFERENCES

Bank, B., Biddle, B., & Good, T. Sex roles, classroom instruction, and reading achievement. *Journal of Educational Psychology*, 1980, *72*, 119–132.

Berscheid, E., & Walster, E. Physical attractiveness. In L. Berkowitz (Ed.), *Advances in experimental social psychology*, (Vol. 7). New York: Academic Press, 1974.

Braun, C. Teacher expectation: Sociopsychological dynamics. *Review of Educational Research*, 1976, *46*, 185–213.

Brophy, J., & Good, T. Teachers' communication of differential expectations for children's classroom performance: Some behavioral data. *Journal of Educational Psychology*, 1970, *61*, 365–374.

Brophy, J., & Good, T. *Teacher–student relationships: Causes and consequences.* New York: Holt, Rinehart, & Winston, 1974.

Clark, K. Educational stimulation of racially disadvantaged children. In A. H. Passow (Ed.), *Education in depressed areas.* New York: Teachers College, Columbia University, 1963, 142–162.

Cohen, J. *Statistical power analysis for the behavioral sciences.* New York: Academic Press, 1977.

Cooper, H. Pygmalion grows up: A model for teacher expectation communication and performance influences. *Review of Educational Research*, 1979, *49*, 389–410. (a)

Cooper, H. Some effects of preperformance information on academic expectations. *Journal of Educational Psychology*, 1979, *71*, 375–380. (b)

Cooper, H. Statistically combining independent studies: A meta-analysis of sex differences in conformity research. *Journal of Personality and Social Psychology*, 1979, *37*, 131–146. (c)

Cooper, H., & Lowe, C. Task information and attributions for academic performance by professional teachers and roleplayers. *Journal of Personality*, 1977, *45*, 469–483.

Dusek, J. Do teachers bias children's learning? *Review of Educational Research*, 1975, *45*, 661–684.

Dusek, J., & Joseph, G. The bases of teacher expectancies: A meta-analysis. *Journal of Educational Psychology*, 1983, *75*, 327–346.

Dusek, J., & O'Connell, E. Teacher expectancy effects on the achievement test performance of elementary school children. *Journal of Educational Psychology*, 1973, *65*, 371–377.

Friedman, P. Comparisons of teacher reinforcement schedules for students with different social class backgrounds. *Journal of Educational Psychology*, 1976, *68*, 286–292.

Glass, G. Primary, secondary and meta-analysis research. *Educational Researcher*, 1976, *8*, 79–82.

Glass, G. Integrating findings: The meta-analysis of research. In L. Schulman (Ed.), *Review of Research in Education.* Itasca, Ill.: Peacock, 1977.

Johnson, E., Maruyama, G., Johnson, R., Nelson, D., & Skon, L. Effects of cooperative, competitive, and individualistic goal structures on achievement: A meta-analysis. *Psychological Bulletin*, 1981, *89*, 47–62.

Mosteller, F., & Bush, B. Selected quantitative techniques. In G. Lindzey (Ed.), *Handbook of social psychology: Volume I. Theory and method*. Cambridge, Mass.: Addison-Wesley, 1954.

O'Connell, E., Dusek, J., & Wheeler, R. A follow-up study of teacher expectancy effects. *Journal of Educational Psychology*, 1974, *66*, 325–328.

Rist, R. Student social class and teacher expectations: The self-fulfilling prophecy in ghetto education. *Harvard Educational Review*, 1970, *40*, 411–451.

Rist, R. *The urban school: A factory for failure*. Cambridge, MA.: MIT Press, 1973.

Rosenthal, R. Combining results of independent studies. *Psychological Bulletin*, 1978, *85*, 185–193.

Rosenthal, R. The "file drawer problem" and tolerance for null results. *Psychological Bulletin*, 1979, *86*, 638–641.

Rosenthal, R., & Jacobson, L. *Pygmalion in the classroom: Teacher expectation and pupils' intellectual development*. New York: Holt, Rinehart, & Winston, 1968.

Stouffer, S. *The American soldier: Volume 1. Adjustment during army life*. Princeton, N.J.: Princeton University Press, 1949.

Weinstein, R., & Middlestadt, S. Student perceptions of teacher interactions with male high and low achievers. *Journal of Educational Psychology*, 1979, *71*, 421–431.

Willis, S. Formation of teachers' expectations of students' academic performance. Unpublished Doctoral Dissertation, The University of Texas at Austin, 1972.

Willis, S., & Brophy, J. Origins of teachers' attitudes toward young children. *Journal of Educational Psychology*, 1974, *66*, 520–529.

REFERENCES USED IN META-ANALYSIS COMPUTATIONS

Adams, G. Racial membership and physical attractiveness effects on preschool teachers' expectations. *Child Study Journal*, 1978, *8*, 29–41.

Adams, G., & Cohen, A. An examination of cumulative folder information used by teachers in making differential judgments of children's abilities. *The Alberta Journal of Educational Research*, 1976, *22*, 216–225. (a)

Adams, G., & Cohen, A. Characteristics of children and teacher expectancy: An extension to the child's social and family life. *Journal of Educational Research*, 1976, *70*, 87–90. (b)

Adams, G., & LaVoie, J. The effect of student's sex, conduct, and facial attractiveness on teacher expectancy. *Education*, 1974, *95*, 76–83.

Algozzine, B. Classroom decision making as a function of diagnostic labels and perceived competence. *Resources in Education*, 1981, *16*, ED 197518.

Algozzine, B., & Stoller, L. Effects of labels and competence on teachers' attributions for a student. *Resources in Education*, 1981, *16*, ED 203588.

Amato, J. Effect of pupil's social class upon teachers' expectations and behavior. *Dissertation Abstracts International*, 1976, *37*, 186–187A.

Archer, P. The influence of pupil's social class on teachers ratings of reading attainment. *Resources in Education*, 1981, *16*, ED 195973.

Bar-Tal, D., & Saxe, L. Teachers' information processing: effect of information about pupils on teachers' expectations and affect. *Psychological Reports*, 1979, *44*, 599–602.

Bennett, C. The effects of student characteristics and task performance on teacher expectations and attributions. *Dissertation Abstracts International*, 1979, *40*, (2-B), 979–980.

Bernard, M. Does sex role behavior influence the way teachers evaluate students? *Journal of Educational Psychology*, 1979, *71*, 553–562.

Bergan, J., & Smith, J. Effects of socio-economic status and sex on prospective teachers' judgments. *Mental Retardation*, 1966, *4*, 13–15.

Borko, H., & Shavelson, R. Teachers' sensitivity to the reliability of information in making causal attributions in an achievement situation. *Journal of Educational Psychology*, 1978, *70*, 271–279.

Carlile, L. Teacher expectations of language delay in black and white head start children. *Dissertation Abstracts International*, 1975, *35*, 2455-A.

Clifford, M., & Walster, E. The effect of physical attractiveness on teacher expectation. *Sociology of Education*, 1973, *46*, 248–258.

Cooper, H. Some effects of preperformance information on academic expectations. *Journal of Educational Psychology*, 1979, *71*, 375–380. (b)

Cooper, H., & Burger, J. How teachers explain students' academic performance: A categorization of free response academic attributions. *American Educational Research Journal*, 1980, *17*, 95–109.

Cooper, H., & Lowe, C. Task information and attributions for academic performance by professional teachers and roleplayers. *Journal of Personality*, 1977, *45*, 469–483.

Cooper, H., Baron, R. & Lowe, C. The importance of race and social class information in the formation of expectancies about academic performance. *Journal of Educational Psychology*, 1975, *67*, 312–319.

Cooper, H., Hinkel, G., & Good, T. Teachers' beliefs about interaction control and their observed behavioral correlates. *Journal of Educational Psychology*, 1980, *72*, 345–354.

Darlega, V., Wang, P. & Colson, W. Racial bias in expectancies and performance attributions. Unpublished manuscript, Old Dominion University, 1981.

DeMeis, D. & Turner, R. Effects of students' race, physical attractiveness, and dialect on teachers' evaluations. *Contemporary Educational Psychology*, 1978, *3*, 77–86.

Deitz, S., & Purkey, W. Teacher expectation of performance based on race of student. *Psychological Reports*, 1969, *24*, 694.

Finn, J., Gaier, E., Peng, S., & Banks, R. Teacher expectations and pupil achievement. *Urban Education*, 1975, *10*, 175–197.

Foster, G., & Ysseldyke, J. Expectancy and halo effects as a result of artificially induced teacher bias. *Contemporary Educational Psychology*, 1976, *1*, 37–45.

Foster, G., Algozzine, B., & Ysseldyke, J. Classroom teacher and teacher-in-training susceptibility to stereotypical bias. *Personnel and Guidance Journal*, 1980, *59*, 27–30.

Foster, G., Ysseldyke, J., & Reese, J. I wouldn't have seen it if I hadn't believed it. *Exceptional Children*, 1975, *41*, 469–473.

Garwood, S. First-name stereotypes as a factor in self-concept and school achievement. *Journal of Educational Psychology*, 1976, *68*, 482–487.

Harari, H., & McDavid, J. Name stereotypes and teachers' expectations. *Journal of Educational Psychology*, 1973, *65*, 222–225.

Harvey, D., & Slatin, G. The relationship between child's socio-economic status and teacher expectations: A test of middle-class bias hypothesis. *Social Forces*, 1975, *54*, 140–159.

Heines, B. Pygmalion's sisters and brothers: The influence of sibling-related teacher expectancies on classroom behaviors and student achievement. Unpublished manuscript, Lake Erie College, 1982.

Helton, G., & Oakland, T. Teachers' attitudinal responses to differing characteristics of elementary school students. *Journal of Educational Psychology*, 1977, *69*, 261–265.

Hendren, T., & Routh, D. Social class bias in psychologists' evaluations of children. *Journal of Pediatric Psychology*, 1979, *4*, 353–361.

Herson, P. Biasing effects of diagnostic labels and sex of pupil on teachers' views of pupils' mental health. *Journal of Educational Psychology*, 1974, *66*, 117–122.

Jensen, M., & Rosenfeld, L. Influence of mode of presentation, ethnicity and social class on teachers' evaluations of students. *Journal of Educational Psychology*, 1974, *66*, 540–547.

Kehle, T., Bramble, W., & Mason, E. Teachers' expectations: Ratings of student performance as biased by student characteristics. *The Journal of Experimental Education*, 1974, *43*, 54–60.

LaVoie, J., & Adams, G. Teacher expectancy and its relation to physical and interpersonal characteristics of the child. *The Alberta Journal of Educational Research*, 1974, *20*, 122–132.

Lenkowsky, R., & Blackman, L. The effect of teachers' knowledge of race and social class on their judgments of children's academic competence and social acceptability. *Mental Retardation*, 1968, *6*(6), 15–17.

Levine, E. Teachers' academic and psycho-social expectations for children from single-parent families. *Dissertation Abstracts International*, 1981, *41*, 5033-A.

Marwit, K., Marwit, S., & Walker, E. Effects of student race and physical attractiveness on teachers' judgments of transgressions. *Journal of Educational Psychology*, 1978, *70*, 911–915.

Mason, E. Teachers' observations and expectations of boys and girls as influenced by biased psychological reports and knowledge of the effects of bias. *Journal of Educational Psychology*, 1973, *65*, 238–243.

Mason, E., & Larimore, D. Effects of biased psychological reports on two types of teachers' ratings. *Journal of School Psychology*, 1974, *12*, 46–50.

Mazer, G. Effects of social class stereotyping on teacher expectation. *Psychology in the Schools*, 1971, *8*, 373–378.

Mertens, D. Expectations of teachers-in-training: The influence of a student's sex and a behavioral vs. descriptive approach in a biased psychological report. *Journal of School Psychology*, 1976, *14*, 222–229.

Miller, H. Race vs. class in teachers' expectations. *Psychological Reports*, 1973, *32*, 105–106.

Miller, C., McLaughlin, J., & Chansky, N. Socioeconomic class and teacher bias. *Psychological Reports*, 1968, *23*, 806.

Palardy, J. What teachers believe—what children achieve. *Elementary School Journal*, 1969, *69*, 370–374.

Parker, R. Teacher expectancy behavior: The impact of several salient student characteristics upon expectations and causal attributions. *Dissertation Abstracts International*, 1980, *40*, 4497-A.

Paulson, R. Expectancy of classroom performance: The effects of students' dialect, students' ethnicity and an introduction to sociolinguistics on teacher candidates' perceptions. *Dissertation Abstracts International*, 1978, *38*, 2200-A.

Phillips, R. Teachers' reported expectations of children's sex-roles and evaluations of sexist teaching. *Dissertation Abstracts International*, 1980, *41*, 995–996 A.

Porter, P. Teacher expectancy: The effect of race, sex, direction of writing performance and trials on the grading of essays. *Dissertation Abstracts International*, 1979, *37*, 1251-A.

Prieto, A., & Zucker, S. The effects of race on teachers' perceptions of education placement of behaviorally disordered children. *Resources in Education*, 1980, *15*, ED 188427.

Pugh, L. Teacher attitudes and expectations associated with race and social class. Paper presented at the Annual Meetings of the American Educational Research Association, Chicago, Ill., April 15–19, 1974.

Purgess, P. Teacher expectancy for academic success in relation to label, sex, and pupil behavior. *Dissertation Abstracts International*, 1979, *39*, 2003–2004 A.

Reschly, D., & Lamprecht, M. Expectancy effects of labels: Fact or artifact? *Exceptional Children*, 1979, *45*, 55–58.

Rich, J. Effects of children's physical attractiveness on teachers' evaluations. *Journal of Educational Psychology*, 1975, *67*, 599–609.

Richey, L. Teachers' expectations for the siblings of learning disabled and non-learning disabled students: A pilot study. *Resources in Education*, 1981, *16*, ED 197516. (a)

Richey, L. Teachers' attitudes and expectations for siblings of learning disabled children. *Resources in Education,* 1981, *16,* ED 203613. (b)

Rivers, J. Older siblings as bases of teacher expectations. *Dissertation Abstracts International,* 1980, *40,* 4253-A.

Roland, C. Students' facial attractiveness as a factor in teacher and counselor expectations. *Dissertation Abstracts International,* 1977, *37.*

Ross, M., & Salvia, J. Attractiveness as a biasing factor in teacher judgments. *American Journal of Mental Deficiency,* 1975, *80,* 96–98.

Rotter, N. The influence of race and other variables on teachers' ratings of pupils. *Dissertation Abstracts International,* 1975, *35,* 7134A.

Salvia, J., Algozzine, R., & Sheare, J. Attractiveness and school achievement. *Journal of School Psychology,* 1977, *15,* 60–67.

Santrock, J. Father absence, perceived maternal behavior and moral development in boys. *Child Development,* 1975, *46,* 753–757.

Santrock, J., & Tracy, R. Effects of children's family structure status on the development of stereotypes by teachers. *Journal of Educational Psychology,* 1978, *70,* 754–757.

Seaver, W. Effects of naturally induced teacher expectancies. *Journal of Personality and Social Psychology,* 1973, *28,* 333–342.

Shavelson, R., Cadwell, J., & Izu, T. Teachers' sensitivity to the reliability of information in making pedagogical decisions. *American Educational Research Journal,* 1977, *14,* 83–97.

Simpson, M., Smith, J., & Means, G. An assessment of differential expectations of performance based on race of student. *Resources in Education,* 1978, *13,* ED 153144.

Smith, J. Ascribed and achieved student characteristics in teacher expectancy: Relationship of socio-economic status to academic achievement, academic self-concept, and vocational aspirations. *Dissertation Abstracts International,* 1979, *40,* 959–960.

Taylor, M. Race, sex and the expression of self-fulfilling prophecies in a laboratory teaching situation. *Journal of Personality and Social Psychology,* 1979, *37,* 897–912.

Tompkins, R., & Boor, M. Effects of students' physical attractiveness and name popularity on student teachers' perceptions of social and academic attributes. *Journal of Psychology,* 1980, *106,* 37–42.

Wiley, M., Eskilson, A. Why did you learn in school today? Teachers' perceptions of causality. *Sociology of Education,* 1978, *51,* 261–269.

Wilkerson, M. The effects of sex and ethnicity upon teachers' expectations of students. *Dissertation Abstracts International,* 1980, *41,* 637-A.

Williams, T. Teacher prophecies and the inheritance of inequality. *Sociology of Education,* 1976, *49,* 223–236.

Wong, M. Model students? Teachers' perceptions and expectations of their Asian and white students. *Sociology of Education,* 1980, *53,* 236–246.

Yoshida, R., & Meyers, C. Effects of labeling as educable mentally retarded on teachers' expectancies for change in student's performance. *Journal of Educational Psychology,* 1975, *67,* 521–527.

Zucker, S. Racial determinants of teachers' perceptions of placement of the educable mentally retarded. *Resources in Education,* 1979, *14,* ED 171051.

Zucker, S., & Prieto, A. Teacher bias in special class placement. *Resources in Education,* 1978, *13,* ED 153389.

10 Social Class, Race and Teacher Expectations

Reuben M. Baron
University of Connecticut

David Y. H. Tom
Harris M. Cooper
University of Missouri-Columbia

Given that teacher expectations influence student performance (Rosenthal & Jacobson, 1968; Rosenthal & Rubin, 1978), it becomes important to identify the determinants of such expectations. Two of the most salient characteristics of students are their social class and racial backgrounds. These may also be large contributors to teacher beliefs about students.

Student race and class may be important influences on teacher beliefs because teachers appear to weigh this information equally with other sources of information when making predictions, even though they realize race and social class are relatively unreliable (Cooper, 1979a). Moreover, other sources of information about students are obviously limited prior to the student's performance. Information about a student's race and social class is directly observable (Cooper, Baron & Lowe, 1975). Along with gender, the race and social class of a student may be among the teacher's first impressions.

Actual differences in the *group* performance of students of different races and social classes are probably at the heart of differential teacher expectations. Both vicarious and direct experiences with children of differing race and class background can create varying generalized expectations for these groups. For instance, teachers may directly observe that lower class students do not do well at lessons or teachers may acquire this belief by modeling the beliefs of fellow teachers. However, the race or class of a particular student may cue the teacher to apply the generalized expectations, therefore making it difficult for the teacher to develop *specific* expectations tailored to individual students. In this manner, the race or class distinction among students is perpetuated. The familiar operation of stereotypes takes place in that it becomes difficult for minority or disadvantaged students to distinguish themselves from the generalized expectation (cf. Deutsch, Katz & Jensen, 1968; Karlins, Coffman, & Walters, 1969; Williams, 1976).

Braun (1976) and Dusek (this volume) have broadly reviewed the bases of teacher expectations. The present review offers a narrower but more exhaustive survey of the individual studies empirically testing the effects on teacher expectations of student race and/or social class. The review and analyses attempt to make two contributions. First, the review utilizes scientific literature reviewing procedures (Cooper, 1982) and quantitative synthesis procedures (Cooper, 1979b; Glass, Smith & McGraw, 1981; Rosenthal, 1980) to retrieve and integrate studies. Second, this review is used as a point of departure for suggesting future directions for research and theory.

The following major hypotheses were tested: (a) Teacher expectations for white students will be higher than for black students or other ethnic minority groups such as Mexican-Americans; (b) Teacher expectations for middle-class students will be higher than for lower-class students; (c) We will also be examining on an exploratory basis, given the limited number of studies available, possible interactions between race and class. For example, does the black or white expectancy difference disappear when comparisons are made between middle-class white and black students?

METHODS

Search Techniques and Outcome

An on-line computer search of *Psychological Abstracts, Educational Research Information Center (ERIC)*, and *Dissertation Abstracts International* served as a basis for an initial bibliography. The descriptors used in the search were crossings of the terms "teacher expect...", "teacher attitudes," or "teacher bias" with "racial," "ethnicity," "class," "socioeconomic," "social background," or "social characteristics." Both titles and abstracts were searched for these terms. The computer search yielded 361 potentially relevant studies.

References from *Psychological Abstracts* and *ERIC* were accompanied by the study's abstract but the computer only provided titles for references from *Dissertation Abstracts International*. This information was used to eliminate obviously irrelevant studies. The full reports of 79 references were examined, except for the studies from *Dissertation Abstracts International*, for which only the abstract was retrieved. Ultimately, 20 reports examining race and/or social class effects on teacher expectations were located. Three more studies were found through an examination of the bibliographies of computer-located studies.

Criteria for Determining Whether a Study was Relevant

A study was considered relevant to the review if it included (a) a measure of teacher expectations, and (b) a measure of either the race or social class of a stimulus student. It was also necessary for the study to contain a testing of the relationship between (a) and (b). Both experimental and nonexperimental studies were included.

Four operational definitions of the term race were found. These were (a) white or Anglican students, (b) black, Afro-American or Negro students, (c) Chicano or Mexican-American students and (d) Asian-American students.

Social Class was most often operationally defined as the occupation of the father of the student. For lower-class students these included auto repairman, waiter, gas station attendant, and truck driver. For middle-class students the father's occupation was either lawyer or accountant. The father's salary, mother's occupation and the terms "disadvantaged" versus "middle class" were also used when a student's social class was manipulated through written material. In addition, four studies manipulated social class by providing a photograph of the student, another used an audiotape, another used videotape, and one study used real children.

The most precise way to describe the students meant to represent higher social classes in these studies would be to call them middle-to upper-middle class. Lower social classes could be described as ranging from lower-to middle-class. For purposes of exposition, however, (and because the small number of studies did not permit a more detailed analysis), the higher social class group in each study was labeled middle class and the lower group was labeled lower class.

Teacher Expectations were defined in terms of how the teacher perceived the student's performance, achievement, or ability. Expectation measures were operationally defined as any measure of a teacher's beliefs concerning a student's likely academic success or performance (such as grades) or ability level (such as IQ scores). More detailed descriptions of each expectation measure can be found in Tables 10.1 and 10.2 to follow.

Characteristics of Studies Retained for Analysis

Each report was examined and coded for each of the following characteristics, related to the study's design:

1. Year of report appearance.
2. Where the report appeared.
3. Whether the study was experimental or nonexperimental.
4. Whether a within- or between-subjects design was employed.
5. Where the study was conducted.
6. How many teachers were involved.
7. Whether or not professional teachers were used.
8. How the stimulus student was presented to the teacher.
9. How many stimulus students were involved.
10. What other variables, in addition to race and social class, were Addressed in the study.
11. What racial or social class comparisons were carried out.

In addition, the direction of each relevant finding, along with its associated significance level and effect size were recorded.

Method for Combining Probabilities

The first method of aggregation involved combining probabilities across studies deemed to have tested the same hypothesis (cf. Cooper, 1979b). The procedure employed, referred to as the Stouffer Method (Rosenthal, 1980) requires that (a) the z scores associated with each study's probability values be computed and (b) the z scores be summed and divided by the square root of the number of tests. The result is itself a z score which can be converted to a p level and interpreted as gauging the probability that the run of study results could have been generated by chance. In the present application, when a study reported a nonsignificant result and no p level was given, a z score of 0.00 was assumed.

Because studies with significant findings are more likely to be published than are studies with nonsignificant findings (Greenwald, 1975), "the file drawer problem" (Rosenthal, 1979) is created. As a means for gauging the potential impact of relevant but unretrieved studies, a failsafe N (N_{fs}) was calculated (Cooper, 1979b). The failsafe N is an estimate of the number null-summing studies needed to increase a combined probability above a chosen level of significance. That is, it indicates the number of additional studies with a summed null finding that would be needed to increase the cumulative probability above, say, the $p < .05$ level. The N_{fs} is calculated by (a) dividing the sum of the z scores associated with known studies by the z score for the critical p level (for $p < .05$ this is 1.65), (b) squaring the result and (c) subtracting the number of known studies. The failsafe N is an approptiate guide only if the assumption of a summed null relation in undiscovered studies is acceptable. It is always possible that a smaller number of studies exist that have a summed z score with a value opposite to the sum of those reviewed.

Effect Size Estimation

The presentation of estimates of the magnitude of effects is an important part of reporting experimental findings (Cooper, 1981; Cooper & Findley, 1982) and is especially important in research reviews. The effect size used in this review was the d index (Cohen, 1977). The d index guages the difference between two group means in terms of their common (average) standard deviation. If d = .3, it means that 3/10 of a standard deviation separates the average persons in the two groups. The d indexes were calculated by the following formula:

$$d = \frac{\bar{X} \text{ white students} - \bar{X} \text{ minority students}}{\text{average SD for both groups}}$$

The d index transforms the results from any two-group comparisons into a common standardized metric. Findings from a number of studies can then be combined and analyzed simultaneously.

Glass et al. (1981) suggest that rather than using the average standard deviation as the denominator for the d index one of the groups be designated the comparison group and its sd be used. This is based on the possibility that the two sds will not be homogeneous, so decidedly different effect sizes would occur dependent on which group was used as the comparison. However, in practice, most reports do not contain means and standard deviations, so effect sizes are often computed through transformation of t and F ratios (cf. Friedman, 1968):

$$d = \frac{2t}{\sqrt{df\ error}}$$

For these studies, the assumption of homogeneity of variance must be made. It is therefore advisable to apply the rule consistently.

Cohen (1977) also presents several measures of distribution overlap meant to enhance the interpretability of effect size indexes. The overlap measure employed in this review, called U_3, tells the percentage of the population with the smaller mean that is exceeded by the average person in the population with the larger mean. For instance, if $d = .3$ then $U_3 = 61.8$, meaning the average person in the higher-meaned group exceeded 61.8% of the people in the lower-meaned group. A table for converting the d index to U_3 is presented by Cohen (1977, p. 22).

RESULTS

Experimental Comparisons of White and Black Students

Sixteen studies involving random assignment of teachers to stimulus students were located which contained comparisons of teacher expectations for white versus black students. Table 10.1 contains a brief description of each study. Ten of the studies were reported in journals, two in *ERIC*, three in *Dissertation Abstracts International* and one was an unpublished manuscript sent to one of the reviewers. The earliest study appeared in 1969, the most recent in 1981.

Ten of the 16 studies employed between-subjects designs in which each teacher or roleplaying teacher evaluated only one student. In the other six studies, each teacher evaluated more than one student in a repeated measures format. Seven studies presented the stimulus student to teachers through written descriptions only. This meant the students were verbally described in a package of written materials. The race manipulation was accomplished through the use of

TABLE 10.1
Experimental Studies of the Effect of Student Race (Black vs. White) on Teacher Expectations

First Author	Year	Presentation Mode	Expectation Measure	Group With Higher Expectations	Significance Level
Deitz	1969	Written description	Academic Performance	Whites	NS
Mazer	1971	Written description	Academic Ability	Blacks	NS
			Mental Ability	Blacks	
			Grades	Blacks	
Miller	1973	Written description	Performance Estimate	Not given	NS
Jensen	1974	Videotape	Test Performance	Whites	NS
			Intelligence	Whites	NS
Kehle	1974	Photographs	Essay Grade	Not given	NS
Pugh	1974	Audiotape	Academic Ability	Whites	$p < .01$
Williams, F.	1974	Videotape	Lang. Arts Performance	Whites	$p < .05$
Cooper	1975	Written description	Grades	Whites	NS
Harvey	1975	Photographs	Completion of Homework	Whites	$p < .01$
Rotter	1975	Photographs	Academic Success	Not given	NS
Simpson	1978	Written description	Grades	Whites	NS
Wiley	1978	Photographs	Expected Quality of Work	Not given	NS
			Native Intelligence	Not given	
Bennett	1979	Real child	Predicted Success	Whites	$p < .05$
Taylor	1979	Written description	Intellectual Potential	Not given	NS
Wilkerson	1980	Not given	Academic Success	Not given	NS
Derlega	1981	Written description	Lesson Performance	Whites	$p < .001$
			Academic Performance	Whites	$p < .001$

photographs in four studies and two studies used video-taped stimulus students. One study used audiotape, accomplishing the race manipulation by varying the dialect of the speaker. One study used actual black and white confederates. One dissertation abstract did not describe how the manipulation of student race was accomplished.

Nine studies employed practicing teachers as subjects and seven used college students taking either psychology or education courses. All studies were conducted in the United States, but many different states of the union were represented (i.e., CT, FL, VA, KY, NM, MI, NY, MA, IL, TX). The average number of teachers per study was 151 with a range from 648 (Rotter, 1975) to 26 (Pugh, 1974).

Eleven studies employed stimulus students described as being in elementary school grades (1 through 6). One study spanned elementary and junior high-aged students (grades 5 through 8; Mazer, 1971). Two studies involved high school-aged stimulus students (Deitz & Purkey, 1969; Pugh, 1974) and one study (Simpson, Smith & Means, 1978) assessed expectations for college-aged students. One dissertation abstract did not report the level of school to which the study pertained (Wilkerson, 1980).

Combined Results of Studies.   While many studies contained multiple teacher perceptions of students (including assessments of personality and causal attributions for performance) only four contained multiple measures of expectations, as defined for use in this review. Three of these studies reported identical results on two indices of expectations. For purposes of synthesis, these studies were counted as each contributing one common result. The fourth study contained three expectation measures and a composite of these plus five other measures. Since all four results were nonsignificant, this study was counted as a single exact null result.

Of the 16 studies, nine reported that teacher expectations favored white students. One study reported black students were expected to perform better than whites, and six studies did not report the direction of their result.

Five studies reported that the results of their comparison were statistically significant. All of these found higher expectations for whites. The combined probability across all 16 studies was $p < .002$, two-tailed (Zma = 3.09), indicating that white students were viewed more favorably than blacks. It would take 50 unretrieved studies with z scores summing to zero to increase the overall probability of the run of studies to above $p < .05$ ($N_{fs} = 49.94$).

Estimates of effect size could be retrieved for only six studies, four of which were associated with significant results. The average of these was d = +.53. If each of the nine studies reporting a null result is considered to have uncovered a d index of zero and the one study (Bennett, 1979) reporting a significant result but no F test is estimated to have a d index of +.36 (by $p < .05$ and df = 1,120), then the average effect size across all sixteen studies was d = +.22. This means the average white student in these studies was given higher expectations by the teacher than about 58% of the black students.

Study Characteristics as Mediators of the Race Effect.   Four study characteristics were examined to determine if they were related to the results of studies. These were whether (a) a between- or within-subjects design was used; (b) a written or other mode of stimulus student presentation was used; (c) professional teachers or college students served as evaluators; and (d) the stimulus student was described as in either elementary school or some more advanced level of schooling.

Only the between- versus within-subjects distinction in study design appeared to be associated with the study's outcome. Specifically, five of six (83%) studies involving presentation of more than one stimulus student to a teacher reported a finding favoring whites while four of ten (40%) studies presenting each teacher with only one student favored whites (phi-coefficient = .41, *p* < .11). Four (67%) within-subject studies reported significant results in favor of whites, but only one (10%) between-subjects study provided significant results (r = .59, *p* < .02). These results probably demonstrate the greater statistical power of repeated measures designs.

The distinction between elementary grade stimulus students and all other students was not formally tested because only four studies involved students past sixth grade. Six of 11 (55%) studies using elementary school-aged students found whites were expected to do better than blacks and four of these (45%) were significant. Three studies employing one college-aged and two high school-aged samples of stimulus students favored white students while the one study at the junior high level favored blacks. Because this result is difficult to explain, further study is needed before it is concluded that the expectation effect favoring whites is reversed at the middle school level.

Nonexperimental Comparisons of White and Black Students.   In addition to the 16 experimental studies, two studies were found in which teachers' naturally occurring expectations for their own students were related to whether the student was white or black.

Finn, Gaier, Peng, and Banks (1975) randomly selected nine schools from the Buffalo, NY school district. From these schools 22 fifth grade teachers were selected. Each teacher filled out several expectation measures about their class. These included measures of (a) how well-prepared they expected their students to be for the year's work; (b) how well they expected this class to perform; and (c) how well the class would perform in the cognitive domain. Finn et al. identified six teachers from predominantly black schools and eight from predominantly white schools and compared their expectations. None of the comparisons proved significant (due to the small sample size) but all comparisons favored the white students and one, involving the students' preparedness for the year's work, revealed a large effect size (d = .78).

Smith (1979) had 16 female elementary school teachers in Chicago, IL complete educational expectation rankings for each of their students. She found expectations to be related to student racial background in the early grades, but not significantly so.

Experimental Comparisons of Middle Versus Lower Class Students

Eleven studies were located in which the social class of a stimulus student was experimentally manipulated prior to assessing teacher expectations. Table 10.2 contains a brief description of each study. Six studies were found in journals, four in *Dissertation Abstracts International* and one in *ERIC*. All reports appeared between 1971 and 1980.

Six studies used within-subjects designs and five used between-subjects designs. Seven studies manipulated the student's social class by providing teachers with a written description of the student's background. Three studies used visual or vocal or vocal cues only to manipulate social class. In each of these studies, social class needed to be inferred by the teacher from variations in how the student looked or spoke. Finally, one study used a real child but the available abstract did not indicate if this manipulation was accompanied by a written description.

Eight studies used practicing teachers and two employed college students. One study (Hendren & Routh, 1979) used clinical psychologists as evaluators. Experiments were conducted in all parts of the country. The average experiment involved 148 participants, ranging in size from 25 to 648.

Nine studies used stimulus students described as being in elementary school, one used junior high-aged students and one used high school students.

Combined Results of Studies.   Eight of the 11 studies contained only a single measure of teacher expectation. Two studies used two relevant measures with each revealing a nonsignificant result. For purposes of synthesis, these studies were treated as revealing a single exact null finding. A study by Mazer (1971) presented a more complex problem. His study contained three measures of expectation, all of which revealed significant effects well below the $p < .01$ level. However, the analyses were based on three degrees of freedom for effect, with two levels of social class and two levels of race employed in a oneway analysis of variance. While it was evident from graphs and discussion that most of the combined effect was due to social class (not race) no decomposition of the variance for effect was presented. For purposes of this synthesis, this study was considered to have contributed one $p < .01$ finding. This was probably a conservative decision.

TABLE 10.2

Experimental Studies of the Effect of Student Social Class on Teacher Expectations

First Author	Year	Presentation Mode	Social Class Manipulation	Expectation Measure	Group With Higher Expectations	Significance Level
Mazer	1971	Written description	Social class labels	Academic Ability	Middle Class	p < .01
				Mental Ability	Middle Class	
				Grades	Middle Class	
Miller	1973	Written description	Father's occupation	Performance Estimate	Middle Class	p < .01
Jensen	1974	Videotape	Visual information only	Test Performance	Middle Class	NS
				Intelligence	Middle Class	
Pugh	1974	Audiotape	Speech dialect	Academic Ability	Middle Class	NS
Cooper	1975	Written description	Father's occupation	Grades	Middle Class	p < .001
Harvey	1975	Photographs	Photographs only	Completion of Homework	Not given	NS
Rotter	1975	Cumulative record	Not described	Academic Success	Not given	NS
Amato	1976	Real child plus written description	Father's occupation	Intelligence	Not given	NS
				Academic Performance	Not given	
Bennett	1979	Real child	Not described	Predicted Success	Middle Class	p < .05
Hendren	1979	Written description	Father's occupation	Level of Achievement	Lower Class	NS
Parker	1980	Written description	Not described	Academic Success	Not given	NS

260

One study (Pugh, 1974) manipulated three levels of social class (through dialect). This study was treated as one nonsignificant finding. Finally, one study (Bennett, 1979) reported a singificant social class effect, but no significance level. A finding of $p < .05$ (df = 1,120) was again assumed.

Six studies reported that teachers held higher expectations for middle-class students, four studies gave no direction for their finding and one study that involved clinical psychologists found lower-class students were favored.

Four studies produced significant social class effects and all of these favored middle-class students. The combined probability for the run of 11 studies was $p < .002$, two-tailed (Zma = 3.14), indicating that teachers held higher expectations for middle-than lower-class students. The number of studies summing to a null result needed to raise the probability for the run of studies to above $p < .05$ was 29 ($N_{fs} = 28.56$).

Effect size information was obtainable only from the four studies reporting significant results. The average of these effects was d = .51. If the remaining seven studies are assumed to have uncovered effect sizes of d = 0, then the average effect size across all studies was d = .19, or, the average middle-class student was expected to outperform about 57% of the lower class population.

Study Characteristics as Mediators of the Social Class Effect.   Because of the small number of studies and the uneven distribution of characteristics across studies, a formal testing of how study characteristics might relate to study results was not undertaken. An informal examination did reveal that all three studies using visual or vocal cues as their only means for presenting social class information produced nonsignificant results.

Nonexperimental Studies.   Three studies were located in which practicing teachers' expectations for their own students were related to the students' social class.

Wong (1980) used a stratified random sample to identify 541 elementary school students and 311 secondary school students. Each student's social class was measured by the father's occupation and teacher expectations were measured by a composite of bipolar adjectives that loaded on a factor called "academic competence." The results showed teacher expectations were higher for students whose fathers held higher status jobs but the relation was significant only for the elementary school sample.

Williams (1976) conducted a correlational study involving 10,530 Canadian high school students and their 351 teachers. He found that the status of the father's occupation, the father's educational level and the mother's educational level each correlated positively with the teacher's rating of the student's academic potential. This was true of both male and female students, with correlations ranging from .14 to .18 (d = .28 to .38).

Finally, the previously described study by Smith (1979) also examined social class, measured by whether or not the student's family was receiving welfare. For primary school students the relation between social class and teacher expectations was significant.

The Interaction of Race and Social Class Information

Studies that simultaneously manipulated the race and social class of stimulus students hold two important sources of information. First, they provide direct comparisons of the relative impact of the two variables on teacher expectations. The examination of main effects presented above revealed the average effect of the student's race (d = .22) and social class (d = .19) on expectations were nearly identical. However, if the two variables appeared in separate studies so that these estimates were based on independent testings, how much of the race effect might be due to teachers *assuming* blacks were lower-class (and whites were middle-class), or how much of the social class effect might be due to assumptions about race, could not be assessed. Second, the interactions effects contained in studies with both race and social class manipulations address whether the effect of one variable is dependent on the level of the other; for example, whether the effect of social class is greater for blacks than whites.

Eight studies manipulated both the race and social class of stimulus students (these are the studies which appear in both Tables 10.1 and 10.2). Four of these studies employed a written description of the student to achieve their manipulations. Of these, three report significant social class effects while none reported a significant race effect. On the other hand, of the four studies that manipulated visual and/or vocal cues from the student, three found significant race effects and only one produced a significant social class effect. It appears, then, that the relative impact of the two students variables on teacher expectations depended on the researcher's choice of how to present the stimulus student.

Six studies tested for the interactive effect of student race and social class but none revealed a significant result. This result may be somewhat misleading, however, since the analysis of variance tests for disordinal or symmetric interactions, rather than the ordinal or asymmetric interactions that are most likely to occur in this case. Put more concretely, it is quite possible that the direction of the social class effect is similar for blacks and whites, but perhaps more dramatic for one group than the other. It is unlikely that the direction of the social class effect reverses itself from one group to the other. The latter effect, however, is tested in the traditional ANOVA design, while the former effect is "spread out" across the interactions and two main effects.

Five studies presented teacher expectation means broken down by race and social groupings. A comparison of mean differences between middle-class and lower-class students within black and white racial backgrounds was conducted to give an indication of the existence of any asymmetric interaction. Three studies revealed a larger mean difference between social classes for blacks than whites and one study revealed the opposite effect. The final study contained two expectation measures and these produced conflicting results.

In sum, no strong evidence was uncovered to indicate that student race and social class had different magnitudes of impact on teacher expectations. Nor was it demonstrated that the impact of one variable differed at different levels of the other variable. However, several methodological problems require that these conclusions undergo more precise testings before firm conclusions are drawn.

Other Variables Interacting with Student Race and Social Class.   Many studies included independent variables other than the student's race or social class. Most frequent among these were the student's sex, past performance, and/or ability. These studies rarely reported that the third variables mediated the relation between the student's race or social class and teacher expectations and few reported relations were replicated in other studies involving the same variable. Many third variables did reveal significant main effects on teacher expectations but these are beyond the scope of this chapter.

Comparisons Involving Other Minority Groups

Three studies examined teacher expectations for Mexican-Americans in comparison to whites and blacks. Williams and Naremore (1974) found that teachers held higher language arts expectations for whites than Mexican-Americans, while expectations for blacks and Mexican-Americans generally did not differ. Wilkerson (1980) reported a similar result. Jensen and Rosenfeld (1974) reported teacher expectations were higher for whites than blacks and for blacks than Mexican-Americans.

Finally, Wong (1980) reported that practicing teachers held higher expectations for their Asian-American than white students and that this effect was stronger at the secondary than primary grade levels.

DISCUSSION

Our discussion is divided into two major subsections. First, the extant research is summarized with regard to (a) its implications for understanding the relationships among race, class, and teacher expectations and (b) with regard to significant omissions in current studies. The second section examines new theoretical directions for teacher expectation formation research.

Overview of Current Findings

In general, the meta-analyses supported the hypothesized relations between race, class, and teacher expectations. White students elicited higher teacher expectations regarding achievement than black students. Similarly, a middle-class background generated higher expectations than a lower-class background. This latter effect appeared across a range of indices of social class. Further, no strong evidence was uncovered to indicate that the social class and race of students had different magnitudes of effect on teacher expectations. And finally, there was no evidence of either symmetrical or asymmetrical interaction effects involving both background variables.

With regard to other racial groups, studies involving comparisons of Mexican-Americans with whites indicated higher expectations were held for whites. Either no difference between blacks and Mexican-Americans (two studies) or lower expectations for Mexican-Americans than blacks (one study) were found.

Extensions and Omissions of Existing Research

An Unexpected Finding.   Perhaps the most intriguing finding of the review concerned the differential efficacy of race and class manipulations depending upon whether a verbal or a perceptual manipulation was used. Specifically, stronger effects were found for the race variable when visual and/or vocal cues were used while stronger social class effects emerged with written descriptions. One explanation of these findings is that the efficacy of the different manipulations corresponds to their ecological validity. Teachers typically receive race information in real situations through perceptual cues whereas social class information is inferred from written records revealing the father's occupation, etc. If this were the case, we would expect the more ecologically valid manipulations to be more impactful.

Although only eight studies are involved in the above comparisons, future studies should systematically vary modes of presentation of race and social class information. Future studies should involve perceptual (i.e., visual and or vocal) manipulations of race and written manipulations of social class. Ideally, all combinations of information should be incorporated with race and class variations in the same study.

Explaining the Lack of Interaction Effect.   As the above discussion indicates, one possible reason for the lack of a significant interaction between race and social class might be the failure of researchers to utilize maximally effective manipulations. For example, the likelihood of a race effect only holding for lower-class students may be more easily detected when race is manipulated by perceptual cues and class by written materials. Two other possible methodological reasons for this failure of the interaction effect are (a) the small sample sizes used in the studies, and (b) the insensitivity of ANOVA designs to asymmetrical interaction effects.

Another possibility worth exploring in future research is that interaction effects emerge only after repeated exposure to students. For example, future expectation formation research in a field setting might gather expectation data at the beginning, middle, and end of the school year (see Cooper, 1982, this volume).

Grade Level. The present review indicated there is a paucity of research involving the effect of grade level on race and social class effects. For example, it might be expected that race, because it is a perceptual variable, has a stronger effect on teacher expectations during the early school years, whereas social class effects may take longer to emerge. Social class effects, however, may persist later into the schooling process.

Theoretical Directions

Present research lacks a coherent theoretical perspective regarding the processes and mechanisms involved in mediating the impact of race and social class on teacher expectations. This lack is of more than academic interest since how expectations are acquired might effect both the mode of communication utilized to shape student behavior and the likelihood that a teacher expectation will be translated into student performance differences. Three theoretical perspectives are applied to suggest future directions for research.

Acquisition vs. Instigation. None of the studies reviewed attempted to distinguish between the acquisition of low expectations versus the instigation of previously acquired expectations. It is possible, for example, that race and social class do not differ in their relative impact on the *acquisition* of low teacher expectations but they do differ in their power to evoke generalized expectations when a student of a certain race or social class is confronted.

While acquisition and instigation are confounded in naturalistic studies, their separate effects should be identifiable in the laboratory. For example, one could vary the performance level information about a variety of black and white students during an acquisition phase. Then teachers could be asked to observe a performance of a particular different black or white student. Teachers differing in their acquisition histories could then be asked to assess the future performance prospects of this student.

Research reported by Darley (1981) designed to test a schema-type model of the operation of class stereotypes, suggests a possible outcome of such an experiment. Specifically, different groups of participants were initially exposed to slides that indicated a target person came from either a well-to-do or poor background. Next, participants were shown a videotape of the target person taking an achievement-type test. The information in the tape contained an equal mixture of cues indicating the student was bright or slow. Participants' subsequent estimates of the target student's ability to perform below, at, or above grade level were strongly biased in favor of well-to-do students. It is of particular interest here, however, that simply asking subjects to guess performance level without the videotape exposure did *not* elicit systematic differences associated with social class. This finding suggests that the "illusion of objectivity" was necessary before participants demonstrated biased information processing in accord with an initial rich–poor schema or prototype (cr. Markus, 1980). Similar constraints are likely to occur regarding teacher expectation effects. That is, expectancies may at times take on schema type properties.

Models of Acquisition.   Two general models appear especially relevant to understanding the acquisition of expectations. One model, derived from the Skinnerian-Operant conditioning approach, highlights the importance of reinforcement schedule parameters. For example, race or social class-based expectations might derive from past observations of different frequencies of black and white successes and failures. To the extent that these distributions of outcomes differ, different expectations will be generated.

A second approach to modeling the acquisition process derives from the impression formation framework (cf. Anderson, 1974, 1965). This perspective would highlight whether past observations regarding the success and failures of different children are integrated according to an averaging or summation rule. More importantly, expectations, because they are based on temporally ordered experiences, raise the possibility that primacy and recency effects are at work (Cooper, Lowe, & Baron, 1976). For example, are the earliest or the most recent observations given most weight in expectation information? Does this effect differ for race as opposed to class-based expectations? Race information, because of its greater perceptual character, might be more likely to produce primacy effects than the more abstract social class information.

Direct vs. Vicarious Expectation Acquisition.   Recent research in the attitude domain suggests that the mode of acquisition of social class and/or race expectations might be an important factor to consider in future research. Specifically, Fazio and Zanna (1981) have demonstrated that the more direct experience one has with an attitude object the greater is the likelihood that the person's attitude will predict his or her behavior toward the object. One explanation for this effect is that the greater the direct experiential basis the more stable and confidently held will be the attitude.

Applied to the present situation, it has already been suggested that expectations are acquired both directly and vicariously. Teachers might have direct experience with students of varying races or classes, or they might vicariously learn group stereotypes through modeling or social comparisons with other teachers. Given Fazio and Zanna's findings, it might be hypothesized that teacher expectations based on direct experience will be more likely to be behaviorally communicated to students (e.g., result in different inputs to student learning).

CONCLUSION

In sum, the confident conclusion of this review that race and social class effects on teacher expectations do exist should not be taken to mean more research is unnecessary. Instead, future researchers should now turn their attention from documenting such effects to examinimg personal and situational variables, which help delineate the basic processes underlying both the acquisition and impact of race and social class based teacher beliefs about students. It is further suggested that current theory and research in the domains of social learning and social cognition might provide fruitful models for extrapolation.

REFERENCES

Anderson, N. H. Averaging vs. adding as a stimulus-combination rule in impression formation. *Journal of Experimental Psychology*, 1965, *70*, 394–400.

Anderson, N. H. Cognitive algebra: Integration theory applied to social attribution. In L. Berkowitz (Ed.), *Advances in experimental social psychology* (Vo. 7). New York: Academic Press, 1974.

Braun, C. Teacher expectations: Sociopsychological dynamics. *Review of Educational Research*, 1976, *46*, 185–213.

Cohen, J. *Statistical power analysis for the behavioral sciences* (revised ed.). New York: Academic Press, 1977.

Cooper, H. M. Some effects of preperformance information on academic expectations. *Journal of Educational Psychology*, 1979a, *71*, 375–380.

Cooper, H. M. Statistically combining independent studies: A meta-analysis of sex differences in conformity research. *Journal of Personality and Social Psychology*, 1979, *37*, 131–146.

Cooper, H. M. On the significance of effects and the effects of significance. *Journal of Personality and Social Psychology*, 1981, *41*(5), 1013–1018.

Cooper, H. M. Scientific guidelines for conducting integrative research reviews. *Review of Educational Research*, 1982, *52*, 291–302.

Cooper, H., & Findley, M. Expected effect sizes: Estimates for statistical power analysis in social psychology. *Personality and Social Psychology Bulletin*, 1982, *8*, 168–173.

Cooper, H. M., Lowe, C. A., & Baron, R. M. Pattern of past performance and expected future performance: A reversal of the unexpected primary effect. *Journal of Applied Social Psychology*, 1976, *6*, 31–39.

Darley, J. M. Talk delivered at Fall meeting of the New England Social Psychological Association, October 17, 1981, Williams College, Williamstown, Mass.

Deutsch, M., Katz, I., & Jensen, A. R. (Eds.). *Social class, race and psychological development.* New York: Holt, Rinehart & Winston, 1968.

Fazio, R. H., & Zanna, M. P. Direct experience and attitude-behavior consistency. In L. Berkowitz (Ed.), *Advances in experimental social psychology.* New York: Academic Press, 1981.

Friedman, H. Magnitude of experimental effect and a table for its rapid estimation. *Psychological Bulletin*, 1968, *70*, 245–251.

Glass, G., McGaw, B., & Smith, M. *Meta-analysis in social research.* Beverly Hills: Sage, 1981.

Greenwald, A. Consequences of prejudice against the null hypothesis. *Psychological Bulletin*, 1975, *82*, 1–20.

Karlins, M., Coffman, T., & Walters, G. On the fading of social stereo-types: Studies in three generations of college students. *Journal of Personality and Social Psychology*, 1969, *13*, 1–16.

Markus, H. The self in thought and memory. In D. M. Wegner & R. R. Vallacher (Eds.), *The self in social psychology.* New York: Oxford, 1980.

Rosenthal, R. The "file drawer problem" and tollerance for null results. *Psychological Bulletin,* 1979, *86,* 638–641.

Rosenthal, R. Summarizing significance levels. *New Directions for Methodology of Social and Behavioral Science,* 1980, *5,* 33–46.

Rosenthall, R., & Jacobson, L. *Pygmalion in the classroom: Teacher expectation and pupil's intellectual development.* New York: Holt, Rinehart, & Winston, 1968.

Rosenthal, R., & Rubin, D. Interpersonal expectancy effects: The first 345 studies. *The Behavioral and Brain Sciences,* 1978, *3,* 377–386.

STUDIES USED IN QUANTITATIVE REVIEW

Journal Articles

Amato, Josephine A. Effect of Pupil's Social Class Upon Teacher's Expectations and Behavior. Dissertation Abstracts International, 1976, 37(1-A) 186-187. (Also paper presented at the 83rd Annual Convention of the American Psychological Association, Chicago, Illinois, August 30, 1975.

Cooper, H. M., Baron, R. M., & Lowe, C. A. The importance of race and social class information in the formation of expectancies about academic performance. *Journal of Educational Psychology,* 1975, *67*(2), 312–319.

Deitz, S. M., & Purkey, William W. Teacher expectation of performance based on race of student. *Psychological Reports,* 1969, *24*(3), 694.

Derlega, V., Wang, P., & Colson, W. *Racial bias in expectancies and performance attributions.* Unpublished manuscript, Old Dominion University, 1981.

Finn, J. D., Gaier, E. L., Peng, S. S., & Banks, R. E. Teacher expectations and pupil achievement. *Urban Education,* 1975, *10,* 175–197.

Harvey, D., & Slatin, G. T. The relationship between child's socio-economic status and teacher expectations: A test of middle-class bias hypothesis. *Social Forces,* 1975, *54,* 140–159.

Hendren, T., & Routh, D. Social class bias in psychologists' evaluations of children. *Journal of Pediatric Psychology,* 1979, *4,* 353–361.

Jensen, M., & Rosenfeld, L. Influence of mode of presentation, ethnicity and social class on teachers' evaluations of students. *Journal of Educational Psychology,* 1974, *66,* 540–547.

Kehle, Thomas J., Bramble, William J., & Mason, E. J. Teachers' expectations: Ratings of students' performance as biased by student characteristics. *Journal of Experimental Education,* 1974, *43*(1), 54–60.

Mazer, G. E. Effects of social class stereotyping on teacher expectation. *Psychology in the Schools,* 1971, *8*(4), 373–378.

Miller, H. L. Race vs. class in teachers' expectations. *Psychological Reports,* 1973, *32,* 105–106.

Taylor, M. C. Race, sex and the expression of self-fullfilling prophecies in a laboratory teaching situation. *Journal of Personality and Social Psychology,* 1979, *37,* 897–912.

Wiley, M. G., & Eskilson, A. Why did you learn in school today? Teachers' perceptions of causality. *Sociology of Education,* 1978, *51,* 261–269.

Williams, T. Teacher prophecies and the inheritance of inequality. *Sociology of Education,* 1976, *49,* 223–236.

Wong, M. C. Model students? Teachers' perceptions and expectations of their Asian and white students. *Sociology of Education,* 1980, *53,* 236–246.

Research in Education (ERIC)

Pugh, L. G. Teacher attitudes and expectations associated with race and social class. American Educational Research Association Annual Meeting, Chicago, Illinois, April 15-19, 1974, EDO94018.

Simpson, M., Smith, J. O., & Means, G. H. An assessment of differential expectations of performance based on race of student. *Research in Education,* September, 1978, ED153144.

Dissertation Abstracts International

Bennett, C. E. The Effects of Student Characteristics and Task Performance on Teacher Expectations and Attributions. *Diss. Abst. Int'l.,* 1979, 40(2-B) 979–980.

Parker, R. N. Teacher Expectancy Behavior: The Impact of Several Salient Student Characteristics Upon Expectations and Causal Attributions. *Diss. Abst. Int'l.,* 1980, 40(8-A), 4497–4498.

Rotter, Naomi G. The Influence of Race and Other Variables on Teachers' Ratings of Pupils. *Diss. Abst. Int'l.,* 1975, 35A, 7134.

Smith, J. A. Ascribed and Achieved Student Characteristics in Teacher Expectancy: Relationship of Socio-Economic Status to Academic Achievement, Academic Self-Concept, and Vocational Aspirations. *Diss. Abst. Int'l.,* 1979, 40(2-B), 959–960.

Wilkerson, M. The effects of sex and ethnicity upon teachers' expectations of students. *Diss. Abst. Int'l.,* 1980, *41,* 637-A.

11 Sex Role Expectations and Achievement

Thomas L. Good
Maureen J. Findley
University of Missouri-Columbia

INTRODUCTION

Sex generally predicts school achievement. Young girls do better in virtually all school subjects whereas adolescent boys generally perform better than girls in mathematics and science. This chapter explores relationships between teacher expectations for, and behavior toward, male and female students and the possible influence of differential expectations and behavior on student achievement. Do certain teachers (e.g., male or female) expect more achievement from boys or girls in particular subjects?

In contrast to the considerable literature that has addressed the relationship between teachers' achievement expectations for students and related behavior toward students, relatively little formal and systematic research has studied the relationship between teachers' expectations and behavior and the differential achievement of boys and girls. There are many studies of teachers' beliefs about boys' and girls' learning styles and classroom needs, but such studies seldom include information about teachers' classroom behavior (Do teachers' beliefs translate into behavior?). Ironically, studies that do measure teachers' behavior toward boys and girls seldom measure teachers' beliefs (Do teachers expect girls to learn more? Do they believe that boys need more or less structure?).

Despite the lack of systematic research, there are signs that teachers' sex-related beliefs about children may influence teachers' classroom behavior. Palardy (1969) studied the reading achievement of students of two groups of first grade teachers. Using a questionnaire, he identified a group of 10 teachers who felt that boys could learn to read as sucsessfully as girls in the first grade, despite the fact that girls are routinely found to do better than are boys in first grade classrooms. He identified another group of 14 teachers who thought that boys could not learn to read as successfully as girls. He identified five teachers from each group for further study (all 10 teachers were experienced and had at least 3 years of teaching in the first grade). All teachers taught in middle-class schools and used the same basal reading series to work with the three reading groups in heterogeneously grouped, self-contained classrooms. Hence, the teachers were teaching reasonably comparable students under similar conditions.

Students had similar reading readiness scores in September; however, differences were found among the boys in reading achievement scores collected in March. In classes where teachers believed boys were as capable of high achievement as girls, boys averaged 96.5 on the tests. In contrast, in classes where teachers did not think boys could achieve as well as girls, boys averaged 89.2. Because these data are correlational it is not possible to argue that teachers' high expectations for boys' reading ability *caused* the higher reading scores. Among the many possible explanations for these findings is the fact that boys' good reading performance in some classrooms may have preceded (and hence influenced), not followed, the development of teachers' positive learning expectations.

Furthermore, Palardy did not measure student–teacher behavior during reading group instruction, so it is impossible to tell if and how teachers' behavior informed boys that they were to "learn to read." Nor can we determine whether teachers who possessed higher expectations provided classroom experiences different from those provided by teachers who held lower expectations for boys' reading ability. Still, it is a carefully controlled study and presents data that indicate teachers may hold sex-related expectations that influence their classroom behavior and student achievement.

Other studies have illustrated that teachers may vary their behavior toward pupils on the basis of student sex. Leinhardt, Seewald, and Engel (1979) provide evidence that male and female students receive differential treatment. These authors studied teacher–student interactions in 33 second grade classrooms and found that in reading, girls had a higher percent of academic contacts with teachers and received somewhat more instructional time than boys. However, in mathematics, boys received more academic contacts and instructional time with teachers than did girls. In all classrooms, boys had more management contacts with teachers than did girls.

Leinhardt et al. (1979) found that differential instructional behavior and student achievement were related in reading. Although there were no differences in initial abilities, significant sex differences were found in end-of-year standardized achievement testing. Presumably, the fact that teachers spent relatively more time with girls in reading was associated with girls' increased reading achievement. However, the results are correlational and hence susceptible to multiple interpretations. Also, the researchers did not measure teachers' beliefs about boys' and girls' abilities and interests in reading and mathematics, but rather assumed that teachers may hold greater expectations for girls in reading and for boys in mathematics. However, other studies suggest that expectations related to students' sex, although important, may not be as powerful a predictor as are other beliefs that teachers hold about students.

Doyle, Hancock, and Kifer (1972) asked first grade teachers to estimate the IQs of their students shortly before an IQ test was given. The teachers' IQ estimates were then compared to the IQs obtained from the tests. The comparisons showed that the teachers tended to overestimate the IQs of girls and to underestimate the IQs of boys, and that these estimates were related to the reading achievement of the children. Even though there was no IQ difference between the boys and the girls, the girls showed higher reading achievement. Furthermore, within both sexes, the children whose IQs had been overestimated by the teachers had higher reading achievement than those whom the teachers had underestimated. All of this might simply mean that the teachers were heavily influenced by the children's reading abilities in making judgments about their general intelligence. However, it is likely that the teachers' expectations affected their teaching of reading. Doyle et al. also discovered that the classes of teachers who generally overestimated their children's IQs achieved more than the classes of teachers who generally underestimated, regardless of sex.

We have seen that there is some reason to believe that teachers' behavior may be related to the beliefs that they hold about young girls and boys. Although countless studies have examined some aspect of teachers' beliefs about individual students, there are few studies that have measured teachers' beliefs and behavior as well as students' classroom behavior and achievement. Due to the extensive literature on school-related sex differences (and the space allocated for this chapter), we review selected but representative studies.

We begin with a discussion of sex-related beliefs that may originate in the home and then examines sex differences in teachers' expectations and perceptions of students. Then we discuss studies of differential teacher classroom behavior and student sex. We also examine two school subjects (mathematics and reading) in which boys and girls may differentially perform. Finally, we offer suggestions for future research.

Influences of Parent and Home

We know that children's interest in, and skills relevant for, academic scholarship begin to develop long before they enter school. Many educators and researchers have attempted to identify family practices (from symbolic appreciation for learning to actual parent instructional behaviors) that contribute to early acquisition of basic academic skills. In particular, many studies have examined students' interest in reading because of the assumed importance of reading to all school subjects. Durkin (1966) found that parents of early readers reported a much stronger interest "in print" (interest in looking at books, etc.) among their children than parents of nonearly readers who were matched on other characteristics such as IQ and SES. Unfortunately, these data do not explain how students become interested in print in the first place.

Other researchers have assessed parents' perceptions of their children's interest in print and knowledge. Hiebert and Coffey (1982) studied parents' views of their young children's print-related development by asking fathers and mothers (individually) to predict their kindergarten children's performances on measures of knowledge and interest in print. While fathers' and mothers' estimates did not differ significantly from one another, both groups significantly underestimated their children's performances on the knowledge of print measure. On the interest in print measure, parents overestimated their children's performances. Although boys and girls scored very similarly on both measures, parents' predictions differed according to gender of child, with parents of boys giving lower estimates than parents of girls. Others too have noted that young girls do not necessarily have superior language skills when they enter school. After reviewing the literature on differences in oral language acquisition related to gender, Macaulay (1978) concluded that the stereotype that girls have a greater propensity for language and acquire it more quickly and fluently is not empirically supported. Rather, studies suggest that boys are as interested and capable with regard to print as girls, at least when they begin school.

However, data on actual school achievement indicate that girls' achievement in reading and verbal skills (as well as other curriculum areas) far surpasses that of young boys by the end of first grade and throughout the elementary school years (see for example the norm data associated with the Iowa Test of Basic Skills, Hieronymus, Lindquist, & Hoover, 1982). Unfortunately, adolescent girls' achievement in certain subjects declines. In part, females' early achievement in reading and their relative decline in performance in some subjects later appear to be due to parental, societal, and teacher expectations.

Parsons, Ruble, Hodges, and Small (1976) suggested that parents and teachers have different expectations for boys' and girls' performances in school and that these differences eventually influence children's self-expectations and actual achievement. Indeed, there is some empirical evidence to suggest that in some classrooms teachers appear to interact with students in sex-specific ways. For example, as noted earlier, Leinhardt et al. (1979) found that boys received more favorable treatment in mathematics, whereas girls received more favorable instruction during reading. It seems clear that students' academic learning may be influenced by social experiences and expectations that are held for them by significant others including parents.

Do parents' beliefs and expectations determine children's interests, or do parents' beliefs merely reflect their awareness of interests that their children have formed independently? It is virtually impossible to separate antecedent from cause in social influence situations because so many variables occur simultaneously and one participant's behavior is always affecting the others'.

As Hiebert and Coffey (1982) noted in their study comparing parents' perceptions of children's interest in print, one difficulty in specifying the relationship between parents' expectations and children's performance is that the process is interactive and the influence is mutual. For example, parents form some of their beliefs about children's interests and capabilities by observing children's performances and by listening to them. However, the data in this study suggest that parents may have some preconceived notions related to gender and developmental status, regardless of the characteristics of individual children.

McGillicuddy-DeLisi (1982) used both observational and interview methods to explore relations between parents' beliefs about children and their behavior toward them. Children in this study were asked to learn two laboratroy tasks that their parents taught. It was found that what mothers believed about children's development predicted their child-rearing behaviors in two different contexts, even after demographic characteristics were taken into account. Also, fathers' beliefs about child development scores were related to their behaviors during interactions with their children, after taking into account family constellation and socioeconomic factors. These data provide evidence that parents' beliefs about child development may guide how they interpret and react to children's behavior.

Many researchers have recently begun to explore parents' influences upon children. Perhaps the major lesson learned from such studies is that it is exceedingly difficult to study family influences on children because so many variables are involved. Sigel (1982) expressed the problem this way: "To return to the geographical metaphor, the terrain is being mapped more accurately than has been the case. What we have also discovered in our mapping efforts is that there is a considerable gap between the models of family functioning and the methods by which to study the models."

There is growing evidence that the study of home instruction is at least as complicated as studying school instruction. Chall and Snow (1982) provide an interesting example of this point. Working in relatively low-SES schools, these investigators identified students who varied in terms of reading skill. They intended to study the homes from which good and poor readers came in order to see if there were systematic differences in home environments (e.g., appreciation of print, resources) that might account for differences in students' reading abilities. When the investigators visited the homes of students who had been identified as good readers, they often found a sibling who was a relatively poor reader, and vice versa. At a minimum, these data suggest that there was about as much variation in reading ability within families as between families. The causes of these differences are not clear. It may be that students in the same family develop different reading abilities because resources (time and energy) are allocated differentially to children in the family. Alternatively, it may be that children read at different levels not because their environments are different, but because they react differentially to similar opportunities. It seems plausible to infer from these data that children from the same home often enter school with different abilities for, and interests in, reading and other subject areas as well.

That students arrive at school with dissimilar interests and abilities may be seen to be a relatively common sense observation at first glance. However, many educators, sociologists, and psychologists implicitly suggest in their writings that home environment, socioeconomic status, and other status variables lead to rather predictable problems and conditions of learning (girls like letters—boys like numbers). As a case in point, it is not uncommon that teachers' expectations and behaviors toward students are related to their knowledge of, and interactions with, older siblings. *Seaver (1973)* conducted a natural, quasi-experiment to see if the achievement of 79 students in first grade was affected by the previous achievement patterns of older siblings. The hypothesis tested was that students would achieve better when taught by the same teacher if their older siblings had been good students and worse when older siblings had been poor students (in contrast to control students, who had a different teacher than the older sibling). It was found that following a sibling who was a good student had positive consequences upon achievement for younger siblings, especially males. It is not entirely clear how teachers' perceptions of home conditions influence their actual behavior, but it does seem possible that some teachers may inadequately assess the potential of students by overusing "status" factors (home background, sex, older siblings, etc.).

Differential Teacher Perception of Student Ability Based on Student Gender

In order to demonstrate that student achievement is affected by teachers' sex-related beliefs and behavior, it must first be shown that teachers *do* hold differing expectations for male and female students. Several researchers have investigated the question, "Do teachers form different kinds of academic expectations for male and female students?" In other words, do teachers perceive male and female students differently in terms of academic ability and do they expect the likelihood of academic success might vary according to the gender of the student? Finally, do teachers evaluate their male and female students according to a different set of criteria? To tap differential academic expectations, Simmons (1980) asked teachers to "attribute various characteristics to either males or females in their classrooms" (p. 250). Along with a number of personality characteristics, teachers were asked to rate the abstract or math reasoning and verbal ability of boys and girls. A majority of the teachers expected that girls and boys would not perform differently on a test of math reasoning. About half of the teachers felt that there was no difference in the verbal ability of males and females either. Thus, as Simmons notes, "a large percentage of the teachers did not give girls credit for having the advantage on a characteristic that contributes positively to school achievement" (p. 252). Still, a number of teachers did differentiate between male and female students in forming their perceptions of ability.

Adams and Cohen (1976) were also interested in how teachers' judgments of students might be affected by student characteristics such as gender. They gave teachers official looking folders containing a variety of information on students (e.g., sex of student, socioeconomic status, attractiveness, general ability, etc.) and asked teachers to make predictions about the student described in each folder. The academic predictions concerned the intellectual ability of the student and the quality of the student–teacher interactions. In addition, they asked teachers to rate the degree of vocational training they expected the student would obtain. Few sex-related differences in ratings were observed beyond the finding that girls were viewed as being more intelligent than boys. Adams and Cohen also compared the ratings of male and female teachers. Only one rating resulted in a significant difference. Male teachers predicted that they would have less supportive teacher interaction than female teachers.

Bernard (1979) attempted to determine if (a) male and female teachers differed in their evaluations of students, and (b) teachers differed in their evaluations of male and female students. In addition to investigating the sex of the student and teacher, Bernard (1979) looked at the students' sex-role behavior and their major course of study. Teachers were asked to read and rate a description of a student who was either male or female, who demonstrated either masculine or feminine sex-role behavior, and whose major course of study was either English or physics. To measure the teachers' perceptions of students' academic ability, the teachers also read and evaluated an essay supposedly written by the students concerning an issue in their course of study. Bernard found that male and female teachers differed in their evaluations of the physics and English essays. Female teachers felt that the English essay was higher in quality than the physics essay, while male teachers tended to evaluate students writing the physics answer as being higher in overall ability.

The sex of the student and of the teacher interacted in a "cross-sex bias." Concerning the physics answer, male teachers evaluated the female students' essays more highly while female teachers rated males' answers as better.

Student gender and sex-role behavior also interacted in terms of teachers' perceptions. Males with masculine sex-role behavior were perceived as less intelligent than a female with masculine behavior. Conversely, males demonstrating feminine behavior were viewed as being more intelligent than a female with feminine behavior.

Finally, there was a sex of student effect for the English essay. Males' answers were judged as more logical and grammatically correct than females' answers.

Finn (1972) was also concerned with whether teachers' evaluations of a student's work might, in part, depend on the student's gender, race, and ability level. He asked teachers to evaluate a pair of essays purportedly written by a student who was either (a) male or female, (b) black or white, and (c) reported to have an achievement-ability level which was either high or low. The teachers who participated in the study were from schools that were classified as either urban or suburban. Finn found that the effects of sex and race were not significant; however, when the locale of the teachers was considered, significant differences did emerge. The suburban teachers did not differentiate among essays written by students of a different race and sex. But, urban teachers rated the essays lowest if they were written by white female students. From the comments that teachers wrote on the essays, it appeared that their expectations for white females were high and they felt that the quality of the essays did not meet their expectations. Urban teachers did not differentiate between the performance of males and females when the students were described as black.

Finally, Wiley and Eskilson (1978) examined teachers' causal attributions for students' performance based on the students' race and gender and the quality of the performance. Causal attributions can be considered an indication of expectation. They found that black students' performances were more likely to be attributed to external causes than were white students', regardless of the quality of the performance. Surprisingly, the sex of the student had no effect on teachers' causal attributions regardless of race or quality of performance.

In conclusion, the research on sex-differentiated expectations is somewhat sparse. As a consequence, it becomes difficult to draw any conclusions with confidence. There do seem to be indications, though, that teachers variably perceive and evaluate male and female students' abilities. The precise nature of these variations is open to question.

Sex Differences and Sex-Role Perceptions of Teachers

Several researchers have investigated teachers' perceptions and expectations of students as a function of the students' gender and sex-role behavior. Recall that Bernard (1979) examined male and female teachers' perceptions of students' sex-role behavior in addition to gauging teachers' evaluations of students' written performance. He found that male and female teachers held different perceptions of students' sex-role behavior depending on the sex of the student. For instance, male teachers evaluated a fictitious male or female student as equally logical, while female teachers perceived the male student as being more logical. But, female teachers rated the male and female students as equally warm, whereas male teachers rated the female students as warmer.

Benz, Pfeiffer, and Newman (1981) examined teachers' expectations of students' sex-role behavior according to the sex, grade level, and achievement level of the students. They wanted to determine if there was a relationship between the achievement level of the students and whether they were rated as masculine, feminine, or androgynous. They were also interested in whether gender would mediate any such relationship. They found that student sex and grade level were generally unrelated to sex-role expectations. But, achievement level was highly related. High achievers were more likely than low achievers to be classified as androgynous. High achievers were also more likely to be classified as masculine than low achievers and low achievers were more likely to be rated as feminine.

Etaugh and Hughes (1975) examined teachers' approval of children's sex-typed behavior. Because it had been found that female teachers tend to approve of and reinforce female sex-typed behavior in both boys and girls, Etaugh and Hughes were interested in testing the hypothesis that male teachers are less likely to reinforce feminine behavior. They found that both male and female teachers approved of dependency, a feminine behavior, more than aggression, a masculine behavior. Also, male teachers approved of dependency more than female teachers. So, it seems that male teachers are at least as likely to approve of feminine sex-typed behavior.

Differential Perception of Students' Personalities Based on Student Gender

A number of studies have been conducted on teachers' perceptions of a variety of personality traits of students as a function of student gender. One interesting question concerns the extent to which teachers perceive their male and female students according to traditional sex-role stereotypes. Motta and Vane (1977) examined teachers' perceptions of the creativity, aggression, dependence, and achievement orientation of their students. They found that girls were perceived as more dependent, creative, and achievement oriented while boys were seen as more aggressive. Simmons (1980) guages teachers' perceptions of a number of personality traits, also. She found that teachers expected boys to be more aggressive, independent, and to have better physical skills. In addition, they expected girls to be more emotional, intuitive, ambitious, and emphathetic.

Brophy and Evertson (1981) assessed teachers' attitudes toward students and the nature of teacher–student interactions as a function of student sex. First, teachers were asked to rank their students on 13 scales that measured student attributes. Significant differences in the ranking of male and female students emerged for 11 of the 13 scales. Girls were seen as "calmer, more careful, more mature, higher achieving, more persistent, happier, more attractive, more likely to maintain eye contact, and more cooperative" (p. 113). Girls were more likely to be seen as objects of attachment and more often described as "helpful, motivated, or sweet, and boys were more likely to be described as aggressive, active, or inattentive" (p. 114). Boys were also described as more humorous, but this category included responses like "silly" so this is not necessarily a positive response category.

Classroom Interaction

Although, for a variety of reasons, the process is poorly understood, boys and girls enter the classroom with beliefs about what constitutes appropriate behavior for them and have distinct preferences for certain school tasks. Children's preferences for particular tasks are also influenced by their experiences with teachers and peers. Hence, at any grade level, students are apt to have beliefs about tasks that may support or hinder their performance. Some of these preferences may be related to student sex.

In a related study, Stein (1971) investigated sixth and ninth graders' reactions to three school subjects identified as masculine (mechanical, athletic, and math) and three identified as feminine (reading, art, and social skills). Again, the students stated that they believed it was more important to do better in the subjects associated with their sex and that they expected to do better in these subjects. They also stated that they would be satisfied with a lower performance in the subjects associated with the opposite sex.

Any evaluation of the appropriateness of classroom interaction for any student or group of students must therefore assess the extent to which differential patterns of classroom behavior are caused by student behavior (and the beliefs associated with these behaviors) or by teachers (and teachers' beliefs that shape—or follow classroom behavior). Unfortunately, most research has assumed a particular casual sequence and often the possibility of reciprocal influence (students influence teachers as well as being influenced by teachers) is seldom considered.

That patterns of school achievement differ for boys and girls is an undeniable fact. Maccoby (1966) and Maccoby and Jacklin (1974) have carefully reviewed the literature on sex differences in intellectual functioning (e.g., general intelligence, numerical ability, verbal ability, spatial ability, problem solving) and report that research does reveal a few consistent sex differences. Others reviewing the same literature have stressed that the few sex differences that are found are very small (Hyde, 1981). Thus, there is *no* reason to believe that boys and girls cannot succeed equally well in different school subjects or subsequently in vocational fields. Simply put, similarities in potential for academic performance between men and women are much more interesting than are differences.

Although boys and girls do achieve in somewhat different ways, available evidence clearly indicates that it is unreasonable to explain differential levels of achievement on the basis of sex (innate biological differences). The performance differences between the sexes are, for the most part, learned behaviors (induced by societal expectations and the behavior of adults). For example, the tendency for girls to read better than boys in elementary school but to avoid mathematics in secondary settings appears to be due to motivational factors related to social expectations and experiences.

In this section we briefly summarize some of the general conclusions that can be made from research in which the interactional opportunities for male and female students are compared. In general, the sharpest differences in the behavior of teachers toward boys and girls have been found in the preschool literature. For example, Biber, Miller and Dwyer (1972); Fagot and Patterson (1969); and

Yarrow, Waxler, and Scott (1971) have all provided evidence that boys appear to be the target of discrimination in preschools (i.e., they receive less supportive teaching).

However, when variations in children's behavior are taken into account, a different picture of cause and effect appears. For example, Brophy and Good (1974) have argued that when child effects are considered, what happens to boys and girls in preschool environments approximates what occurs in elementary schools (no apparent gross favoritism).

As a case in point, Serbin, O'Leary, Kent, and Tonick (1973) measured child behavior as well as teacher behavior and noted the following sex differences:

1. Boys showed more aggression and ignoring of teachers and less proximity to teachers; there were no differences in crying or solicitation of teacher attention.

2. Teachers reacted more often to aggression (significantly) and to destruction and ignoring (nonsignificant trends) by boys than girls. Boys also were given many more loud reprimands per behavior than girls. Thus, teachers were more attentive and punitive towards male misbehavior, although such behavior probably was typically more intense and disruptive.

3. There were no significant sex differences for praise, hugging, or brief conversation, although each mean score was higher for boys. Also, teachers significantly more often reacted to boys' solicitations for attention and had significantly higher rates of extended conversations, brief instructions, and extended instruction with boys. All 15 teachers had significantly higher rates of attention to positive behavior for boys, as well as to negative behavior.

As Brophy and Good (1974) have argued, Serbin et al.'s (1973) data suggest that student sex differences are due to student differences in salience, with boys being more salient and therefore more likely to receive teacher attention and response to *either* positive or negative behaviors. As a result, their data often suggest mistreatment of boys by female teachers, when a broader data base would have shown that the teachers were merely reacting to more frequent and intense initiations by boys, thus "favoring" boys in positive as well as negative reactions.

For a comprehensive review of particular studies examining the literature on sex differences, the reader can consult Brophy and Good (1974). For a variety of reasons, classroom observational research turned away from teacher expectation questions and individual student issues to studies of teacher effectiveness. There continues to be a strong interest in classroom interaction, but the frequency of such research has dropped in the past decade. Most importantly, the general conclusions from the earlier review (Brophy & Good, 1974) still appear to hold.

Although individual studies suggest that classroom interaction varies for individual students in particular settings, there are some reasonably general findings that result from classroom interaction studies (Brophy & Good, 1974). Data from many different studies and diverse educational levels show certain common sex differences in classroom interaction patterns. The primary difference is quantitative: Boys tend to have more interactions of all kinds with their teachers than girls. This difference is especially pronounced, however, for interactions involving behavioral criticism and control of misbehavior. Boys are much more often warned or criticized for misbehavior than girls. The data of several studies show clearly that this finding is not attributable to discrimination against boys by female teachers; male teachers also criticize and warn boys more frequently about misbehavior. Thus, the sex difference is due to the more frequent breaking of classroom rules by boys. However, it should be clear that boys as a group do not share teacher criticism equally.

Brophy and Good (1970) found that boys had more interactions of all kinds with teachers than girls and received more teacher criticism. However, a finer analysis of the teacher criticism data from this study showed that most of the teachers' criticism was directed toward the boys in the low-expectation group. Of the contacts that these boys had with their teachers, 32.5% involved criticism, while the corresponding figures for high-expectation boys were 13.3%, for low-expectation girls 16.2%, and for high-expectation girls 8.3%, respectively. Thus, teachers criticized the low-expectation boys in almost a third of their interactions with them, while their criticism rates for the other three groups were much lower. It is clear that relative to other students low-achievement girls receive more aversive and less stimulating contact with teachers. Low-expectation girls also received teacher contacts that varied notably from those received by high-expectation boys and girls. The fact that boys also have more frequent work and procedural interactions with their teachers is probably related to the more general finding that boys tend to be more active and assertive than girls (Maccoby, 1966). Most of the boys' advantage here is in student-initiated contacts. That is, boys are more active and probably more forceful in asserting themselves and gaining their teachers' attention.

This points to another general research finding and one which we believe helps to explain the results of other investigators: Teachers appear to be primarily reactive rather than proactive in their interpersonal interactions with students. Individual differences in students make differential impressions on teachers and condition them to respond differentially. Most differential teacher behavior toward students appears to be of this reactive variety. As Jackson (1968) has vividly described, the pace of classroom interaction is so rapid, and the teacher is so continually bombarded with complex and sometimes conflicting demands, that he or she may be able to do nothing more than simply react just to keep up. Thus, most teacher behavior is reactive; relatively little of it is proactive in the sense that it reflects deliberate planning and control. Taken together, the data suggest that student sex differences are to be explained by differences in the attitudes and behavior of the students themselves, and these in turn are to be explained largely by variations in the sex-role expectations and socialization practices that are prevalent in different cultures.

Recent classroom data on teacher–student interaction are consistent with these trends. In a large study involving classrooms Brophy and Evertson (1981) found significant sex differences for 22 of the 73 variables measured. Boys had higher rates of total contacts with teachers than girls, partly because teachers initiated more contact with them, but mostly because they had more behavioral contacts. Girls had higher percentages of contacts that were private and non-academic, indicating that the bulk of the boys' contacts with teachers were related either to their academic work or their misbehavior.

Boys were more likely than girls to call out answers in general class settings, but girls were more likely to raise their hands and wait to be called on as volunteers. Girls were more likely to be called on after having waved their hands to gain attention rather than after merely raising their hands quietly. These data indicate that students of both sexes were willing to contribute to lessons and discussions but they used contrasting styles to gain response opportunities.

Girls initiated more private contacts with teachers than boys did, especially approval-seeking and housekeeping contacts. Approval-seeking contacts occurred when students who had completed an activity or assignment and brought the work up to the teacher to show off. They were not seeking help or direction, but instead were showing completed work and the expectation of getting praise, approval, or other positive teacher response. The sex difference on this variable indicates that girls were more teacher-oriented than boys and were more interested in pleasing the teacher. Data on student-initiated housekeeping contacts indicate that girls were more likely than boys to request permission to run errands or perform housekeeping chores.

Even though girls frequently initiated contacts with teachers, the teachers did not reciprocate in this regard. In fact, teachers initiated more private contacts with boys, especially academic and personal contacts. Teachers intervened and provided direction more frequently with boys. Data on behavioral contacts indicate that boys misbehave not only more often, but more disruptively. Yet they were no more likely than girls to express hostility or respond sullenly to the teachers. These classroom observation data support the teacher adjective description data suggesting that, even though the boys' difficulties in conforming to the student role required that teachers discipline boys more frequently, this did not lead to alienation or strong negative affect. Measures of teacher praise and criticism showed no sex differences for praise, but a greater frequency of criticism during teacher-initiated academic contacts with boys. Brophy and Evertson (1981) argue that the classroom observational data suggest that girls were more successfully adjusted to student roles than were boys and, hence, were perceived more favorably by teachers. Girls also appeared to be oriented more positively toward teachers and initiated more contacts with them, including showing off their work to seek approval and offering to run errands or perform housekeeping chores for them. Girls also conformed more to classroom rules and apparently worked on their assignments more efficiently and successfully. They conclude:

> Boys misbehaved much more often and more disruptively, but were no more likely than girls to be alienated from the teachers or to express negative affect toward them. Nor were teachers alienated from them, although they were slightly more likely to express negative affect in interactions with boys than in interactions with girls. All in all, the sex difference data reviewed here reinforce and extend the patterns observed in earlier research: Teachers perceive girls more positively than boys and share more positive patterns of interaction with them; but most, if not all, of these differences are attributable to differences in the behavior of the students themselves and not to significant teacher favoritism of girls or rejection of boys [p. 118].

Parsons et al. (1980) studied 600 students in grades five to twelve, their parents, and their teachers in the attempt to understand why the mathematics achievement performance of females declines (relative to males) in secondary schools. These investigators' results are directly comparable with those obtained in the Brophy and Evertson (1981) study since in both studies a modified version of the Brophy/Good Dyadic System was utilized. Of the 51 variables measured, significant effects were found on only three, each of which was a main effect due to sex. Girls received consistently less criticism than did boys. Girls received less work-related criticism than did boys and less criticism of the quality plus form of their work. Surprisingly, boys and girls did not differ in the amount of criticism directed to their conduct or on any of the forms of praise. Furthermore, classroom interactional measures did not emerge as significant predictors of student attitudinal variables. However, teachers' expectancies, measured by the teacher questionnaire, were predictive of student expectancies. Thus, while the proposed relations between teachers' expectancies and students' expectancies were supported, the mediating effects of classroom behavior on expectancies were not demonstrated.

It is possible that the effects of classroom behaviors are dependent on teacher style. For example, some teachers may treat boys and girls differently while others may not. By collapsing across all of the teachers, these effects would have been masked. To explore for this possibility, Parsons et al. (1980) selected a sample of five classrooms with the largest sex differences in the students' self-reported expectancies and a sample of the five classrooms with no significant sex differences in expectancies and reanalyzed the data using raw frequency scores to allow for classroom comparisons. As was true for the previous analyses, most variables did not yield significant differences. Those effects that were significant were divided into three types: behaviors characteristic of teacher style (teacher behaviors under primary control of the teacher, e.g., use of praise following the correct answer), behaviors characteristic of student style (behaviors under primary control of the student, e.g., student-initiated dyadic interactions), and behaviors dependent on both teachers' and students' styles. Teachers in high sex-differentiated classrooms were more critical, were more likely to use a public teaching style, and less likely to rely on more private dyadic interactions, and were more likely to rely on student volunteers for answers than to direct the class participation by calling on specific children.

Girls interacted more, received more praise, and had higher expectancies in the low sex-differentiated classrooms. Boys, on the other hand, interacted more and received more praise in the high sex-differentiated classrooms but had equal expectancies in both classrooms. These data suggest that teachers' praise is facilitative of girls' expectancies for success in math. To test this hypothesis, they correlated teacher praise and the other teacher style variables that discriminated the low from the high sex-differentiated classrooms with the following student's attitudinal variables: future expectancy, current expectancy, self-rated ability, interest in math, plans to go on in math, utility of advanced math, ratings of the difficulty of their present and future math courses, and their stereotypes of the sex-linkage. Few correlations were significant. As was true with the whole sample, teachers' expectancies had the most significant effect.

In the next attempt to find classroom behaviors that might relate to student attitudes, the investigators divided the sample into two groups: those students for whom the teacher had high expectations (bright students) and those students for whom the teacher had low expectations. In general, they found that both bright males and bright females were treated differently in each of the two classroom types. Bright girls interacted the most, answered more questions, and received more praise and less criticism in the low sex-differentiated classrooms. In contrast, bright boys were afforded the most praise and interacted the most in the high sex-differentiated classrooms. Bright girls were afforded the least amount of praise of *any* of the eight groups in the high sex-differentiated classrooms.

Since bright girls were treated so differently in these two classroom types, Parsons et al. (1980) recalculated the correlational analyses of the sample of bright and less bright girls. A few interesting relationships emerge from this reanalysis. Amounts of both praise and work criticism were predictive of perceptions of current and future math difficulty. In addition, the total number of interactions was predictive of both perceptions of future difficulty and plans to continue taking math. Apparently bright girls who have a large number of teacher-initiated interactions followed by evaluative feedback see math as easier, and bright girls who have a large number of teacher-initiated interactions, regardless of feedback, are more likely to plan to continue taking math. This pattern was not evident for girls considered less bright by the teachers.

In concluding, these additional points are important to stress. The frequency rates of all these interactive variables are quite low and the interactional variables are not as predictive of students' expectancies as are other variables that were measured in the study (e.g., students' sex and teachers' expectancies). Consequently, while classroom interactions may have an effect on children's expectancies, the effect is not large and may be as much a function of the children as the teacher.

Lockheed (1982) has noted that previous research has examined the equity of classroom life for male and female students primarily from the perspective of teacher–student interactions. Specifically, she argues that both student to student communication and teacher response to comparable student behavior have been ignored. Her research, a 2 year longitudinal study of 29 fourth and fifth grade classrooms, addresses the following questions: (1) Are there differences in the sequences of interactions experienced by boys and girls?; (2) Are there sex differences in student behavior in the classroom?; (3) Do teachers respond differently to the same behavior exhibited by girls and boys?; (4) Do other students respond differently to the same behavior exhibited by girls and boys?; (5) Do different teacher behaviors precede the behaviors of girls and boys?; and (6) Do different behaviors on the part of other students precede the behaviors of girls and boys?

Preliminary findings from the first year of study, which focused on the behavior of 356 boys and 362 girls, include the following:

1. No differences in the types of interaction chains in which male and female student behavior is embedded were found.

2. The average number of events observed for boy target students (35.1) was greater than the average number of events observed for girl target students (30.6).

3. A higher proportion of boys' events (21.0%) than girls' events (14.1%) were coded as inappropriate, and a higher proportion of girls' events (55.2%) than boys' events (46.3%) were coded as appropriate.

4. Sex differences in behaviors were noted, with boys engaged in more negative and neutral micro-events associated with orientation to instruction, interactions, and affect than were girls.

5. Overall, teachers responded to the inappropriate behaviors of boys more frequently than they did to the inappropriate behaviors of girls, but responded to neutral and appropriate behaviors equally.

6. Some differences in types of teacher responses to types of student behaviors exhibited by girls and boys were noted, and were found for neutral or inappropriate academic performance, neutral or inappropriate affective behavior, and for neutral orientation to instruction. No differences in teacher responses to inappropriate orientation to instruction or to neutral or inappropriate interactions were noted.

7. No sex differences in teacher response to student behavior within subject matter areas were found.

8. Other pupils responded to the appropriate, inappropriate, and neutral

behaviors of girls more frequently than they responded to these behaviors of boys.

9. Teacher antecedent behaviors differed for girls and boys, with girls receiving more teacher eliciting behavior.

10. Other pupil antecedent behaviors differed for girls and boys, with girls receiving fewer negative antecedent behaviors from boys than expected and boys receiving more negative antecedent behaviors from boys than expected.

Her data amply illustrate that classroom interactions are quite different for boys and girls. However, as she notes, the findings are complex and suggest a more intricate network of sex equities and inequities than studies of teacher behavior alone would have suggested.

Sex Differences and Reading Achievement

As has been noted elsewhere (Bank, Biddle, & Good, 1980; Brophy & Good, 1974), substantial differences appear in the play behavior of 1 year old boys and girls (Goldberg & Lewis, 1969) and these differences continue throughout childhood. Separating children's and parents' influences on one another is a complex task.

After they enter school, boys and girls continue to behave differently and to achieve in different ways. Even when IQ is held constant, achievement differs between boys and girls in basic subjects, both at the primary and secondary levels. On the average, American boys do not read as well as American girls, although boys tend to outperform girls in other subjects such as mathematics. Variations across the sexes in reading achievement also are affected by aptitude and ethnicity, for boys who have lower aptitude and those from minority groups may fall even further behind in expected reading level than other pupils. Data consistently indicate that girls' greater achievement persists into high school and beyond.

There is no doubt that females (and young girls in particular) do better on verbal measures of achievement than do males. What accounts for these differences? Can they be attributed to school factors or do achievement differences arise from other conditions? Bank et al. (1980) suggest six different hypotheses that might account for differences in boys' and girls' achievement. They discuss the relative weaknesses and strengths of each hypothesis and the reader can find extended treatment of the topic there.

Two popular hypotheses that Bank et al. discount are the physical maturation and female teacher bias hypotheses. Some educators have argued that girls do better than boys because they physically mature more quickly, and that girls develop longer attention spans, needed for learning to read, more quickly than boys. However, the plausibility of this hypothesis is seriously challenged by crosscultural studies, which illustrate that in some societies boys read as well as girls, and suggest that societal or instructional factors must be involved (Good & Brophy, 1978).

Others contend that girls achieve better than boys because female teachers are biased against males or insensitive to their needs. However, as Bank et al. note, it seems improbable that all female teachers would hold expectations or have biases that differ from all male teachers. Furthermore, it appears that both male and female teachers interact with boys in comparable ways. Hence, hypotheses that link student performance to teacher expectations and behavior can better explain student differences than variables such as teacher sex. Extant data suggest that it is not likely that the reading performance of boys will be improved by increasing the number of male teachers in elementary schools (see Brophy & Good, 1974 for a review of this literature).

Four other hypotheses presented by Bank et al. appear more plausible, considering the existing literature. One of these hypotheses is discrimination. Proponents of this argument note that boys are often treated differently in the classroom (boys are more likely to be praised, etc.); however, as we noted previously, it is often impossible to tell whether differences in teacher behavior are due to discrimination or to differences in student behavior. Do students receive more criticism because they misbehave more (student influence), because of teacher favoritism (teacher influence), or because of the timing of the misbehavior? Research indicates that differences in contact with teachers are apt to be due more to differences in student behavior than they are to differences in teachers' reactions to student behavior (Brophy & Evertson, 1981).

Another hypothesis, feminization of reading, suggests that pupil behaviors may be influenced by pupils' own expectations and interests as well as by the behavior of teachers. Here both teacher and student expectations and behaviors are assumed to vary across subject areas as well as across the sexes (e.g., Leinhardt et al., 1979). This hypothesis assumes that teachers and students view certain subject areas as feminine and others as masculine and that student achievement depends on the perceived sex-appropriateness of the task at hand. Stein and Smithells (1969) found that pupils viewed reading as a feminine task, while mathematics was seen as a masculine task. However, at present this seems a plausible but unproven argument. We noted earlier that in some countries young boys read as well as young girls. If the feminization hypothesis is correct, however, reading will be seen as feminine in countries where girls achieve better than boys, and will be viewed as masculine or sex-neutral in those countries where girls' verbal achievement does not surpass that of boys. It would be important to collect such information.

In order to show an association between the perceived sex-role appropriateness of subject matter and achievement, researchers would have to collect longitudinal data. It is possible that present beliefs about the femininity of reading may be a consequence, rather than a cause of, differential achievement. As a case in point, it would be especially important to see if girls whose mathematics achievement begins to drop in adolescence alter their perceptions of sex-role appropriateness of mathematics.

Despite the plausibility of the feminization of reading hypothesis (or masculinity of mathematics, as will be argued later), students and teachers enter the classroom with many other expectations and behaviors. It is unlikely that students' perceptions of the sex-role appropriateness of reading (or mathematics) would be the major determinant of achievement. Two other factors likely combine with sex-role appropriateness to affect student performance. First, the differential response hypothesis notes that teachers see and react to students' behaviors and interests. Teachers' responses to students are also related to assumptions teachers hold about what boys and girls can do or should do in the classroom. As Bank et al. have noted, the discrimination and feminization of reading hypotheses acknowledge that teachers often behave toward pupils in ways that reflect their expectations about those pupils. However, the differential response hypothesis is unique in its conceptualization that teachers do not necessarily assume that most teachers like girls more than boys (or vice versa), or that students perceive certain subjects as sex-specific (masculine or feminine).

The differential response hypothesis suggests that teachers form a broad range of expectations for students and that these expectations may be based on actual differences in students' behaviors. This hypothesis cannot be tested with available data, but it does seem to be potentially descriptive of variation in reading achievement (and mathematics achievement) that occurs not only across the sexes, but also within. It should be clear that if this hypothesis is to be tested, measurement will have to occur at the individual level (a particular student) rather than at the group level (girls).

The last hypothesis argued by Bank, Biddle, and Good (1980) is that teachers instruct in varied ways and that some instructional styles may have more advantages for certain types of students than others, at least at a certain point in time. The sex-relevant teaching style hypothesis suggests that the average teaching style in American classrooms (pace, warmth, cooperation, etc.) may facilitate the verbal achievement of girls rather than boys.

Obviously, the implications for classroom practice vary depending on which hypothesis is considered, and the reader is encouraged to see Bank et al. for a detailed discussion of implications. The point here is that past research has not been conducted in a way that allows one to choose among the competing hypotheses. All four of the hypotheses (excluding physical maturation and teacher bias) probably account for differences in classroom behavior and achievement. We will be able to test these hypotheses seriously only when crosscultural and longitudinal data have been collected in replicated studies in which both teachers' and students' expectations, beliefs, and behaviors are measured across a number of dimensions. Comprehensive designs must be used to determine whether students' and teachers' beliefs and preferences are best explained by previous experience and socialization (e.g., parent behavior, teacher education programs).

It is likely that many factors mediate achievement gains for males and females in American classrooms. Despite the various beliefs and behaviors that students bring to the class, the quality of instruction they receive will affect their learning to some extent. Hence, if research is to determine why and how boys and girls learn in the classroom, it must combine the best substantive and methodological knowledge about general instructional effects on students (e.g., Brophy, 1979), the effects of students on teachers (e.g., Weinstein, 1983), as well as the effects of classroom ecology (e.g., Bossert, 1979; Doyle, 1979; Hamilton, 1983) on both teachers and students.

SEX DIFFERENCES AND MATHEMATICS ACHIEVEMENT

Sex Differences in Mathematical Achievement

Several noted reviewers of the sex difference literature (c.f. Anastasi, 1958; Maccoby & Jacklin, 1974) have reported that while girls excel in verbal ability and linguistic skill, boys tend to show superiority in mathematical ability and spatial visualization. These findings are well documented and much work has been devoted to the search for explanations for these gender differences. In reference to the gender difference in mathematical ability, a number of non-biological factors have been cited as contributing to this disparity in performance.

One important qualification of the finding that males tend to show superior math ability concerns the age at which this sex difference begins to emerge. Maccoby (1973) has suggested that the onset of adolescence marks the turning point. Prior to adolescence, sex differences in mathematical ability appear to be insignificant. But, at adolescence, male superiority begins to manifest itself. Several studies cited by Maccoby and Jacklin (1974) have demonstrated sex differences in mathematical ability in favor of males during adolescence and adulthood (e.g., Keating & Stanley, 1972; Svensson, 1971).

Given that male superior math ability begins to emerge at adolescence, a number of researchers have attempted to identify variables that might moderate the relation between gender and math achievement. Meece, Parsons, Kaczala, Goff, and Futterman (1982) have reviewed the more popular explanations for this phenomenon in an attempt to account for sex differences in the pursuit of careers in scientific, mathematical, and technical fields. They describe four types of explanations, each relying on either: (1) biological factors, (2) socialization factors, (3) attitudinal factors, or (4) affective factors.

As Meece et al. (1982) point out, biological explanations rely on three assumptions. These are that: (1) Sex differences in math ability are consistently demonstrated; (2) these differences in ability are a consequence of biological differences among the sexes; and (3) the differential rate of enrollment in math courses and the selection of math-related careers by males and females are due to innate differences in math ability. Socialization explanations are concerned with cultural stereotypes that regard males as having superior mathematical ability and the perpetuation of these stereotypes via the attitudes of parents and teachers. Explanations relying on attitudinal factors center on sex differences in students' views of themselves as learners of mathematics and the sex-typing of mathematics as a male domain. Finally, Meece et al. (1982) describe affective explanations as those that cite math anxiety as a causal factor in demonstrated sex differences.

Meece et al. (1982) note that "no one explanation has emerged with unequivocal support" and "sex differences in math achievement and enrollment patterns are determined by a complex set of causative factors" (p. 334). In this paper, research investigating a variety of explanations is reviewed. While biological factors have not been presently considered, the research covered can be categorized as directed at testing some aspect of the latter three explanations. The reader interested in biological factors as causes of sex differences in mathematics achievement can consult Hier and Crowley (1982) and Kagan (1982).

VARIABLES CITED AS CONTRIBUTING FACTORS TO SEX DIFFERENCES IN MATHEMATICS ACHIEVEMENT

Cultural Influences

Schratz (1978) has suggested that cultural influences may account for sex differences in mathematical ability. She found a female superiority in spatial and mathematical skills in an adolescent Hispanic population. And, in testing an adolescent black population, similar but nonsignificant results were found. But, white adolescent males were found to outperform their female peers, though this difference in performance was not statistically significant. She suggests that the different "societal experiences" of Hispanic, black, and white persons may account for these observed sex differences. Thus, she sites culture as a contributor to differential mathematical achievement among male and female adolescents.

Previous Mathematical Experience

Fennema and Sherman (1977, 1978) proposed that the most important variable in explaining sex differences in mathematics achievement is the previous study of mathematics. They controlled for math background while investigating sex differences in mathematical achievement and spatial visualization. They found that males tended to score higher on tests of math achievement and spatial visualization but the differences in performance on these tests were significant in only two of the four schools tested. Furthermore, differences between the sexes did not increase with age or math difficulty. They interpret their findings as supporting sociocultural explanations for sex differences in math achievement. They state that "at least a moderately convincing case can be made for the importance of variables associated with the female sex-role as negatively influencing the election of mathematics courses" (p. 167).

Pedro, Wolleat, Fennema, and Becker (1981) have also suggested that the difference in the number of math courses taken can account for sex-related differences in the math achievement of adults. They investigated a number of attitudinal and attributional variables that might be related to the decision to take math courses by male and female students. They found that students' views of the usefulness of mathematics was significantly related to plans to take more math courses. Math anxiety was also related to math plans but this relationship was stronger for males. In addition, effectance motivation and the view of math as a male domain were related to math plans for males. The relative strength of these relationships varied depending on the grade level of the students.

Interest in Mathematics

Hilton and Berglund (1974) suggested that sex-typed interests are a possible cause of sex differences in math achievement. In a longitudinal study, they investigated mathematical achievement as a function of gender, comparing it to changes in math interest among male and female students. Hilton and Berglund found support for the generally accepted belief that males and females do not differ in math ability at early ages, but males begin to excel at adolescence. Concerning interest in math, they found that "more males are interested in mathematics and more females are of the opinion that the math classes were boring to them" (p. 234). Furthermore, Hilton and Berglund point out that the "real question" in studying the relationship between math interest and achievement concerns the direction of causality. Does interest spark greater achievement or does success in math spur interest? The most likely answer is that a reciprocal influence process is involved.

Related to math interest, Christopolos and Borden (1978) hypothesized that girls would do better on math problems that were female-oriented and boys would do better on male-oriented problems. They presented students with problems, half of which were stereotypically relevant to boys and half relevant to girls. They found that girls did significantly better on the female-oriented problems than on the male-oriented problems. Likewise, boys did better on the male-oriented questions. There were no overall differences in performance between males and females. Christopolos and Borden gained support for their belief that females' performance in math would improve if their attitudes toward or interest in math was strengthened. Providing girls with problems put into a feminine context spurred their interest in math.

Math Related Attitudes

Wilhelm and Brooks (1980) noted the importance of attitudes toward mathematics in accounting for the variability in mathematical achievement. They investigated the relationship between parents' and children's attitudes toward math. They were also interested in determining if sex differences in math attitudes exist and if math attitudes vary across grade level. The particular attitudes tested were (1) perception of the mathematics teacher, (2) anxiety toward mathematics, (3) value of mathematics in society, (4) self-concept in mathematics, (5) enjoyment of mathematics, and (6) motivation in mathematics. They found that for several of the attitudes measured, there was a relationship between the parent and student responses. For example, in the low ability level group there was a relationship between the parent's anxiety about math and the same-sex child's anxiety. For the medium ability level group, the parent's and the opposite-sex child's anxiety were related. These relations were all positive. In terms of sex differences in students' attitudes, males appeared to have more positive attitudes toward the teacher, while females demonstrated higher anxiety about mathematics. Finally, there were differences in the attitude data based on grade level, but sex differences by grade level were not examined.

Norman (1977) measured attitude toward arithmetic and mathematics in a sample of students from grades two through ten and college. He also suggested that sex differences in attitudes toward math may account for associated differences in achievement. He found that from grade six on, males have better attitudes toward math than females. He also found that there was an increasing dislike for math from grade two through college for both sexes, but females' attitudes declined more dramatically. From grade nine on, sex differences in math attitude were increasingly greater.

Fennema and Sherman (1977) related eight attitude variables to sex differences in math achievement in a population of ninth to eleventh graders. They found sex differences for three of the attitude variables: attitude toward success in mathematics, usefulness of mathematics, and number of mathematics activities engaged in. The nature of the differences varied across the four different schools tested. Fennema and Sherman (1978) also investigated these attitude variables in a younger population of sixth to eighth graders. They found two significant sex-related differences. Males were more confident of their ability to learn math and males stereotyped math as a male domain more than females. Also, recall that Pedro et al. (1981) used this set of attitude variables to help predict the decision to continue the study of mathematics. They also found sex differences in their research.

Finally, Merkel-Keller (1977) developed a scale tapping math-related attitudes to determine if sex differences exist. Her scale measured the student's attitude toward math as a subject, the student's self-concept or self-esteem, parental expectations, peer pressures, and teacher appraisals by the student. She found a nonsignificant tendency for girls to have more positive attitudes toward mathematics than boys.

Sex-Role Standards of Students

Dwyer (1974) suggested that sex differences in arithmetic test scores are partly a function of the student's perception of arithmetic as sex-appropriate or sex-inappropriate. In other words, it was thought that students who felt that arithmetic-related activities were appropriate to their sex were more likely to do better on arithmetic tests. She found that the sex-role standards of children did account for a significant amount of the variability in arithmetic achievement scores for both sexes.

Stein and Smithells (1969) also hypothesized that sex differences in performance in a variety of areas might be mediated by sex-role standards of students concerning achievement in these areas. They gauged the sex-role standards of students at three grade levels (second, sixth, and twelfth) for six achievement areas: athletic, spatial and mechanical, arithmetic, reading, artistic, and social skills. They found that the areas of reading, artistic, and social skills were rated as more feminine. Athletic, spatial and mechanical, and arithmetic were rated as more masculine. Also, girls tended to make more feminine judgments than boys. Furthermore, as age increased, sex differences decreased.

STUDENTS' CAUSAL ATTRIBUTIONS OF PERFORMANCE IN MATHEMATICS

Wolleat, Pedro, Becker, and Fennema (1980) have stated a belief that differences in math achievement of adults can be accounted for by differences in the number of math courses taken in high school. They describe the failure of females to persist in taking math courses as "math avoidance." To partially explain math avoidance they have invoked the principles of attribution theory. They hypothesized that females are more likely to attribute successful performance in math to unstable or external causes and unsuccessful performance to stable or internal causes. This pattern of attributions decreases the likelihood of persisting in mathematical study. Furthermore, Wolleat et al. cite Deaux (1976) in stating that differences between the sexes in attributions are more pronounced when the task of interest is sex-typed as masculine. On such tasks, expectations for males to succeed are stronger than those for female success. Since math is considered by many to be a male domain, it is not unreasonable to expect male and female students' causal attributions for success in mathematics to vary. Wolleat et al. investigated students' attributions for success in math as a function of the students' sex and level of mathematics achievement. They found that males attribute their success experiences in mathematics to ability more so than females. Females attribute their success more strongly to effort than do males. As the achievement level of the student goes up, females become more likely to cite effort as the cause of their success and males became less likely to do so.

In a similar study, Pedro et al. (1981) measured students' causal attributions in an attempt to identify variables that related to the election of math courses in high school by male and female students. Like Wolleat et al. (1980), they believed that differences between male and female adults in math achievement could be accounted for by differential course taking. Causal attributions were thought to affect course taking which, in turn, affects math achievement differences in adults. They found that for females, success-environment, success-ability, and failure-ability were attributional patterns that explained some of the variability in mathematics plans in some of the groups tested. For males, the attributional pattern of success-ability explained some of the variability in their plans to enroll in math courses in some of the groups tested.

Students' Expectations for Their Mathematics Performance

Parsons, Kaczala, and Meece (1982) have suggested that the expectancies for success that students hold may be partly responsible for their patterns of achievement. Such a hypothesis is particularly significant in light of the finding that females tend to have lower expectancies than males. Parsons et al. again found that female students, on the average, had lower future expectancies for math and also believed that math was more difficult.

Teachers' Expectations for Students' Mathematics Performance

Only one study identified at this time has tested differential teacher expectations for students' mathematical ability as a function of sex. Simmons (1980) gauged teachers' perceptions of their students' abstract or math reasoning skills, in addition to their perceptions of their students' verbal abilities. In this study, it was found that teachers did not hold higher expectancies for their male students with respect to these kinds of skills.

Differential Teacher Treatment of Male and Female Students

As noted earlier, Leinhardt, Seewald, and Engel (1979) suggested that sex differences in reading and math achievement might be related to differential teacher treatments of students during math and reading classes. They found that teachers did make more academic contacts with girls in reading and with boys in math. Furthermore, teachers spent more "cognitive time" with girls in reading and boys in math. And, in general, teachers made more managerial contacts with boys than girls.

Parsons, Kaczala, and Meece (1982) also coded teacher–student interactions in math classes, suggesting that the nature of these interactions might vary depending on the student's sex and relate to the student's attitude toward math. They found that females received less criticism and asked more questions than males. When sex and the level of the teachers' expectancies were both considered, it was found that females in the high-expectancy group had fewer of their interactions praised than other groupings of students. Females in the high-expectancy group also had a lower self-concept of their ability to do math than males in the high-expectancy group. Low-expectancy males received more criticism than the other groups. Finally, the low-expectancy males received the most teacher-initiated dyadic interactions.

Future Research

As Lockheed (1982) suggests, the creation and maintenance of sex-role behavior and status in the classroom are complex issues that are not easily studied. There is also reason to believe that student gender per se is perhaps not as salient as some have argued. Teacher and parental reactions toward girls who are aggressive and bright or those who are passive and slow are likely to vary. Beliefs about appropriate sex-role behavior are no doubt mediated by student personality and aptitude as well as by status characteristics of the adult who is making the judgment (e.g., social class).

Prawat and Jarvis (1980) studied elementary school teachers' perceptions of students and found that student ability and achievement exerted more influence on teacher perceptions than did student gender. In a recent study, Cooper and Good (1983) found that elementary school girls initiated more interactions with teachers and that boys misbehaved more often. However, they essentially found no significant differences in teacher behavior toward boys and girls across a variety of interactional measures. When one compares teacher–student classroom interaction data collected in the 1960s with interaction data collected in the late 1970s and subsequently, the more recent literature suggests less of a tendency for teachers to vary their behavior toward students as a function of student sex.

This difference may be due to the fact that teacher training programs have made teachers more sensitive to these issues. However, more equitable treatment in general classroom interactions may be due to the fact that boys and girls enter school with fewer behavioral differences than they did 20 years ago. These findings are consistent with Brophy and Evertson's (1981) contention that differences in teacher–student interactions are due more to differences in student behavior than they are to teacher bias.

There is evidence that students who vary in perceived ability receive differential teacher behavior in some classrooms and that students are aware of such behavior. Weinstein (1983) noted that students believed to be low achievers by their teachers are perceived by fellow students to receive more frequent negative feedback and teacher direction and more work and rule orientation than high achievers. However, student sex was not a particularly important issue. Rohrkemper (1981) also found that student sex in general was not a powerful predictor of student reactions to classroom events.

Research indicates that if educators are to understand more fully why boys and girls sometimes achieve differentially, we must develop more complex models than those used in the past. Researchers must explore several explanations simultaneously (Bank et al., 1980), and more attention needs to be paid to student factors that maintain sex-role beliefs (Lockheed, 1982) as well as more complex interaction models. Finally, the contexts (especially subject matter) in which interactions occur need to be explored more fully (Leinhardt, et al., 1979). In particular contexts, teachers may behave in ways that allow certain sex-role behaviors to develop or be maintained. Given extant information and general societal beliefs, classroom opportunities afforded to boys and girls appear to be at least as important (and probably more so) as classroom factors in explaining differential achievement.

ACKNOWLEDGMENT

The authors want to acknowledge the support provided by the Center for Research in Social Behavior. The authors want to especially thank Patricia Shanks for her careful professional typing of the manuscript, and Gail Hinkel for her valuable editorial assistance.

REFERENCES

Adams, G. R. & Cohen, A. S. An examination of cumulative folder information used by teachers in making differential judgments of children's abilities. *The Alberta Journal of Educational Research,* 1976, *22*(3), 216–225.

Anastasi, A. *Differential psychology: Individual and group differences in behavior.* New York: Macmillan, 1958.

Bank, B., Biddle, B., & Good, T. Sex roles, classroom instruction, and reading achievement. *Journal of Educational Psychology, 1980, 72,* 119–132.

Benz, C. R., Pfeiffer, I., & Newman, I. Sex role expectations of classroom teachers, grades 1–12. *American Educational Research Journal,* 1981, *18*(3), 289–302.

Bernard, M. E. Does sex role behavior influence the way teachers evaluate students? *Journal of Educational Psychology,* 1979, *71*(4), 553–562.

Biber, H., Miller, L. B., & Dwyer, J. L. Feminization in preschool. *Developmental Psychology,* 1972, *7,* 86.

Bossert, S. Task and social relationships in classrooms: A study of classroom organization and its consequences. American Sociological Association, *Arnold and Caroline Rose Monograph Series.* New York: Cambridge University Press, 1979.

Brophy, J. Teacher behavior and its effects. *Journal of Educational Psychology,* 1979, *71,* 733–750.

Brophy, J. E. & Evertson, C. M. *Student characteristics and teaching.* New York: Longman, 1981.

Brophy, J. & Good, T. Teachers' communication of differential expectations for children's classroom performance: Some behavioral data. *Journal of Educational Psychology,* 1970, *61,* 365–374.

Brophy, J. & Good, T. *Teacher–student relationships: Causes and consequences.* New York: Holt, Rinehart & Winston, 1974.

Chall, J. & Snow, C. A study of family influences on literacy acquisition in low-income children in Grades 2–8. Paper presented at the annual meeting of the American Educational Research Association, New York, 1982.

Christopolos, F. & Borden, J. Sexism in elementary school mathematics. *Elementary School Journal,* 1978, *78*(4), 275–277.

Cooper, H. M. & Good, T. L. *Pygmalion grows up: Studies in the expectation communication process,* New York: Longman, 1983.

Deaux, K. *The behavior of women and men.* Monterey, Calif.: Brooks/Cole, 1976.

Doyle, W. Classroom tasks and students' abilities. In P. Peterson & H. Walberg (Eds.), *Research on teaching: Concepts, findings, and implications.* Berkeley, Calif.: McCutchan, 1979.

Doyle, W., Hancock, G. & Kifer, E. Teachers' perceptions: Do they make a difference? *Journal of the Association for the Study of Perception,* 1972, *7,* 21–30.

Durkin, D. *Children who learn to read early: Two longitudinal studies.* New York: Teachers College Press, 1966.

Dwyer, C. A. Influence of children's sex role standards on reading and arithmetic achievement. *Journal of Educational Psychology,* 1974, *86,* 811–816.

Etaugh, C. & Hughes, V. Teachers' evaluations of sex-typed behaviors in children: The role of teacher sex and school setting. *Developmental Psychology,* 1975, *11*(3), 394–395.

Fagot, B. I. & Patterson, G. R. An in vivo analysis of reinforcing contingencies for sex-role behaviors in the preschool child. *Developmental Psychology,* 1969, *1,* 563–568.

Fennema, E. & Sherman, J. Sex-related differences in mathematics achievement, spatial visualization and affective factors. *American Educational Research Journal,* 1977, *14*(1), 51–71.

Fennema, E. & Sherman, J. Sex-related differences in mathematics achievement and related factors: A further study. *Journal for Research in Mathematics Education,* 1978, *9,* 189–203.

Finn, J. Expectations and the educational environment. *Review of Educational Research,* 1972, *42*(3), 387–410.

Goldberg, S. & Lewis, M. Play behavior in the year old infant: Early sex differences. *Child Development,* 1969, *40,* 21–31.

Good, T. & Brophy J. *Looking in classrooms* (2nd ed.). New York: Harper & Row, 1978.

Hamilton, S. The social side of schooling: Ecological studies of classrooms and schools. *Elementary School Journal,* 1983, *83,* 313–334.

Hiebert, E. & Coffey, M. Parents' perceptions of their young children's print-related knowledge and interest. Paper presented at the annual meeting of the American Educational Research Association, New York, 1982.

Hier, D. & Crowley, W. Spatial ability in androgen-deficient men. *New England Journal of Medicine*, 1982, *306*, 1202–1205.

Hieronymus, A., Lindquist, E., & Hoover, H. Iowa Test of Basic Skills, Manual for school administrators. Riverside 1982.

Hilton, T. L. & Berglund, G. W. Sex differences in mathematics achievement: A longitudinal study. *Journal of Educational Research*, 1974, *67*(5), 231–237.

Hyde, J. How large are cognitive gender differences? *American Psychologist*, 1981, *36*, 892–901.

Jackson, P. *Life in classrooms*. New York: Holt, Rinehart & Winston, 1968.

Kagan, J. The idea of spatial ability (an editorial). *New England Journal of Medicine*, 1982, *306*, 1225–1226.

Keating, D. P. & Stanley, J. C. Extreme measures for the exceptionally gifted in mathematics and science. Study of the Mathematically and Scientifically Precocious Youth, 1972 (cite as correspondence in Maccoby, E. & Jacklin, C., *The psychology of sex differences*).

Leinhardt, G., Seewald, A. & Engel, M. Learning what's taught: Sex differences in instruction. *Journal of Educational Psychology*, 1979, *71*, 432–439.

Lockheed, M. E. Sex equity in classroom interaction research: An analysis of behavior chains. Paper presented at the annual meeting of the American Educational Research Association, New York, March, 1982.

Macaulay, R. The myth of female superiority in language. *Journal of Child Language*, 1978, *5*, 353–363.

Maccoby, E. E. *The development of sex differences*. Stanford, Calif.: Stanford University, 1966.

Maccoby, E. E. Sex differences in intellectual functioning. In *Assessment in a pluralistic society, Proceedings of the 1972 Invitational Conference on Testing Problems*. Princeton, N. J.: Educational Testing Service, 1973.

Maccoby, E. E. & Jacklin, L. *The psychology of sex differences*. Stanford, Calif.: Stanford University, 1974.

McGillicuddy-DeLisi, A. The relation between family constellation and parental beliefs about child development. In L. Laosa & I. Sigel (Eds.), *Families as learning environments for children*. New York: Plenum, 1982.

Meece, J. L., Parsons, J. E., Kaczala, C. M., Goff, S. B., & Futterman, R. Sex differences in math achievement: Toward a model of academic choice. *Psychological Bulletin*, 1982, *91*(2), 324–348.

Merkel-Keller, C. Sex differences in mathematics: An investigation of sex-differentiated attitudes toward mathematics and sex-differentiated achievement in mathematics on the ninth grade level in eight schools in New Jersey. Paper presented at the annual meeting of the American Educational Research Association Conference, 1977.

Motta, R. W. & Vane, J. R. An investigation of teacher perceptions of sex-typed behaviors. *Journal of Educational Research*, 1977, 363–368.

Norman, R. D. Sex differences in attitude toward arithmetic-mathematics from early elementary school to college levels. *Journal of Psychology*, 1977, *97*, 247–256.

Palardy, J. What teachers believe—what children achieve. *Elementary School Journal*, 1969, *69*, 370–374.

Parsons, J. Addler, P., Futterman, R., Goff, S., Kaczala, C., Meece, J. & Midgley, C. *Self-perceptions, tasks perceptions and academic choice: Origins and change*. NIE Grant, NIE–G–78–0022, Final Report, University of Michigan, Ann Arbor, 1980.

Parsons, J. E., Kaczala, C. M., & Meece, J. L. Socialization of achievement attitudes and beliefs: Classroom influences. *Child Development*, 1982, *53*, 322–339.

Parsons. J. E., Ruble, D. N., Hodges, K. L., & Small, A. W. Cognitive-developmental factors in emerging sex differences in achievement-related expectancies. *Journal of Social Issues*, 1976, *32*, 46–61.

Pedro, J. D., Wolleat, P., Fennema, E., & Becker, A. D. Election of high school mathematics by females and males: Attributions and attitudes. *American Educational Research Journal*, 1981, *18*(2), 207–218.

Prawat, R. & Jarvis, R. Gender differences as a factor in teachers' perceptions of students. *Journal of Educational Psychology*, 1980, *72*, 743–749.

Rohrkemper, M. Classroom perspectives study: An investigation of differential perceptions of classroom events. Unpublished dissertation, Michigan State University, East Lansing, Mich., 1981.

Schratz, M. M. A developmental investigation of sex differences in spatial (visual-analytic) and mathematical skills in three ethnic groups. *Developmental Psychology*, 1978, *14*(3), 263–267.

Seaver, W. B. Effects of naturally induced teacher expectancies. *Journal of Personality and Social Psychology*, 1973, *28*, 333–342.

Serbin, L. A., O'Leary, K. D., Kent, R. N., & Tonick, I. J. A comparison of teacher response to the preacademic and problem behavior of boys and girls. *Child Development*, 1973, *44*, 796–804.

Sigel, I. The relationship between parents' distancing strategies and the child's cognitive behavior. In L. Laosa & I. Sigel (Eds.), *Families as learning environments for children*. New York: Plenum, in press.

Simmons, B. Sex role expectations of classroom teachers. *Education*, 1980, *100*(3), 249–253.

Stein, A. H. The effects of sex-role standards for achievement and sex-role preference on three determinants of achievement motivation. *Developmental Psychology*, 1971, *4*, 219–231.

Stein, A. H. & Smithells, J. Age and sex differences in children's sex-role standards about achievement. *Developmental Psychology*, 1969, *1*(3), 252–259.

Svensson, A. *Relative achievement. School performance in relation to intelligence, sex, and home environment*. Stockholm: Almquist & Wiksell, 1971.

Weinstein, R. Student perceptions of schooling. *Elementary School Journal*, 1983, *83*, 287–312.

Wiley, M. G. & Eskilson, A. Why did you learn in school today? Teachers' perceptions of causality. *Sociology of Education*, 1978, *51*, 261–269.

Wilhelm, S. & Brooks, D. M. The relationship between pupil attitudes toward mathematics and parental attitudes toward mathematics. *Educational Research Quarterly*, 1980, *5*, 8–16.

Wolleat, P. L., Pedro, J. D., Becker, A. D., & Fennema, E. Sex differences in high school students' causal attributions of performance in mathematics. *Journal for Research in Mathematics Education*, 1980, 357–367.

Yarrow, M., Waxler, C., & Scott, P. Child effects on adult behavior. *Developmental Psychology*, 1971, *5*, 300–311.

Section 4
Communicating and Receiving Expectancies

Teachers, like any of us, may have expectancies for the behavior of others with whom they have contact. What makes the study of teachers' expectancies so important is that the "others" are our students. Indeed, students represent the other half of the teacher expectancy effect. In order for teacher expectancies to influence student achievement first the expectancies must somehow be communicated to the student and then the student must somehow understand the teacher's behavior as involving an expectancy for performance. The two chapters in this section address these issues.

Brophy (Chapter 12) has long been involved in the study of teacher–student interaction in the classroom. In his chapter, Brophy reviews research on teacher–student interaction as it pertains to the communication of teacher expectancies for student achievement. His discussion deals with the difficult issue of the nature of the interaction between the teacher and students who are high versus low expectancy. The importance of considering teacher behaviors toward groups of students, as well as toward individual students, is highlighted. In his review, he further notes that some forms of differential treatment are appropriate. Brophy also discusses individual differences in teachers as related to teacher expectancy effects.

Whereas most researchers have emphasized the role of the teacher in the communication of expectancy effects, Weinstein (Chapter 13) has placed her emphasis on the role of the student in the expectancy process. The focus of her chapter is the processes within the student that may mediate teacher expectancy effects on achievement. Research on this aspect of the teacher expectancy phenomenon addresses questions concerning student perception and interpretation of the teacher's behavior. As Weinstein points out, teacher behaviors, such as the use of praise and criticism, may differ, not only in frequency, but also in quality. Teacher behaviors not only influence the individual student but also reflect a classroom atmosphere that is interpreted by the student and is related to learning. Unraveling how students perceive and interpret teacher behavior, and how those interpretations relate to teacher expectancy effects, is an important component in our understanding of teacher expectancy effects.

In a sense, the two chapters in this section represent the sum and substance of the impact of teacher expectancies on the student's achievement. Expectancies must somehow be communicated to students, who must interpret them. Until we have a greater understanding of the meaning of differential teacher behaviors and student comprehension of those differential behaviors we shall not come close to fully understanding or explaining teacher expectancy effects.

12

Teacher–Student Interaction

Jere E. Brophy
Michigan State University

This chapter considers research on teacher–student interaction as it relates to teacher expectations for student achievement, especially research designed to identify the teacher behaviors (differential treatment of different students) that mediate self-fulfilling prophecy effects of teachers' expectations. It assumes, as established in previous chapters, that teachers' expectations can have such effects on student achievement, so that the emphasis is not on the existence or strength of such effects, but on how they are mediated when they do occur. Also, the emphasis is on teachers' achievement expectations because previous chapters deal with the consequences of teachers' perceptions of sex, social class, and race.

The chapter also assumes that the nature and extent of self-fulfilling prophecy effects of teachers' expectations depend on the accuracy and rigidity of those expectations and the degree to which teachers use them as guides to instructing the student. Expectation effects will be minimal when teachers hold their expectations lightly (i.e., change them in response to changes in the students) or when they concentrate on the content rather than the students when planning instruction. Conversely, significant expectation effects can be expected when teachers harbor more rigid expectations for student achievement and take these expectations into account when planning instruction and interacting with the students. If these expectations are largely accurate, they are likely to lead to behavior that sustains and reinforces the status quo, and result in some degree of increase in the variance in student achievement but little change in the relative placement of individuals in the distribution. Finally, where teachers' expectations are both rigid and inaccurate, and where the teachers act on these expectations in planning instruction and interacting with students, some degree of self-fulfilling prophecy

303

effect of the kind originally defined by Merton (1948) can be expected: Originally false expectations are made to come true by the actions taken in response to those expectations.

THE CLASSROOM CONTEXT

Before considering the data on teacher–student interaction, it is important to consider the context within which these data should be understood. In particular, it is important to note that the results of brief social-psychology experiments in which college-student "teachers" interact briefly with strangers designated as "learners" have only limited generalization to the classroom context in which inservice teachers interact continuously over long periods of time with the students in their classes.

Accuracy and Flexibility of Teachers' Expectations

Experimental subjects given only limited information and little or no opportunity to interact with "students" have been shown to base performance expectations not only on records of prior achievement but on such dubious cues as physical appearance, race, speech characteristics, and various diagnostic labels (see Chapter 9 and reviews by Braun, 1976; Brophy & Good, 1974; and Persell, 1977). However, studies of inservice teachers' expectations for their actual students reveal that most teacher perceptions of students are accurate and based on the best available information, and most of those that are inaccurate are corrected when more dependable information becomes available (Borko, Cone, Russo, & Shavelson, 1979; Brophy & Good, 1974; Shavelson, Cadwell, & Izu, 1977; Willis, 1972). Most of the data in school records are accurate, and the impressions that teachers form, even in the first few days of the year, are based mostly on students' participation in academic activities and performance on assignments, and not physical or other status characteristics (Willis, 1972).

Consequently, teachers' expectations are generally accurate, reality based, and open to corrective feedback. Powerful biasing effects of the kind seen in some experiments are infrequent in ordinary classrooms, because few teachers can sustain grossly inaccurate expectations for many of their students in the face of daily feedback that contradicts those expectations. Furthermore, whether they are initially accurate or not, the fact that teachers' expectations are usually open to correction in response to newer or better information limits their potential for self-fulfilling prophecy effects. Averaged across all teachers and students, teacher expectations probably make about a 5% difference in student achievement (Brophy, 1982), although in this case the variance is more meaningful than the average. That is, the data suggest that teacher expectation effects on student achievement are minimal except for those teachers who hold rigid expectations and allow these expectations to guide their interactions with their students.

Student Effects on Teachers

Students differ in intelligence, achievement motivation, classroom conduct, and other variables relevant to teaching and learning and these exert differential pressures on teachers. For example, compared to low achievers, high achievers are more likely to: be attentive to lessons and engaged in tasks; volunteer to answer questions or offer comments; respond correctly when called on; complete independent work assignments without help; desire a businesslike emphasis on teaching academic content; and cooperate with the teacher's rules and expectations most of the time (Brophy, Evertson, Anderson, Baum, & Crawford, 1981; Brophy & Good, 1974; Evertson, 1982; Metz, 1978; Noble & Nolan, 1976).

Because teacher expectations are largely accurate, these differences between high and low *achieving* groups occur in comparisons between high and low teacher *expectation* groups (in effect, the high expectation students *are* the high achievers, and the low expectation students *are* the low achievers). Consequently, one cannot interpret differential teacher interaction with high versus low-expectation groups by assuming that all differences are due to teachers' expectations. Clearly, if teachers merely react consistently to the student behavior that confronts them, high expectation students will: receive more response opportunities (because they volunteer more often); have more academic and fewer behavioral interactions (because they are oriented more toward academic learning; work more independently without supervision, and seldom become disruptive); and receive more praise and less criticism (because they are generally well behaved and academically successful).

The extent and intensity of the differential pressures that students exert on their teachers will vary with the makeup of the classroom, so no single set of norms can be used to judge the degree to which teachers are exacerbating, merely reacting to, or compensating for, existing student differences. In most classrooms, some degree of group difference along the lines discussed here, and not equality or lack of group difference, should be expected, and should be interpreted as evidence of student effects on teacher behavior rather than evidence of biased teacher treatment related to self-fulfilling prophecy effects. Furthermore, to the extent possible, teacher behavior measures should be adjusted for differences in the frequencies and types of opportunities that students present to their teachers. Praise following correct answers, for example, can be interpreted more meaningfully when expressed as the percentage of correct answers followed by praise than when expressed merely as a frequency measure that does not take into account how often students answer correctly and thus present the teacher with opportunities to praise.

Situational Constraints on Teacher Behavior

Interpretation of differential patterns of teacher–student interaction is also complicated by situational or context factors (Brophy & Evertson, 1978). Grade level is one example. In the upper elementary and secondary grades, most teachers use a whole-class lesson format, and the emphasis is on teaching the content. Dyadic interactions with individual students are infrequent, except when the teacher calls on a student to contribute to a recitation or discussion. Probably because of the public setting, teacher praise and criticism are infrequent, as is interaction for social or personal rather than academic reasons. Consequently, most group differences are quantitative—differences in the sheer frequency of interaction with the teacher (Brophy, Evertson, Anderson, Baum, & Crawford, 1981; Brophy & Good, 1974).

In the early grades, however, most teachers spend a lot of time developing personal relationships with their students and socializing them to the role of pupil in addition to teaching them academic content. Furthermore, there is much individualized and small group instruction, where teachers have more opportunity to compensate for the tendency of high achievers to dominate whole-class activities. Consequently, there may be few if any differences in total contacts with the teacher, although more of the high achievers' interactions with the teacher occur in public, large group settings and are initiated by the students themselves. In any case, the most striking group differences in these early grades are usually in qualitative measures. High achievers (and thus, high-expectation students) may not interact with the teacher more often, but when they do, they may be treated with more warmth, support, encouragement, or respect (Brophy & Good, 1974).

Group size and pacing factors are also relevant. Whole-class activities have to be kept moving at a good pace to minimize inattention and disruption (Kounin, 1970). Thus, in this setting it is more difficult for the teacher to wait patiently for a response or take time to reteach a confused individual than it is in small group or individualized settings. Consequently, although whole-class data often suggest teacher favoritism of high-expectation students, small group data often show few differences or even suggest teacher attempts to work more intensively with low-expectation students (Alpert, 1974; Weinstein, 1976).

Time of year is another factor. Early in the year, teachers may hold expectations loosely and allocate extra time to low achievers in an attempt to keep the class together. As time goes on, however, teachers may become discouraged when their best efforts with certain students consistently fail. Furthermore, as time begins to run out and pressures to get through the curriculum increase, teachers may begin to step up pacing and concentrate on high achievers (Good, Cooper, & Blakey, 1980; Lundgren, 1972). Thus, data taken early in the year are likely to suggest teacher attempts to compensate for existing student differences, but data taken later may suggest self-fulfilling prophecy effects (Brophy & Good, 1974; Persell, 1977).

The nature of the content is also relevant. With tasks of familiar content and predictable difficulty level, both teachers and students can draw on experience to form accurate expectations. However, when new content or skills are being introduced (Braun, 1976), and especially when students are dependent on the teacher rather than out-of-school experiences or their own independent learning efforts to master the new content or skills (West & Anderson, 1976), there is more opportunity for self-fulfilling prophecy effects to occur.

In summary, then, situational or context factors affect the degree to which teachers are likely to be oriented toward, or presented with opportunities for, differentiating in their interactions with different students. These factors affect both the likelihood of such differentiation and the form it takes if it does occur. Only a portion of such differentiation will be due to teachers' expectations exerting self-fulfilling prophecy effects.

THE MEDIATION OF SELF-FULFILLING PROPHECIES

Rosenthal and Jacobson (1968) did not address the issue of how expectation effects are mediated, but Beez (1968) included observational data in his study of tutors working with *Head Start* children. He showed that tutors with high expectations tried to teach more words to their children than tutors with low expectations did. This demonstrated that teacher expectations can have direct effects on student opportunity to learn: Expectations shape what is taught, which determines what is ultimately learned.

Brophy and Good (1970b) hypothesized that teacher expectations could also affect student outcomes indirectly through teacher behaviors that condition student attitudes, expectations, and behavior. They conducted a series of studies linking teachers' naturalistic expectations for different students to differential patterns of teacher–student interaction, guided by the following model:

1. Early in the year, teachers form differential expectations for student performance.

2. Consistent with these differential expectations, teachers behave differently toward different students.

3. This differential teacher behavior communicates to each individual student something about how he or she is expected to behave in the classroom and perform on academic tasks.

4. If teacher treatment is consistent over time, and if students do not actively resist or change it, it will likely affect student self-concept, achievement motivation, level of aspiration, classroom conduct, and interactions with the teacher.

5. These effects generally will complement and reinforce the teacher's expectations, so that students will conform to these expectations more than they might have otherwise.

6. Ultimately, this will make a difference in student achievement and other outcomes, indicating that teacher expectations can function as self-fulfilling prophecies.

The Brophy and Good (1970b) study revealed several differences in dyadic teacher–student interaction patterns between high-and low-expectation groups. Many of these apparently represented student effects on teachers rather than teacher expectation effects on students: High expectation students more often volunteered to answer questions, initiated interactions with the teachers, and gave correct answers; had fewer problems in reading during reading groups; were criticized for misbehavior less often; and received more praise and less criticism generally. In addition, however, there were several differences that did not seem explainable as student effects on teachers. First, differences in teacher praise and criticism appeared not only in frequency measures but also in percentage measures adjusted for student performance. Even though they succeeded much more often, high-expectation students (highs) were more likely than low-expectation students (lows) to be praised when they did succeed (percentage of success responses followed by praise), and less likely to be criticized when they failed (percentage of failures followed by criticism). Another difference was in teacher failure to give specific feedback as to the correctness of student responses. This happened only 3% of the time with highs, but 15% of the time with lows. Finally, there were differences in teachers' tendencies to seek an improved response when students failed to answer a question or answered incorrectly. Compared to their behavior with lows, the teachers were more likely to repeat the question, give a clue, or simplify through rephrasing for highs, and less likely to give up by providing the answer or calling on someone else. Such differential teacher treatment should increase, and not merely maintain, existing student differences, thus producing self-fulfilling prophecy effects of teacher expectations on student achievement.

Differential Treatment of Individual Students

Other research focused on differences in dyadic teacher–student interaction revealed a variety of potential mediators of teacher expectation effects. Rosenthal (1974), hypothesized that positive expectation effects on student achievement will occur when teachers:

1. Create warm social-emotional relationships with students (climate).
2. Give them more feedback about their performance (feedback).

3. Teach them more (and more difficult) material (input).
4. Give them more opportunities to respond and ask questions (output).

This model subsumes many of the findings concerning mediation of expectation effects, and probably is sufficient for purposes of developing social psychological theory. Educators, however, need a longer and more specific list of mediation mechanisms for educating teachers. Furthermore, because of concern about low-expectation students, and because teachers unfortunately are more affected by negative than positive information (Mason, 1973; Persell, 1977; Seaver, 1973), there is a need for focus on how low expectations can cause teachers to limit students' progress. Brophy and Good (1974) listed the following as mechanisms through which teachers might minimize the learning progress of lows. The list was originally compiled on the basis of research published through 1973, but more recent references are included.

1. Wait less time for lows to answer (Allington, 1980; Bozsik, 1982; Rowe, 1974; Taylor, 1979).
2. Give lows the answer or call on someone else rather than trying to improve lows' responses by giving clues or repeating or rephrasing the question (Brophy & Good, 1970b; Jeter & Davis, 1973).
3. Inappropriate reinforcement: rewarding inappropriate behavior or incorrect answers by lows (Amato, 1975; Fernandez, Espinosa, & Dornbusch, 1975; Kleinfeld, 1975; Rowe, 1974; Taylor, 1977; Weinstein, 1976).
4. Criticizing lows more often for failure (Brophy & Good, 1970b; Cooper & Baron, 1977; Good, Cooper, & Blakey, 1980; Good, Sikes, & Brophy, 1973; Jones, 1971; Medinnus & Unruh, 1971; Rowe, 1974; Smith & Luginbuhl, 1976).
5. Praising lows less frequently than highs for success (Babad, Inbar, & Rosenthal, 1982; Brophy & Good, 1970b; Cooper & Baron, 1977; Firestone & Brody, 1975; Good, Cooper, & Blakey, 1980; Good, Sikes, & Brophy, 1973; Martinek & Johnson, 1979; Medinnus & Unruh, 1971; Rejeski, Darracott, & Hutslar, 1979; Spector, 1973).
6. Failure to give feedback to the public responses of lows (Brophy & Good, 1970b; Good, Sikes, & Brophy, 1973; Jeter & Davis, 1973; Willis, 1970).
7. Generally paying less attention to lows or interacting with them less frequently (Adams & Cohen, 1974; Blakey, 1970; Given, 1974; Kester & Letchworth, 1972; Page, 1971; Rist, 1970; Rubovits & Maehr, 1971).
8. Calling on lows less often to respond to questions (Davis & Levine, 1970; Mendoza, Good & Brophy, 1972; Rubovits & Maehr, 1971).
9. Seating lows farther away from the teacher (Rist, 1970).
10. Demanding less from lows. This shows up in a variety of ways. Beez (1968) found that tutors with high expectations not only tried to teach more

words, but taught with more rapid pacing and less extended explanation and repetition of definitions and examples. Evertson, Brophy, and Good (1973) found that when teachers tried to improve students' responses, they were more likely to simply repeat the question to highs but to give help or clues to lows. The studies of inappropriate reinforcement mentioned above indicate that teachers may accept low quality or even incorrect responses from lows.

11. General differences in type and initiation of individualized interactions with students: Teachers interact with lows more privately than publicly, and monitor and structure their activities more closely (Brophy & Good, 1974 discuss these differences in detail).

Teachers may also impede the learning progress of lows in the following ways, which were omitted from the Brophy and Good (1974) list or were identified since that list was compiled:

12. Differential administration or grading of tests or assignments, in which highs but not lows are given the benefit of the doubt in borderline cases (Cahen, 1966; Finn, 1972; Heapy & Siess, 1970).

13. Less friendly interaction with lows including less smiling and other nonverbal indicators of support (Babad, Inbar, & Rosenthal, 1982; Chaikin, Sigler, & Derlega, 1974; Kester & Letchworth, 1972; Meichenbaum, Bowers, & Ross, 1969; Page, 1971; Smith & Luginbuhl, 1976).

14. Briefer and less informative feedback to the questions of lows (Cooper, 1979; Cornbleth, Davis, & Button, 1972).

15. Not only less smiling and nonverbal warmth, but less eye contact and nonverbal communication of attention and responsiveness (forward lean, positive head nodding) in interaction with lows (Chaikin, Sigler, & Derlega, 1974).

16. Less intrusive instruction of lows/more opportunity for them to practice independently (Anderson & Rosenthal, 1968; Beez, 1968; Allington, 1980; Brophy, et al., 1981).

17. Less use of effective but time consuming instructional methods with lows when time is limited (Swann & Snyder, 1980).

Differential Treatment of Intact Groups or Classes

The research discussed so far, and in fact most research on teacher expectations, has concentrated on teachers' differential interactions with students in the same group or class. Rosenthal and Jacobson (1968) established this as a pattern in experimental studies, and Brophy and Good's (1970a) development of a system for coding dyadic teacher–student interaction influenced most naturalistic studies. Yet, teachers' differential expectations for individuals in the same class are but variations around the norms established by their expectations for the class as a whole. The potential for self-fulfilling prophecy effects is probably at least as great for these more general expectations as it is for expectations about individuals.

Research on teacher effectiveness (Brophy & Evertson, 1976; McDonald & Elias, 1976) and school effectiveness (Brookover, Beady, Flood, Schweitzer & Wisenbaker, 1979; Edmonds, 1979; Rutter, Maughan, Mortimore, Ouston, & Smith, 1979) indicates that higher expectations for student achievement are part of a pattern of differential attitudes, beliefs, and behaviors that characterize teachers and schools that maximize their students' learning gains. Brookover, et al. (1979), for example, found that in effective schools the teachers not only held higher expectations but acted on them by setting goals expressed as minimally accepted levels of achievement (floor levels), and not by using prior achievement data to establish arbitrary ceiling levels beyond which the students would not be expected to progress. They also responded to failure as a challenge, requiring students to redo failed work (with individualized help if needed) rather than writing the students off or referring them to remedial classes. They responded to failure with appropriate feedback and reinstruction rather than lowering of standards or inappropriate praise.

Research on differential treatment of reading groups also suggests potential mediators of expectation effects. Teachers tend to give longer reading assignments (Pflaum, Pascarella, Boswick, & Auer, 1980), to provide more time for discussion of the story (Bozsik, 1982), and to be generally more demanding (Haskett, 1968) with their high groups than with their low groups. They are quicker to interrupt low group students when they make reading mistakes (Allington, 1980), and more likely to simply give them the word or prompt them with graphemic (phonetic) cues rather than semantic or syntactic cues designed to help them intuit the word from the context (Allington, 1980; Pflaum, et al., 1980). They are also less likely to ask low groups higher level, comprehension-oriented questions (Bozsik, 1982).

Research is also beginning to accumulate on differential teacher treatment of intact classes that differ in student achievement level due to tracking. Evertson (1982) identified several ways in which low-track students slowed down academic pacing and shifted time allocation from academic to procedural or behavioral matters. However, she also noted teacher behaviors in low-track classrooms that suggest teacher expectation effects rather than student effects. Compared to their behavior in higher track classrooms, many teachers were observed to be less clear about their objectives, to introduce material less clearly or completely, to make less attempt to relate the content to student interests and backgrounds, and to be less reasonable in their work standards, consistent in their discipline, and receptive to student input in low-track classes.

In general, tracking tends to have minor benefits for high-track students but major disadvantages for low-track students. Despite ideology indicating that students should move back and forth between tracks as their needs dictate, there is usually remarkably little movement between tracks once students have been assigned, and most of what does occur is downward movement (see reviews by Brophy & Good, 1974, and Persell, 1977).

Teachers plan and implement more independent projects and introduce more high level or integrative concepts with high-track classes (Heathers, 1969), but stress more structured assignments dealing with basic facts and skills in low-track classes (Borko, Shavelson, & Stern, 1981). They also appear to plan more thoroughly for high-track classes, wanting to be prepared for the academic challenges they present. In contrast, in low-track classes, they are more likely to correct papers or allow students to do activities of their own choosing rather than to spend the time teaching academic content (Brookover, et al., 1979; Keddie, 1971; Leacock, 1969; Rosenbaum, 1976).

In addition to these differences documented in systematic research, the more general literature on tracking, educational equity, and related issues suggests a variety of other ways in which expectations may lead to differential treatment producing self-fulfilling prophecy effects: testing and diagnostic labeling practices, special education placement and instruction practices, counseling practices concerning later educational or occupational opportunities, and frequency of contact with parents and responsiveness to their concerns.

Opportunities for undesirable self-fulfilling prophecy effects are maximized when low-expectation students are segregated into separate classes or (through *de facto* segregation) separate schools. Under these conditions, such students will not even have the opportunity to find out about what they are missing, and low expectations can become entrenched norms that channel teacher and student behavior without ever being seriously questioned. In any case, differential teacher treatment of intact groups and classes may well be a much more widespread and powerful mediator of self-fulfilling prophecy effects on student achievement than differential teacher treatment of individual students within the same group or class, even though it has received less attention in the expectation literature. A simple but instructive example of how powerful such effects can be is seen in the study by Pidgeon (1970), who found that British fourth graders learned considerably more mathematics than comparable American fourth graders simply because of differences in the expectations of curriculum developers in the two nations. That is, the British students learned more because they were taught more, due to differences in content coverage and expected pacing built into the curricula they were using.

Mediation of Expectation Effects: Conclusions and Cautions

To the extent that teachers interact differentially with individuals, groups, or classes in ways that seem likely to affect achievement progress, the teachers' expectations for student achievement may function as self-fulfilling prophecies.

Several qualifications and complications must be kept in mind in drawing implications from this conclusion, however.

First, although the forms of differential treatment listed above have been documented in at least one study, they do not occur in all teachers' classrooms. As noted previously, the potential for self-fulfilling prophecy effects of teacher epxectations depends on the degree to which teachers consistently project relatively inaccurate expectations to students. Teachers differ considerably in whether and how they do this, and consequently in the degree and nature of expectation effects they have on their students.

Second, most teacher expectation effects are mediated not only by teacher behavior but by student reaction to that behavior, as Brophy and Good (1970b) noted in their original model. Students differ in their susceptibility to being conditioned by teachers' expectations.

Third, despite appearances to the contrary, many of the differential teacher–student interaction patterns discussed in this section may represent student effects on teachers rather than teacher expectation effects on students, at least in part. Some low-expectation students are both behind in achievement and unresponsive to or alienated from their teachers. If so, sustained determination and perhaps extraordinary efforts may be required to involve them in academic activities in ways comparable to the involvement of higher achieving and more compliant students. Thus, the absence of group differences or even a pattern of small differences seemingly favoring highs may actually represent considerable teacher effort to compensate for student differences, and not merely the absence of bias against lows.

Finally, *some forms of differential treatment are appropriate.* Just as we cannot assume that all differential patterns represent teacher effects on students rather than vice versa, we cannot assume that even those differences that do involve teacher effects on students necessarily represent inappropriate favoritism of highs or bias against lows. For example, both experimental work on aptitude-treatment interactions (Tobias, 1976) and classroom process–product studies (Brophy & Evertson, 1976; Ebmeier & Good, 1979) indicate that low achievers seem to require, and to learn relatively more when provided with, more structured and redundant instruction in basic concepts and skills (delivered within a meaningful context by their teachers, however—not through endless worksheets or other materials that require the students to learn mostly on their own). Thus, even though this means exposing low achievers to less content than high achievers are exposed to, they nevertheless will retain more content when taught with this approach (which is effective with them) than they would retain if taught with approaches more effective for high achievers. Similarly, within a given grade level, slow readers may profit more from frequent teacher interruptions to cue them to graphemic features of words than from being allowed more opportunity to correct their own errors or to intuit words from context cues.

Given that findings from research on effective teaching complicate the interpretation of even seemingly obvious relationships between the amount of content to which students are exposed and the amount that they retain, it is not surprising that interpretation becomes even murkier when attention is shifted to teacher behaviors believed to mediate self-fulfilling prophecy effects indirectly through students attitudes, beliefs, and expectations. Teacher praise, for example, is often treated as an important determinant of student learning, but it usually does not even correlate significantly with learning outcomes, and when it does, it sometimes correlates negatively. The same is true of the cognitive level of questions that teachers ask students (Brophy, 1979; Good, 1979).

Teacher effectiveness researchers will have to make much more progress in identifying linkages between teacher behavior and student learning before teacher expectation researchers will be able to interpret differential patterns of teacher–student interaction unambiguously. In the meantime, it behooves us all to avoid jumping to the conclusion that all differences in interaction with high- versus low-expectation students are undesirable differences. Many teachers not only are not biased against low-expectation students but are systematically compensating for the problematic behavior of these student and maximizing their achievement through appropriately individualized instruction.

THE ROLE OF INDIVIDUAL DIFFERENCES IN TEACHERS

Brophy and Good (1974) noted that each of their studies on teacher expectations contained some teachers who conformed to predictions based on the self-fulfilling prophecy hypothesis, and some who did not. They concluded that susceptibility to teacher expectation effects is an individual difference variable in teachers, and characterized teachers as proactive, reactive, or overreactive. Proactive teachers are guided by their own beliefs about what is appropriate. If they are experienced and perceptive enough to set realistic goals, and skilled enough to overcome frustrations or obstacles, they are likely to move students systematically toward fulfilling the expectations associated with these goals. This would have variable outcomes depending on the teachers' beliefs about teaching and learning (see below), but in any case it is these proactive teachers who are most likely to have positive expectation effects on their students, especially low achievers.

At the other extreme are overreactive teachers who develop rigid expectations and treat their students as stereotypes rather than individuals. This is almost certain to lead to undesirable expectation effects on low achievers. Effects on high achievers would vary, depending on the teachers' beliefs about teaching and learning (see below) and their skills in instructing those students for whom they have high expectations.

In between the extremes are reactive teachers (the majority) who neither consistently strive to mold students to conform to expectations that they (the teachers) project on them, nor consistently treat the students as if they were exaggerated stereotypes of their own previous records. Reactive teachers hold their expectations more lightly, adjusting them in response to new feedback and emerging trends. Consequently, they have few self-fulfilling prophecy effects on their students, and mostly maintain existing differences between highs and lows.

Babad, Inbar, and Rosenthal (1982) studied "high bias" and "no bias" physical education student teachers. Bias classifications were based on responses to an earlier task involving grading drawings allegedly made by students from families of contrasting social status background. The no bias student teachers were not influenced by social status information, but the high bias student teachers assigned higher scores to the drawings allegedly produced by high status students. These student teachers were then observed conducting physical education classes with pupils whom they had previously rated for degree of skill. The data indicated that differences between high- and low-expectation students were much larger in the classes of high bias student teachers. The no bias student teachers made accurate predictions about differential student performance and were affected to some degree by differential student behavior during the classes, but unlike the high bias student teachers, they did not exaggerate these existing student differences through self-fulfilling prophecy effects of expectations mediated through preferential treatment.

Brattesani, Weinstein, Middlestadt & Marshall, (1980) reported similar findings for inservice teachers. "High differentiation" teachers are perceived by their students as communicating higher expectations and allowing more opportunities to participate and more choice of task to high achievers, while being more directive, restrictive, and negative in their treatment of low achievers. "Low differentiation" teachers were not perceived to treat high and low achieving students so differently. Analyses indicated that teacher expectations added only about 3% to the variance in yearend achievement accounted for by prior achievement in the classes of the low differentiation teachers, but added about 15% in the classes of the high differentiation teachers. Again, we see that self-fulfilling prophecy effects are minimal in some classes but substantial in others.

It is clear at this point that the nature and degree of teacher expectation effects likely to be observed in a particular classroom will vary with the teacher's personal characteristics and beliefs about teaching and learning. We are only beginning to understand what some of these important characteristics and beliefs are, and how they interact to produce predictable outcomes.

Teachers' Personal Characteristics

Among the factors already mentioned are teachers' role definitions (degree to which the teacher is willing to assume personal responsibility for student learning), the rigidity versus flexibility of teachers' expectations, and the degree to which these expectations are salient and taken into account in planning and delivering instruction versus held lightly and adjusted in response to current student behavior. Other potential candidates include general intelligence, cognitive complexity, locus of control, sense of efficacy, cognitive style, tolerance for ambiguity, and various coping and defense mechanisms.

Babad, Inbar, and Rosenthal (1982) reported no differences between their high bias and no bias student teachers on structured self-report measures, but found that high bias teachers wrote more dogmatic statements and showed more concern about authority and failure issues in responding to hypothetical classroom events, and were described by observers and supervisors as more autocratic, rigid, distant, impulsive, and preferential, and as less trusting, in their classroom behavior. It is worth noting not only that the high bias student teachers produced most of the self-fulfilling prophecy effects found in this study, but that most of these were what the authors call Golem effects (undesirable, negative effects indicating that low expectations retarded achievement) rather than Galatea effects (desirable, positive effects, indicating that high expectations enhanced achievement). Furthermore, the data suggest that the exaggeration of student differences seen by the high bias student teachers was due more to mediocre instruction of high achievers combined with poor or inappropriate instruction of low achievers than to optimal instruction of high achievers combined with mediocre instruction of low achievers. Similar conclusions can be drawn from the data on high differentiators and low differentiators studied by Brattesani, et al. (1981); from Palardy's (1969) study of teachers who did or did not expect sex differences in reading achievement; from Seaver's (1973) study of the fate of students whose older siblings had been taught by the same teachers; and indeed, from most of the research reviewed by Brophy and Good (1974) and Persell (1977). In practice, then, it appears that most expectation effects observed in classrooms are Golem effects rather than Galatea effects, and are produced by teachers variously labeled as overreactive (Brophy & Good, 1974), high bias (Babad, Inbar, & Rosenthal, 1982), or high differentiating (Brattesani, et al., 1981).

Other teacher characteristics that affect teachers' potential for expectation effects are needs to control the timing, duration, and outcomes of interactions with low achievers (see Chapter 6; Cooper, 1979; and Cooper & Good, 1983); patterns of causal attribution for student success and failure (Cooper, 1979; Weiner, 1979), and trust in one's own judgments about students' abilities (Wise, 1972).

Teachers' Beliefs About Teaching and Learning

To predict how teachers will treat students, we need information not only about their expectations and personal characteristics, but also about their beliefs about teaching and learning. Research on teacher expectations and teacher effectiveness suggests several mediating mechanisms. One of these involves teachers' role definitions (Good & Brophy, 1978, 1980) or beliefs about what constitute the central functions of the teacher role and about how these functions should be accomplished. Many teachers, especially at the secondary level, believe that instruction in subject matter is their primary teaching function. Other teachers, especially at the elementary level, place as much or more emphasis on student socialization (promoting their students' general mental health or personal adjustment). The subject matter specialists organize most of their interactions with students around the content, and run businesslike, academically oriented classrooms. Most of their affect and reinforcement is likely to be directed to high achievers, especially those who participate often and communicate both comprehension and enjoyment of the content. Low achievers may be slighted and low participators ignored in these classrooms. However, if such teachers use a mastery learning approach, they may invest more time with the low achievers than the high achievers.

Teachers who stress student socialization are more likely to get to know their students individually, and to interact with them on personal or social matters. They move through the curriculum at a slower pace, because they allocate more time to nonacademic activities. The class as a whole is likely to show less achievement progress under this type of teacher than a more content oriented teacher (Brophy, 1979; Good, 1979; Fisher, Berliner, Filby, Marliave, Cahen & Dishaw, 1980), because of less exposure to content and thus less opportunity to learn. Given the content that is presented, however, these socialization oriented teachers are most likely to have expectation effects on low achievers. To the extent that these teachers see the low achievers as capable of learning (but in need of extra encouragement and instruction), the low achievers may end up doing better than their previous achievement records would predict. On the other hand, if the teachers see these low achievers as inherently limited in potential, they may treat them in ways that are well intended but nevertheless likely to further retard their achievement progress (encouraging them through overly effusive, noncontingent, or otherwise inappropriate praise; calling on them only when they are certain to know the answer, in order to protect them or avoid putting them on the spot).

Teachers' responses to student performance also will vary according to the causes to which that performance is attributed. Teachers who attribute student failure to their own failure to explain the material adequately are likely to repeat their explanation or try to accomplish their objectives in another way, but those who attribute student failure to inherent limitations in ability are likely to give up.

Interactions Among Teachers' Personal Characteristics, Beliefs, Attitudes and Expectations

Various combinations of personal characteristics, beliefs, and attitudes interact with teachers' expectations in determining teachers' reactions to those expectations. For example, some teachers feel much more sense of responsibility than others to "do something" about their low achievers, but these teachers differ in what they see as appropriate and thus in what their ultimate effects on their low achievers will be.

Some teachers seem to redouble their efforts with low achievers, arranging to monitor and interact with them more often (Brophy, et al., 1981; Brophy & Good, 1974; Rejeski, Darracott, & Hutslar, 1979) and to work with them in smaller reading groups (Weinstein, 1976). This should be beneficial to the low achievers if the extra attention and instruction is appropriate to their needs.

Teacher praise and criticism are involved in many of the unusual patterns that have been reported. For example, high-expectation students usually receive more praise and less criticism than lows. However, two studies found that highs received both more reinforcement for success and more punishment for failure. Presumably they were seen as more salient or as more relevant as objects of teaching effort than the lows were. In any case, to the extent that teachers' beliefs about effective instruction include demanding the most from students and criticizing them for failure to deliver maximal effort, highs may receive more criticism as well as more praise.

Several studies suggest that, even in classrooms where high achievers get more praise because they succeed more often, teachers make the most of the opportunities that low achievers present to them. Thus, low achievers may get more (or more lengthy or intensive) praise on those occasions when they do respond correctly (Jeter & Davis, 1973; Rejeski, Darracott, & Hutslar, 1979; Taylor, 1979; Weinstein, 1976). Similarly, two studies revealed that, although teachers were more likely to repeat or rephrase questions for highs following failure, they were more likely to ask followup questions of lows when they had answered the first question correctly (Good, Sikes, & Brophy, 1973; Evertson, Brophy, & Good, 1973).

Given that most teachers see lows as needing more encouragement and approval than highs (Good & Dembo, 1973; Hersh, 1971; Rothbart, Dalfen, & Barrett, 1971), it is surprising that such "strike while the iron is hot" phenomena are not observed more often. Cooper (1979) provides one explanation with his suggestion that teachers may be unresponsive or even hypercritical toward lows in public situations as a way to inhibit their initiation rates. Other (not mutually exclusive) possibilities are that unexpected success by lows may not be noticed as regularly (because expectations tend to structure attention to competing stimuli and interpretation of events that are attended to); that teachers are often temporarily confused by unexpected success (simply because it is unexpected) or are suspicious of it (maybe it stems from copying or cheating); that unexpected events are somehow troubling even when desirable (because we tend to adjust to and eventually prefer what we have come to expect); or that unexpected success is threatening to teachers (especially teachers who have given up on particular students and rationalized this decision by concluding that the students lack ability). Whatever the dynamics, several studies indicate that teachers sometimes react negatively to unexpected success by lows (Leacock, 1969; Rosenthal & Jacobson, 1968; Rubovits & Maehr, 1971; Shore, 1969; Spector, 1973). Thus, under some circumstances, teacher response to student behavior will depend not so much on whether the behavior is objectively desirable, but on whether it agrees with the teachers' expectations.

THE ROLE OF INDIVIDUAL DIFFERENCES IN STUDENTS

Although they have not received as much attention as individual differences in teachers, individual differences in students also mediate the effects of teacher expectations. For example, some students are more sensitive to voice tone or other subtle communication cues than other students, and thus may be more affected by teachers' expectations (Conn, Edwards, Rosenthal, & Crowne, 1968; Zuckerman, DeFrank, Hall, & Rosenthal, 1978).

Brophy and Good (1974) noted that some students are active, initiatory, and generally salient in the classroom, and that these students are likely to be perceived accurately by their teachers (although not necessarily positively). It is easier for teachers to sustain incorrect expectations about less salient students because they give the teachers less frequent and striking evidence about what they are like. Also, salient students are likely to condition the teacher, but less salient students are more likely to be conditioned by the teacher.

Students who are dependent, adult-oriented, and generally ''other directed'' are more susceptible to expectation effects than other students (Asbury, 1970; Johnson, 1970). Also, younger students (Persell, 1977) or students who are heavily dependent upon the teacher for information (c.f. West & Anderson, 1976) are more likely to be affected by teacher expectations than students who have more information or experience available to draw on in forming their own opinions. Disruptive students who threaten teachers' control needs (Cooper, 1979) tend to structure teacher–student interaction around issues of conduct rather than achievement, and thus are likely to get less academic encouragement than similar-achieving but more compliant students get. In general, where students and teachers are mutually hostile, the potential for positive self-fulfilling prophecy (Galatea) effects seems minimal, but the probability of negative (Golem) effects is high.

Finally, student motivational and attributional patterns interact with differential patterns of teacher treatment to determine outcomes. The output of some students is increased by praise and decreased by criticism, but other students show the opposite pattern. Thus, similar teacher expectations leading to similar treatment of students (in this case, praise for success) may augment achievement in some students, but not others. Similarly, teacher praise may augment achievement in students who attribute their success at least in part to their own efforts, but not in students who attribute success purely to ability or to uncontrollable external factors such as luck.

CONCEPTUALIZING SELF-FULFILLING PROPHECY EFFECTS IN THE CLASSROOM

Models of the self-fulfilling prophecy process will not be discussed at length here (see Chapter 6). However, I do want to note that such models need to address not only expectation phenomena, but the complexities involved in the linkages between teachers' expectations, teachers' beliefs about students needs, objectives that teachers formulate based on those beliefs, behaviors intended to meet those objectives, and the actual effects of these behaviors on students. The possibility of slippage between any one of these steps and the next makes predictions risky.

For example, a teacher may have high expectations and thus set lofty objectives for a particular student, and yet fail to see these expectations fulfilled for lack of knowledge or misinformation about effective teaching. Or, the teacher may formulate firm expectations about differential student achievement but do very little to generate self-fulfilling prophecy effects because he or she relies on whole class instructional methods that minimize interaction with individuals. Or, the teacher may be impressed with certain students but may believe that these students will make the most progress if allowed to work independently, so the students may achieve less than they might have achieved with more guidance. Or, the teacher may believe that certain students have such low potential that they will need as much extra attention and help as possible. The extra attention and help afforded these students is likely to cause them to achieve much more than they would have otherwise, possibly more than some of their classmates whose entry levels were not low enough to cause the teacher to place them into this special group. In this example, the teachers' original low expectations lead to behavior that produces disconfirming rather than self-fulfilling prophecy effects.

In summary, a comprehensive conceptualization of self-fulfilling prophecy effects of teachers' expectations for student achievement in ordinary classroom settings requires attention not only to teacher behavior related directly to the communication of expectations, but to teacher beliefs about curriculum, instruction, and student motivation; to the quality of the personal relationship between the teacher and the student; and to a variety of teacher and student individual difference variables.

RESEARCH IMPLICATIONS

There is a need for more information about how inservice teachers develop and respond to expectations about student achievement. In particular, information is needed about the formation of normative expectations for students in general. Who decides what content is appropriate for students at each grade level to master, and on what basis? Who selects the curriculum packages that appear most appropriate for students in a particular school or classroom, and on what basis? Expectations operating at this general level may have much more profound consequences than individual teachers' differential expectations for students in their classes, but this topic has not received much attention in the expectation literature.

There is also need for more information about teachers' expectations over the course of the school year (c.f. Good, 1980). We know that teachers can produce (largely accurate) expectations on demand, but do they draw on this information in planning and delivering instruction? Research on teacher planning (reviewed by Clark & Yinger, 1979, 1980) suggests that teachers concentrate mostly on procedures, with little attention to objectives. Judgments about whether the class is likely to "respond" to the activity tend to be based on its potential management difficulties or appeal to the students, rather than on the degree to which its difficulty level and academic content fit the students' current achievement progress.

Research on teachers' perceptions and decision making during actual interaction with their students suggests similar conclusions (Shavelson & Stern, 1981; Brophy, 1981). Most thoughts are about the flow of instruction of the activity itself, and most expectations concern the anticipated group response to the activity. To the extent that individuals are considered, teachers focus more on their attentiveness and participation than on their immediate learning needs or more general personal or status characteristics. Thus, existing research on teachers' preactive planning and interactive decision making reveal little spontaneous mention of student achievement expectations.

However, these lines of research have not yet been adopted by researchers specifically interested in teacher expectations. Thus, a great deal of information about the role of teacher expectations in planning and delivering instruction might be revealed by researchers who specifically looked for it.

Good (1980) has noted that most research on communication of expectations has concentrated on teachers' public interactions with students during recitations and discussions. More attention is needed to other contexts and mechanisms for communicating expectations: Grouping decisions and rationales, differential assignments, and individualized comments written on returned assignments, etc. More information is also needed about how students mediate such teacher behavior (see Chapter 13).

To date, research on teacher expectations has focused almost entirely on expectations for student achievement. Yet, as Good and Brophy (1978, 1980) have pointed out, the success of teachers' classroom management efforts is probably determined in part by the expectations that teachers communicate about student conduct; classroom atmosphere probably depends in part on the expectations teachers communicate about student cooperation; and student responsiveness to assignments probably depends in part on the expectations teachers communicate about the meaningfulness or value of those assignments. In short, teachers routinely model and communicate expectations likely to affect not only achievement, but students' attitudes, beliefs, attributions, expectations, achievement motivation, and classroom conduct. Yet, such expectation effects have received little attention to date.

Finally, we need more information about whether and how teachers can have positive ("Galatea") self-fulfilling prophecy effects on their students. In theory, consistently projecting positive expectations in the process of instructing students should produce more positive outcomes than comparable instruction presented more neutrally. This may not be true in practice, however. First, expectations may have nontrivial effects only in the short run or in new situations. Perhaps the potential for self-fulfilling prophecy effects is not great enough to bother with when the same teacher is working with the same students across the school year. Second, this approach to improving student achievement may be too complex to be cost/effective. Recall that self-fulfilling prophecy effects require consistent projection of *inaccurate* expectations (in this case, treating students as if they were brighter than they actually are). This may be too difficult to do consistently, because we are accustomed to responding to our real expectations, and not to acting as if we actually had somewhat more optimistic expectations than we do. Third, even if this approach should ultimately prove feasible and cost/effective, we need much more information about how teachers can communicate positive expectations in ways that will have the desired effects on students. As the complications reviewed in this chapter indicate, we are presently a long way from having an organized body of such knowledge.

TEACHING IMPLICATIONS

In the meantime, the literature on expectations does afford some suggestions to teachers. First, it is not appropriate to try to maintain very high expectations for all students. Unrealistically high expectations will lead to inappropriate instruction and ultimately depress rather than enhance achievement. Nor is it appropriate to try to maintain equal expectations for all students, or to treat all students the same way. Optimal instruction implies some degree of individualization, and also implies that treatment of low achievers will differ from treatment of high achievers. Instruction of low achievers should be judged on the degree to which it meets their needs and maximizes their achievement progress, and not on its degree of similarity to the teacher's treatment of higher achievers.

However, expectations and instruction must be adjusted to take into account emerging developments. To the extent that teachers begin with appropriate expectations and instruction that help students make rapid progress, this very progress will propel the students toward new levels of mastery that imply higher level needs and associated instructional strategies. Thus, the low reading group presently needs more basic content and structured teaching than the middle group, but as the low group makes progress, their activities should become more like those presently used with the middle group.

More generally, teachers can expect to minimize negative (Golem) expectation effects, and perhaps maximize positive (Galatea) expectation effects, if they:

1. Concentrate on how to teach (and where necessary, reteach) the content to the class or group as a whole, rather than worry too much about individual differences.

2. Keep expectations for individuals current by monitoring their progress closely; stress present performance over past history.

3. Set goals in terms of floors (minimally acceptable standards), not ceilings.

4. Stress continuous progress relative to previous levels of mastery rather than normative comparisons or comparisons between individuals.

5. Give informative feedback, not merely evaluation of success or failure.

6. When students do not understand, diagnose their learning difficulty and follow through by breaking down the task or reteaching it in a different way, rather than merely repeating the same instruction or giving up in frustration.

7. In general, think in terms of stretching the students' minds by stimulating them and encouraging them to achieve as much as they can, and not in terms of protecting them from failure or embarrassment.

ACKNOWLEDGMENT

This chapter is based on a paper delivered as part of a symposium entitled "The self-fulfilling prophecy: Its origins and consequences in research and practice," at the 1982 annual meeting of the American Educational Research Association in New York, in March, 1982. The author wishes to thank Tom Good, Neelam Kher, and Rhona Weinstein for their comments on earlier drafts, and June Smith for her assistance in manuscript preparation.

This work is sponsored in part by the Institute for Research on Teaching, College of Education, Michigan State University. The Institute for Research on Teaching is funded primarily by the Program for Teaching and Instruction of the National Institute of Education, United States Department of Education. The opinions expressed in this publication do not necessarily reflect the position, policy, or endorsement of the National Institute of Education. (Contract No. 400–81–0014)

REFERENCES

Adams, G. & Cohen, A. Children's physical and interpersonal characteristics that affect student–teacher interactions. *Journal of Experimental Education*, 1974, *43*, 1–5.

Allington, R. Teacher interruption behaviors during primary-grade oral reading. *Journal of Educational Psychology,* 1980, *72,* 371–377.

Alpert, J. Teacher behavior across ability groups: A consideration of the mediation of Pygmalion effects. *Journal of Educational Psychology,* 1974, *66,* 348–353.

Amato, J. Effect of pupils' social class upon teachers' expectations and behavior. Paper presented at the annual meeting of the American Psychological Association, 1975.

Anderson, D. & Rosenthal, R. Some effects of interpersonal expectancy and social interaction on institutionalized retarded children. *Proceedings of the 76th Annual Convention of the American Psychological Association,* 1968, *3,* 479–480.

Asbury, D. The effects of teacher expectancy, subject expectancy, and subject sex on the learning performance of elementary school children. *Dissertation Abstracts International,* 1970, *31,* 4537A.

Babad, E., Inbar, J., & Rosenthal, R. Pygmalion, Galatea, and the Golem: Investigations of biased and unbiased teachers. *Journal of Educational Psychology,* 1982, *74,* 459–474.

Beez, W. Influence of biased psychological reports on teacher behavior and pupil performance. *Proceedings of the 76th Annual Convention of the American Psychological Association,* 1968, *3,* 605–606.

Blakey, M. The relationship between teacher prophecy and teacher verbal behavior and their effect upon adult student achievement. *Dissertation Abstracts International,* 1970, *31,* 4615A.

Borko, H., Cone, R., Russo, N., & Shavelson, R. Teachers' decision making. In P. Peterson & H. Walberg (Eds.). *Research on teaching: Concepts, findings, and implications.* Berkeley, Calif.: McCutchan, 1979.

Borko, H., Shavelson, R., & Stern, P. Teachers' decisions in the planning of reading instruction. *Reading Research Quarterly,* 1981, *16,* 449–466.

Bozsik, B. A study of teacher questioning and student response interaction during pre-story and post-story portions of reading comprehension lessons. Paper presented at the annual meeting of the American Educational Research Association, 1982.

Brattesani, K., Weinstein, R., Middlestadt, S., & Marshall, H. Using student perceptions of teacher behavior to predict student outcomes. Paper presented at the annual meeting of the American Educational Research Association, Los Angeles, April, 1981.

Braun, C. Teacher expectation: Sociopsychological dynamics. *Review of Educational Research,* 1976, *46,* 185–213.

Brookover, W., Beady, C., Flood, P., Schweitzer, J., & Wisenbaker, J. *School social systems and student achievement: Schools can make a difference.* New York: Bergin, 1979.

Brophy, J. Teacher behavior and its effects. *Journal of Educational Psychology,* 1979, *71,* 733–750.

Brophy, J. Teachers' cognitive activities and overt behaviors. Occasional Paper No. 39, Institute for Research on Teaching, Michigan State, 1981.

Brophy, J. Research on the self-fulfilling prophecy and teacher expectations. Paper presented at the annual meeting of the American Educational Research Association, 1982.

Brophy, J. & Evertson, C. *Learning from teaching: A developmental perspective.* Boston: Allyn & Bacon, 1976.

Brophy, J. & Evertson, C. Context variables in teaching. *Educational Psychologist,* 1978, *12,* 310–316.

Brophy, J. & Evertson, C., with Anderson L., Baum, M., & Crawford, J. *Student characteristics and teaching.* New York: Longman, 1981.

Brophy, J. & Good, T. Brophy-Good System (teacher-child dyadic interaction). In A. Simon & E. Boyer (Eds.). *Mirrors for behavior: An anthology of observation instruments continued, 1970 supplement. Volume A.* Philadelphia: Research for Better Schools, Inc., 1970a.

Brophy, J. & Good, T. Teachers' communication of differential expectations for children's classroom performance: Some behavioral data. *Journal of Educational Psychology,* 1970b, *61,* 365–374.

Brophy, J. & Good, T. *Teacher-student relationships: Causes and Consequences.* New York: Holt, Rinehart, & Winston, 1974.

Cahen, L. An experimental manipulation of the halo effect. Unpublished doctoral dissertation, Stanford University, 1966.

Chaikin, A., Sigler, E., & Derlega, V. Nonverbal mediators of teacher expectation effects. *Journal of Personality and Social Psychology,* 1974, *30,* 144–149.

Clark, C. & Yinger, R. Teachers' thinking. In P. Peterson & H. Walberg (Eds.). *Research on teaching: Concepts, findings, and implications.* Berkeley, Calif.: McCutchan, 1979.

Clark, C. & Yinger, R. The hidden world of teaching: Implications of research on teacher planning. Research Series No. 77, Institute for Research on Teaching, Michigan State, 1980.

Conn, L., Edwards, C., Rosenthal, R., & Crowne, D. Perception of emotion and response to teachers' expectancy by elementary school children. *Psychological Reports,* 1968, *22,* 27–34.

Cooper, H. Pygmalion grows up: A model for teacher expectation communication and performance influence. *Review of Educational Research,* 1979, *49,* 389–410.

Cooper, H. & Baron, R. Academic expectations and attributed responsibility as predictors of professional teachers' reinforcement behavior. *Journal of Educational Psychology,* 1977, *69,* 409–418.

Cooper, H. & Good, T. *Pygmalion grows up: Studies in the expectation communication process.* New York: Longman, 1983.

Cornbleth, C., Davis, O., & Button, C. Teacher–pupil interaction and teacher expectations for pupil achievement in secondary social studies classes. Paper presented at the annual meeting of the American Educational Research Association, 1972.

Davis, D. & Levine, G. The behavioral manifestations of teachers' expectations. Unpublished manuscript, Hebrew University of Jerusalem, 1970.

Ebmeier, H. & Good, T. The effects of instructing teachers about good teaching on the mathematics achievement of fourth grade students. *American Educational Research Journal,* 1979, *16,* 1–16.

Edmonds, R. Effective schools for the urban poor. *Educational Leadership,* 1979, *37,* 15–18.

Evertson, C. Differences in instructional activities in higher- and lower-achieving junior high English and Math classes. *Elementary School Journal,* 1982, *82,* 329–350.

Evertson, C., Brophy, J., & Good, T. Communication of teacher expectations: Second grade. Report No. 92, Research and Development Center for Teacher Education, University of Texas at Austin, 1973.

Fernandez, C., Espinosa, R., & Dornbusch, S. Factors perpetuating the low academic status of Chicano high school students. Memorandum No. 13, Center for Research and Development in Teaching, Stanford University, 1975.

Finn, J. Expectations and the educational environment. *Review of Educational Research,* 1972, *42,* 387–410.

Firestone, G. & Brody, N. Longitudinal investigation of teacher-student interactions and their relationship to academic performance. *Journal of Educational Psychology,* 1975, *67,* 544–550.

Fisher, C., Berliner, D., Filby, N., Marliave, R., Cahen, L., & Dishaw, M. Teaching behaviors, academic learning time, and student achievement: An overview. In C. Denham & A. Lieberman (Eds.). *Time to learn.* Washington, D. C.: National Institute of Education, 1980.

Given, B. Teacher expectancy and pupil performance: The relationship to verbal and non-verbal communication by teachers of learning disabled children. *Dissertation Abstracts International,* 1974, *35,* 1529A.

Good, T. Teacher effectiveness in the elementary school: What we know about it now. *Journal of Teacher Education,* 1979, *30,* 52–64.

Good, T. Classroom expectations: Teacher-pupil interactions. In J. McMillan (Ed.). *The social psychology of school learning.* New York: Academic Press, 1980.

Good, T. & Brophy, J. *Looking in classrooms,* Second edition. New York: Harper & Row, 1978.

Good, T. & Brophy, J. *Educational psychology: A realistic approach,* Second edition. New York: Holt, Rinehart, & Winston, 1980.

Good, T., Cooper, H., & Blakey, S. Classroom interaction as a function of teacher expectations, student sex, and time of year. *Journal of Educational Psychology,* 1980, *72,* 378–385.

Good, T. & Dembo, M. Teacher expectations: Self report data. *School Review,* 1973, *81,* 247–253.

Good, T., Sikes, J., & Brophy, J. Effects of teacher sex and student sex on classroom interaction. *Journal of Educational Psychology,* 1973, *65,* 74–87.

Haskett, M. An investigation of the relationship between teacher expectancy and pupil achievement in the special education class. *Dissertation Abstracts,* 1968, *29,* 4348A–4349A.

Heapy, N. & Siess, T. Behavioral consequences of impression formation: Effects of teachers' impressions upon essay evaluations. Paper presented at the annual meeting of the Eastern Psychological Association, 1970.

Heathers, G. Grouping. In R. Ebel (Ed.). *Encyclopedia of educational research, Fourth edition.* New York: MacMillan, 1969.

Hersh, J. Effects of referral information on testers. *Journal of Consulting and Clinical Psychology,* 1971, *37,* 116–122.

Jeter, J. & Davis, O. Elementary school teachers' differential classroom interaction with children as a function of differential expectations of pupil achievements. Paper presented at the annual meeting of the American Educational Research Association, 1973.

Johnson, E. Pygmalion in the testing setting: Nonverbal communication as a mediator of expectancy fulfillment. *Dissertation Abstracts International,* 1970, *31,* 6716A.

Jones, V. The influence of teacher–student introversion, achievement, and similarity on teacher–student dyadic classroom interactions. Unpublished doctoral dissertation, Department of Educational Psychology, University of Texas at Austin, 1971.

Keddie, N. Classroom knowledge. In F. Young (Ed.). *Knowledge and control: New directions for the sociology of education.* London: Collier-Macmillan, 1971.

Kester, S. & Letchworth, J. Communication of teacher expectations and their effects on achievement and attitudes of secondary school students. *Journal of Educational Research,* 1972, *66,* 51–55.

Kleinfeld, J. Effective teachers of Eskimo and Indian students. *School Review,* 1975, *83,* 301–344.

Kounin, J. *Discipline and group management in classrooms.* New York: Holt, Rinehart, & Winston, 1970.

Leacock, E. *Teaching and learning in city schools.* New York: Basic Books, 1969.

Lundgren, U. *Frame factors and the teaching process: A contribution to curriculum theory and theory on teaching.* Stockholm: Almqvist & Wiksell, 1972.

Martinek, T. & Johnson, S. Teacher expectations: Effects of dyadic interaction and self-concept in elementary-age children. *Research Quarterly,* 1979, *50,* 60–70.

Mason, E. Teachers' observations and expectations of boys and girls as influenced by biased psychological reports and knowledge of the effects of bias. *Journal of Educational Psychology,* 1973, *65,* 238–243.

McDonald, F. & Elias, P. *Beginning Teacher Evaluation Study: Phase II Technical Summary, Final Report.* Princeton, N. J.: Educational Testing Service, 1976.

Medinnus, G. & Unruh, R. Teacher expectations and verbal communication. Paper presented at the annual meeting of the Western Psychological Association, 1971.

Meichenbaum, D., Bowers, K., & Ross, R. A behavioral analysis of teacher expectancy effect. *Journal of Personality and Social Psychology,* 1969, *13,* 306–316.

Mendoza, S., Good T., & Brophy, J. Who talks in junior high classrooms? Report No. 68, Research and Development Center for Teacher Education, University of Texas at Austin, 1972.

Merton, R. The self-fulfilling prophecy. *Antioch Review,* 1948, *8,* 193–210.

Metz, M. *Classrooms and corridors: The crisis of authority in desegregated secondary schools.* Berkeley, Calif.: University of California Press, 1978.

Noble, C. & Nolan, J. Effect of student verbal behavior on classroom teacher behavior. *Journal of Educational Psychology,* 1976, *68,* 342–346.

Page, S. Social interaction and experimenter effects in the verbal conditioning experiment. *Canadian Journal of Psychology,* 1971, *25,* 463–475.

Palardy, J. What teachers believe—what children achieve. *Elementary School Journal,* 1969, *69,* 370–374.

Persell, C. *Education and inequality: The roots and results of stratification in American schools.* New York: The Free Press, 1977.

Pflaum, S., Pascarella, E., Boswick, M., & Auer, C. The influence of pupil behaviors and pupil status factors on teacher behaviors during oral reading lessons. *Journal of Educational Research,* 1980, *74,* 99–105.

Pidgeon, D. *Expectation and pupil performance.* Slough, Great Britain: NFER, 1970.

Rejeski, W., Darracott, C., & Hutslar, S. Pygmalion in youth sport: A field study. *Journal of Sports Psychology,* 1979, *1,* 311–319.

Rist, R. Student social class and teacher expectations: The self-fulfilling prophecy in ghetto education. *Harvard Educational Review,* 1970, *40,* 411–451.

Rosenbaum, J. *Making inequality.* New York: Wiley-Interscience, 1976.

Rosenthal, R. *On the social psychology of the self-fulfilling prophecy: Further evidence for Pygmalion effects and their mediating mechanisms.* New York: MSS Modular Publications, 1974.

Rosenthal, R. & Jacobson, L. *Pygmalion in the classroom: Teacher expectation and pupils' intellectual development.* New York: Holt, Rinehart & Winston, 1968.

Rothbart, M., Dalfen, S., & Barrett, R. Effects of teacher's expectancy on student–teacher interaction. *Journal of Educational Psychology,* 1971, *62,* 49–54.

Rowe, M. Wait-time and rewards as instructional variables, their influence on language, logic, and fate control: Part One—Wait-time. *Journal of Research in Science Teaching,* 1974, *11,* 81–94.

Rubovits, P. & Maehr, M. Pygmalion analyzed: Toward an explanation of the Rosenthal-Jacobson findings. *Journal of Personality and Social Psychology,* 1971, *19,* 197–203.

Rutter, M., Maughan, E., Mortimore, P., Ouston, J., & Smith, A. *Fifteen thousand hours: Secondary schools and their effects on children.* Cambridge: Harvard, 1979.

Seaver, W. Effects of naturally induced teacher expectancies. *Journal of Personality and Social Psychology,* 1973, *28,* 333–342.

Shavelson, R., Cadwell, J., & Izu, T. Teachers' sensitivity to the reliability of information in making pedagogical decisions. *American Educational Research Journal,* 1977, *14,* 83–97.

Shavelson, R. & Stern, P. Research on teachers' pedagogical thoughts, judgments, decisions and behavior. *Review of Educational Research,* 1981, *51,* 455–498.

Shore, A. Confirmation of expectancy and changes in teachers' evaluations of student behaviors. *Dissertation Abstracts,* 1969, *30,* 1878A–1879A.

Smith, F. & Luginbuhl, J. Inspecting expectancy: Some laboratory results of relevance for teacher training. *Journal of Educational Psychology,* 1976, *68,* 265–272.

Spector, P. The communication of expectancies: The interaction of reinforcement and expectancy instructions. Unpublished manuscript, Washington University of St. Louis, 1973.

Swann, W. & Snyder, M. On translating beliefs into action: Theories of ability and their application in an instructional setting. *Journal of Personality and Social Psychology,* 1980, *38,* 879–888.

Taylor, D. Second grade reading instruction: The teacher–child dyadic interactions of boys and girls of varying abilities. Unpublished Masters thesis, Rutgers, The State University of New Jersey, 1977.

Taylor, M. Race, sex, and the expression of self-fulfilling prophecies in a laboratory teaching situation. *Journal of Personality and Social Psychology,* 1979, *37,* 897–912.

Tobias, S. Achievement treatment interactions. *Review of Educational Research,* 1976, *46,* 61–74.

Weiner, B. A theory of motivation for some classroom experiences. *Journal of Educational Psychology,* 1979, *71,* 3–25.

Weinstein, R. Reading group membership in first grade: Teacher behaviors and pupil experience over time. *Journal of Educational Psychology,* 1976, *68,* 103–116.

West, C. & Anderson, T. The question of preponderant causation in teacher expectancy research. *Review of Educational Research,* 1976, *46,* 613–630.

Willis, B. The influence of teacher expectation on teachers' classoom interaction with selected children. *Dissertation Abstracts,* 1970, *30,* 5072A.

Willis, S. Formation of teachers' expectations of students' academic performance. Unpublished doctoral dissertation, Department of Educational Psychology, University of Texas at Austin, 1972.

Wise, R. Teacher and pupil factors related to teacher expectations for children. *Dissertation Abstracts International,* 1972, *33,* 6191A.

Zuckerman, M., DeFrank, R., Hall, J., & Rosenthal, R. Accuracy of nonverbal communication as determinant of interpersonal expectancy effects. *Environmental Psychology and Nonverbal Behavior,* 1978, *2,* 206–214.

13 Student Mediation of Classroom Expectancy Effects

Rhona S. Weinstein
University of California, Berkeley

In much of the research literature on the self-fulfilling prophecy in the classroom, relatively little attention has been directed toward an investigation of the mechanisms by which certain patterns of teacher treatment result in the enhancement or deterioration of student performance. How different treatment leads to different performance is the question at issue. Existing theory about the mediation of the self-fulfilling prophecy in the classroom has distinguished between direct and indirect effects of teacher expectations on student performance (Brophy, 1982; Brophy & Good, 1974; Good, 1980).

Recently, studies of classroom expectancy effects are beginning to examine processes within the student which may mediate between hypothesized differential teacher treatment and student performance. This chapter reviews and integrates the growing body of literature concerned with such student processes and suggests directions for future research.

STUDENT MEDIATION THEORY

Since the Rosenthal and Jacobson study (1968) of *Pygmalion in the Classroom*, much research has been directed toward specifying the components of the causal process underlying classroom expectancy effects. Explicated in Brophy and Good (1970, 1974) and expanded upon in Braun (1973, 1976), the causal sequence includes teacher input factors, such as possible sources of teacher expectations and the differential susceptibility of teachers to input information; teacher output factors, in the form of teacher behaviors that transmit expectancy cues; and finally, learner output factors, which include learner responses to the expectancy cues, learner self-expectations, and learner performance. Until recently, the bulk of the research has addressed teacher variables, with student achievement outcomes as the only learner variable measures (Weinstein & Middlestadt, 1979a,b). Although student response to differential treatment by the teacher was implied in the underlying model, such responses were rarely studied. One exception to this pattern was the Entwisle and Hayduk investigation (1978) of the development of young children's academic expectations. Their study addressed the way in which the school experience shapes children's early expectations for themselves.

That student perceptions of teacher feedback could provide a missing link in understanding the transmission of expectations became clearly evident in this author's study of the process and outcomes of grouping for reading in three first grade classrooms (Weinstein, 1976). In this study, findings about teacher–child interaction patterns and about student outcomes proved difficult to reconcile. On the one hand, observations of teacher treatment toward reading groups suggested that the teacher favored low reading group members with more praise and less criticism than that accorded high reading group members. On the other hand, over the course of the school year, the gap in achievement, in peer status, and in experienced anxiety about school performance widened significantly between high and low reading group members. Of note, the classroom observers reported that the praise to lows was qualitatively different form the praise to high. It was hypothesized that the more frequent critical comments concerning performance directed toward highs might suggest high expectations to students and that the high rates of praise for lows (and as the observers also pointed out, for less than perfect answers) conveyed an indiscriminate "fine, fine, fine" to those from whom less was expected. What did the students think? At issue was the perception of these differences and its resultant impact.

Braun (1973, 1976) further delineated the student role in the dynamics of the self-fulfilling prophecy by outlining several propositions about the probable course of events following differential teacher treatment. He suggested that if student self-image and motivation are influenced by such treatment differences, students must first perceive and interpret the meaning of teacher behavior. He argued that students are capable of interpreting the verbal and nonverbal cues expressed by the teacher, and further, that student awareness of teacher cues about expectations informs the development of their own expectations for performance. Braun (1976) also hypothesized that students' self-expectations affect the degree to which students volunteer answers or persist in trying. These behaviors, in turn, determine ultimate student performance.

In addition, Braun (1976) pointed to individual differences in students that may be reflected in differential susceptibility to expectancy effects. He argued that there was little reason to expect that "all learners will read and internalize the same cues any more than that they will act upon these cues to the same degree" (p. 203). As one example of such a difference, the self-image of the learner may affect the potency of expectancy cues. If a student already views himself or herself as a competent learner, the student may be able to resist attempts to change this image. Thus, the student will behave in ways consistent with his or her self-image.

The teacher cues that Braun (1976) identified followed the lead of classroom observational studies which focused on differences in the frequency of a variety of teaching behaviors accorded high- and low-expectation students in the classroom. For example, praise from the teacher was expected to improve a student's self-image and a series of such confirmations would likely ensure this change in self-view.

Cooper (1979) has suggested an alternative model of the influence process, and in it, he, too, stresses the student role in the mediation of the self-fulfilling prophecy in the classroom. He hypothesized that teachers' expectations for students influence their perceived control over student performance and further, that teachers choose feedback patterns to maximize interaction control. With slower students, teachers might be less likely to praise strongly for effort expenditure because this feedback pattern would encourage future student initiations. The teacher becomes motivated to control interactions in order to maximize the possibility of successful outcomes. In evaluating higher achieving students, the teacher can reward effort because the more likely positive interactions alleviate the need for teacher control.

Cooper (1979) has speculated that the differing feedback contingencies used by teachers, such as noncontingent praise and criticism, affect student perceptions of their own personal control over academic performance. Greater use of feedback by teachers, independent of student effort but geared to the control of student interaction, may lead to less of a belief on the part of students that personal effort is instrumental in their success and hence, less demonstration of effort. Such feedback contingencies shape student perceptions of effort–outcome covariation and subsequently, student performance.

In contrast to the formulation of Braun (1976), Cooper's explanatory model highlights student attention to the contingencies of teacher feedback rather than the frequency with which praise and criticism are provided. Further, he identified student locus of control beliefs as critical determinants of reduced effort expenditure by the student. Perceived locus of control and self-evaluations, however, are intimately linked constructs. For many theorists (see Harter, 1983, for review), the roots of self-esteem and the basis for future expectations lie in a developing sense of control over events.

These theoretical formulations apply specifically to the self-fulfilling prophecy in classroom settings. However, recent theorizing about expectancy processes across a wide variety of social settings has also underscored the importance of the target person's (the recipient of the expectation) interpretation of the treatment (Darley & Fazio, 1980). As well, in the case of experimenter expectancy effects, others have argued that the process may require not only the expression of expectations but subjects' attention to the comprehension of these cues, (Rosenthal & Rosnow, 1975; Finkelstein, 1976).

The target person's own response is based on his or her interpretation of the treatment. Darley and Fazio (1980) have noted that different forms of expectancy maintenance and confirmation can occur, with the classic self-fulfilling prophecy as only one possible outcome. They point to a variety of attributions that the target of expectations may use to explain the treatment. These include attributions to dispositional characteristics of the holder of the expectation, to elements of the situation, to the self or to some combination of these features. Further, they add an additional loop to the influence process by suggesting that targets interpret not only the perceiver's behavior but also their own response to the perceiver's treatment. Thus, their own behavioral response becomes an additional element in shaping the nature of their attributions. Each of these attributions has different implications for subsequent behavior in this situation as well as in the future. Thus, the target of the expectation is thought to play a critical role in determining the outcome of the social interaction. Different attributions for the treatment underlie the differential susceptibility of targets to expectancy effects. To date, however, little is known about the conditions under which the target of expectations will accept the other's impression; reject it; or attempt to disprove it. These conditions might be created by target characteristics, such as the strong self-concept of learners which Braun (1976) identified as a mitigating factor in expectancy effects, or they might reflect aspects of the situation that may reduce the impact of expectancy cues.

Despite several underlying differences, the theoretical formulations of Braun (1973, 1976), Cooper (1979) and Darley and Fazio (1980) all highlight the important role of the student as mediating the impact of the self-fulfilling prophecy in the classroom. Student perceptions and cognitions about teacher behavior emerge as critical factors underlying the dynamics of expectancy effects.

This interest in student thought, as students engage in instruction and in classroom life, has intensified in other areas of educational research as well. In the study of teacher effectiveness, there exists much disillusionment with simple input–output models of instructional effects, where students have been largely viewed as the passive recipients of instruction. There is growing recognition that students influence instruction and its outcomes as much as teachers do. Both Berliner (1976) and Doyle (1977) have argued for a mediating-process paradigm in the study of teaching that views variations in student learning outcomes as a function of specific student responses to instructional stimuli. There is much to be learned here. As Berliner (1976) suggested, "Researchers do not know how much of what is called skilled teaching is even perceived by the learner" (p. 10).

Interest in student thought has also been stimulated by the development of the field of social cognition. Recent advances have extended Piaget's theory of cognitive development to include the construction of social as well as physical reality (Flavell, 1977). Developmental social cognitive theory has much to teach us about the capabilities and limits of students' cognitive capacities for understanding classroom life (Gordon, 1981; Swarthout, 1980). The student perspective on schooling has been highlighted in two recent special issues of the *Educational Review* (Meighan, 1978) and the *Elementary School Journal* (Weinstein, 1982), addressed in a conference concerned with both student and teacher perceptions of success and failure (Levine & Wang, 1983), and reviewed by Duke (1977) and Weinstein (1983). More specific studies of student perceptions of classroom learning environments have also been extensively reviewed (Fraser, 1980; Fraser & Walberg, 1981; Moos, 1979).

Relatively few of these studies, however, answer the specific questions concerned with explicating the role of the student in the expectancy process. Research about student-mediation of self-fulfilling prophecies is still in its infancy. The research evidence to date will be reviewed here under four general topic areas that follow from the theoretical formulations proposed: (1) student perceptions of teacher behavior; (2) perceived teacher behavior as influencing student beliefs; (3) links between self-other perceptions and performance; and (4) student susceptibility to teacher expectations.

STUDENT PERCEPTIONS OF TEACHER BEHAVIOR

Student Perceptions of Teacher Feedback in General

Several studies provide evidence that students can make sophisticated interpretations of teacher behavior. For example, in a series of studies of boys' perceptions of simulated verbal reinforcers, Solomon and Yaeger (1969a,b) found that content and interaction both singly and in concert had significant effects on the perceived meaning of reinforcers. Sechrest (1962) also reported students' awareness of teachers' nonverbal ways of giving them information about performance.

Students were also found to acknowledge the differential meaning of grading by the teacher; for example, one student reported that "the meaning of an F depends on the kind of pupil one is" (Boehm & White, 1967). Students were able to articulate their feelings about a variety of teacher behaviors and to describe the information that these behaviors provided them. Zahorik's (1970) findings suggested that if students are to feel good about answers and to know that their answer is correct, the teacher's verbal feedback must contain such phrases as "All right," "Fine," or "Good." Morine-Dershimer (1982) investigated student perceptions of the function of teacher praise and found students could distinguish between praise as deserved and praise as having an instructional purpose. Their awareness of these differences matched teacher use of praise in the classroom.

Students have also been asked to rate the psychosocial climate or teaching environment of the classroom. The instruments tap student perception of a wide variety of both teacher behavior and peer behavior (see Fraser & Walberg, 1981; Moos, 1979; Walberg, 1976; Walberg & G. Haertel, 1980). This area of research represents the most well developed use of student perceptions as a methodology. However, the classroom climate studies have typically relied upon the classroom mean of student observations as a measure of perceived climate. With regard to implications for within-classroom expectancy effects, this method masks the possibility that different environments exist for high and low achievers within one classroom setting and that these differences are perceived by the students.

Student Perceptions of Teacher Treatment Toward High and Low Achievers

Weinstein and Middlestadt (1979a,b) developed the Teacher Treatment Inventory to assess student perceptions of teacher interactions with high and low achievers in the classroom. Items were derived from reviews of the literature on the relationship between teaching behaviors and student achievement; on the expression of teacher expectations in behavior; on student perceptions of classroom environments; and from pilot interviews with students. They asked younger and older elementary school children to rate the 60 teacher behaviors as descriptive of the treatment of a hypothetical male student, either a high or low achiever. Each student completed only one form of the inventory in order to provide an independent assessment of perceived teacher treatment that would most closely match the conditions under which classroom observers assess teacher interaction, that is, without awareness of the specific comparisons being drawn between types of students. Male stimulus children were chosen for study because of boys' greater salience in classroom interaction (Brophy & Good, 1974). In comparing the treatment profiles of the two types of students, it was found that differential treatment was perceived by students across one-quarter of the teacher behaviors studied. Student-perceived teacher treatment of male high achievers reflected high expectations, academic demand, and special privileges. Male low achievers were viewed as receiving fewer chances but greater teacher concern and vigilance.

In a subsequent study, a fourth through sixth grade sample of students from eight open and eight traditional classrooms was asked to rate the frequency with which 44 teacher behaviors were accorded one of four types of students (Weinstein, Marshall, Brattesani, & Middlestadt, 1982). In this study, student perceptions of teacher treatment toward female as well as male high and low achievers were measured, with the achievement level comparison of treatment assigned to students within classrooms and the sex comparison assigned across classrooms. In this study, the revised and shortened Teacher Treatment Inventory was factor analyzed to yield four types of teacher behaviors that were perceived by the students. The results were largely supportive of the earlier investigation. Students described low achievers as the recipients of more negative feedback and teacher direction, and more work and rule orientation than high achievers. High achievers were perceived as receiving higher expectations, more opportunity and choice than low achievers. No differences were documented in the perceived degree of supportive help. These findings underscore the perceived differential usage of teacher direction versus student autonomy. Students are clearly aware of the greater teacher input, help, and structure accorded low achievers in contrast to the more autonomous learning context accorded high achievers.

Sex of the Target Subject.   In the Weinstein et al. study (1982), the teacher treatment differences between highs and lows were perceived both for male and female target students. Further, no differences were reported by students in the treatment of boys and girls across different classrooms. In a third study, now currently in progress, both sex as well as achievement level comparisons of treatment were obtained within classrooms. Here again, students reported few sex differences in teacher treatment on the Teacher Treatment Inventory. In a sample of 30 classrooms of first, third and fifth graders, no sex differences were documented in the perceived provision of negative feedback and teacher direction, and in expectations, opportunity, and choice. However, students did report that boys and girls differed in the frequency of work and rule oriented behavior they received from the teacher, with first and third grade students perceiving girls as the more frequent recipients and fifth graders perceiving boys as the more frequent recipients.

Several earlier studies examined within-classroom differences in the treatment of boys and girls as perceived by students using a pupil nomination technique. Meyer and Thompson (1956) found that three sixth grade teachers showed more disapproval for the boys than for the girls and that the children recognized this differential in teacher response. McNeil (1965) reported that boys were named more often by classmates as receiving negative comments from the teacher and as having fewer opportunities to respond in reading groups, and that their teachers believed boys were less ready for reading. In a first grade sample (Davis & Slobodian, 1967; Slobodian & Campbell, 1967), using a similar pupil nomination technique, boys were viewed as receiving more negative comments, few opportunities to read, and as being poorer readers than girls. In this study, these differences were not confirmed in observational data nor were significant differences in achievement documented.

It may well be that the types of teacher behavior differentially accorded boys and girls in the classroom are not the same as those behaviors differentially accorded high and low achievers, and that differences in treatment toward boys and girls are more context-specific (both subject matter as well as age level).

Stability of Perceived Treatment Toward High and Low Achievers.   Test–retest data were collected for the Teacher Treatment Inventory on a sample of first, third, and fifth graders in order to ascertain the stability of student perceptions of teacher treatment toward a high or low achiever over a 2 week period (Weinstein & Marshall, 1981). The test–retest reliability coefficients over both high achiever and low achiever forms and over all grades were .73, .70, and .80 for all three scales of the Teacher Treatment Inventory. They were also adequate within each grade level, suggesting relative stability in perceived treatment over a 2 week period. Of interest, an examination of test–retest coefficients across the 26 classrooms revealed enormous classroom differences in the stability of perceptions, with some classrooms showing much change in perceptions and other classrooms virtually no change in perceptions (coefficients in the .90s) over the 2 week period.

Classroom Differences in Perceived Differential Treatment.   The results to date from classroom observational studies of teacher treatment suggest that not all teachers exhibit differential treatment toward high- and low-expectation students (Good, 1980). This variability between classrooms in the occurrence of differential treatment has most often been explained in terms of individual differences in teacher type of personality (Brophy & Good, 1974; Cooper, 1979; Rubovits & Maehr, 1973). However, a growing body of research suggests that the activity structure adopted for classroom instruction also functions to both facilitate and constrain the opportunities available for certain kinds of teacher–child interactions (Bossert, 1979; Doyle, 1980).

In the Weinstein et al. study (1982), perceptions of teacher treatment toward highs and lows were gathered from students in eight open and eight traditional classrooms. A classroom structure comparison was included in order to investigate the hypothesis that perceptions of differential treatment would be more likely in traditional than in open classrooms, because in traditional classrooms teacher feedback to students was apt to be more comparative and more public. Contrary to this hypothesis, differential treatment toward highs and lows (at a classroom level) was perceived in both open and traditional classrooms (as measured by principal nominations or teacher ratings). The extent of perceived differential treatment was also found to be unrelated to the mean achievement level of the students in the classroom. Differential treatment was perceived by students in high as well as low achievement classes.

However, classrooms were found to vary in the extent of differential treatment perceived by students, with large differences in treatment perceived in some classrooms and little difference in others. Further, teachers were perceived to differ more in their treatment of low achievers than in their treatment of high achievers. Not surprisingly, in interviews, students from high differential treatment classes reported more public communication about poor performance from the teacher and more public cues about smartness than did students from low differential treatment classrooms (Weinstein, 1981). Hence, public comparability of performance was an important differentiating factor perhaps not captured by the open/traditional distinction, at least as measured by principal and teacher ratings.

Direct Assessments of Perceived Differential Treatment. In contrast to the Weinstein et al. (1982) methodology of obtaining independent assessments of the perceived treatment of highs and lows, students have also been directly asked whether teachers treat learners differently. In a study of second graders (Clements, Gainey, & Malitz, 1980), 57% of the children interviewed said that the teacher did treat good readers differently from poor readers. Thus, a little more than half of the students responded that the treatment was different. Classroom differences in response patterns concerning this single judgement were not documented. The most frequently cited differential teacher behavior concerned the provision of greater rewards to good readers and helping poor readers more. These reported treatment differentials are congruent with the Weinstein et al. findings (1982).

Weinstein and Marshall (1981) also directly asked a sample of first, third, and fifth grade students whether the teacher treated high and low achievers differently with regard to each of 44 teaching behaviors on the Teacher Treatment Inventory. The results suggested that when students are asked directly about differential teacher treatment, they are likely to respond that the treatment is the same. First graders reported on the average that 82% of the teaching behaviors were the same for high and low achievers. Similar treatment was also reported for 75% of the behaviors by third graders and 80% of the behaviors by fifth graders.

Student Perceptions of Their Own Treatment from the Teacher

Self-ratings of the Frequency of Teacher Behavior. A sample of third, fourth, and fifth graders completed the Teacher Treatment Inventory as a self-rating, that is, students indicated how often their teacher worked with them in the ways described (Brattesani & Weinstein, 1980; Brattesani, Weinstein, & Marshall, 1984). In addition, they described the teacher treatment of a high or low achiever. Low-expectation students perceived more negative feedback and teacher direction, and less opportunity and choice than did high-expectation students. Further, these perceived expectation related differences in one's own treatment appeared in perceived high-differential treatment classes and not in low-differential treatment classes.

Self-ratings of Differential Teacher Treatment. In a study by Cooper and Good (1983), fourth through sixth grade students (highs, middles, and lows from each class) described their own treatment by rating nine teacher–student interactions for whether these occurred more often, about the same amount, or less often than classmates. Teachers completed a parallel questionnaire for each of the 12 target students in their classroom and classroom observations of the frequencies of these same interactions with each of the target students were also available.

Students who were the recipients of higher expectations from the teacher saw themselves as engaging in more frequent teacher-initiated public interactions, less frequent teacher-initiated private interactions, more appropriate (correct) responding, and less frequent criticism from the teacher. Teachers were aware of these differences as well, except that in the case of praise, high-expectation students tended to perceive more frequent praise from the teacher whereas teachers perceived low-expectation students as the more frequent recipients.

Cooper and Good (1983) also examined the "accuracy" of student perceptions of interactions as compared to observed frequencies of interactions. Student estimates of teacher treatment matched the observational records on only one of the nine behaviors compared—however, all the means were in the observed direction. There was a greater correspondence between student and teacher perceptions of interaction. Two possible sources of difficulty were noted by Cooper and Good. First, teachers took part in all the interactions whereas students had to estimate the frequency of their peers' interactions as well as their own. Second, students may over or underreport certain interaction patterns with teachers in order to protect their teachers.

Support for such protecting behaviors is found in a study by Gustafsson (1977). She documented that fourth grade students (85% of the sample) were most likely to say that they got the same number of questions or same amount of help from the teachers as did other students. Pupils made comments such as "Miss X does as good as she can. She comes to all of us."

In sum, these studies of student perceptions of teacher behavior suggest that (1) students are sensitive to verbal as well as nonverbal cues from the teacher; (2) they perceive differences in the functions of teacher behavior; (3) they perceive the teacher treatment of high and low achievers differently; (4) these perceptions of teacher treatment are relatively stable over a 2 week period; (5) the extent of perceived differential teacher treatment is great in some classes and minimal in others; (6) when students are asked directly about their awareness of differential teacher treatment toward highs and lows or about their own differential treatment relative to others, students might underreport differential treatment; (7) expectation effects are perceived by students in their own treatment from the teacher; that is, students who are the recipients of high or low expectations perceive correspondingly more or less of particular teacher behaviors both in general as well as relative to peers; (8) student perception of interactional frequencies do not match observed ratings of interactional frequencies but they match teacher judgments.

PERCEIVED TEACHER BEHAVIOR AS INFLUENCING
STUDENT BELIEFS

Relationships with Self-Expectations

In studies using the Teacher Treatment Inventory to tap student perceptions of treatment toward high and low achievers, it has been found that the extent to which the teacher was perceived by students to differentiate treatment was related to the degree of congruence between student and teacher expectations (Brattesani, Weinstein, & Marshall, 1984). Students in perceived high differential treatment classrooms had expectations for themselves that were more strongly related to their teachers' expectations than did students in perceived low differential treatment classrooms. For example, in perceived high differential treatment classrooms on the dimension of high expectations, opportunity, and choice (where highs were perceived to get more favorable treatment than lows), teacher expectations predicted an additional 12% of the variance in student expectations over and above prior student achievement whereas teacher expectations explained only an additional 1% of the self-expectation variance in perceived low differential treatment classrooms. These findings suggest that students in classrooms with perceived high differential treatment have access to more information about their teachers' expectations for them and incorporate this information into their own expectations for performance.

There is a growing literature on student perceptions of ability that suggests both developmental constraints and classroom structural influences on students' ability to develop realistic perceptions of ability relative to others (see review by Blumenfeld, Pintrich, Meece & Wessels, 1982). While this literature has not yet linked the development of self-perceptions to the perception of teacher behavior, it has implications for further research in this area.

The developmental literature suggests that young children see ability or intelligence as a changeable entity that can be improved with effort (Dweck & Elliott, 1981; Yussen & Kane, 1980). Only with increasing age, are children able to embrace a stable internal trait theory of intelligence. Younger children do not distinguish ability, effort, and outcome and believe that those who try harder are smarter (Nicholls, 1978). Nicholls suggests four levels of reasoning about ability and effort which culminate in children's belief that ability may limit or increase the effectiveness of effort. Younger children are also less able to integrate information about previous outcomes in making predicitons for future performance (Parsons & Ruble, 1977). In the assessment of performance, younger children rely on absolute and individual standards rather than normative standards, that is, children's achievement-related evaluations are not affected by social comparisons. Blumenfled and colleagues (1982) argue that these developmental patterns bias young children's self-perceptions in a positive direction.

There also exists compelling evidence that teacher feedback patterns and classroom conditions that maximize the differences between high and low achievers affect student perceptions of ability, particularly after fourth grade. Young children's academic expectations appear to be highly resistant to negative teacher feedback in the form of marks or reading grade placement (Entwisle & Hayduk, 1978; Stipek, 1977). With age, student perceptions of their ability become more congruent with teacher perceptions of their ability (Nicholls, 1978; Stipek, 1981). In a study of junior high school classrooms (Parsons, Kaczala, & Meece, 1982), the discriminative use of criticism for academic work had a positive impact on student self-perceptions of ability. Blumenfeld and colleagues (1982) also found relationships between feedback patterns and self-perceptions of ability. Further, in classrooms with competitive versus cooperative reward structures (Ames, 1981); in classrooms with narrow task structures and an emphasis on public and comparable performance evaluation (Rosenholtz & Wilson, 1980); and as described earlier, in classrooms where students perceived greater differential treatment toward high and low achievers (Brattesani et al., 1984), self-perceptions of performance differences were accentuated.

Relationships with Effort—Outcome Covariation Beliefs

Student perceptions of feedback contingencies have been directly measured in a study by Kennelly and Kinley (1975). In a sample of male students, they found that boys who perceived their teacher to be contingently critical were more internal in their perceived locus of control beliefs. This relationship did not hold for the provision of praise. Research on locus of control or self-efficacy beliefs has also suggested developmental milestones in children's ability to hold an internal orientation of control (Crandall, Katkovsky & Crandall, 1965).

Cooper and Good (1983), in their study of expectancy effects in a fourth through sixth grade sample of students, did not find a relationship between teacher expectations and student-effort-outcome covariation beliefs. Further, only limited support was found for a relationship between actual feedback patterns and student self-efficacy beliefs and between student perceptions of the differential frequency of these feedback patterns and student self-efficacy beliefs. However, in this study, the contingencies of teacher feedback were not assessed, either in student perceptions or in observer ratings.

LINKS BETWEEN SELF—OTHER PERCEPTIONS AND ACADEMIC PERFORMANCE

Student perceptions of teaching behavior have been found to mediate the effect of teaching behavior on achievement. For example, Stayrook, Corno, and Winne (1978) found that beyond the effects that student aptitude and teacher usage of the specific behaviors had on achievement, student perceptions of teacher structuring and reacting (but not soliciting) had a direct causal link to student achievement. These results suggest that student perceptions of the occurrence of specific teaching behaviors can be related to subsequent learning. Further, the mediating effect may be behavior-specific.

In a meta-analysis of predictive validity studies using student perceptions of psycho-social climate, Haertel, Walberg, and Haertel (1979) found with remarkable consistency of effects, that classroom environment perceptions accounted for variance in learning outcomes beyond the variance accounted for by ability. Learning gains were positively associated with student-perceived cohesiveness, satisfaction, task difficulty, formality, goal direction, democracy, and the material environment and negatively associated with friction, cliqueness, apathy, and disorganization.

In the previously cited Brattesani et al. study (1984), student perceptions of differential treatment at a classroom level moderated the relationship between teacher expectations and student achievement. In classrooms with perceived low differential treatment, where it was hypothesized that little information about differential student ability is communicated by the teacher, student achievement was best predicted by a previous measure of achievement, accounting for 64% to 77% of the variance. In other words, students continued to perform at about the same levels, relative to their classmates, as they had performed before. In contrast, in classrooms with perceived high differential treatment, where it was hypothesized that teachers give more differential information about students' abilities, student achievement was less effectively predicted by prior achievement, accounting for 47% to 62% of the variance. In these high differentiating classrooms as perceived by students, teachers' expectations explained an additional 9% to 18% of the variance in student achievement, whereas teacher expectations explained only an additional 1% to 4% of achievement variance in low differentiating classrooms.

Research addressing the relationship between student self-perceptions and student outcomes has a much longer history. Many studies have shown positive relationships between students' perceptions of personal control and achievement (for recent reviews, see Findley & Cooper, 1983; Stipek & Weisz, 1981; Uguroglu & Walberg, 1979). That is, more internal beliefs have been associated with greater academic achievement. Based on a recent meta-analysis (Findley & Cooper, 1983), this relationship was found to be stronger in adolescent populations, among males, and with specific locus of control measures and standardized achievement tests. Stipek and Weisz (1981) also point to the substantial differences underlying the three major conceptualizations of locus control which are derived from social learning theory, attribution theory, and competence motivation theory. Although very few studies have examined the causal relationship between locus of control beliefs and achievement, the findings do suggest personal control beliefs as making a causal contribution to achievement (Stipek & Weisz, 1981). Further, locus of control beliefs have also been associated with a variety of behaviors that underlie successful achievement, such as persistence at tasks and preference for tasks (Findley & Cooper, 1983).

Positive relationships have also been demonstrated between self-esteem measures and achievement (as reviewed by Hansford & Hattie, 1982; Wylie, 1979). Overall, the results from these studies suggest that achievement influences one's self-evaluation in the academic domain (Calsyn & Kenny, 1977; Harter, 1983). Expectation of success on a task, or confidence level, has also been found to show positive relationships to academic performance, task persistence, and task choice (as reviewed by Meece, Parsons, Kaczala, Goff & Futterman, 1982). Further sex differences in achievement expectations have been demonstrated and these differences in expectancies have been found to be related to patterns of achievement.

STUDENT SUSCEPTIBILITY TO TEACHER EXPECTATIONS

Some students may be more resistant than others to expectancy effects in the classroom. Given the student-mediation model outlined, student individual differences may be reflected at various points of the process. Research on the perceptual process suggests that perceptions of others appear to be jointly determined by characteristics of both the perceiver and perceived (Jones, 1977). Thus, perceptions may not be entirely accurate representations of the environment and intraindividual factors may play a role in what is perceived. Students may therefore differ in their perceptions of teacher behavior toward others or toward themselves. As well, students may differ in their interpretations of the behavior, in their incorporation of teacher cues about expectations into their own self-perceptions, and/or in their behavioral response.

To date, some studies have addressed student individual differences in perceptions of teacher behavior. For example, in studies of student perceptions of classroom environments, student achievement level differences have been documented as affecting perceptions of the favorable nature of the classroom climate (Moos, 1979). Girls and students from higher social classes have been found to perceive their teachers' feelings more positively (Davidson & Lang, 1960). However, since these studies focus on student reports of teacher treatment toward the self or treatment in general, these studies cannot distinguish between two possible explanations for the different perceptions reported by different types of students: (a) student individual difference effects and (b) within-classroom differential treatment effects. That is, the ability level of students may alter their capacity to perceive dimensions of classroom climate or alternatively, the actual classroom subenvironments for high and low achievers may indeed be different.

By examining students' perceptions of teacher treatment toward targeted types of students (such as a low achiever), agreements and disagreements between high and low achieving students in their perceptions of the treatment of the same target student can be tested. In the Weinstein et al. study (1982), fourth through sixth grade students, regardless of achievement level, were found to similarly perceive the treatment differences towards high and low achievers across three general types of teacher behavior. In two other studies, achievement level differences have been found to influence the perception of differential treatment and the perceived function of praise. Clements et al. (1980) reported that low reading group members as compared to high reading group members were more likely to perceive the teacher as treating the groups similarly. Low achievers more than high achievers have also been found to perceive the function of standardized examples of praise as instructional rather than deserved (Morine-Dershimer, 1982).

With regard to sex differences in perception of treatment, boys and girls were found to agree in their perceptions of the differential allocation of the types of teacher behaviors toward high and low achievers (Weinstein et al, 1982). However, at an individual item level of teacher behaviors, sex differences in the perceptions of treatment did occur on some of the items (Weinstein & Middlestadt, 1979a,b). Cooper and Good (1983) found that perception differences between boys and girls were not strong. In two cases, boys thought they received less praise and more behavioral interventions than girls. Classroom observational data documented that boys did indeed receive more behavioral interactions than girls, but not less praise. Other individual differences in perceptions of teacher behavior have also been documented: for example, self-concept of ability (Weinstein & Middlestadt, 1979a,b); locus of control and anxiety (Solomon & Yaeger, 1969).

The findings to date are rather sparse and inconsistent. Further, they do not address the subsequent processes of differential interpretation of teacher behavior, differential incorporation of the cues into self-perceptions and differential action. Hence, it is difficult at this point to conclude which student individual differences might be most important to consider.

ISSUES FOR FUTURE RESEARCH

This review of research concerned with student mediation of expectancy effects in the classroom clearly underscores the fact that students are aware of differential treatment by the teacher in the classroom. Students can describe these differences in the treatment of others as well as in their own treatment from the teacher. There is also evidence to suggest classroom differences in the extent of differential treatment as identified by students are associated with different outcomes—in self-perceptions as well as achievement. Differences between students in how they view themselves and in how they achieve are accentuated in classrooms where students perceive differential treatment.

To date, however, we know far more about what students perceive in teacher behavior than about the impact of such perceptions on other processes. Future research must address several important issues.

First, the linking of student perceptions of treatment to student self-perceptions and behavioral responses is an important priority for future research. But in forging such links, the studies available are not particularly helpful in delineating what aspects of student perceptions of teacher treatment are important. Is it the perception of *absolute levels* of certain teacher behaviors (e.g., a great deal of praise), or of the *relative frequency* of teacher behaviors compared to classmates (e.g., differential treatment such as more praise than others) or of the *contingent use* of teacher behaviors, that impacts on self-perceptions?

One limiting factor has been that the theoretical formulations concerning student mediation of the self-fulfilling prophecy have not yet been fully tested. The studies by Weinstein and colleagues have examined student perceptions of differential treatment at the level of the classroom only. Individual students' perceptions of differential treatment are being assessed in their current study and will (for the first time) allow the investigation of individual susceptibility to the effects of teacher expectations. As well, Cooper's (1979) theoretical notions about student mediating process have only received partial examination. In Cooper & Good (1983), student locus of control beliefs were related to student perceptions of the differential (relative to peers) interactions they had with teachers rather than their perceptions of teacher feedback contingencies as was hypothesized. Finally, the possibility that students may make alternative attributions other than to self in response to perceived treatment (Darley & Fazio, 1980) has not yet been studied. Hence, conclusions about which perceptions of teacher interaction may be critical require a more thorough and complete investigation of the range of attributions that individual students might make in interpreting the meaning of teacher treatment.

Second, the issue of individual differences in susceptibility to teacher expectations must be more directly assessed at the point of behavioral response, as well as in perception and interpretation. To date, the moderating influence of self-concept on the impact of teacher expectations as suggested by Braun (1976) has not yet been tested. Minority status may also play a role in the vulnerability with which students respond to teacher expectations. Differences in cultural values (family compared to school) may serve to immunize some children from the impact of teacher views of their performance or alternately to heighten their susceptibility to the dominant viewpoint. Parental beliefs may also serve an important mediating role. In addition, investigations need to look beyond individual factors to aspects of the social setting that may be critical in discounting or minimizing the impact of teacher expectations.

Third, in our studies of student-mediation effects, we must examine the developmental capacity of children to process social information from classroom interaction and the ability to apply such information to themselves in the form of stable self-perceptions. The tasks of integrating findings from developmental social cognition studies as well as of building developmental comparisons into our research on expectancy effects are necessary steps in order to make sense of what has been described as young children's resistance to negative feedback (Blumenfeld et al., 1982; Entwisle & Hayduk, 1978; Stipek, 1977). There are distinct developmental milestones in the child's capacity to process social information. As Turiel (1978) suggests, the place to look for structural age-related changes is within delimited domains of knowledge. That is, it is likely that children's reasoning about the social system of the classroom proceeds on a different timetable than their knowledge of self and others. The emergence of concepts of stable, internal dispositions also appears at a much later date. Hence, the unfolding of these processes has implications for the staying power of feedback from the teacher and its translation into a stable self-image or set of beliefs about self-efficacy. Future research on student mediation of classroom expectancy effects must examine the process at different developmental stages.

Finally, future research investigations need to build on the results of recent interview studies with students in addition to being influenced by researcher-derived classroom observation systems. Our interviews with fourth grade students (about how children learn about their own level of smartness in the classroom and how they perceive the consequences of relative smartness) (Weinstein & Middlestadt, 1979; Weinstein, 1981; Marshall, Weinstein, Sharp & Brattesani, 1982) suggest several limitations with regard to how and what we focus on in dyadic interaction.

In spontaneous descriptions of the cues they use to determine their own smartness, students are likely to refer to critical incidents (single events) rather than the frequency of events. Students also make distinctions about teacher behavior far beyond what researchers measure (Weinstein & Middlestadt, 1979). For example, interview responses revealed at least four varieties of the teacher behavior "calls on": The teacher "calls on the smart kids for the right answers . . . She expects you to know more and won't tell answers" whereas with regard to the low achievers, the teacher calls on them sometimes "to give them a chance" or "because they goof off," or often "she doesn't call on them because she knows they don't know the answer."

As well, the teacher behaviors that students describe as providing cues are more complex, and more subtle than the teacher behaviors that the classroom observers are recording or students are asked to rate. For example, students talk about teacher statements such as:

I'm very disappointed in you.
> She makes me feel like I just started school that day. It makes me feel like I'm stupid, just dumb, crazy, stupid.

I know you'll do better on your next report.
> And that kind a gives you a hint that you didn't do that well.

Just try and you can do it.
They give me courage.

In a current study, we are noting the occurrences of these expectation statements in the classroom observational records. While Blumenfeld and colleagues (1983) have reported few examples of the direct expression of expectations in their observations of second and fifth grade classrooms, we might argue that frequency is not the issue, rather their importance lies in what is conveyed in these messages to individual students, to reading groups, to the class as a whole. That is, content and the tone of these statements create an ideology about learning and about mistakes that can influence the development of student expectations. For example, in one low differential treatment classroom (as perceived by students), students reported feeling that they can become smart. In their class, "people who used to not be smart, they're smart now."

Students also pay attention to cues other than teacher feedback statements. For example, particularly when students described teacher behaviors that informed them about poor performance, the structure of learning activities became a more salient cue. Here, twice as many children (31% of the sample) reported structuring strategies that alerted them to poor performance in the classroom. The most frequent structural strategy cues about poor performance were the assignment of remedial work and the amount of help given.

The subtle nature of student descriptions of teacher behavior needs to be integrated into our conceptualization of differential teacher treatment before we can fully understand student mediating processes. Our instruments need some refinement.

Despite this early state in our knowledge about student-mediation effects, we can conclude that students' perceptions and interpretations of the classroom reality are an important focus for further study—not only to the extent that their views of teacher treatment influence subsequent student outcomes, but also that the student perspective can alert us to salient classroom processes about which researchers and teachers have been unaware. Our earlier conceptualizations of expectancy effects in the classroom have not enabled us to easily learn from the perspective of students. Perhaps, this growing body of research will help us to hear what they have to say.

ACKNOWLEDGMENT

This chapter is based on an invited address (Division C) entitled "Expectations in the classroom: The student perspective" which was delivered at the annual meeting of the American Educational Research Association, in New York, March 1982. The author wishes to thank Hermine Marshall, Karen Brattesani, Lee Sharp, and Susan Middlestadt for their contributions to the ideas and to the research described in this chapter, and Peggy Moffett for her help in preparing the manuscript.

This work is supported in part by the National Institute of Education (Grants NIE-G-79-0078 and NIE-G-80-0071) and the National Institute of Mental Health (I ROI MH 34379.) The opinions expressed here do not necessarily reflect the position or policy of these agencies and no official endorsement should be inferred.

REFERENCES

Ames, C. Competitive versus cooperative reward structures: The influence of individual and group performance factors on achievement attributions and affect. *American Educational Research Journal,* 1981, *18,* 273–287.

Berliner, D. C. Impediments to the study of teacher effectiveness. *Journal of Teacher Education,* 1976, *27,* 5–13.

Blumenfeld, P. C., Hamilton, V. L., Wessels, K. & Meece, J. Teacher talk and student thought: Socialization into the student role. In J. Levine & M. C. Wang (Eds.). *Teacher and student perceptions: Implications for learning.* Hillsdale, N.J.: Lawrence Erlbaum Associates, 1983.

Blumenfeld, P. C., Pintrich, P. R., Meece, J. & Wessels, K. The formation and role of self-perceptions of ability in elementary classrooms. *Elementary School Journal,* 1982, *82,* 401–420.

Boehm, A. E. & White, M. A. Pupils' perceptions of school marks. *Elementary School Journal,* 1967, *67,* 237–240.

Bossert, S. *Task and social relationships in classrooms: A study of classroom organization and its consequences.* American Sociological Association, Arnold & Caroline Rose Monograph Series. New York: Cambridge University, 1979.

Brattesani, K. A. & Weinstein, R. S. *Children's perceptions of teacher behavior: Their role in a model of teacher expectation effects.* Paper presented at meeting of the Western Psychological Association, Honolulu, May 1980.

Brattesani, K. A., Weinstein R. S., & Marshall, H. H. Student perceptions of differential teacher treatment as moderators of teacher expectation effects. *Journal of Educational Psychology,* 1984, *76,* 236–247.

Braun, C. Johnny reads the cues: Teacher expectation. *The Reading Teacher,* 1973, *26,* 704–712.

Braun, C. Teacher expectation: Socio-psychological dynamics. *Review of Educational Research,* 1976, *46,* 185–213.

Brophy, J. Resarch on the self-fulfilling prophecy and teacher expectations. In L. Shulman (Chair), *The self-fulfilling prophecy: Its origins and consequences in research and practice.* Symposium presented at the meeting of the American Educational Research Association, New York, March 1982.

Brophy, J. & Good, T. Teachers' communication of differential expectations for children's class-room performance: Some behavioral data. *Journal of Educational Psychology,* 1970, *61,* 365–374.

Brophy, J. & Good, T. *Teacher–student relationships: Causes and consequences.* New York: Holt, Rinehart & Winston, 1974.

Calsyn, R. & Kenny, D. Self-concept of ability and perceived evaluation of others: Cause or effect of academic achievement? *Journal of Educational Psychology,* 1977, *69,* 136–145.

Clements, R. D., Gainey, L. M. & Malitz, D. *The accuracy of students' perceptions of themselves and their classroom.* Paper presented at the meeting of the American Educational Research Association, Boston, April, 1980.

Cooper, H. M. Pygmalion grows up: A model for teacher expectation communication and performance influence. *Review of Educational Research,* 1979, *49,* 389–410.

Cooper, H. M. & Good, T. L. *Pygmalion grows up: Studies in the expectation communication process.* Longman, 1983.

Crandall, V. C., Katkovsky, W., & Crandall, V. J. Children's beliefs in their own control of reinforcements in intellectual-academic achievement situations. *Child Development,* 1965, *36,* 91–109.

Darley, J. M. & Fazio, R. H. Expectancy confirmation processes arising in the social interaction sequence. *American Psychologist,* 1980, *35,* 867–881.

Davidson, H. H. & Lang, G. Children's perceptions of their teachers' feelings toward them related to self-perception, school achievement and behavior. *Journal of Experimental Education,* 1960, *29,* 107–118.

Davis, O. L. & Slobodian, J. J. Teacher behavior toward boys and girls during first grade reading instruction. *American Educational Research Journal,* 1967, *4,* 261–269.

Doyle, W. Paradigms for research on teacher effectiveness. In L. S. Shulman (Ed.), *Review of Research in Education* (Vol. 5). Itasca, Ill.: Peacock, 1977.

Doyle, W. *Student mediating responses in teaching effectiveness.* NIE Final Report. North Texas State University, Denton, Tx., 1980.

Duke, D. L. What can students tell educators about classroom dynamics. *Theory into Practice,* 1977, *16,* 262–271.

Dweck, C. S. & Elliott, E. S. *A model of achievement motivation: A theory of its origins and a framework for motivational development.* Unpublished manuscript, Harvard, 1981.

Entwisle, D. & Hayduk, L. *Too great expectations: The academic outlook of young children.* Baltimore: John Hopkins University, 1978.

Findley, M. J. & Cooper, H. M. Locus of control and academic achievement. *Journal of Personality and Social Psychology,* 1983.

Finkelstein, J. C. Experimenter expectancy effects. *Journal of Communication,* 1976, *26,* 31–41.

Flavell, J. H. *Cognitive development.* Englewood Cliffs, N.J.: Prentice-Hall, 1977.

Fraser, B. J. Research on classroom learning environment in the 1970's and 1980's. In B. J. Fraser (Ed.). *Studies in Educational Evaluation* (Vol. 6). Oxford: Pergamon Press, 1980.

Fraser, B. J. & Walberg, H. J. Psychosocial learning environment in science classrooms: A review of research. *Studies in Science Education,* 1981, *8,* 67–92.

Good, T. Classroom expectations: Teacher-pupil interactions. In J. McMillan (Ed.). *The social psychology of school learning.* New York: Academic Press, 1980.

Gordon, N. J. Social cognition. In F. H. Farley & N. J. Gordon (Eds.). *Psychology and education: The state of the union.* Berkeley: McCutchan, 1981.

Gustafsson, C. *Classroom interaction: A study of pedagogical roles in the teaching process.* Stockholm, Sweden: Gruppen, 1977.

Haertel, G. D., Walberg, H. J., & Haertel, E. H. *Socio-psychological environments and learning: A quantitative synthesis.* Paper presented at the meeting of the American Educational Research Association, San Francisco, April 1979.

Hansford, B. C. & Hattie, J. A. The relationship between self and achievement performance measures. *Review of Educational Research,* 1982, *52,* 123–142.

Harter, S. Developmental perspectives on the self-system. In M. Hetherington (Ed.). *Carmichael's manual of child psychology, Volume on social and personality development.* New York: Wiley, 1983.

Hartup, W. The social worlds of childhood. *American Psychologist,* 1979, *34,* 944–950.

Jones, R. A. *Self-fulfilling prophecies.* Hillsdale, N.J.: Lawrence Erlbaum Associates, 1977.

Kennelly, K. & Kinley, S. Perceived contingency of teacher administered reinforcements and academic performance of boys. *Psychology in the Schools,* 1975, *12,* 449–453.

Levine, J. & Wang, M. (Eds.). *Teacher and student perceptions: Implications for learning.* Hillsdale, N.J.: Lawrence Erlbaum Associates, 1983.

Marshall, H. H. Weinstein, R. S., Sharp, L. & Brattesani, K. A. *Students' descriptions of the ecology of the school environment for high and low achievers.* Paper presented at the meeting of the American Educational Research Association, New York, March 1982.

McNeil, J. D. Programmed instruction versus usual classroom procedures in teaching boys to read. *American Educational Research Journal*, 1964, *1*, 113–119.

Meece, J. L., Parsons, J. E., Kaczala, C. M., Goff, S. B., & Futterman, R. Sex differences in math achievement: Toward a model of academic choice. *Psychological Bulletin*, 1982, *91*, 324–348.

Meighan, R. (Ed.). The learners' viewpoint: Explorations of the pupil perspective on schooling. Special Issue of *Educational Review*, 1978, *30*, 91–191.

Meyer, W. S. & Thompson, G. C. Sex differences in the distribution of teacher approval and disapproval among sixth grade children. *Journal of Educational Psychology*, 1956, *XLVII*, 385–396.

Moos, R. H. *Evaluating educational environments*. San Francisco: Jossey-Bass, 1979.

Morine-Dershimer, G. Pupil perceptions of teacher praise. *The Elementary School Journal*, 1982, *82*, 421–434.

Nicholls, J. G. The development of the concepts of effort and ability, perception of academic attainment, and the understanding that difficult tasks require more ability. *Child Development*, 1978, *49*, 800–814.

Parsons, J. E., Kaczala, C., & Meece, J. Socialization of achievement attitudes and beliefs: Classroom influences. *Child Development*, 1982, *53*, 322–339.

Parsons, J. E., & Ruble, D. The development of achievement related expectancies. *Child Development*, 1977, *48*, 1075–1079.

Rosenholtz, S. & Wilson, B. The effect of classroom structure on shared perceptions of ability. *American Educational Research Journal*, 1980, *17*, 75–82.

Rosenthal, R. & Jacobson, L. *Pygmalion in the classroom: Teacher expectations and pupils' intellectual development*. New York: Holt, Rinehart & Winston, 1968.

Rosenthal, R. & Rosnow, R. L. *The volunteer subject*. New York: Wiley, 1975.

Rubovitz, R. & Maehr, M. Pygmalion black and white. *Journal of Personality and Social Psychology*, 1973, *25*, 210–218.

Sechrest, L. B. The motivation in school of young children: Some interview data. *Journal of Experimental Education*, 1962, *30*, 327–335.

Slobodian, J. & Campbell, P. Do children's perceptions influence beginning reading achievement. *Elementary School Journal*, 1967, *67*, 423–427.

Solomon, D. & Yaeger, J. Effects of content and intonation on perceptions of verbal reinforcers. *Perceptual and Motor Skills*, 1969, *28*, 319–327. (a)

Solomon, D. & Yaeger, J. Determinants of boys' perceptions of verbal reinforcers. *Developmental Psychology*, 1969, *1*, 637–645.

Stayrook, N. G., Corno, L., & Winne, P. H. Path analyses relating student perceptions of teacher behavior to student achievement. *Journal of Teacher Education*, 1978, *29*, 51–56.

Stipek, D. J. *Changes during first grade in children's social-motivational development*. Unpublished Ph.D. dissertation, Yale University, 1977.

Stipek, D. J. Children's perceptions of their own and their classmates' ability. *Journal of Educational Psychology*, 1981, *73*, 404–410.

Stipek, D. J. & Weisz, J. R. Perceived personal control and academic achievement. *Review of Educational Research*, 1981, *51*, 101–137.

Swarthout, D. *Applying four social-cognitive perspectives to the study of classroom life*. Paper presented at the meeting of the American Educational Research Association, Boston, April 1980.

Turiel, E. Social regulations and domains of social concepts. In W. Damon (Ed.). *New directions for child development: Social cognition*. San Francisco: Jossey-Bass, 1978.

Uguroglu, M. & Walberg, H. Motivation and achievement: A quantitative synthesis. *American Educational Research Journal*, 1979, *16*, 375–389.

Walberg, H. J. The psychology of learning environments. In L. S. Shulman (Ed.). *Review of research in education*. Vol. 4. Itasca, Illinois: Peacock, 1976.

Walberg, H. J. & Haertel, G. D. Validity and use of educational environment assessments. *Studies in Educational Evaluation*, 1980, *6*, 225–238.

Weinstein, R. S. Reading group membership in first grade: Teacher behaviors and pupil experience over time. *Journal of Educational Psychology*, 1976, *68*, 103–116.

Weinstein, R. S. *Student perceptions of differential teacher treatment*. (Final Report to National Institute of Education). Berkeley, Calif.: University of California, 1980.

Weinstein, R. S. Student perspectives on "achievement" in varied classroom environments. In P. Blumenfeld (Chair), *Student perspectives and the study of the classroom*. Symposium presented at the meeting of the American Educational Research Association, Los Angeles, April 1981.

Weinstein, R. S. (Ed.) Students in classrooms. Special Issue of the *Elementary School Journal*, 1982, *82*, 397–540.

Weinstein, R. S. Student perceptions of schooling. *Elementary School Journal*, 1983, *83*, 287–312.

Weinstein, R. S. & Marshall, H. H. *Ecology of students' achievement expectations*. (First year report to National Institute of Education). Berkeley, Calif.: University of California, 1981.

Weinstein, R. S., Marshall, H. H., Brattesani, K. A. & Middlestadt, S. E. Student perceptions of differential teacher treatment in open and traditional classrooms. *Journal of Educational Psychology*, 1982, *74*, 678–692.

Weinstein, R. S. & Middlestadt, S. E. *Learning about the achievement hierarchy of the classroom: Through children's eyes*. Paper presented at meeting of the American Educational Research Association, San Francisco, April 1979.

Weinstein, R. S. & Middlestadt, S. E. Student perceptions of teacher interactions with male high and low achievers. *Journal of Educational Psychology*, 1979, *71*, 421–431.

Wylie, R. *The self concept*. Vol. 2: *Theory and research on selected topics*. Lincoln, Neb.: University of Nebraska, 1979.

Yussen, S. R. & Kane, P. T. *Children's conception of intelligence*. Technical Report No. 546, Wisconsin Research and Development Center for Individualized Schooling, July, 1980.

Zahorik, J. A. Pupils' perception of teachers' verbal feedback *Elementary School Journal*, 1970, *71*, 105–114.

Section 5
Teacher Expectancies:
Backward and Forward

The previous chapters present a plethora of both specific and general information, all of which is central to our understanding of the broad area of teacher expectancy effects on student achievement. The theoretical developments, methodological advances, and substantive descriptions presented earlier reflect both the rapid growth of the area and the types of advances that occur whenever a number of researchers from various perspectives undertake the task of clarifying the nature of some phenomenon. Many questions have been answered and, though the phrase often is trite, many more have been raised. Again, as is usually the case, we know much more now than we did previously, but we also in a sense know less, for we have uncovered new questions that are critical to our understanding.

This discovery and requestionning is the theme of Meyer's summary perspective of the field (Chapter 14). After reviewing and summarizing the substantive contributions, he uses as an analogy in evaluating the state of the field the earlier research on project *Head Start*. In so doing, he questions the emphasis that researchers look to teacher expectancy effects within the restricted domain of student achievement and aptitude test performance. He suggests that the more important questions may be those dealing with how students learn to adapt to school or extraschool environmental demands as a function of the expectancies under which they performed in the school environment. His suggestions for better definitions of variables, the further integration of research from other areas of education and psychology, and a focus on individual differences, likely reflect the trends we shall see in the future.

14 Summary, Integration, and Prospective

William J. Meyer
Syracuse University

Judging from the sheer volume of research studies and efforts to conceptualize these research findings, this volume has earned a place on the shelves of interested scholars. The origins and subsequent development of the research area are interestingly traced by the only person who could do so in a personal way, the author of *Pygmalion in the Classroom*, Robert Rosenthal.

It has been suggested that somewhere between 300–400 papers have been published examining teacher-expectancy and teacher-expectancy effects. One suspects that at least another 400 studies exist that have not been published for one reason or another. Clearly the original impetus for this outpouring of research struck a responsive nerve for researchers interested in teacher behavior and teacher–pupil interactions. It is equally clear that this reaction was based initially on some intuition that a powerful effect had been uncovered that, if removed from the school environment, would serve to remove bias from classrooms and significantly improve the performance and status of children adversely affected by this bias. Now some 15 years later, the original promise seems not to have been met. In this sense the history of research on teacher-expectancy effects and research on the effects of Head Start programs on poor children are similar. In both cases researchers initially concentrated on narrow academic outcomes (IQ test scores, achievement test scores) but these variables proved to be difficult to interpret and often the outcomes were not as robust as expected. Recent work in evaluating the long term effects of preschool programs for the poor have concentrated more on non-cognitive variables with remarkable success. It appears that research on teacher-expectancy effects is also moving away from the initally narrow outcome variables and this work holds great promise. Later in the chapter the recent efforts in examining the long term outcomes of programs for poor children are examined in detail for clues about where we might find promising variables for future teacher-expectancy research.

An overview of the research studies suggests that most of the student variables that might mediate teacher expectancies, and many of the teacher variables, have been examined several times over. Most of these variables seemed to have been selected in a common sense sort of way (gender, race/ethnicity, ability) but some variables were derived from a broader conceptual view; teacher or student perceptions, for example. It is also the case that different investigators have different definitions of teacher expectancy, so that often it appears that some are really talking about teacher bias. And, as one would expect, with different views about teacher expectancy there are different methods used in studying the phenomena. Without a doubt, the mix of variables, methods, and outcome measures has made the construction of this chapter a formidable task indeed. Actually the major problem has been one of organization and how one might, or, more precisely should attempt to deal with the multitude of issues. In the case of the organization, the chapter title provides a hint on that score but those headings turn out to be too limiting (besides what can one do with a summary of summaries?). The material is summarized and simultaneously integrated, from which, hopefully, perspectives will become fairly apparent, if not logical. With respect to the second problem, it was simply decided to deal with a limited number of issues that were either of interest to me or that seemed to provide the greatest promise for future work.

SUMMARY AND INTEGRATION

Empirical Results

The research findings reviewed in those studies focusing directly on teacher expectancies and teacher expectancy effects leave no doubt that teachers do have expectancies about the children in their classrooms. What is more, these expectancies are quite accurate; that is, whatever cues or information teachers use in forming their expectancies, those expectancies reflect the children's actual performance. These apparently reassuring results are uniformly associated with naturalistic studies; studies of real teachers dealing with real information about real students. Many of these studies (those which are poorly conceived) relate teacher expectancies to achievement or aptitude measures but do not examine how the teachers' behaviors toward the children mediated the effects; that is, variation in achievement or aptitude. Fortunately there are many well-conceived studies that in fact examine in detail teacher behaviors that may mediate student performance. There is a major problem with this research, even when teacher behaviors are examined. Specifically, there is the difficult problem of determining causal links. Although tempting, and many fell to the temptation, it is inappropriate to conclude that the teacher behavior mediated the students' performance. Obviously, student performance could well have mediated teacher behaviors. To complicate the problem even more, it is found that, as often as not, teacher behaviors tend to be not only different from children who have high or low expectancies but there is general agreement that the differential behaviors are justified and appropriate. In those instances, there is not only the problem of causal direction, there is a question of whether anything relevant to expectancy effects in fact occured. And what are the effects we are talking about? This turns out to be an interesting and complex issue, but at a somewhat superficial level the problem concerns how to index achievement or aptitude effects. Hall and Merkel (Chapter 4) believe that researchers define expectancy-free teaching as being reflected in essentially zero variance in achievement performance. This view is similar to Bloom's (Bloom, 1976) definition of the success of Mastery Learning; namely no variation in performance. For a variety of reasons, I don't agree with this definition. I suspect that *poor* teaching is associated with either restricted or expanded variance, depending on which end of the distribution is subjected to the negative consequences. Cooper (Chapter 6) seems to disagree with my position in that he views maintenance of the variance as a prime symptom of teacher expectancy in operation. His position is interesting and logical, but it seems to occur in those instances where teacher behaviors tend to be adapted to the needs of the children.

Experimental studies of teacher expectancy effects, studies in which fictitious information about selected students is provided to people who serve as teachers but are typically not trained teachers, show that the information about the students often does influence teacher behavior in anticipated ways. In examining these studies, Dusek (1975) has correctly concluded that they should more appropriately be called "biasing effects." Briefly, his case is that the "teachers" had no other information on which to determine their behavior so that the incorrect information given them had to serve as a basis for behaving toward the subjects. But there are very few, if any, instances of biasing effects in natural classrooms because, in fact, the information that teachers have at their disposal is accurate and they have infinitely more feedback from students about the accuracy of their expectancies than occurs in the experimental studies. In fact, the experimental studies have been strongly criticized for lacking external validity (see Mitman & Snow, Chapter 5). In this context it should be noted that in a few studies real teachers were given inaccurate information about real students (in this case, poor students were described as late "bloomers"). The effects of this manipulation have been mixed and do not provide strong support for teacher-expectancy effects.

In view of the fact that experimental studies have not been very productive, we must rely on naturalistic studies in spite of the causal direction problems that are involved. I want to briefly note here that Mitman and Snow (Chapter 5) have provided a detailed description of the problems involved and have further asserted that currently available solutions are inadequate. Specifically, they take the view that the cross-lagged panel correlation method is of little value in solving the problem. They do find path analyses to be a more promising approach but they persuasively argue that this method requires a complete theoretical model and an awareness of, and the ability to measure, all the major variables contributing to outcome measures. As we shall see, the current state of our theories is inadequate to carry that burden. Despite the protestations of leading methodologists and despite the fact that hardly anyone ever earned a research degree without being told that cause-and-effect statements derived from correlational designs are inappropriate, many published papers and textbook summaries carelessly infer causality.

So, the presence of teacher-expectancy effects appear, so far, to be somewhat ephemeral and maybe even more complex than just effects on achievement and aptitude. But all this work started, as noted at the beginning of this chapter, with the assertion that teacher behavior generates "self-fulfilling prophesies" (Rosenthal, 1966). It should be understood that this effect actually requires that teachers ignore child performance and behave in ways that are antithetical to the child's actual performance. We have already noted that evidence for this effect derives from experimental studies but generally not from naturalistic studies. Nevertheless we are often left with the inference that Pygmalion effects occur with respect to gender, race, and socioeconomic status. Although the research evidence is contradictory and often relies upon cultural differences, the strongest case for the effect seems to be with respect to reading differences often found among young males and females (see Good & Findley, Chapter 11 and Dusek & Joseph, Chapter 9). Hall and Merkel (Chapter 4) direct their attention on the Pygmalion effect and enumerate the commission and omission errors in that research as well as the logic of expecting changes in ability and achievement performance as a function of teacher expectancies. The view that disturbs them is that the performance of low-expectancy children (who are typically low-achieving children) will be substantially improved by changing the teacher's expectancy. I am sympathetic with their concerns especially when researchers assume that negative teacher expectancies and positive teacher expectancies are mirror images of each other in terms of the dynamic processeses involved in their effects on children (see Mitman and Snow for an extended discussion of this problem). Hall and Merkel may well take solace from Brophy's recent (1983) conclusion that about 5% of the variance in achievement can be accounted for in terms of the self-fulfilling prophecy. Brophy further notes that a 5% effect on educational outcomes is important but it is equally clear that 5% is not the key to educational equality. Hall and Merkel clearly would like to see this softer interpretation of the self-fulfilling prophecy appear in textbooks—and hopefully it will.

There is another problem with the generalizations drawn from some of the research cited in this volume. Many research studies report average differences among groups on achievement and aptitude measures that are presumably mediated by teacher expectancies (boys, blacks, receive lower expectancy ratings than girls, whites). Almost no attention is paid to individual differences, suggesting that teacher expectancies and their effects are uniform within categories of children. This suggests that race, gender, socio-economic status, or any other group characteristic contain, within themselves, the cues teachers require in forming their expectancies. This is not only illogical, it is incompatible with the data. An early study by Meyer and Thompson (1957) showed that even though fifth grade boys received considerably more blame from their teachers than girls, the variation in the distribution of blame for boys was considerably larger than it was for girls. Some years after the paper was published, a noted investigator, who was preparing an anthology, noted the discrepant variances, among males & females, and wrote (me) asking for an explanation. The facts are as follows: (1) About 30% of our sample of boys accounted for almost 80% of the observed variance; and (2) of the boys receiving the blame, most, but not all, were below average in achievement and aptitude. The distinctive feature characterizing the high-blame boys, keeping achievement and aptitude constant, was their tendency to be disruptive in class. The low-achieving boys who received little or no teacher blame—they even received some praise—sat passively and quietly in their seats throughout the school year. To a lesser degree the same dynamics occurred with the girls. A few of the girls received blame and they also tended to be more disruptive.

The importance of considering individual differences was demonstrated in an intensive study of 12 Head Start classrooms (Meyer & Lindstrum, 1969). The distribution of teacher-initiated praise and blame was observed in terms of children's gender and race (black and white). The classes were homogeneous with respect to both gender and race. Extensive observations were also made of the children's behavior. This information was used to determine if teacher behaviors were consistent with the children's behaviors (aggressive disruptive behavior evoked teacher blame). There was no evidence whatsoever that teachers blamed or praised one group more than another nor was their evidence that one group behaved more or less acceptably than another. This latter result was surprising with respect to gender differences and is not consistent with other studies of preschool children. Of relevance to this discussion is that within-group variations in behavior were substantial and that between-teacher variations were quite small. It is worth noting that the teachers in this study used substantially more blame than praise but there was one teacher who almost never used blame. Teacher blame occurred in response to disruptive behaviors (but not always, and not contingently) and teacher praise occurred for achievement and effort (again, not always and certainly not contingently). We don't know what the teacher expectancies might have been but we do know that the teachers' behaviors were consistent with the quality of the children's behaviors. Thus if they had had positive or negative expectancies about any of the groups they would have been clearly inaccurate in *terms of the group*. It occurs to me that some of the studies about expectancy effects relative to student groups may, in fact, reflect experimenter expectancies.

Even though it seems preferable to examine individual differences within student categories, nevertheless important information has been obtained from examining the dynamics of teacher expectancies with groups differing on some variable. Brophy (Chapter 12) does examine in a careful analytic fashion the dynamics of expectancy effects as mediated by teachers with respect to high-and low-expectancy children. In particular, he focuses on differences in academic aptitude among students that he believes define teachers' high and low expectancies. Brophy makes the reasonable assertion that given the accuracy of teachers' expectancies one would *expect* differences in their behaviors towards the high-and low-aptitude and expectancy groups. In this analysis he is saying that in all probability the direction of causality is from the student to the teacher. Most analyses of teacher effectiveness assume that teachers should be sensitive to children's performance characteristics and make appropriate adjustments to them. Apparently that is what happens. Obviously, teachers must also be sensitive to possible errors on their part and, more importantly, alert to changes in the children's performance. The research evidence does not support a position that says teachers are insensitive to either high-or low-expectancy children and that they in fact do use different teaching strategies with each group. Despite these encouraging results there are nevertheless several studies showing that teachers use many inappropriate teaching methods with low-expectancy children. The use of inappropriate teaching methods with high-expectancy children has not received much attention. Although Brophy identifies some 17 negative teacher behaviors that are directed toward low-expectancy children, these behaviors are probably not typical of teacher behaviors in general. Whether or not these negative approaches will be used appears to be less a function of teacher expectancies but more related to how powerful an effect teachers believe they can have on the learning of children; The more powerfully they perceive their influence on learning, the less likely they will use negative behaviors.

Brophy's discussion of teacher–student interactions also raises an issue about the unit of measurement; within-class differences as opposed to between-class differences. This issue attacks the question of whether teachers form expectancies for entire classrooms of children and whether these expectancies can effect the larger unit of children. Typically this research examines the effects of classrooms where the children are homogeneously grouped. This issue is raised several times in this volume and will be examined again later. Brophy concludes that ability grouping at the classroom level has little effect on the high group but serious disadvantages for the low group. The research on teacher behavior in intact classrooms would be more persuasive if there had been an opportunity to observe the same teachers working with the different levels of ability. A knowledge of class assignments in schools suggests the real possibility that they are not random. Thus less adequate teachers may be assigned at a greater rate to the low ability group and the best teachers to the high ability group. Although one might infer that administrators are engaged in self-fulfilling prophecy behavior, it seems more likely that many other variables, unfortunately nonacademic in nature, operate in these situations. In any event, the outcome for the lows is still adverse but without a knowledge of how teachers are assigned the question of causal direction remains open.

The consequences of ability grouping at the classroom level was strikingly demonstrated in a study by Meyer and Barbour (1968). These investigators found that the "slowest" classroom in their sample were characterized by poor morale and almost uniformly lower self-concepts. These children indicated that the students they admired most were in the "fastest" group and the students they admired least were their own classmate. What makes this study particularly interesting is that the so-called lowest groups of children were, in fact, above average on both intelligence tests and standardized tests of achievement. This study also suggests another problem related to expectancy effects. My guess is that even if teachers behaved in some optimal way to avoid expectancy behavior on their part with all its subsequent negative effects, we would still see some children struggling to maintain positive self-concepts. The fact is that teacher behaviors reflect our culture so that academic achievement will create problems for those children at the lower end of the distribution. According to Weinstein (Chapter 13) children are aware of how teachers treat them and their peers. Meyer and Barbour (1968) show that children are aware that certain classroom groups, the high achievers, are more positively viewed than others. My guess is that children can define their own relative performance without the help of teachers. The use of cute names for identifying reading groups in the primary grades is simply a convenience for the teacher, the children *know* that those groups differ in reading performance. Thus, although it may be possible to reduce teacher expectancies, there will continue to be society-initiated expectancy effects that will impact on children.

These descriptions of how low-expectancy (low-ability) children are adversely influenced by teachers is certainly unfair and pedagogically counterproductive. The fact is that these behaviors simply reflect bad teaching. But the crucial question implicit throughout this book is the degree to which the children's aptitude and achievement would change if all the adverse behaviors were removed. On this issue, most authors in this book are careful not to suggest what magnitude of improvement would occur under ideal conditions. Readers should also be careful in inferring what would happen under these conditions.

There are two issues with respect to the question of what would happen to the status of low-expectancy children if classroom conditions changed in some positive way. The first issue involves relative standing and the meaning conveyed by relative standing. While authors (not necessarily those in this volume) talk about improving teaching in general, the focus is really on the low achievers. Some authors contend that low- and high-expectancy children probably require different teaching methods to optimize their performance. In this case, and forgetting for now the question of how much improvement would occur, we might assume that all children in a classroom would benefit from optimal teaching. The assumption is further made, by me anyway, that improvement would not interact with entering level of achievement or aptitude. Thus, under ideal conditions the group mean would incease but relative position in the group would remain the same. My hypothesis is that teacher-expectancies are formed on the basis of relative position; relative in most cases to the best children in the room. An alternative hypothesis is that expectancy is formed on relative position to the classroom mean or some hypothetical average population developed by teachers over the years. These alternative hypotheses are testable and would add an important piece of information about expectancy formation. However, it appears that in general, relative position is important and that it does not change when ideal teaching is available to children at all levels of ability or achievement. If these assumptions are correct then there would be no reason to anticipate that expectancies would change. Is it possible, however, that teacher behaviors would change as a reflection of the higher performance they are experiencing from their students?

The second issue relevant to changes in achievement and expectancy relates directly to the magnitude of change that can reasonably be expected. This discussion begins with a few postulates about variance that occurs on aptitude and achievement tests. My guess is that my colleagues on this book do not agree with many of these postulates because they did not include them in any of their discussions: (1) the development of general and specific academic skills is a function of environmental and genetic factors; (2) performance is a function of the interaction of environment and genetic factors; (3) developmental patterns within and between individuals are relatively, but by no means totally, constant and stable; and (4) major environmental trauma (e.g., war, famine, physical abuse, severe sensory deprivation) will seriously and permanently interrupt normal developmental patterns. Postulates three and four are empirically based and infer that in the general case experiental events will have relatively little impact, either positive or negative, on either the course of development or relative position. The estimate of the 5% effect of the self-fulfilling prophecy on achievement *variance* seems a little high from this perspective but appropriate if one refers to *average* performance. In effect the question comes down to how much importance one can attribute to a gain of six points in average performance on an IQ test in terms of how children perform on achievement measures or are perceived by teachers? (Admittedly, there are children who show much more dramatic gains or losses than six points but these children are often in the middle of some major event in their lives or are coming out of some severe detrimental event.) Thus whether one attacks the problem in terms of relative position or in terms of actual performance the same conclusion emerges: It is unlikely that teacher expectancies will be significantly altered.

The four postulates represent the bare outlines of what is often called the organismic view of behavior as opposed to the mechanistic view. The organismic view is often associated with a more conservative view of the power of environmental manipulation than the mechanistic view. In a sense this is correct in that the organismic view filters environmental stimulation through an organism that has its own unique characteristics. Thus this view takes quite seriously the assertion that children with different patterns of development, different aptitudes, and different academic skills require different treatment. This view does not dictate what those treatments might be but if the evidence suggests that low-aptitude children require more guidance, less freedom of exploration, or whatever, then such evidence is congruent with the organismic view. In the case of high- and low-aptitude children, it is not surprising that teacher behaviors are different, so long as they are adaptive for the children. Thus the second postulate seems tailor-made for conceptualizing teacher–student interactions and teacher expectancies. For example, we noted earlier that sometimes expectations can be set too high for a child. The organismic view can handle that problem because it explicitly recognizes that there are limits beyond which the organism is incapable of responding. When that occurs, the consequence can be serious. The organismic view might also play a role in understanding how children acquire the social awareness of events happening in classrooms, not only to themselves but to others. This issue is discussed at greater length later. In general, it seems that placing the stable and more flexible characteristics of children in the expectation process makes it possible to more realistically assess expectancy effects and opens the possibility of moving toward trait by treatment kinds of research designs (Cronbach & Snow, 1977).

Up to this point this summary and integration suggests that teacher expectancies exist and that they are quite accurate. The effects of teacher expectancies on students are less clear but surely they occur, although not with the frequency or intensity that was suggested by earlier investigators. This is also probably another way of saying that there are bad teachers in the real world. The reasons we seem unable to get a good handle on expectancy effects involve the inadequacy of research designs and methods; problems in confidently determining causal links and directions; theoretical deficiencies that do not allow the use of more sophisticated research designs and analytic methods; and an overly narrow philosophical view about the nature of human behavior and development. It is quite obvious that I am very concerned about the focus on aptitude and achievement either as outcomes of teacher expectancy effects or as child characteristics that will be positively influenced if or when we rid the schools of expectancy effects. I started this chapter by commenting about the perceived similarity of histories of Head Start and teacher expectancy research. There is a lesson to be learned from the Head Start experience: A narrow focus on aptitude and achievement, on those measures, is not likely to be productive. In the next section, I document these assertions and at the same time show how productive broader based outcome measures can be. I attempt to integrate the already growing efforts to look at expectancy outcomes for children and teachers from a broader viewpoint.

Theoretical Issues

Hall and Merkel, as already noted, point out that Head Start did not generate the anticipated gains in intelligence. There were some gains but the pessimists attributed them to regression and other artifacts and the optimists thought they saw a new dawn for poor children. Similar events occurred with respect to achievement scores, particularly during the primary grades when it appeared that the Head Start children were performing better. These modest gains later disappeared.

Early in the history of Head Start, Zigler (1970) pointed at the need for broader based outcome measures. An effort was made to develop a set of outcome measures that examined social and emotional behaviors (Anderson & Messick, 1974) but these measures were unable to define a concept of "social competence" and researchers were unable to develop the methodology to assess it (Zigler & Trickett, 1978). Zigler and Trickett attempted to define social competence and it should be noted that in their development of the concept they recognized that cognitive ability plays a role. According to Zigler and Trickett there are two criteria for measures of social competence: "The first is that social competence must reflect the success of the human being in meeting societal expectancies. Second, these measures of social competence should reflect something about the self-actualization or personal development of the human being" (p. 795). It turns out then when one begins to analyze social competence at a micro level the task is extraordinarily complex. The authors in this volume who have attempted to develop these measures are indeed hearty souls who deserve our gratitude. Among some of the measures included in the Zigler and Trickett paper are effectance motivation, including mastery motivation; positive reactions to social reinforcement; locus of control; expectancy of success; a variety of indices about self-concept and self-image, and attitude toward school. Most of these variables are discussed by our authors. In addition to the micro behaviors, Zigler and Trickett call for a series of molar behaviors: being in the appropriate grade for age; being in a regular classroom rather than a special education class; not dropping out of school.

The usefulness of macro-variables was demonstrated in a recently published monograph in which the longterm effects of early education programs were examined. (Lazar & Darlington, 1982). This report examines data from 12 wellknown preschool programs. There were no Head Start programs included in the sample of programs. Each of the included programs contained an appropriate control group. Outcome variables included: School Competence, defined in terms of percent placement in special education classes and frequency of grade retention; Developed Abilities, defined by performance on achievement and intelligence tests; Children's Attitudes, defined by analyses of interviews focusing on achievement orientation, school adjustment, and enhancing self-concepts, and Impact on the Family, defined from maternal interviews related to satisfaction with children's school progress and vocational aspirations for their children. The children were uniformly from low-income families.

In considering the outcome data it should be remembered that the programs were designed to improve achievement and intellectual aptitude; that is, to prepare the children for successful academic experiences. With respect to intellectual performance, the evidence shows some improvement over controls but predominantly in the elementary grades. However, the differences between the treatment and control children were typically on the order of five IQ points. The group IQs were below the average of the general population; in fact, for four of the studies that most nearly approximated randomized designs, both treatment and control groups were about one standard deviation below the general population. Achievement effects were less substantial. The authors concluded that the data did not warrant the conclusion that achievement differences occurred (there were some method problems that may have been responsible for the weak effects). These results relate to the concerns raised in this chapter in that they show that concerted efforts by very talented early childhood educators did not produce large gains in either intelligence test or achievement test performance.

Findings of considerable relevance to the present discussion include the macro-variables. With respect to social competence, it was found that 13.8% of the treatment children and 28.6% of the control children were assigned to special education. Among the four most nearly randomized design programs 5.3% and 29.4% of the treatment and controls, respectively, were assigned to special education. Grade retention outcomes are less clear. All but one program found that fewer treatment than control children were retained, but the effect was significant for only one program. However, pooling across projects resulted in a significant difference, with stronger effects emerging for the four randomized design programs. What makes these results important, obviously, is that there were generally no differences in the variables usually associated with assignment to special education or grade retention.

Examination of the children's attitudes toward the self produced the strongest effects for this outcome variable. Specifically, treatment children were more likely to link their positive self-evaluations to school or job achievement than the controls. This effect was stronger for the younger children and for the older females. There were no differences, however, in terms of educational expectancies or occupational aspirations for the treatment and control groups. The family variable indicated that the mothers of the treatment children were more satisfied with their children's progress and achievement levels than the control mothers. The treatment mothers also had consistently higher aspirations for their children, in fact higher than the children themselves, than the control mothers.

Considering the overall results of this major undertaking, including the methodological problems encountered, Lazar and Darlington's (1982) conclusion seems reasonable: "Apparently, the children with early education experience were more able to adapt to the intellectual, social, and behavioral demands of their schools'' (p. 56). An explanation of the conclusion is more complex. One obvious variable is that the treatment children appeared to be more achievement-oriented and that their mothers perceived them as being successful. Thus we have a self-perception that apparently developed in school which is also supported by the children's mothers (unfortunately we shall never know the role of the teachers). There remains the problem of explaining why the treatment children escaped the consequences of below average IQs and below average achievement. Ramey (1982), in the same monograph, offers an interesting hypotheses that just happens to be very much related to expectancy effects. He points out that the treatment children did evidence somewhat better performance in the earlier grades. He then states: ''Their better earlier adaptation may have earned them reputations that buffered them from placements in special education classes, particularly if they continued to appear academically more interested and vocationally more motivated than their controls'' (p. 148). Note that the term ''teacher expectancies'' can be substituted for the term ''reputation'' in the quote and that the references to motivation and aspirations are constructs that are examined by authors in this volume as possible student behaviors that mediate expectancies.

The relevance of this work to the study of teacher expectancy and teacher expectancy effects seems obvious. First the evidence from these very special educational programs demonstrates the stability of aptitude and achievement performance. In this context I should mention that the case developed by Eccles and Wigfield, (Chapter 8) urging that we think in terms of skill deficits rather than low aptitude, does not really solve the problem. Briefly, they assert that the crucial issue for school performance is the level of skill development and that skills, unlike aptitude, can be taught or remediated. This assumes of course that skill levels are unrelated to aptitude. A careful examination of the various Head Start programs indicate that many of them were very directly and explicitly designed to foster skill development. As we have seen, their effects were marginal and transient. To repeat once more, if skill training is applied equally over levels of skill groups, relative position will remain unchanged and thus, presumably, teacher expectancy.

The second implication of the Head Start report is that a narrow aptitude/achievement based set of outcome or dependent variables may underestimate the effects of a remedial program or the negative or positive effects of something like teacher-expectancies. The Head Start study clearly demonstrates that a positive self-image and maintenance of academic interest with parental support can overcome some of the problems associated with below average aptitude. These results are consistent with all learning and cognitive theories that agree a learner must be motivated to actively engage the environment in order for any learning to occur. It seems to me the real issue in the study of teacher expectancy effects is not whether these effects depress or enhance aptitude, skills, or achievement, but rather how expectancy effects influence the psychological functioning of children and their ability to adapt to environmental demands both in school and out of school. For example, if it were demonstrated that learned helplessness can be generated by teacher behavior then we might expect those children to leave school earlier and be unable to adapt to the demands of the adult social and economic world. I do not disagree with Zigler and Trickett that inadequate social competence is somewhat related to intellectual aptitude (they suggest a correlation on the order of $+.30$), but this leaves considerable room for the operation of other variables.

The need for a broader view of expectancy and expectancy effects is shared by many of the authors in this volume. In order to accomplish this objective it will be necessary to develop, or at least adapt, theories relevant to expectancy. It should be noted that many of the studies cited throughout this volume are totally lacking any theoretical view and, though possibly helpful for identifying important variables, these studies do not enhance our understanding of the psychological processess involved. For the purpose of developing new measures, it would seem that the broader based theories are more likely to be helpful than those that are empirically based and narrowly focused on teacher-expectancy effects. Although Zuroff and Rotter (Chapter 2) were referring to developments with another theoretical position where new measureable variables were not forthcoming, I am in agreement with their conclusion that in order for a research area to continue to develop new variables there is a need to create systematically developed theories. A more detailed statement about the views of Zuroff and Rotter appears later.

A detailed discussion of the various theories and hypotheses offered by the authors will not be attempted here. What I shall attempt is a general description of the various views as they seem to coalesce into a broader conceptualization. Before doing so, however, there are a few observations about the theories that seem necessary. An important problem that emerges from many of the theoretical formulations is either a failure to develop satisfactory operational definitions of concepts or the use of circular definitions; definitions of the kind: ''The child does poorly on achievement tests because of poor motivation as shown by low scores on achievement tests.'' The two problems are really quite related. In the case of poor operational definitions, the problem lies in the failure to obtain measures of a particular construct that are independent of the behavioral outcome. Part of the problem is that often concepts are inadequately defined. For example, sometimes a teacher expectancy effect refers *operationally* to the teacher's behavior toward children with particular characteristics. Sometimes the expectancy effect is defined operationally in terms of what it does to children's aptitude, achievement, motivation, or self-concept. In this case teachers' behaviors are viewed as mediational variables but not effects. Even in the situation where care is taken to observe teachers' behaviors, concepts about those behaviors are few and where they exist are not explicitly related to outcome variables, whatever they may be. The problem is not a simple one as the description of the task presented by Zuroff and Rotter makes clear, but nevertheless, it is crucial. A second problem seems to be a failure to incorporate the work of other investigators into the process of theory building. This is not so widespread, I think, but it does occur. Perhaps the relevent investigators should come together for a working conference at which they can more clearly see how different concepts fit (or do not) into their work, come to agreement on the definitions of terms (or agree on how each definition differs), and agree about the data. An example of this last situation is the insistence in one paper that teacher expectancy attributions are associated with perceived *student ability* and another paper insisting, with equal fervor, that expectancy attributions emerge from *perceived effort*. Obviously both variables can and probably do contribute to teacher attributions but it is disquieting to see each view being argued without an apparent awareness of the other position. Surely such inconsistencies could be resolved in a 5 day session. Finally a comment made earlier in a slightly different way seems again pertinent. I find the failure, in general, to use broad based psychological theories in connection with teacher-expectancy work as a detriment to the evolution of research in this area.

Despite my general concerns there is not doubt that the last 3–4 years have seen an important growth in efforts to develop theories and hypotheses to explain previously observed relationships and to stimulate new hypotheses. The work on attribution theory described by Peterson and Barger (Chapter 7) is a good example. This theoretical description of what factors are related to teachers' attributions and the behavior associated with these attributions are interesting and well documented. One unique contribution that emerges from the authors' broadly conceived attribution theory is the inclusion of the role of *teacher affect* as a mediating link between the attribution and the teacher's action or behavior. The reader should review this material and in so doing will note that it is here, among other places, that scholars disagree about the source of teacher attributions— ability or effort. What seems to be missing from the Peterson and Barger conceptual analyses is a linkage with student behaviors, of whatever sort seem relevant.

While Peterson and Barger concentrated on teacher behaviors, Cooper (Chapter 6) and Weinstein (Chapter 13), describe, from different perspectives the students' involvement in the teacher-expectancy effect process. Cooper in fact deals with a number of interesting issues that have been previously alluded to in this chapter. His major focus is on the communication to students of teachers' expectancies, particularly as they are mediated through teachers perceptions of their control of the classroom situation. In a subsequent modification of the model, characteristics of the children, self-efficacy beliefs, for example, were included. The most recent iteration of the model reflects a concern with a broader array of theoretical constructs involving both teachers and their students. The model, as Cooper concedes, needs elaboration and refinement especially with respect to student perceptions of the process.

Understanding student perceptions of the teacher-expectancy behavior process is, according to Weinstein (Chapter 13) a complex task. This chapter is an impressive review of work related to student perceptions of teachers' behaviors and the consequences for student behavior. Weinstein includes in the review the very current, and potentially fruitful, work on social cognition theories that have been widely used in the study of socialization. It seems that incorporation of this sort of theory, a theory that has definitive developmental concepts, would be extremely useful in a model of student perceptions of teachers' behaviors. For example, research described in this chapter indicates that there are age differences in teacher-expectancy effects; younger children seem less influenced by teacher behaviors. Another issue raised in the chapter is extremely interesting. It appears that children change, developmentally, in their concept of the stability of aptitude. Thus older children seem to accept that ability is stable and their relative standing will remain more or less constant. Younger children do not share that view. In terms of a cognitive analyses of this phenomena, it would be interesting to know how such a belief (understanding) occurs. From my view, of course, this is interesting in itself, but I also wonder if at the time this knowledge occurs would it not also be possible to help children understand their own self-worth regardless of their relative position. As Weinstein notes, there is a decided need to build developmental social cognition theory into work on teacher-expectancy effects. The past work on student perceptions is important, future work looks even more promising. We should not forget, however, that we are after an explication of the total process beginning with teacher expectancies.

A general theme throughout this chapter has been the need for more general measures of teacher effects on students. One variable that is repeatedly mentioned is motivation. This topic is exhaustively examined by Eccles and Wigfield who review a large number of teacher and student variables. Of conceptual interest, there is material on effectance-motivation-theory, which is related to the success–failure experiences of students. From this work, it again appears that extensions of developmental social-cognitive theory would be most helpful in understanding how students' assess their own abilities and their academic successes and failures. This work is also related to the concept of personal efficacy and other concepts developed by Bandura and his students. Another conceptual formulation that receives attention by Eccles and Wigfield is derived from Atkinson's model of achievement behavior. This model, as Zuroff and Rotter note, seems particularly useful in understanding student motivation. In this model the potential reinforcement value of achievement, and the behaviors required, plays a key role; that is, the cost of success or failure. The potential of this model is amply demonstrated in the chapter and will hopefully be considered by other theorists in their subsequent conceptual formulations. As noted earlier, my problem with a small part of this paper is the insistence that if teachers would regard academic skills as amenable to modification and independent of ability, which is not amenable to modification, then the so-called Golem effects would dissipate. While I still disagree with the premise, I can now see that if one looks at this position in terms of how it might influence teacher behavior in sustaining children's motivation, the purpose of the case is acceptable. Simply stated, if teachers believe that a child with modest or lower skills can be taught, then they will work hard to teach them and in so doing they will maintain the child's willingness to work. My guess is that the successes of the economically deprived children who had preschool experiences derived from teachers who believed they (teachers) could make a difference. Without becoming involved in a debate about skills and abilities, it seems that if we can train teachers who believe they can make a difference regardless of the child's current performance, then the objective of sustaining the child's motivation will be achieved.

PROSPECTIVE

In an effort to estimate where research in the area of teacher expectancy and teacher-expectancy effects is going, it might be useful for me to briefly review the road it has already traveled. That road started with certain generally held beliefs that low-expectancy children, typically thought to be children of minority groups or low social status but not restricted to them, were being harmed by teachers implementing their low expectations for these children. Typically the implementation was viewed more in terms of biasing effects; effects whereby the low-expectancy child would be treated negatively without regard to their actual behavior of performance. This supposition triggered many studies, some of which lent support to the hypothesized effect but many more which did not. Indeed we learned that teachers are quite accurate in their assessment of the abilities of the children in their classrooms and that in many instances their teaching strategies are entirely consistent with the state of our current knowledge about teaching effectiveness. We even discovered that teachers very often blamed themselves for the failures of their children and attributed success to the children's efforts and possibly, abilities. Despite this rosy picture, we also discovered that *some* teachers in fact evidence behaviors that seemed destined to harm low-expectancy children, a finding that must be of concern to all of us. The percentage of teachers who behave this way toward children has not been estimated (as near as I can tell) but the effects of low expectancies has been estimated to be about 5% of the achievement variance. As more investigators became involved in the research area and as some investigators began to dig below the surface, theoretical efforts began to emerge. These efforts were initially empirically based and, while they had some explanatory value, their usefulness in stimulating research was limited. As research publications increased to their current volume, we notice that investigators started to pay less attention to the original hypotheses and more attention to the dynamics of classroom interactions. Now it appears to me researchers are concentrating their efforts on what is happening in classrooms and the horizons have broadened to include not only achievement outcomes but social and emotional outcomes as well. Finally, we are seeing more investigators attempting to develop broader theoretical perspectives.

I believe that the current movement toward better understanding of classroom dynamics and theory building is precisely the way to go. I also believe that we should take the recommendations of Zuroff and Rotter about how best to engage in the enterprise of theory building seriously. I realize that a strict adherence to their rules of theory construction is difficult when working in naturalistic settings (operational definitions are always easier to develop when one has complete control over the operations). Nevertheless I feel certain that we can develop measures, observational schemas, and other assessment techniques that have operational precision and external validity. For example, I suspect that there are scaling techniques available by which we can assess children's levels of aspiration for subject matter that would substantiate the findings of Pauline Sears' now classic study of the effects of academic achievement on level of aspiration (Sears, 1940). More effort must be given to theory development and measurement procedures.

In reviewing the efforts to construct theoretical constructs it occurred to me that we are seeing fragmented attempts to develop the process model suggested by Brophy and Good. Thus some people are writing about the teacher (expectancies, attributions, etc.), others are writing about mediating effects with respect to teachers or students, while others are writing about students, especially student perceptions. This is important work. But clearly as one sits back and examines these efforts it becomes obvious that theoretical constructs linking the various components of the process model are needed. These linkages are necessary to develop the kind of important set of interrelated constructs described by Zuroff and Rotter and also to enhance the thinking of those enveloped in their particular component of the process. I know that better research will emerge from such a successful endeavor because it will be possible to not only develop external validity measures it will also be possible to determine the generalizability of hypothesized processes, attributions, and any other theoretical construct. The success of this enterprise would also provide us with a better approximation of the variables, and their related measures, involved in teacher–student interactions, and their mutual effects, in order to appropriately use path-analytic techniques in identifying causal relationships. Finally I would suggest, with some trepidation, that investigators broaden their perspective of their work and view it more in terms of approaches such as attribution theory, social learning theory, achievement behavior theory, or any theory that is broader than the classroom context but which can include classroom dynamics. This recommendation may open up whole new areas that have not seen relevant because of the focused concern with the classroom. (Recent work, derived from attribution theory, on the role of teacher affect is a good example of what I have in mind.)

A final note. It occurs to me that like so many other areas of psychological and educational research there is often a social and a scientific agenda. This is the case with teacher-expectancy research and in my opinion the social agenda did not help except to define the scientific agenda. I believe that if we can communicate our *scientific* work to teachers we will have made an important social contribution to both children and teachers.

REFERENCES

Anderson, S., & Messick, S. (1974). Social competency in young children. *Developmental Psychology, 10,* 282–293.

Bloom, B. S. (1976). *Human characteristics and school learning.* New York: McGraw-Hill.

Brophy, J. E. (1983). Research on self-fulfilling prophecy and teacher expectations. *Journal of Educational Psychology, 75,* 636–661.

Cronback, L. J., & Snow, R. E. (1977). *Aptitudes and instructional methods.* New York: Irvington.

Dusek, J. (1975). Do teachers bias children's learning? *Review of Educational Research, 45,* 661–684.

Lazar, J., & Darlington, R. (1982). Lasting effects of early education: A report from the consortium for longitudinal studies. *Monographs Society for Research in Child Development, 47,* (Serial No. 195), 151 pp.

Meyer , W. J., & Thompson, G. G. (1956). Sex differences in the distribution of teacher approval and disapproval among sixth grade children. *Journal of Educational Psychology, 7,* 385–396.

Meyer, W. J., & Lindstrum, D. (1969). *The distribution of teacher approval and disapproval of Head Start children.* Final Report, Mimeo.

Meyer, W. J., & Barbour, M. (1968). Generality of individual and group social attractiveness over several rating situations. *Journal of Genetic Psychology, 113,* 101–108.

Ramey, C. T. (1982). *Commentary.* In Lazar, J., & Darlington, R., Lasting effects of early education: A report from the consortium for longitudinal studies. *Monographs Society for Research in Child Development, 47,* (Serial No. 195), 151 pp.

Rosenthal, R. (1966). *Experimenter effects in behavioral research.* New York: Appleton-Century-Crofts.

Sears, P. S. (1940). Levels of aspiration in academically successful and unsuccessful children. *Journal Abnormal & Social Psychology, 35,* 498–536.

Zigler, E., & Trickett, P. K. (1978). IQ, social competence, and evaluation of early childhood programs. *American Psychologist, 33,* 789–798.

Zigler, E. (1970). The environmental mystique: Training the intellect versus development of the child. *Childhood Education, 46,* 402–412.

Author Index

Numbers in *italics* indicate pages with complete bibliographic information.

A

Abrami, P. E., 119, *130*
Abramson, L. Y., 193, *220*
Adams, G. R., 233t, 234t, 234, 237t, 240, 243, 247, *249*, 277, 297, 309, *323*
Addler, P., 284, 285, *299*
Adler, T. F., 187, 189, 190, 191, 192, 194, 195, 202, 205, 208, 212, 217, 218, *222, 224*
Ajzen, I., 27, *33*
Algozzine, B., 233t, 237, 237t, 245, *247, 248, 250*
Allen, V., 149, *158*
Allington, R., 309, 310, 311, *324*
Allport, J. L., 83, 87t, *91*, 109, *127*, 306, *324*
Alpert, J. L., 83, 87t, *91*, 109, *127*, 306, *324*
Amato, J. A., *247*, 260t, *268*, 309, *324*
Ames, C., 340, *347*
Ames, R., 172, 173, *182*
Anastasi, A., 290, *297*
Anderson, A. H., 179, 180, *324*
Anderson, L., 305, 306, 310, 318, *324*
Anderson, N. H., 266, *267*
Anderson, S., 362, *370*
Anderson, T. H., 93, 97, 112, *131*, 146, *158*, 307, 319, *328*
Andrews, G., 197, *220*
Archer, D., 59, *64*
Archer, P., *247*

B

Badad, E. Y., 59, *62*, 149, *156*, 185, *220*, 309, 310, 315, 316, *324*
Bailey, M. M., 204, *225*
Baker, J. P., 52n, 53, *62*
Bales, R. F., 69, *91*
Bandura, A., 15, 16, 23, *32*, 97, *127*, 193, 198, 199, *220*
Bank, B., 235, 244, *246*, 287, 289, *298*
Banks, R. E., 102, *129, 248*, 258, *268*
Bar-Tal, D., 118, *127, 247*
Bar-Tal, Y., 118, *127*
Barber, T. X., 50, 52n, 53, *62*
Barbour, M., 359, *370*
Barker Lunn, J., 71, *91*
Baron, R. M., 82, 86t, *91*, 115, *128*, 169, 170, 177, 178, 179, *183*, 248, 251, 266, *267, 268*, 309, *325*
Barr, A. S., 40t, *63*

371

Subject Index